CW01390764

Totally Wired

Totally Wired

The Rise and Fall of the Music Press

Paul Gorman

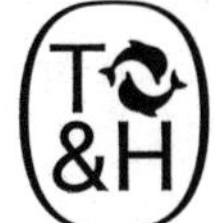

Contents

Prologue

This book examines an extraordinarily fertile branch of the media, one that grew from humble beginnings nearly a hundred years ago to become a multi-million-pound business that tested the very limits of what was understood to be journalistic endeavour.

Along the way it was established as one of the most potent breeding grounds in popular culture, producing scores of writers, photographers, designers, image-makers and even music-makers who made an impact on the wider worlds of film, media and pop.

And the title of this book takes its cue from a song by British avant-punk group the Fall, referring to the fact that many publications incorporating music as a central strand of their coverage in the last near-century were, at least at one stage or another, totally wired for information, for sound and for mind-altering journalism.

My 2001 music press oral history, *In Their Own Write*, represented a first attempt at encapsulating this chaotic world. This book takes in a far wider brief, seeking to provide a more rounded portrait and shining a spotlight on those marginalized publications and individuals – inevitably women, people of colour and those of non-normative sexuality – whose contributions have often been unfairly overlooked. By incorporating their narratives, the conflicting stories of unbound talent, blind ambition and bitter rivalry that pepper these pages are undoubtedly enhanced.

The concentration on the years between 1950 and 2000 is based on an understanding that the music press was atomized and fragmented into unrecognizability not just by the onset of the online era, with its free downloads and predominance of unlettered, critique-free social network commentary, blogs and tweets, but also by the waning potency of popular music itself. Here corporate exploitation has long since called a halt to pop's status as the central nexus for self-expression and the dissemination of vanguard ideas to mass audiences. It is a fact that music outside of niche interests has become the soundtrack for *the selling of things*.

Of course, the commercial imperative was always a significant force in the music press, never more so than in the early autumn of 1926 when the songwriter Lawrence Wright struck on the idea of promoting his wares by circulating copies of the first issue of his new monthly publication, *The Melody Maker*.

The year 1926 is notable in modern memory in America for the death of the great silent screen star – and one of the first international super-celebrities – Rudolph Valentino, and in Britain for the General Strike, the industrial action by nearly two million unionized workers to prevent governmental wage restraint and alleviate the harsh conditions suffered by the country's beleaguered coal miners. That this was ultimately unsuccessful only added to the misery of a nation about to be plunged into the Western world's recessionary period, characterized by the Great Depression in the US.

But Lawrence Wright was not a person to be deterred by widespread economic malaise. He not only understood that an era of modernism and mass communication was under way – 1926 is also marked by the first demonstration of John Logie Baird's invention, the television – but had deep insight into the public appetite for popular music, as a prominent host of so-called 'song booths' in the northern seaside resort of Blackpool.

This drew eight million holidaymakers to its delights every summer. Among them was the author Anthony Burgess, who recalled Wright many decades later as an extremely charismatic figure: 'the ginger-haired master of ceremonies, clad in a white coat as though song-plugging were a surgical operation, shouting from his large fund of Lancashire energy'.

And Lawrence Wright's application of this energy to the launch of *The Melody Maker* in London's Tin Pan Alley is where our story starts ...

1 In the Beginning

The Melody Maker and the Origins of the Music Press

In the Beginning

In the beginning was *The Melody Maker*, a monthly launched in 1926 by one of the successes of the period's popular song publishing scene: thirty-eight-year-old jack-of-all-trades Lawrence Wright.

The cover star of that first issue (pl. 1) was one Horatio Nicholls, trumpeted as 'the world's greatest popular composer'. According to *The Melody Maker*, 'all England is now demanding and soon the civilised world will clamour' for Nicholls's songs 'Babette' and 'Sunny Havana'.

These were by no means objective journalistic judgments: Horatio Nicholls was Lawrence Wright's songwriting nom de plume. Not for the last time was a music paper used to foreground the interests of its principals. But in printing and circulating 7,000 copies of volume 1, issue 1 of *The Melody Maker*, Wright had made an important step in the inauguration of the music press.

There were already specialist music periodicals. In America, *The Etude* and *Metronome* had catered to music students and marching bands since the 1880s and *Billboard* had been founded midway through the next decade, focusing on the advertising and bill-posting industries – and, later, radios and record players. In the UK, the theatrical press – such as *The Era*, *The Performer* and *The Stage* – began covering popular music after the First World War, while the classical-oriented *The Gramophone* occasionally featured dance music and jazz.

The Melody Maker's first issue was distributed free to subscribers of Wright's 'Orchestral Club', which sent out song-sheets of the latest tunes. The paper quickly established authority over Britain's dance band scene, dominated by musicians adapting jazz from across the Atlantic for local consumption. By issue 3 – cover price sixpence – sales hit 8,000 a month.

Wright ran his music publishing company in London's Tin Pan Alley, Denmark Street, and had deep experience and many contacts, having operated a sheet music shop in the Midlands in the early 1900s. A prolific songsmith in his own right, his compositions included a wartime propaganda tune written with a fellow serviceman in the barracks they shared: 'Are We Downhearted? No!'

This bullish attitude informed Wright's publication, edited in a basement office by Edgar Jackson (né Cohen). He paid homage to

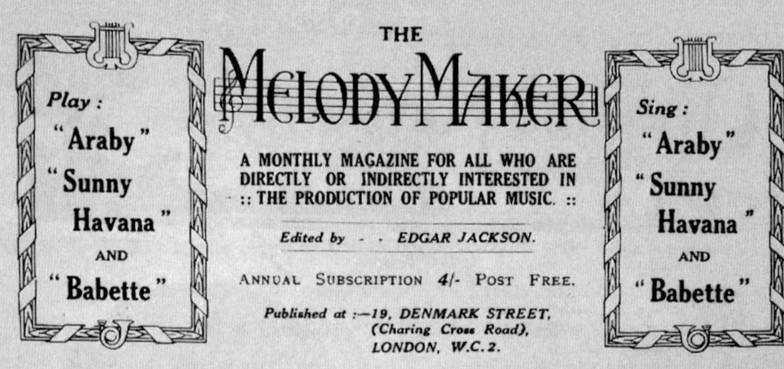

Play: "Araby" "Sunny Havana" AND "Babette"

THE MELODY MAKER

A MONTHLY MAGAZINE FOR ALL WHO ARE DIRECTLY OR INDIRECTLY INTERESTED IN :: THE PRODUCTION OF POPULAR MUSIC. ::

Edited by - - EDGAR JACKSON.

ANNUAL SUBSCRIPTION 4/- POST FREE.

Published at :—19, DENMARK STREET, (Charing Cross Road), LONDON, W.C. 2.

Sing: "Araby" "Sunny Havana" AND "Babette"

No. 1. VOL. I. JANUARY 1926. PRICE 3d.

THE MELODY MAKER

EDITORIAL TELEPHONE - REGENT 4147.

Members of the Profession and all others are Cordially Invited to submit MSS. Information and Photographs for Publication.

*** Whereas every care is taken, we cannot be responsible for the loss of any matter submitted.

Stamped and addressed envelope should be enclosed if return of any matter submitted is desired.

RATES FOR ADVERTISING SPACE WILL BE SENT ON REQUEST.

INDEX.

EDITORIAL.

It is usual, we believe, when introducing a new publication, to say a few words before the curtain as it were. Whereas we do not propose after this to adhere to any example already set by others, but rather to branch out for ourselves in our own way, we feel it due to our readers to give briefly the *raison d'etre* of our existence.

We must confess that we have, on more occasions than we like to admit, noticed a lack of co-ordination between the many branches of the entertainment profession, when the closest co-operation ought, in the interests of all concerned, to have existed.

Which brings us to our point. By giving in an interesting manner, between these two covers, up-to-date information of as many branches of popular entertainment as space will permit, we hope to let each section know exactly on what the other is concentrating, so that concerted efforts may enhance the success of all.

If we succeed in only a small measure we shall feel our humble effort has not been made in vain.

We have decided to devote our frontispiece each month to some prominent member of the musical profession.

In this, our first issue, we are indebted to the famous British composer, Mr. Horatio Nicholls, for allowing us the privilege of publishing his photograph.

Born in Leicester, Mr. Nicholls rapidly came to the fore and is now admittedly one of the finest and most popular composers of lighter music, not only in England, but throughout the world.

THE EDITOR.

— 1 —

The Melody Maker, vol. 1, no. 1, January 1926, page 3

his boss in the first issue by thanking 'the famous British composer Mr Horatio Nicholls for allowing us the privilege of publishing his photograph'. A Nicholls composition topped This Month's Hits of the Season, one of two charts in the first edition (the other being The Most Popular Dance Orchestrations).

Jackson, a drummer, led his own dance band. He was not, according to jazz chronicler Jim Godbolt, well disposed to the African American originals: 'Over-conditioned by the easily grasped arrangements on typical dance-band records,' Jackson failed to appreciate 'the free-flowing lines springing from the quintessential New Orleans instrumentation of trumpet, clarinet, trombone, piano, guitar, bass and drums'. The result: 'When records by black bands were released, the editor of the *Melody Maker* in his role as record critic was persistently virulent in his denunciation.'[1]

The 'wildly opinionated' Jackson, noted critic John Fordham, initially endorsed 'a highly arranged and fashionable style of smooth jazz in preference to rougher, improvisational works from New Orleans he already regarded as "dated". History, of course, came to treat the latter as classics and consigned most of the smooth forms to oblivion, but *The Melody Maker* was nonetheless a symbolic arrival, confirming jazz music's now unshakeable presence.'[2]

Racial tensions were baked into popular music. 'Hot' jazz was played by, or paid homage to, the music's African American performers. Its European counterparts were watered-down 'syncopated' music and a 'symphonic' orchestral sound that relied on sentimentality and novelty (among Wright's 'comedy song hits' in the first issue were 'I've Never Wronged an Onion' and 'The Girl's Got Long Hair'). Such was the controversy surrounding the music that Jackson was initially reluctant to refer to it as 'jazz', because the word derived from the erotically charged slang 'jasm'.

In the first issue, Jack Hylton – the era's biggest British dance band star – railed against critics of syncopated sounds: 'Syncopation is the compromise between rhythm and harmony, between savagery and intellectualism. It will live in this country because British dance orchestras are becoming some of the finest in the world. We have produced a People's Music which satisfies every musical need of those for whom it is intended.'[3]

Jackson's copy was replete with the N-word, as was other text printed during his editorship. An anecdote in the first issue from Hylton's guitarist concerned a recording session by a 'red hot' band whose 'coloured' drummer completed a take with a cymbal crash: 'It came with perfect musicianship, followed by the words, "Say, Bo!! If that ain't just fine, I'll eat my hat." As it was [pub] opening time, we didn't wait to see whether our n***** friend left with his hat on his head, or in his inside.'[4] Jazz historian Hilary Moore pointed to the dilemma of the first British jazz fans: 'Support for the "whitening" of jazz and extreme distaste for the music's black roots' versus 'guilty enjoyment of the transgressive Negro rhythms'.[5]

Meanwhile, Jackson used his prominence to push his views. His editorship was flagged beneath the masthead, and he took to the front page to warn of the threat to musicianship posed by gramophones and the matter of labour permits being issued to overseas musicians in the UK. He even weighed in on a controversial portrait by artist JB Souter in the 1926 summer show at London's Royal Academy of Arts. Entitled *The Breakdown*, it depicted a Black saxophonist in top hat and evening dress playing for a dancing, naked, White female.[6] 'Because of the signified jazz of the saxophone, and probably also for the pragmatic reason that he wished his new publication to be recognized as a mouthpiece for the scene, Jackson felt it his duty to speak out against the painting on behalf of all British jazz musicians,' wrote academic and musician George McKay, who quotes from Jackson's editorial: 'We jazz musicians ... protest against, and repudiate, the juxtaposition of an undraped white girl with a black man ... We demand also that the habit of associating our music with the primitive and barbarous negro derivation shall cease forthwith ... In the degradation it implies to modern white woman there is the pervasive danger to the community and the best thing that could happen to it is to have it ... burnt!'[7] Such was the resulting furore that the painting was withdrawn from the show and destroyed by the artist.

A year after the launch of *The Melody Maker*, owner Lawrence Wright threw himself deeper into the music business as a show promoter. Under Jackson, the *Maker* gradually changed course, stating, 'Modern popular music is the form in which it was and is most popularly demanded – syncopated.'[8] But although the editor played both sides, he began to accentuate authenticity, decrying a licensing restriction imposed upon a venue: saxophones – considered suggestive owing to the blowsy nature of their tone – were not permitted.

In a history of *Melody Maker*, Nick Johnstone pointed out that Jackson now lambasted 'straight' ensembles for refusing to play 'hot' music (which they often blamed on British audiences' demand for familiar – i.e. White – material). In 1927, the editor advocated more adventurous music policies, with a report direct from the home of jazz. A visit to New York by contributor Mr Jos Geo. Gilbert led to the new columns 'What's doing across the pond' and 'Who's who in American bands'. Contrasts and comparisons between American originators and their British successors were to dominate the *Maker* for years to come.

Meanwhile, women in bands, or all-female groups, were tolerated only 'because they are cheap and look nice', according to a contributor credited as Anonymous (likely to have been Jackson, who used several pseudonyms).[9] This was countered by one Miss Molly Pearl, whose article 'The case for the fair sex' hailed 'the progress which woman is making in every walk of life – the art of syncopation included'. Jackson, however, allowed Anonymous to have the last word: 'As hopelessly illogical as you expect from a woman.'

It would be a long time before the music press shed such sexism, despite the pioneering work of singers such as Ma Rainey, Bessie Smith and Sophie Tucker. Their blues music was provided little space in *The Melody Maker* until the 1930s. Women featured instead included Jack Hylton's wife, Ennis Parkes, who sang with pianist Madge Mullen. The latter, according to the *Maker*, was 'taken very seriously even by the boys, which is a great tribute coming from the harassed trousered sex to a lady musician'.

'It was socially unacceptable to simply say Mullen was a talented artist,' noted Nick Johnstone. 'Her gender had to be highlighted and placed within the context of unquestionable male supremacy. Along with Mullen, a musician called Agnes Rogers was reported to be at the forefront of a new breed of youthful female jazz musicians. This talented twenty-one-year-old was degradingly summarized as a "jazz mistress".'[10]

14

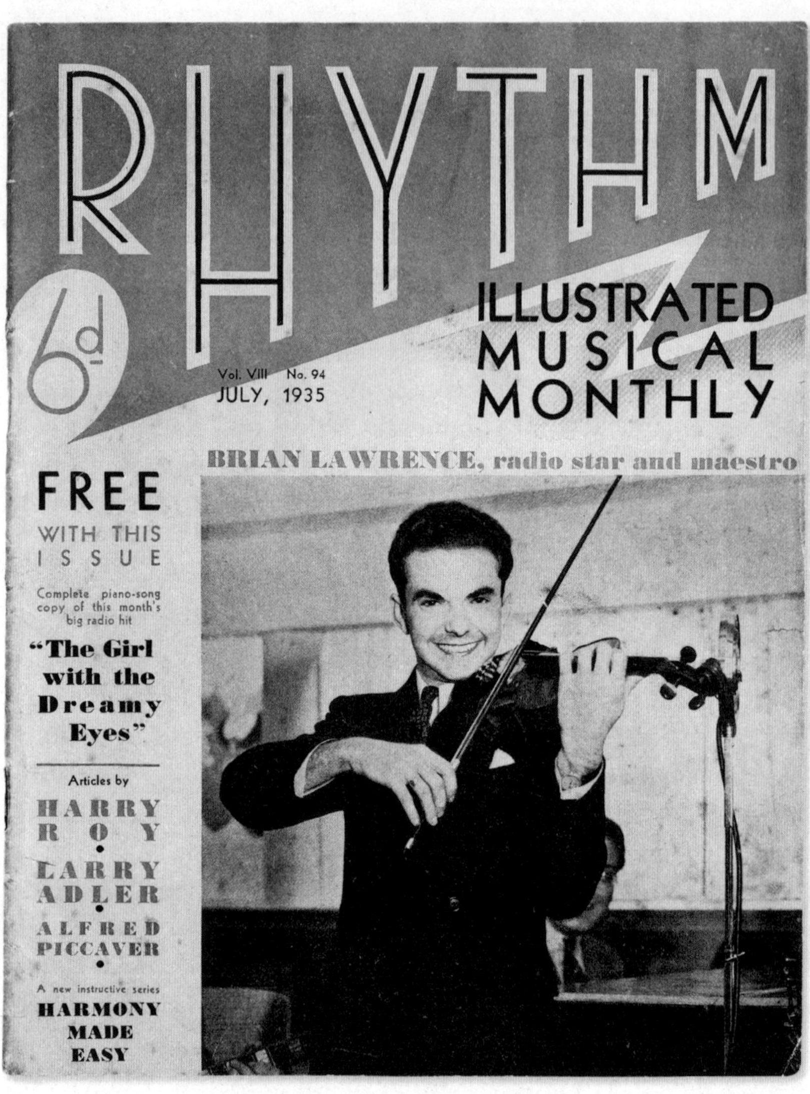

Rhythm Illustrated Musical Monthly, vol. 8, no. 94, July 1935

Two years after *The Melody Maker*'s debut came a rival. Like Lawrence Wright's crafty promotion of his song publishing, *Rhythm Illustrated Musical Monthly* dedicated space to equipment sold by the company that had launched it, John E. Dallas & Sons. Otherwise, it focused on saccharine domestic dance bands and orchestras, thereby sidestepping the race debates that flared around jazz in the *Maker*.

Edgar Jackson visited New York in 1929. Amid the resultant articles, 'Harlem – the Negro quarter' described the neighbourhood as 'a veritable paradise for enthusiasts of hot music'. According to Jim Godbolt, Jackson was 'shaken by the scanty clothing on the Black dancers in Harlem's night spots', but his Manhattan reports highlighted an edginess lacking in Britain. A month after they were published, he resigned to be Jack Hylton's manager – though it wasn't long before this irrepressible figure returned to journalism. The editor's departure coincided with Lawrence Wright's decision to sell *The Melody Maker* for £3,000 to publisher Odhams, whose portfolio included *Sporting Life* and *Ideal Home*.

Jackson's dedication, however misdirected at times, had been the making of the paper. 'At the end of the twenties,' wrote Godbolt, '*The Melody Maker* could – not without a blush of embarrassment – look back on its highly significant contribution to jazz appreciation in Britain, and most of the credit was due to its editor and first record critic, the extraordinary, polymorphous and pseudonymous Edgar Jackson.'

His replacement was Percy Mathison Brooks. A former manager of the Covent Garden Ballroom, Brooks was less of a provocateur. The publication became calmer and embraced popular new jazz stars. British tours in the early 1930s by trumpeter Louis Armstrong, bandleader Duke Ellington and saxophonist Coleman Hawkins stoked *The Melody Maker*'s monthly circulation to 25,000. When Armstrong arrived for a visit that included twenty-eight sell-out shows at London's Palladium, Brooks snared the first British interview. During the encounter, he inadvertently conjured the trumpeter's soon-to-be famous sobriquet 'Satchmo': the posh Englishman's pronunciation of Armstrong's nickname 'Satchelmouth'.

Brooks cemented *The Melody Maker*'s place at the centre of the action by recruiting young American writer and DJ John Hammond as New York correspondent. Later to make his name as a civil rights activist and keystone in the careers of Benny Goodman, Bob Dylan, Aretha Franklin and Bruce Springsteen, Hammond noted that the demand for American jazz in Britain far outstripped supply. He persuaded Columbia Records to increase the flow of releases to the UK and produced sessions by saxophonist Benny Carter and pianist Fletcher Henderson, providing them with much-needed income as the Great Depression bit hard. And, within a year of starting at the British publication, Hammond arranged for seventeen-year-old Billie Holiday to make her recording debut.

The Melody Maker went weekly as its demographic expanded to fans as well as players and music became a comfort to the millions despairing of recession and political instability. A report on a crack-down on Jewish musicians in Germany noted that UK players were being forced to return to their own country, while stateless performers sought sanctuary in neutral Switzerland.[11] Yet the paper still wrestled with race. Columnist Spike Hughes hailed 'Old Man Harlem' by the Dorsey Brothers as 'a record made by white men for white men. No jungle nonsense I tell you, but music to show who's the master of these upstart natives once and for all, egad!'[12] In fairness, this was a parody of racism, and music writer Simon Frith has identified Hughes as an important contributor to jazz criticism. In a review of Duke Ellington's first British performance, Hughes cited the pianist as 'the first genuine jazz composer' and proclaimed jazz 'the music of the Harlem gin mills, the Georgia backyards and New Orleans street corners – the music of a race that plays, sings and dances because music is its most direct medium of expression and escape'.[13]

Demand for 'rhythm music' gave rise to record clubs dedicated to the genre. 'The general procedure is for the club's members to congregate periodically and listen to hot records,' wrote Percy Mathison Brooks in a 1933 editorial. 'That the self-same records are owned by ninety per cent of the club members, and have already been played over and over again in the seclusion of their own homes, is no deterrent, apparently, to listening to them again in public. It is peculiar but, from our point of view, praiseworthy.'[14]

These clubs cemented jazz's respectability. 'Once a popular, hedonistic craze with connotations of excess and moral degeneracy, jazz was increasingly understood to have artistic depth similar to western "art" music, and to require focused attention,' wrote academic Lawrence Davies.[15] Brooks and his *Melody Maker* predecessor Edgar Jackson – then writing the column 'Dance and popular rhythmic records' for *The Gramophone* – became co-presidents of an association representing the nation's clubs: the No 1 Rhythm Club.

Jazz's mainstream acceptance was boosted by the rise of record labels, eroding the domination of sheet music that tended towards the staid and sentimental. Meanwhile, 'the talkies' replaced silent cinema and disseminated jazz and its performers far and wide.

In 1934, *Melody Maker* – now minus the definite article – became a sixteen-page broadsheet, with one page dedicated to musicians' classified ads. The latter, soon expanded, were to be a *Maker* staple for the next sixty years. Now wholeheartedly promoting Black American culture, the paper featured blues artists and even hipster slang and occasional drug references. Coleman Hawkins was described affectionately as 'a reefer man' with 'weed-smoker's riffs'. British musicians' penchant for pot, however, was condemned as 'insanity and death'.[16]

No longer considered adornments, female artists such as blues singer Alberta Hunter and jazz performers Pat Hyde and Ina Ray Hutton were granted more exposure. This was underlined, Nick Johnstone noted, 'by the paper's first truly revolutionary act: the Christmas 1934 issue, with its trademark gallery of stars, included for the first time a black and a female musician (the Guyanese clarinetist Rudolph Dunbar and Ennis Hylton, née Parkes, who was nevertheless credited as Mrs Jack Hylton).'[17] Former editor Edgar Jackson, now enlightened, returned to publish a review that asserted, 'True jazz is neither crooning nor Gershwin's concert hall syncopation – it is nothing a white man plays. It is the stuff the Negro plays and sings.'

The paper was strengthened by the acquisition of its closest competitor, *Rhythm*, from John E Dallas & Sons, which had built a solid readership over seven years. Incorporating the title made *Melody Maker*, its cover declared, 'a super-modern magazine ... the best way to spend sixpence'.[18]

Having made progressive strides in its first decade, the paper still stumbled. It is hard to reconcile the prominence of Jews in the British music business and associated with *Melody Maker* – not least Edgar Jackson – with a 1936 piece by critic Stanley Nelson that denigrated Jewish musicians' contribution to jazz. 'The Jew is not a great creator,' he wrote. 'The Jew is the complete masochist.' Yet Nelson had published one of the first books in Britain about the genre, in which he opined that White appropriation 'has led us into a cul de sac. We lack the spontaneity of the coloured people and their innate feel for the idiom'.[19]

Bandleader Benny Goodman – one of the Jewish musicians accused by Nelson of appropriating black music – was at the forefront of the highly popular swing genre. Meanwhile, another craze – for squeezeboxes – gave rise to the launch of *Accordion Times*. A White DIY culture antithetical to the soul and grit of jazz and blues, it produced popular figures such as Harry Bidgood. He was featured regularly on *Whistle While You Work*, a programme begun by the BBC in 1939 to support the war effort at factories and workplaces.

The Second World War forced *Melody Maker* – with Edgar Jackson back in the fold as jazz critic – to revert to a monthly cycle. Reporter Chris Hayes, who joined the editorial team in 1929, enlisted with the Royal Artillery, but would ultimately remain with the *Maker* until the New Romantic era in 1981.

Editor Percy Brooks joined the Royal Air Force, though he wrote about the role the paper would play as 'a watchdog over the temporary ruins of a profession and an industry until they are rebuilt'.[20] His place was taken by Ray Sonin, who had been judged unfit for military service. Educated at London's Regent Street Polytechnic, he had written popular songs such as 'Gertie the Girl with the Gong'.[21] And for the BBC, who aimed to uplift the populace at a time of crisis, Sonin wrote scripts for the comedy *ITMA* – 'It's that man again', referring to Hitler – and produced shows featuring Noël Coward and Vera Lynn.

In wartime, paper stock was limited and advertising all but collapsed. *Melody Maker* shrank from broadsheet to slightly larger than A4, though it went back to weekly publication within months, reporting on the impact on venues and musicians of the Blitz: the German air assault that pummelled British cities from the summer of 1940 to the spring of '41. As American professor Christina Baade has pointed out, dance halls and clubs, and the ongoing broadcast of music, reinforced a sense that the Luftwaffe could not disrupt daily life and its pleasures: '*Melody Maker* provided guidance to its readership on survival in the changing landscape of wartime entertainment with articles like "If your band is blitzed ...". To the extent it could do so without revealing strategic information, it chronicled the dramas, disasters and everyday bravery of the dance music profession during the period. *Melody Maker*'s coverage not only reinforced a sense of unity but also sutured dance musicians into national narratives of the Blitz.'

One such was British Guyanan bandleader Ken 'Snakehips' Johnson, killed in a direct hit on London's Café de Paris in March 1941. '*Melody Maker* devoted extensive coverage to the loss of "England's swing king", along with the death of his tenor saxophonist Dave Williams,' wrote Baade, who noted that the BBC was slower to acknowledge Johnson's death. 'A week after *Melody Maker* had devoted most of its front page to the news, the *Radio Times* (the BBC's listing magazine) offered "a belated word of regret for Ken Johnson". His fans must have flooded the weekly with tributes because the next week it published three, which not only expressed regret but advocated for a special programme to memorialize Johnson.' The BBC did however broadcast a tribute to the White South African singer Al Bowlly, who died in an air raid a month after Johnson.

For the next four years of the war, *Melody Maker* hovered around eight to twelve pages as it marked time without a domestic live scene. Visits to the UK by American stars such as Glenn Miller helped maintain positivity, and the tone remained defiant, even after a flying bomb damaged the *Melody Maker* offices in September 1944. Editor Ray Sonin noted that not one issue was lost to the hostilities despite 'all that Hitler has tried to do'.[22]

The paper played its part in boosting relations with the US. When Bing Crosby visited Britain to tape a performance for the BBC, Sonin gushed: 'He bounded on stage, beaming, and stood there while the biggest reception ever accorded an artist in my memory thundered through the vast hall. Men and girls [*sic*] alike were completely captivated by him. Tough commandos and burly sergeant majors were among those who yelled out for him to sing "White Christmas", not hysterical girls.'[23]

All publications were hit by paper rationing, but *Accordion Times* also suffered from the waning popularity of its titular instrument. A change of direction resulted in a new weekly in October 1946: *Accordion Times & Musical Express*. By February 1948, the masthead was slimmed to *Musical Express*. Throughout, it tracked Britain's still fertile dance band scene while serving up showbusiness tidbits. A 1950 issue of what was then billed as 'Britain's largest weekly entertainment newspaper' previewed a BBC show featuring future jazz giant Johnny Dankworth and, 'of special interest to the younger set', a regular jiving contest.[24]

'*Musical Express* exuded raffishness and Bohemianism,' wrote Pat Long, who tracked the paper's history in a largely laudatory book. It was, Long said, 'a cosmopolitan and glamorous paper that transcended the mood of the threadbare, gloomy Britain of bombsites and ration cards. *Musical Express* dealt with music like it was the most important thing in the world, and that the people who played it were an elect group, apart from everyday society.'[25]

Black American music was revered at *Melody Maker*, particularly after the 1944 recruitment of semi-pro saxophone player Ronald 'Max' Jones. The music press's first star – identifiable by an after-hours look of dark glasses and black beret – 'published work by people such as George Padmore, pioneer of pan-Africanism, and the black American writer Langston Hughes, as well as the "Negrophile" Nancy Cunard,' said Val Wilmer, a jazz-mad teenager who was to meet Jones and write for *Melody Maker*. 'The music's early chroniclers wrote in isolation in Britain. Not having to confront the Black reality in their presence to any extent, they could afford to be liberal, and it became increasingly apparent that the role whites played in defining the music irked many people within the culture. Nevertheless, tribute is due to those pioneering white spirits who went beyond the affair with the "Negro" that existed from the days of Blackface minstrelsy, to realize there was more to the music than fashion or instant thrills. Max Jones was certainly one of those.'[26]

'Jones came to be regarded as among the leading writers on New Orleans, swing and mainstream jazz,' wrote *Jazz Journal* and *Melody Maker* columnist Steve Voce. 'The pieces he wrote for the paper were amazing both in their proliferation and their perception.'[27]

'*Melody Maker* seemed incredibly hip,' says Chris Welch, who joined the paper in the 1960s. 'It carried weekly coverage of an almost underground scene, which made you feel like you were part of a secret society. Max Jones was the great authority. I discovered later, when I worked for it, that most of the people he wrote about were personal friends.'[28]

Stars such as Dinah Washington and Billie Holiday relied on Jones for help during their visits to London. Early one morning, Jones received a call from a distressed Washington, who had been accosted by a staff member at her hotel: 'She had sent out for a bottle of whisky in the small hours and the night man – delivering same and discovering our singer bare except for a nightie – had drawn a perilously false conclusion.' Steve Voce wrote that Jones helped calm the situation and Washington ensured that the man was sacked.[29]

While Jones and the *Melody Maker* team engaged with heavyweights, *Musical Express* focused on British bandleaders. Two such stars – Joe Loss and Cyril Stapleton – were on the roster of young manager-turned-promoter Maurice Kinn, who sometimes advertised in the weekly. In 1952, Kinn received a call from the ad manager at *Musical Express*, whose circulation was struggling around 18,000 as a paucity of advertising restricted its size to just four pages. 'The paper had lost so much money, it was going to close down if they couldn't find a buyer by the following Monday,' recalled Kinn. 'I wasn't really that interested. They were asking for £1,000.' But a visit to the publisher's offices changed his mind. 'I went to talk to them because they owed me money and got caught up with this idea of running the paper.'[30]

Backed by a loan from his parents-in-law, Kinn decided to branch into publishing. And so began events that transformed his fortunes and shaped the future of the music press.

2
‘Everyone thought I was crazy’

16, *NME* and the Birth of Rock

'Everyone thought I was crazy'

A quarter of a century after the founding of *The Melody Maker* in London's Denmark Street, Maurice Kinn installed new staff at offices across the road. Here, in 1952, they set about producing the renamed *New Musical Express*.

Kinn aggressively poached *Melody Maker* staffers, including advertising manager Percy Dickins, assistant editor Jack Baverstock and reporter Les Perrin, later to make his name as a publicist for the likes of the Rolling Stones. The editor was another *Melody Maker* alum, Ray Sonin, who – having won a 'respectable sum of money on the British football pools'[1] – had retired to write novels. But his track record as editor of the *Maker* lent credence to his later claims that it was he, not Kinn, who drove the transformation of what became *NME*.

'Everybody said we'd last five minutes,' said Dickins. 'The target was £100 worth of advertising a week, and I did it. I'd built up contacts and some weeks I did more than that.'[2]

'Percy had a slightly rarified air about him – his nickname was "Sir Percy",' recalled songwriter Don Black, then an office boy at the paper. 'Maurice seemed very authoritarian but I think that was because he was a very shy man.'[3]

The first issue of the recharged publication hit British newsstands on 7 March 1952. 'The presentation and contents will be fresh and stimulating,' declared editor Sonin, 'because *The New Musical Express* will be produced by a brand new, handpicked staff of editorial experts with long experience in music journalism and an overall knowledge of the business.'[4]

With issues expanded to sixteen pages, the front page emphasised photography in place of the jumble of stories posted by the previous regime. Moving the letters page upfront increased engagement with readers, while an expanded classified ads section brought in a much needed three pence per word. The back page was dominated by 'Tail-pieces': music industry gossip from Kinn, in the guise of 'the Alley Cat' – a persona he used over the years to break news, spread tittle-tattle, promote his own acts and sometimes settle scores.

Takeup of the new version proved slow. 'The paper kept on losing money hand over fist,' Kinn admitted. 'I had to borrow money from my mother-in-law to keep it afloat. I felt like an idiot, like I'd made a mistake.' But he persevered. '[Kinn] thought of the idea of sending out free copies to show people what it was like and had his mum and dad in one of the rooms sending them out,' said Percy Dickins. 'He put new life into it and it started to look better.' Kinn also invested in ads on Radio Luxembourg, a broadcaster that challenged the BBC's monopoly. 'That did it,' said Dickins.[5]

As *Musical Express*, the paper had included an unobtrusive chart of sheet music sales. 'There were names there like Johnny Ray, Frank Sinatra [and] Nat "King" Cole, but they weren't getting the coverage,' Kinn noted. 'Instead it had been all about the big-band scene, which was fading away. So I got hold of the chart and said, "These are the people we should be covering. The chart should be the reason why people buy the paper."'

In 1952, a deal was struck to license so-called 'music popularity' charts from *Billboard*. The American trade journal had made strides towards desegregating popular music by replacing the title 'Race' with 'Rhythm & Blues' for its listing of African American songs. This opened White fans' ears to pre-rock 'n' roll Black music in the US, but *NME* chose four other charts, each with twenty-five places: Records Most Played by Disc Jockeys, Best Selling Pop Singles, Best Selling Sheet Music and Top Tunes in Britain.

NME's course, however, was changed by the decision in November 1952 to print a chart based on sales from twenty British outlets. Sonin claimed credit for this, noting that he had an understanding of the commercial potential of charts from his twelve years at *Melody Maker*. Dickins claimed the chart was *his* idea: 'I said to Ray, "This would be a good idea, to have the best-selling records," and he said, "Good idea, you set it up."'[6]

Dickins oversaw the collection of information from record shops, many of which were in London. 'For the first time in the history of the British popular music business, an authentic weekly survey of the best selling "pop" records has been devised and instituted,' trumpeted the intro to the 'Record Hit Parade'.[7] But amid post-war austerity, so small was the release schedule that the debut *NME* chart featured just twelve releases. Number one was 'Here in My Heart' by Al Martino, who had fled the US mafia to live in England and would play a role based on his experiences in Francis Ford Coppola's *The Godfather*. Also represented were big names that Kinn was keen to include in the paper: Nat 'King' Cole, Doris Day, Bing Crosby, Vera Lynn, Guy Mitchell, Johnny Ray and Jo Stafford.

The initial list of twenty chart reporting outlets was expanded to fifty-three, taking in northern hubs such as Liverpool and Manchester. 'Each member of the paper's staff was allocated a list of shops to call every Monday morning,' wrote Pat Long. 'The results of these calls were passed to *NME*'s staff accountant, who took time from his duties on the payroll to collate and process the week's research.'[8]

The chart boosted *NME*'s profile sufficiently for it to become the basis of a show on Radio Luxembourg. That forced *Melody Maker* to follow suit, according to Mark Williams, 'using its financial muscle to undermine *NME* by licensing its own pop charts to daily newspapers'.[9]

In 1953, Kinn introduced what became a magazine standard: an annual awards event. He declared the first *NME* Poll Winners' Concert 'the night of the year' and, although the show was notionally based on readers' votes, the paper's editors and heavyweight music managers clearly had a hand in who appeared. A packed audience at London's prestigious Royal Albert Hall witnessed winners' crowns being placed on bandleader Ted Heath, jazzers Johnny Dankworth and Ronnie Scott and singers Lita Roza and Dickie Valentine.

'Everyone thought I was crazy,' said Kinn. 'They couldn't see why kids would want to come along to see these acts on the same bill. To me, after years of packaging artists, it seemed obvious. The readers' polls started to help push up the circulation.'

NME's rising fortunes elevated Kinn to celebrity status. When Frank Sinatra arrived in London in 1953 after the collapse of his marriage to Ava Gardner (which had led to him being admitted to hospital suffering from 'mental strain and exhaustion'), the singer poured his heart out in an *NME* interview. 'He'd had a disastrous tour of Italy, where the fans had booed and called for Ava, but we gave him his chance to put his side of the story,' said Kinn. 'He never forgot our support. A couple of years later my wife and I visited him in LA on the set of a movie he was making, and he flew us to Las Vegas and paid for our stay at the Sands.'

By the mid-1950s *NME*'s circulation was 100,000. 'I bought my first Rolls-Royce,' recalled Kinn. Meanwhile, *Melody Maker* rose to 97,000 in 1955. The boom stemmed from an explosion in releases – and accompanying ads – from labels such as EMI, Columbia, HMV, MGM and Parlophone.

Represented by their own youth cult – neo-Edwardian peacocks the Teddy Boys – and targeted by records, films and new fashions, British teenagers had come to the fore. And so were born opportunities for publishers who catered to their tastes. Among the new weeklies was *Record & Show Mirror* (its title soon to be abbreviated), launched in 1954 by Isidore Green, who lured columnists such as Peter Hepple, future editor of *The Stage*, 'for little in the way of reward'.[10]

Record Mirror, wrote British academic Peter Mills, 'was the first weekly to assume the reader as non-musician and furthermore to be as interested in the lives and preferences of the performers as their music. It became a respected if more lightweight companion to *NME*, the "poppiest" of the weeklies.'[11] The new title riled the market leaders by establishing its own singles chart, followed by the UK's first album chart. Undaunted by a legal challenge – mounted on the basis that the younger magazine had infringed *NME*'s trademarks – Isidore Green declared *Record Mirror*'s charts 'the most authentic'.[12]

Nevertheless, *Record Mirror* failed to dent either *NME*'s or Maurice Kinn's standing. Kinn came to know major players in the music business, including Elvis Presley and his notoriously protective manager Colonel Tom Parker: 'He used to organise interviews with Elvis for me, always provided front row tickets and used to take regular adverts.' Parker later had Presley record a message to be played at a 1964 *NME* awards show. In it, the star wished 'much continued success' to the Beatles, 'as well as the other great recording artists in England'.

Melody Maker's predilection for jazz, blues and folk left it unmoved by the emergence of rock 'n' roll. A review of Presley's UK breakthrough single 'Heartbreak Hotel' dismissed him as 'a very mannered singer' with 'extremely poor diction'.[13] Steve Race was equally unimpressed by 'Hound Dog': 'Many times I have heard bad records, but for sheer repulsiveness coupled with the monotony of incoherence, "Hound Dog" hit a new low.'[14]

NME's letters page gave young fans a forum to torment jazzers and, by association, *Melody Maker* readers. 'Rock 'n' roll provides excitement,' noted one. 'What better music for young cats to jump to?'[15]

The new genre went mainstream with the excited response to the film *Rock Around the Clock* in 1956. Newspapers seized on reports of public disorder in cinemas and demonized the Teddy Boys. Kinn leapt to the defence of his readers, accusing the press of 'exaggerating and distorting the situation, instead of recognising the riots as the hooliganism of an undisciplined minority'. And that autumn, according to Pat Long, 'The paper was full of pieces on Fats Domino, Elvis, Bill Haley, Carl Perkins and the thirteen-year-old Frankie Lymon. Reading these interviews with wonder were hundreds of the children – among them John Lennon, Malcolm McLaren and Marc Bolan – who would later shape British pop music.'[16]

A force in the 1960s counterculture and a music journalist in the seventies, Mick Farren hailed Kinn's paper as 'tougher than *Melody Maker*. It ran articles on Gene Vincent and Jerry Lee [Lewis], while the *MM* still had that jazzer, snotty attitude.'[17] Even the staid John Major, later one of Britain's Conservative prime ministers, was swayed. 'In my youth,' he told Kinn, 'the weekly copy of *NME* was an absolute must.'[18]

'If any new artist came into the chart, it was almost the duty of the paper to cover them,' said broadcaster-to-be Charlie Gillett, who became so fixated with the charts that he cut them out each week. These proved useful when he wrote *The Sound of the City*, the first authoritative account of rock 'n' roll in the post-war years.[19]

Strained relations between Kinn and his editor Ray Sonin reached breaking point in 1957. The latter emigrated to Canada and launched his own paper, *Music World*, before switching to a distinguished career in radio. His replacement at *NME* was Andy Gray, a Canadian living in London. Meanwhile, Kinn and his wife entertained homegrown and visiting stars at cocktail parties in their Mayfair apartment. When Sammy Davis Jr was booked to play a season in London, the singer asked Kinn – who had met Davis during his residencies in Las Vegas – to throw him a gathering where he could meet British performers. 'Everybody came along,' recalled

Kinn. 'Lonnie Donegan, Russ Conway, Janet Scott, Connie Francis, Lionel Blair, Alma Cogan, Dickie Valentine ... everybody. That night [Davis] put on an impromptu performance. He sang, danced and told stories for forty minutes. That was his UK debut. Then he persuaded all the others to each do a turn. It helped launch his career here.'

Since *Record Mirror* had seen off Kinn's attempts to close its chart, others entered the fray; notably *Disc*, founded by Charlie Buchan, a soccer star turned journalist who had established a publishing empire. There are stories that the young British singer Cliff Richard worked as an office assistant for Buchan. Certainly he would have been a member of the new record-buying demographic at whom the weekly was aimed. '*Disc* will live up to its name, spotlighting discs, the artists who make them and all the interesting backroom secrets from the recording studios,' proclaimed the first issue, which included three charts: a Top Twenty ('compiled from dealers' returns all over the country'), American Top Tunes and a Juke Box Top Ten, with figures provided by the US trade magazine *World's Fair*.

Columnists included DJ Pete Murray, a presenter of the BBC's first pop television show, *Six-Five Special*. He was among the high-profile entertainment names who gathered to launch *Disc* in February 1958. The mood was dampened when Buchan announced that he would not make a celebratory speech because news had broken that eight Manchester United footballers had died in an air crash in Munich.

Nonetheless *Disc* soon won an audience, thanks to cover stars such as Nat 'King' Cole and the Native American-style singer Marvin Rainwater. The 'Big Beat' page – news from America – featured unknowns such as the young African American quartet the Blossoms, later to become the voices of producer Phil Spector's early hits. Advertisers included Britain's first male boutique, Vince Man's Shop, and Sherrick, the makers of an American-cut, denim 'rock suit'.

Six-Five Special producer Jack Good was a popular contributor. 'Good would take the whole column – probably 1,000 words – to write about "Duke of Earl" by Gene Chandler or "Hey! Baby" by Bruce Channel,' recalled *Disc* reader Richard Williams. 'Although they were hits, they were nonetheless quite extreme in their own way, and he would write, "These are the best things you've ever heard." I really responded to that.'

Rather than cannibalizing each other's sales, the four weeklies, each with different takes on the potent pop scene, stoked interest among a growing band of British fans. Elton John, in the late 1950s, 'copied all the different singles charts out of *Melody Maker*, the *New Musical Express*, *Record Mirror* and *Disc*, then compiled the results, averaging them out into a personal chart of charts'.[20]

But *Disc*'s emergence underlined *Melody Maker*'s lack of agility. The homemade skiffle craze – which went mainstream in Britain in 1957 when Lonnie Donegan scored chart-toppers with 'Cumberland Gap' and 'Gamblin' Man' – was within *Melody Maker*'s purview, because it combined jazz, blues and folk, genres the paper had long championed. However, the *Maker* remained hostile to rock 'n' roll; a stance, according to Nick Johnstone, 'rooted in the question of musical ability. The cult of the idol was growing, but critics accustomed to praising the merits of being able to play well found this hard to stomach.'[21] Writer Steve Race railed against the new music as 'sexually suggestive, simplistic and lacking melody'. Citing the Imps' tawdry novelty B-side 'Dim Dumb Blonde', Race lashed out at British youth for buying into 'the cheapest music even America has produced' – overlooking the fact that the group were skiffling Lancastrians.

The paper's first editor, Edgar Jackson, was brought out of retirement in 1958 to applaud the new wave of jazzers such as saxophonist Sonny Rollins and pianist Thelonious Monk. 'A cultural war developed between the jazz intellectuals and the rock 'n' roll hedonists,' noted Nick Johnstone. 'Some of the finest jazz records of all time were made in the coming period, and it was only natural that the paper should enthusiastically endorse the growing diversity of jazz styles.'[22]

* * *

Across the Atlantic, contemporary music had been the preserve of trade titles such as *Billboard* and *Cashbox*, while the jazz journal *DownBeat* – founded in Chicago in 1934 – rode the waves from big band music and swing to modern jazz. John Hammond, New York stringer for *Melody Maker* at the start of the 1930s, personified its fiercely critical and intellectual approach, though *DownBeat* took heat for not featuring African American musicians such as Lester Young and Charlie Parker on its front pages until the 1950s.

DownBeat's defenders, however, note that, between the covers, 'There was no music magazine of the period more progressive or aggressive on the race issue, or in making sure that its readers understood the Black innovators.'[23] And it was a hotbed for talent: among those who published their first journalism in *DownBeat* were the Turkish American brothers Ahmet and Nesuhi Ertegun, who would champion Black music with Atlantic Records, where artists ranged from John Coltrane and Charles Mingus to Ray Charles and Aretha Franklin.

According to the Los Angeles musicologist Harvey Kubernik, Phil Spector – Kubernik's Fairfax High School pal – wrote to *DownBeat* in the mid-1950s to protest the exclusion of jazz guitarist Barney Kessel from an article. 'A lot of people had letters printed in magazines before they jump-started their careers in music or the press,' said Kubernik. 'It was a way of showing interest in the subject as well as being their only outlet.'[24]

Intentionally devoid of *DownBeat*'s critical sensibilities was *Seventeen*, a bimonthly launched by the Hearst Corporation in 1944 to provide role models for teenage girls and school-leavers. On the back of the bobbysoxer phenomenon – fandom for crooners such as Frank Sinatra – *Seventeen* sold 500,000 copies an issue by 'offering a non-patronising approach that hit a chord by focusing on the barely recognized purchasing power of adolescents'.[25] And it proved an important stepping stone for a generation of American talent: art director Marvin Israel, who had studied at Yale under the Bauhaus's Josef Albers, commissioned work by photographers Diane and Allan Arbus, Robert Frank and Lee Friedlander.

Israel also took stunning portraits of James Dean and Elvis Presley. 'In the context of a mainstream publication aimed at teenage girls,' wrote Martin Harrison, 'Israel's stark, uncompromising black and whites must have appeared unsettling, and only two of his 500 photographs of Elvis were published at the time.'[26]

The teen market spawned a slew of vibrant newcomers – notably *Dig*, *Hit Parader* and *16*, which laid the foundations for US music criticism in the 1960s and '70s. *Dig*'s target market was made clear by the name of its publisher: Teenage Magazines. It emerged from Hollywood in 1955 alongside other bids to exploit the new demographic, such as *Modern Teen* and *Teen Scene*. 'In sharp contrast with the moralistic flavor of earlier youth magazines,' one sociologist of the period concluded, 'the post-war group is distinguished by its hedonistic values within an essentially amoral setting: the teen years are not ones of preparation for responsible adulthood, but of play and diversion.'[27]

'*Dig* was America's hippest magazine, one in tune with what was really happening with fifties teens,' music critic Alan Betrock declared. 'It was frequently a leader, rarely a follower. Early issues had rhythm and blues inserts – the first issue had an R&B flexidisc! – and a string of youthful reporters who were part of the scenes they covered.'[28]

A *Mad* magazine-like humour permeated *Dig*'s pages, which documented the rock 'n' roll lifestyle, from custom cars and movies to fashion and hairstyles. Among the contributors was songwriter and producer Kim Fowley, later the man behind the Runaways. 'He used it as an entrée into the record business,' says Harvey Kubernik. 'Kim went to Goldstar Studios to interview the Champs when they were recording "Tequila". It was his way of getting in.' Fowley followed his *Dig* gig with a stint in record promotions, and topped the US chart with 'Alley Oop' by his ensemble the Hollywood Argyles.

Dig itself fared less well. 'By the early sixties, it deteriorated into just another teen idol mag,' lamented Betrock. But as *Dig* fell, *Hit Parader* rose. '*Hit Parader* evolved from a pop to a rock 'n' roll magazine in the late fifties,' wrote Betrock. 'Once there, it never looked back, always managing to cover whoever was in the charts, local favourites, deejays, movies and song lyrics. In its '55 to '63 years it was never too radical or adventurous, and there was less Black coverage than there should have been, but a good run of *Hit Paraders* profile just about anyone in rock 'n' roll and are a good mirror of the charts and the times.'[29]

'It was written intelligently, taking music away from the teeny-boppers and putting it in a more serious context,' agreed record label operator and music magazine publisher Greg Shaw. Kubernik favoured *Hit Parader* for 'the newsprint – it was black and white, gritty. There were really good photos. I went for it rather than the trades like *Cashbox* and *Billboard*. They were expensive but not true to the music. I didn't like seeing phrases like "race music" with all these guys with phony smiles holding plaques up.'

But the title that can truly lay claim to inaugurating the era of rock writing was *16* magazine, despite its origins in the mid-1950s as a cash-in on *Seventeen*'s popularity by literary agent Jacques Chambrun. This thoroughly bad egg had embezzled a fortune from novelist W. Somerset Maugham, screenwriter Ben Hecht and *Peyton Place* author Grace Metalious. One element of Chambrun's long con was to make much of his background: he claimed to have been born into the French aristocracy, though it is likely that he hailed from the Bronx. 'He could be elegant or oily, depending on whom you asked,' noted *The New Yorker*. 'Knox Burger, an editor and agent, once described Chambrun as a "feral character" and said he would be perfect "if you were casting an unctuous Levantine villain in a 1950 film noir". He dyed his hair a deep black and threw Hugh Hefner-style parties in his basement pool.'[30]

Having fleeced his clients, Chambrun scored a publishing sensation in 1956 with the one-off cash-in *All About Elvis*, built around previously published stories and photos of Presley bought from a newspaper editor in Memphis. When this sold out, Chambrun established a new magazine for teenage girls. Fellow agent Desmond Hall and journalist George Waller contributed, using female pseudonyms: editor-in-chief 'Georgia Winters', for example.

The first issue of *16*, with Presley on the cover, appeared in 1957. Billed as 'The magazine for girls', it resembled, said American writer Margaret Moser, 'one of those 1950s Hollywood scandal sheets minus the dirt. Plenty of Elvis coverage, snaps of Hollywood stars like Natalie Wood and Debra Paget, a quiz asking "Are your parents delinquent?" and a feature on the Million Dollar Quartet [the retrospective name for a gathering of stars at an Elvis session in December 1956]. How honed-in was *16* on its audience in its first issue?

Those iconic photos of Jerry Lee Lewis, Carl Perkins, Elvis Presley and Johnny Cash at a piano in Sun Studios were *16*'s exclusively.'[31]

This set the tone for successive issues. 'While Waller filled its pages with such hot young performers as Elvis, Pat Boone, even James Dean, he did not personally interview any of the subjects but worked from press releases, previously published material and some commissioned stories,' wrote Randi Reisfeld and Danny Fields in their history of the magazine. 'From the get-go, *16* was done on the cheap. Waller worked from home and, while some funds were spent on photos and stories, Chambrun's iron-clad rule was always, "Get it for as little as you can."'[32]

These economies didn't stop the circulation's steady rise. And *16* steadfastly shunned third-party advertising, despite the clamour from record labels, managers, agents and producers of goods aimed at the burgeoning teenage market. For the first twenty years of its existence, non-editorial space was reserved for in-house promotions. This would have deep-sixed any other title, but it honed the magazine's appeal. 'Fans were quick to realize *16* was the only place they could go to find information (such as it was) and photos,' wrote Reisfeld and Fields. 'It was a fanbook for them, a *Photoplay* or *Life*, filled with the young stars they cared about.'[33]

As subscription forms and readers' letters poured in, the middle-aged men producing the copy and licensing the photography cast around for someone to assist. Chambrun's chance encounter at a New York party with glamorous model Gloria Stavers was to lead *16* in a brave new direction. The seeds were sown for the development of what critic Dave Marsh described as 'rock and pop culture journalism'[34] and for the decades-long task of wresting dominance of the music press from White male writers.

3 'Everything was possible'

Gloria Stavers and the Teen Scene

It is likely that *16*'s saturnine publisher Jacques Chambrun was more persuaded by Gloria Stavers's appearance than her editorial potential when he hired the ex-model to handle the magazine's subscriptions and mail at 50¢ an hour in 1958.

'Gloria Stavers was one of the most beautiful people I have known,' gushed critic Dave Marsh. 'Her skin was the most beautiful I have ever seen, her jet black hair could mesmerize almost as much as her piercing eyes, and her leggy elegance never wavered.'[1]

Stavers had fled a dull marriage in upstate New York to make her name in Manhattan. Her looks clinched fashion work, but it was her ready wit and intellect that secured entry to the upper echelons of the city's café society. Among those with whom she broke bread at highfalutin nightspots were Marilyn Monroe and baseball's Mickey Mantle (she was rumoured to have had an affair with the latter). 'Gloria read voraciously and widely,' noted Marsh, 'but she didn't dwell on book learning ... When you are that sharp, that insightful, that beautiful, you don't have to worry about being hip – your existence defines it.'[2]

16 magazine's chroniclers Randi Reisfeld and Danny Fields relate that she swiftly grasped how it could better engage with the hopes and desires of its readers: 'She began to read the letters in the envelopes she was assigned to open. Most were full of breathless declarations of adoration for the idols of the day. All were full of questions, but not about the process that goes into making a record or how much money a star was raking in. The new stars (mostly boys) were young – the readers (mostly girls) were young. The readers cared about things they could relate to: how old was the performer, did he have a girlfriend, what did he eat for breakfast, what was his favourite TV show, or subject in school, what music did he listen to?'

Stavers suggested the magazine replace standard press bios with Q&As. Chambrun gave her the go-ahead for 'Forty intimate questions' and agreed for her to take photographs with her Rolleiflex. The results appeared alongside other Stavers-led sections: 'Hates & Loves', 'At home with ...' and 'Baby pix' (photographs of the stars as infants).

'Girls from ten to fifteen are in a period of development more intense than any other in their lives,' she explained. 'They are hungrier than they'll ever be, so they eat more. They see something they want, a skirt or a pair of boots, and they want it more than they'll ever want anything in their lives. By the time a girl reaches sixteen, she's ready to leave the dreamworld, and *16* is way behind her.'[3]

Within months, *16*'s sales rose to 250,000 and Chambrun appointed Stavers editor-in-chief – a post she was to hold for seventeen years. And the fans weren't all female. 'Gloria Stavers brought in a vibe and us readers picked up on music people that way,' said Harvey Kubernik. Her questionnaires were emulated in copycat titles such as *Tiger Beat*.[4] And a Stavers-created lingo – photographs were 'pix', issue 'ish', because 'cos' and favourite 'fave' – ensured *16* retained its innocence. There were no references to drinking, smoking or drugs, and sex was only hinted at in stories such as 'Our perfect night together'.

'Early *16* readers adored Troy Donahue, Paul Petersen, Paul Anka, Bobby Vee, Bobby Vinton, Bobby Rydell – such clean-sounding young men!' wrote Margaret Moser. 'Even the girls had bouncy names: Annette! Shelley Faberes! Sandra Dee! Connie Stevens! The magazine was packed full of big black-and-white pictures ("Kute-n-kuddly pix") and, later, colour pinups of the male stars, advice columns emphasizing character and inner beauty from female stars, glossy interviews, and always the contests: "You can be Miss 16!" "Win a record hop for your school!" and "Would you like to be friends with Annette?"'[5]

Drawing on her modelling background, Stavers gave young performers styling suggestions, while her insights into teen girls helped labels decide which releases to prioritise. But she was, as Moser noted, 'no saint, terrorizing under-assistants from both coasts ("Do I have to do your fucking job for you, man?"). She was known to rage over personal quests, threatening to print Paul Revere's real name if he didn't play a benefit for a dying girl (he was born Paul Revere Dick). Nor was Stavers above dipping her pen in company ink: she slept with a few of the idols between *16*'s pages. But Stavers wasn't about wielding pussy power even though she had it. She was about ambition and drive and being the first to get the story right. What she did with *16* altered the female psyche in America.'

The formula Stavers created for *16* 'matured into today's rock music journalism', noted Karen Steele: 'Gloria encouraged millions of young people to follow their dreams and presented them with a glimpse into a groovy adult world where everything was possible.'[6]

Such acknowledgment was a long time coming. 'I remember *16* being sneered at by the music press at large for its unabashed worship of all things young and pretty, for its unconditional embrace and acknowledgment that teenage love is real,' recalled Moser. 'It was the anti-standard for rock criticism, but its acceptance of an impressionable readership that simply loved and wanted to be loved made its enthusiastic approach guileless. That understanding existed because of one woman.'[7]

* * *

The saccharine performers celebrated by *16* threatened to usurp rock 'n' rollers in the late 1950s. Elvis Presley's air of danger diminished when he entered the US army in 1958. Little Richard renounced rock as the devil's music and enrolled in college to study theology. Jerry Lee Lewis's debut UK tour ended in disarray when it transpired that the twenty-two-year-old had married his thirteen-year-old cousin. Chuck Berry was arrested for the sex trafficking of a fourteen-year-old girl. Buddy Holly died in an air crash.

The major labels duly focused on tamer fare, and the readership and revenue of the *New Musical Express* started to sink. As issues shrank to forty pages, ad manager Percy Dickins resorted to featuring front-page advertisements. Increasingly out of touch, publisher Maurice Kinn gravitated to pop's more mature performers. His censorious side was evinced in attacks on young stars such as Cliff Richard and Billy Fury; Kinn wrote that the latter displayed 'revolting mannerisms' during a TV performance. 'Early evening viewers should be catered for,' he declared, 'not offended.'

'The Fleet Street [London media] moralists and MPs had won their battle to control rock 'n' roll,' wrote Pat Long. 'As 1960 became 1961, Kinn took stock of his business interests. His prognosis was pessimistic: this pop music lark's over ... Time to get out while the going's good.'[8]

Meanwhile, the Mirror Group – publisher of the UK's biggest-selling newspaper, the *Daily Mirror* – set its sights on the country's five million teenagers. The post-war baby boom meant people between the ages of ten and nineteen comprised close to fifteen per cent of the UK population.[9] 'In an era of plentiful jobs, British teenagers had double the spending power that they had in 1939,' wrote Jon Savage. 'Temporarily free of responsibilities, they bought a wide range of items: cosmetics, magazines, clothes, soft drinks, cinema tickets, and – most of all – records and record players.'[10]

As baby boomers flashed their cash, the media swooped. The Mirror Group swallowed Odhams, which had owned *Melody Maker* since the late 1920s. By now selling 110,000 copies a week, the paper featured five charts and included more rock and pop, though jazz remained its main constituent and race remained among its concerns. Frank Sinatra submitted an article titled 'Jazz has no colour bar!' about the civil rights turmoil that centered on African American students attending White schools in newly desegregated Arkansas. 'My debt to Negro performers', he wrote, 'can never be repaid.'[11] And when Miles Davis was savagely beaten on the streets of New York by racist policemen, *Melody Maker* put a photograph of the bloodied trumpeter in handcuffs on the cover, with the headline, 'This is what they did to Miles Davis.'[12]

Disc, meanwhile, introduced a promotional device that became an industry standard: the presentation of silver and gold sales discs. The first recipients, announced in May 1959, were Elvis Presley ('I Need Your Love Tonight'), Buddy Holly ('It Doesn't Matter Anymore') and pianist Russ Conway ('Side Saddle'). But publishers played it safe, either focusing on the 'trad jazz' boom (Humphrey Lyttelton, Chris Barber, Kenny Ball and Acker Bilk) or, taking a cue from across the Atlantic, aiming titles at teenage girls.

'I was ghosting disc columns for *Marilyn*, *Roxy* and *Valentine*,' recalled Keith Altham, later a publicist for big groups of the 1970s. 'They were teenage love story comics sandwiched with articles on pop stars. This was the era of Marty Wilde, Billy Fury, Adam Faith, Cliff Richard, Jess Conrad. Most of them were pale imitations of Elvis: people like Larry Page "the teenage rage". You'd end up with innocuous copy – "Duane Eddy is a mid-tempo shuffler that I love to listen to when I shave in the morning," that kind of crap. We weren't competing with *NME* and *Melody Maker*. This was kids' stuff.'[13]

Fans seeking tougher fare gravitated to the rural and urban blues of Black Americans stretching back to the 1930s. School pals John Broven, Mike Leadbitter and Simon Napier published the specialist magazine *Blues Unlimited*. 'The first issue was 200 copies done on a stencil machine in the attic of Simon's parents' antiques shop,' said Broven. 'Mike said, "You've got the records. You can write it."'[14]

Seeds for the blues boom were sown by visits to the UK by American artists, some now entering middle age, who had been largely ignored in their own country. The American Folk Blues Festival – held in October 1962 at Manchester's Lesser Free Trade Hall – blew the doors open. Willie Dixon, John Lee Hooker, Memphis Slim, Shakey Jake, T-Bone Walker, Sonny Terry and Brownie McGhee attracted an audience that included Mick Jagger and Brian Jones. Also in attendance was Nigel Waymouth, later to make his mark as co-founder of the psychedelic London boutique Granny Takes A Trip and half of the graphic design duo Hapshash and the Coloured Coat. 'After the gig I was chatting to Shakey Jake,' he recalled. 'This young boy comes up and says, "Can I have a go?", picks up the harmonica and starts blowing. Shakey Jake looks him up and down and goes, "Hey, you a star, man!" Of course, it was Mick Jagger. Him and Brian had travelled up in a little Mini-Minor. Anybody who was into the music had made the effort to get there and meet our heroes.'[15]

Blues fans were mostly young, middle class and male. Val Wilmer was virtually alone among White teenage females in having investigated Black music, from pre-war jazz to folk and blues, since her school days in the mid-1950s. *Melody Maker*'s Max Jones, she recalled, 'was understandably surprised to receive a letter from a fifteen-year-old schoolgirl. This, he said, he just had to see, and invited me to his office off Long Acre and gave me a stack of old magazines. Max's "Collector's corner" and "World of jazz" columns were packed with information on many of the lesser known musicians.'

Among the performers she invited to her family home was the blues artist Jesse Fuller. In Wilmer's highly recommended memoir *Mama Said There'd Be Days Like This* is a photograph of Fuller cooking breakfast in the family's kitchen, while her first published journalism was a piece on him for *Jazz Journal*.

Excited at the prospect of the American Folk Blues Festival, Wilmer was heartbroken to miss it: 'My friend's motorbike broke down soon after we set off from London, so I had to make do with reading Max Jones's report the following week.'[16] She would, however, become a *Melody Maker* contributor. This she credits to her friendship with fellow photographer and counterculture mover and shaker John 'Hoppy' Hopkins: he introduced her to the avant-garde likes of saxophonist Albert Ayler, pianist Cecil Taylor, composer/multi-instrumentalist Frank Zappa and bandleader Sun Ra. 'Hoppy was always ahead of the game,' she said. 'It was through meeting these musical revolutionaries that I started writing for *Melody Maker*.'

In the meantime, October 1962 proved an auspicious month. The Beatles released their first single, 'Love Me Do', beginning their transformation of popular culture. Meanwhile, *Melody Maker*'s dynamic features editor Jack Hutton was installed as editor. Determined to assert his paper's dominance over *NME*, he instituted a redesign and assembled a formidable team. A particular asset was assistant editor Ray Coleman, who coined the phrase 'Beatlemania'. 'Ray was merciless when it came to getting interviews,' said Hutton. 'He'd tell a prevaricating PR, when he was trying to get hold of John Lennon, "Don't give me all that. Somewhere he's within three yards of a telephone." He was a master at tracking people down. If people weren't co-operative, he'd ignore them and go his own way. We used to beat *NME* every week with his exclusive interviews. And people trusted him. He never misquoted people and never fantasised. He never used fancy phrases but managed to convey the artists' feelings in an honest and straightforward way and in some depth.'[17]

Such was *Melody Maker*'s reputation in America that Bob Dylan made a pilgrimage to its offices on his first visit to the UK in December 1962. 'He came into *MM* to find Max Jones,' said writer Michael Watts. 'But Max wasn't there and they threw him out of the office, thinking he was what was then known in the vernacular of the times [as] a "lumber", or a pest.'[18]

Eventually interviewed by Jones, Dylan namechecked the *Melody Maker* man in his 1965 album track 'Ballad of a Thin Man': 'Something is happening here and you don't really know what's going on, do you, Mr Jones?' The song, Dylan told one audience, was 'a response to people who ask me questions all the time. You just get tired of that every once in a while. You just don't want to answer no more questions. I figure a person's life speaks for itself, right? So every once in a while you got to do this kind of thing; you got to put somebody in their place. So this is my response to something that happened over in England.'[19]

Female music journalists were few and far between. Most prominent was Penny Valentine, of the retitled *Disc & Music Echo*. 'She was probably the first woman to write about pop music as though it really mattered,' said Richard Williams, who came to know her during his time at *Melody Maker* in the 1960s and '70s. 'When the Beatles travelled to London to promote their early records, one of the ports of call was *Disc*'s offices in Fleet Street. In the words of Andrew Loog Oldham, then acting as their press officer, they went to "ogle and fawn" over Penny, who had become Britain's most influential reviewer of new pop singles.'[20]

Val Wilmer initially disregarded Valentine: '*Disc* was rather downmarket compared to the *MM*, and I think I tended to dismiss her as a kind of dollybird. Eventually we became friends and confidantes, helping each other cross the precipices that opened up as women began increasingly to question our status as second-class citizens. The music press is a bastion of male chauvinism, and when I got to know a woman who worked there as a staffer, and survived it, I wanted to throw my hat in the air.'[21]

A soul music fan, Valentine championed Aretha Franklin and Marvin Gaye long before they became stars, and spotted the potential of Elton John and David Bowie during their years as 1960s marginals. Richard Williams believes the key to her copy was 'an unguarded enthusiasm. She was writing for the kids who bought and danced to the records ... "It's a girl's song with incredibly feminine words," she wrote in a review of Rita Wright's "I Can't Give Back the Love I Feel for You", "and I felt it so much I wanted to cry."'[22]

Meanwhile, at *Melody Maker*, production editor Bob Houston oversaw a conversion to a bold tabloid format in 1963. 'Bob played a central role in modernising the publication's look, and was equally influential in balancing its content to satisfy the demands of the jazz audience and the rising tide of rock music – with the Beatles on the front page and Ornette Coleman in the centre section,' wrote critic Dave Laing. 'He immediately understood the importance of such work as Val Wilmer's pioneering interviews with Archie Shepp, Sun Ra and other exponents of the new jazz, and gave them due prominence. He was enthusiastic about what was genuinely new in the rock scene, embracing the work of artists such as Frank Zappa.'[23]

According to Chris Welch, who joined the paper in 1963, Houston was a 'Glaswegian with a strong Marxist streak'. Another staffer, Bob Dawbarn, was 'well educated, public school but rebellious'. These qualities earned him a role as the paper's gossip columnist, competing with Kinn's Alley Cat at *NME* and reflecting the hive of activity the music business had become. His acerbic column 'The Raver', said Bob Houston, 'gave *Melody Maker* an edge its rivals conspicuously lacked'. And, the production editor noted, 'His annual "Old Dawbarn's Almanac" was eagerly awaited – and dreaded – in both jazz and rock scenes. All the while, he contributed perceptive, sometimes hilarious contributions; of American blues pianist Les McCann he wrote that "Les McCann M'Can't".' According to Houston, it was Dawbarn who sent Dylan packing: 'It was, after all, press day.'[24]

In this period of upheaval, Chris Welch recalls, 'They were throwing away files and photographs from the dance band era: literally dumping pictures of Ted Heath, Henry Hall, Billy Cotton. They wanted to bury the past. Some people were outraged because a lot of those who bought *Melody Maker* were professional musicians and their livelihoods were disappearing under the onslaught of the guitar groups.'

New editor Jack Hutton became a notable presence; spotting him at a New York press conference in 1964, John Lennon shouted, 'There's fucking Hutton!' That year the editor joined the Rolling Stones' US tour, visiting New York jazz clubs with Charlie Watts and accompanying the group to Chicago's Chess Studios, where they recorded the hit 'It's All Over Now' and met their idol Chuck Berry.

As Hutton took hold of *Melody Maker*, Maurice Kinn was approached by the Mirror Group. For a whopping £500,000 (£9 million today), *NME* joined *Melody Maker* and *Disc* as part of the Mirror's new magazine group International Publishing Company

(IPC). Kinn remained as executive director and continued to file his Alley Cat column, with an expense account to fund foreign travel and showbiz parties.

NME began to address the coming beat boom (while *Melody Maker* fretted, 'The new wave: is it killing jazz?'). Helpfully, Kinn had met the Beatles and their manager Brian Epstein at an EMI party soon after they were signed. 'Even then it was obvious they were going to be huge,' he recalled. 'I knew Brian because he had gone to school with my brother-in-law. He became a great friend; my wife, Berenice, got on very well with him.'

Berenice Kinn sympathized in particular with Epstein's struggle with his sexuality; England didn't legalize homosexuality until 1967, the year of his death. 'Brian was a sad person, somehow unfulfilled,' she said. 'The gay world was so different then. We all knew and accepted him, but I think it was very tough for Brian. In 1964 we were staying at the Beverly Hills Hotel and he called up in an awful state. I went to his room. He'd been smoking marijuana, was suicidally depressed and needed a shoulder to cry on. I sat up with him for four hours, talking and talking.'[25]

NME ran its first piece on the group in February 1963, ahead of the release of their debut album *Please Please Me*. Liverpudlian reporter Alan Smith, who had been canvassing support for them at the paper, announced, 'Things are beginning to move for the Beatles,' and pointed out that the title of a new track, 'From Me to You', was inspired by the banner across *NME*'s letters page: From You to Us.

'I was in the US when *Please Please Me* started to really take off,' recalled Maurice Kinn. 'I called Percy Dickins and told him to book them immediately for the Poll Winners Concert. They played every one between 1963 and 1966.'

Rivalry marred the 1965 event when Mick Jagger insisted to John Lennon that the Rolling Stones headline, as they had scored a run of chart-toppers. 'Lennon turned the air blue, enraged at Jagger's ingratitude after all the help the Beatles had given the nascent Stones (even penning "I Wanna Be Your Man" to help them get into the charts),' wrote Steve Sutherland, who edited *NME* in the 1990s. 'Jagger insisted he would pull the Stones out of the show if they didn't headline and was crestfallen when Maurice Kinn reminded him he would be in breach of contract with ABC [who broadcast the concerts] if he did so. The upshot was that the Beatles won the day; though, characteristically, Lennon then decided it would be far too dangerous for his band to finish the show as the audience would gather outside the venue and tear them apart. So it was that the Kinks closed the '65 show.'[26]

The following year's concert featured one of rock's greatest bills: the Who, Dusty Springfield, the Yardbirds, the Walker Brothers, Roy Orbison, the Spencer Davis Group with Stevie Winwood, Cliff Richard, the Shadows, Herman's Hermits, the Small Faces, the Stones and the Beatles. After the previous year's row, both of the top groups refused to allow their performances to be filmed. Consequently, the Beatles' final British performance – bar their rooftop farewell in 1969 – went unrecorded.

Mick Farren was in the audience for the Beatles' first appearance at the event. 'This was a real crossover point,' he said. 'They were on the same bill as Adam Faith, which showed how things were changing, and that was reflected in the magazine's coverage.'

The young musicians also attended parties at the Kinns' Mayfair apartment. 'Once Ringo brought Michael Crawford, then an aspiring actor, and one of the others came with Richard Burton's first wife,' said Maurice Kinn. When George Harrison and his girlfriend Pattie Boyd went missing while a party was in full swing, Kinn recalled, 'I found them performing on the bed in my daughter's room and said, "This is neither the time nor the place."'

A year after he sold *NME*, Kinn dined with music publisher Dick James, whose interests included the Beatles' company Northern Songs. James told Kinn that he would be prepared to sell his share. 'He wanted £250,000 because he thought the bubble was about to burst,' said Kinn. 'I was always interested in getting into music publishing – which, as everyone knows, is where the real money is in the music business.' According to Kinn, they shook hands on a deal. However, 'The next morning Dick called me: "Maurice, when I got home I told my wife and she's not happy about it. I know that we shook on it but I've changed my mind." I had to let it go. Needless to say, when he eventually sold Northern Songs, he got something like £9 million.'

The Beatles were sometimes horrified by Kinn's snipes at them in his gossip column –particularly John Lennon, who is believed to have begun a fling with singer Alma Cogan after meeting her at a Kinn soirée. 'Lennon could be a real handful, quite troublesome and rude sometimes,' said Kinn. 'He didn't really like me because I revealed the existence of his son in Alley Cat at a time when it was secret.' The group were also needled by Alley Cat's question, 'Did the Beatles leave their tarts in San Francisco?' after Kinn was told, by *NME* news editor Chris Hutchins, 'They were screwing everything in sight.'

The group's rapid success prompted a clampdown on access. Before they scored the five top positions in the US chart in April 1964, 'You kind of knew everyone was winging it,' says Keith Altham, then covering pop for Fleetway magazines. 'There were PR people like Les Perrin, but it was chummy, not cutthroat. The big money hadn't fully come in yet. It took nearly two years for British bands to fully break in America, so during that time it was still 'amateur night out' and everyone was having a great time. When the Beatles cracked America it all began to change, as the realization hit that there was huge money involved. It became more serious: more accountants, lawyers, press agents. It also became more specialized. Money was available and you realized you could make a career out of being a music journalist.'

Altham joined *NME* as a reporter. For the laid-back Andy Gray, he said, 'golfing correspondent' was a more fitting title than 'editor', but 'there were a few people who were cut-and-thrust. Chris Hutchins, who went to Fleet Street and later became PR for Tom Jones and Gilbert O'Sullivan, was hard-nosed and tough.' Of Kinn, Altham says, 'Because he'd owned it, he was a headmasterly figure. I made the mistake of calling him Maurice on my third day and received a phone call from his secretary telling me I had to call him Mr Kinn. So I always did. His response was to call me "M'lord" for the four years I was there.'

Kinn's tendency to prudishness was exposed when he wrote about singer PJ Proby's habit of deliberately splitting his tight trousers to delight his squealing fans. 'Proby mortally offended Maurice,' says Altham. 'He virtually caused PJ Proby's downfall when he put the accidentally-on-purpose trouser stuff in Alley Cat. That got into the nationals and, at the time, it wasn't considered on, so Proby was carved up.'

Kinn's profile rose when he guested on the TV show *Juke Box Jury*, on which celebrities judged new singles. Participants weren't supposed to know the records, but Kinn was primed by *NME* news and reviews editor Derek Johnson. 'Derek would put together a résumé and Maurice would pontificate, "Of course, this was a song first recorded by the Shirelles in 1961 at Muscle Shoals. I think it was raining at the time,"' said Altham. '[Host] David Jacobs would say, "Thank you very much, the Memory Man."'

Despite such minor deceptions and more serious charges of chart manipulation by record companies and promoters, Kinn claimed he held hard against pressure from Brian Epstein in regard to another of the manager's clients, singer Cilla Black. Her version of 'You've Lost That Lovin' Feeling' was released in Britain at the same time as that of the duo who originally recorded it, the Righteous Brothers. 'Brian called, absolutely out of his skin, and said, "It is very important to me that Cilla isn't outdone by them. What would it cost to ensure that?" I said, "I can't believe you're serious. You, EMI and the Beatles could put all their money together, but it wouldn't move me. I don't entertain changing chart positions in *NME* for anybody."' In the event, Black came second.

Meanwhile, in 1964, at least a dozen weeklies sold a total of a million issues a week to Britain's youngsters. Girls' comic *Jackie* featured substantial music coverage and Fleetway's weekly pop paper *Fabulous* soon rivalled *Melody Maker* in shifting 200,000 copies a week. A colourful new monthly, *Rave*, was created by IPC to cater to female teenagers, whether school-leavers or workers. '*Rave* was five times as expensive as the weekly music papers,' noted Jon Savage, 'but in return you got an eighty-page or so A4-size monthly, with excellent quality paper, meaty content and great photographs.'

With advertising from cosmetics and fashion companies, *Rave* marked out its territory with photography by Terry O'Neill and text by Cathy McGowan, the presenter of TV's *Ready Steady Go!* 'The first issue showed the cross-media spread of British pop culture with a front cover shot of the Beatles with 007 badges,' said Savage.

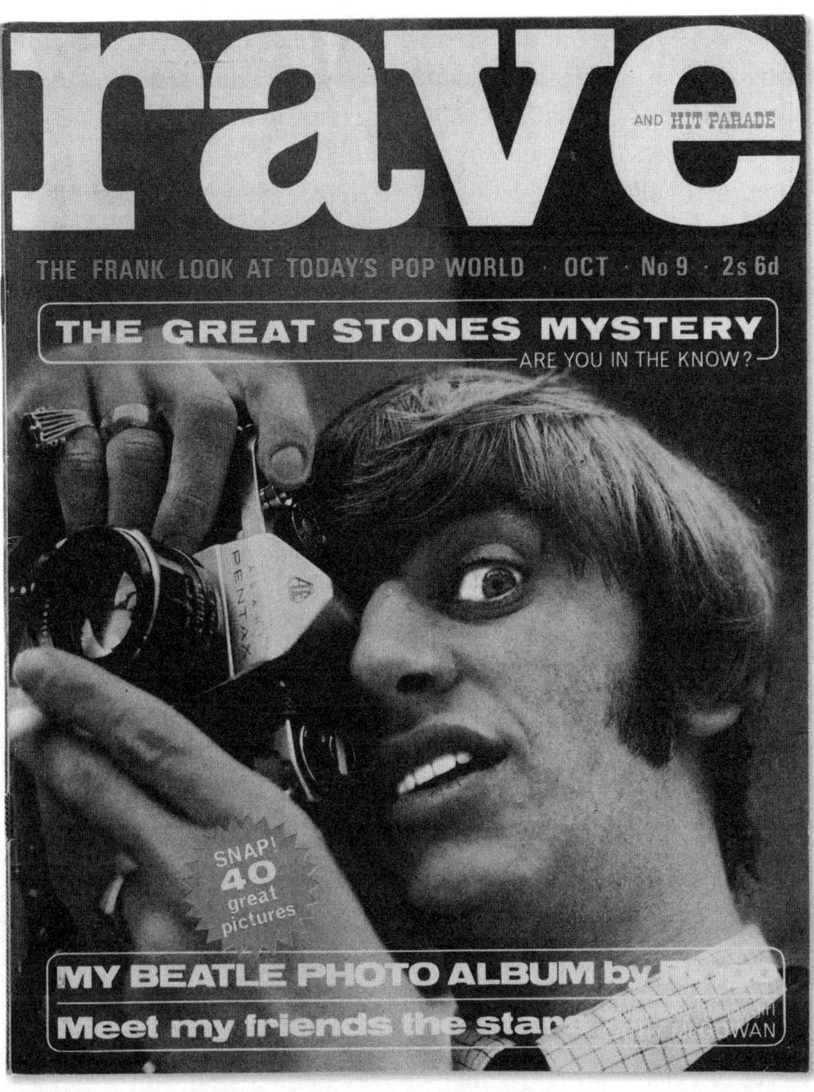

Rave, no. 9, October 1964

'*Rave* went further and deeper with articles about Stuart Sutcliffe, the lost Beatle, a fashion round table with John Stephen and the Pretty Things, and notices about up-and-coming groups such as the Yardbirds. Photo shoots were set in (for then) unusual locations, like Portobello Road or Covent Garden, and stars including Jeff Beck were used to model gear such as PVC overcoats.

'Like *Fabulous*, *Rave* prominently featured young women writers. However, if the ads for guitars were anything to go by, *Rave* also appealed to young men. Balancing teen pop with groups like the Yardbirds, the Byrds and the Who, it acquired a circulation of 125,000 by 1966.'[27]

NME's weekly circulation had risen to 300,000, though it continued to lack the command of its principal rival. '*Melody Maker* was very much like a traditional newspaper,' said Richard Williams, who joined as a reporter in the mid-1960s. 'They recruited strictly from local newspapers, as far as I could see, and that was good. It meant that everybody pitched in on Monday, doing news stories. People were prepared to go to the printer's and read proofs.'

However, one recruit – Max Jones's sixteen-year-old son Nick – caused consternation during his three years as a reporter. 'Nick was a huge fan of the Who and Eric Clapton and put us at the forefront again with those people,' said Chris Welch. 'But Nick was very opinionated, like his dad, and fell out with Jack [Hutton, editor] over asking for more money and complaining about having to interview groups like the Honeycombs, who he thought were beneath his dignity. Eventually he shouted and complained once too often. We were all quite shocked at this teenager berating the editor!'

Tony Tyler – an avid reader who became assistant editor of *NME* in the 1970s – believes tensions between the likes of Jones and the paper's old guard created an unbeatable mix: 'The jazz rump of *Melody Maker* was fighting a rearguard action and probably owned about half of the editorial, but no other paper covered what was happening in the pop world with such authority. *Melody Maker* was mandatory reading, especially if you worked in a music store and played gigs with a half-assed blues band in the evenings, as I did.'[28]

4 The Aesthetic of Rock

Jann Wenner Launches *Rolling Stone*

The buzzing music journalism of Britain was not yet mirrored across the Atlantic. The geographic scale of America stopped individual magazines dominating from coast to coast, and heavyweight music publications – *Billboard*, *Cashbox*, *DownBeat* – were focused on industry matters and musicianship. But while pop periodicals were condemned as ephemera, there were exceptions. *Broadside* and *Sing Out!* rose from the leftist movements of the 1950s and documented folk music but became conflicted when the genre's figurehead, Bob Dylan, turned to electric sounds in the sixties.

Paul Nelson, a pioneer of popular music criticism and later an A&R manager, turned Dylan on to folk when he met the singer at the University of Minnesota in the early 1960s – a factor that contributed to Nelson's appointment as *Sing Out!*'s editor. *Time* journalist Jay Cocks paid tribute to Nelson's 'gentleness and compassion – I think it was unique in rock writing',[1] while the self-titled 'dean of American rock critics', Robert Christgau, identified him as 'a neurotically painstaking writer who wasted years on unfinished articles, books, and screenplays ... He was also a hopeless romantic silently tormented by both guilt (over his split with his high school sweetheart and their son) and rejection (by the other woman, a beguiling folk singer who [said], "He wasn't a complete person. You know, Paul's interests really were in three areas: music, books, and movies."). But none of this negates how readily artists took to his laconically encyclopedic cool, or how awestruck colleagues were by his high-principled, dryly humorous, reference-dropping style.'[2]

'When the folk revival took off, *Sing Out!* was the most serious music magazine in the world,' said Nelson. 'All of a sudden they needed a managing editor and offered me the job, so I took it. I later quit because I knew they were going to nail Dylan to the wall for not writing protest songs, and I didn't want any part of it. I kept on watching Dylan's shows. At one, a *Sing Out!* critic left after the acoustic section in protest. A lot of people left, except me. I made it a point to applaud.'[3]

At the commercial end of music publishing, *16* thrived under Gloria Stavers, who embraced the British Invasion groups. 'Gloria wanted to make *16* the Beatles magazine of record,' wrote Randi Reisfeld and Danny Fields. 'It certainly had the best American coverage of them in their mop-top years. Through her friend Nat Weiss, a business associate of Brian Epstein's, Gloria made contact with the group's road managers Neil Aspinall and Malcolm Evans, and contracted them to write a series of articles. She also got stories from Johnny Hamp, a TV producer in London. This was one of the few times when Gloria had to be truly aggressive to get material on a popular phenomenon, and she welcomed the challenge. Eventually she did get access to each Beatle.'

Such triumphs confirmed Stavers as 'a pioneer in rock journalism's infancy', according to writer Margaret Moser. But her success was begrudged by the male-dominated establishment, which later extracted revenge in a depiction of her in *The Idolmaker*, Taylor Hackford's 1980 movie about music business machinations. Moser noted 'the disgraceful portrayal of the thinly disguised Stavers character [as] a ruthless pop-press prima donna. It should have portrayed her as a woman completely in love with her job and the world she created for adolescent girls.'[4]

The rise of guitar groups in the early 1960s led to an overhaul of *Hit Parader*. 'At that time there was an extremely boring music scene and fake stories like "The secret life of Connie Stevens" were published on a regular basis,' writer Jim Delehant lamented. 'The only source of information used to create these articles came from record company bios and publicity material. In 1964 the Beach Boys and Beatles changed everything. Suddenly other groups were happening: the Byrds, [Joan] Baez, Dylan, Donovan ... I hooked up a tape recorder to my phone and started interviewing. Now it was exciting!'[5]

'*Hit Parader* became America's finest rock magazine in both words and their many exclusive photos,' agreed Alan Betrock. 'Besides the heavy rock 'n' roll coverage, there was added emphasis on folk, R&B, blues and Black artists, spotlights on people in the industry like songwriters and producers, and in-depth Q&A interviews, which set *HP* apart.'[6]

Mass uptake of music magazines remained relatively low. 'There was very little rock 'n' roll press,' recalled Danny Fields. '*The Village Voice* was the underground paper. They had Richard Goldstein writing his Pop Eye column, which must have been the first ever, certainly in New York, but it was a very small world.' Goldstein pitched the idea of regular pop coverage to *The Village Voice* in 1966, proposing himself as a 'rock 'n' roll critic'. When editor Dan Wolf asked what that entailed, Goldstein set about defining the role. 'With its equal interest in the audience, the media and emerging social trends, Pop Eye in many ways prefigured the pop culture landscape we know today,' wrote journalist Darren Reidy in 2015. 'Goldstein understood the pimpled, fanboy/rock star dynamic, the mooning eyes of the front row screechers ready to stampede. He too wished to be transformed.'[7]

Before Goldstein, noted academic Evelyn McDonnell, 'Popular music was considered too déclassé for serious consideration, but he used the writings of Walter Benjamin and Herbert Marcuse to embrace the explosion of culture and activism that was being driven by rock 'n' roll.' Particularly strong was the influence of Benjamin, the German philosopher who believed that coherent views of culture emerge from the investigation of material that is otherwise considered detritus. 'With the *Voice* we were starting with his premises, and trying to apply that kind of reasoning to music and other forms of pop culture,' Goldstein declared. 'Benjamin's idea was that mechanical reproduction – or mass reproduction – changes perception and creates its own aesthetic experience and values ... We tried to discern what the unique aesthetic of the popular form was, and how it was changing the way we perceive reality.'[8]

Goldstein communed with the musicians about whom he wrote: 'Interviewing rock stars, you got stoned with them. There were no press agents – no publicists of any sort. It was you and the person. Rarely was there anybody else in the room. So getting stoned with them was a sort of a rite of trust. If you didn't get stoned with them, they would think you were straight, [which] meant "normal" back then.'[9]

Pop Eye reader Danny Fields – then a proofreader for a Manhattan publisher – was to take his cue from Goldstein, though his entry into music writing was via a job ad to edit the teen magazine *Datebook*. 'It mentioned "pop magazine",' he remembered. 'I was hanging out with Andy Warhol's crowd and thought "pop" meant pop art so answered the ad with a very extravagant letter describing how fabulous I was, about the people I knew, and the parties I went to.'

At Fields's interview for the job, *Datebook* executives revealed that, like Gloria Stavers, they had acquired Neil Aspinall's stories about being on the road with the Beatles. 'I lied and said, "Sure, I know all about pop music,"' said Fields, who had witnessed the Beatles' first New York performance and liked them 'because they had long hair'.

Fields's first issue of *Datebook* as editor caused a worldwide furore: it republished a March 1966 interview with London's *Evening Standard* in which John Lennon declared, 'Christianity will go. It will vanish and shrink ... We're more popular than Jesus now.' In the same issue, Fields published Paul McCartney's view that America was 'a lousy country where anyone Black is a dirty n*****!', but it was Lennon's quote that led to protests, boycotts and record-burning.

'I didn't know how to be a magazine editor,' Fields confessed. 'I lost my job after three months when the owner asked me to do a story on Paul Revere and the Raiders. I said, "I can't run one because I haven't interviewed them." He knew that was not what an editor is about; you get the story even if you cut and paste it, make one up, whatever, to get it in there. That was what *16* was doing.'

Before he was removed from the job, Fields had a memorable first encounter with Gloria Stavers: 'I went to see a friend at *16*'s offices. They took me in and said very politely, "Gloria, this is Danny, the editor of *Datebook*," and she started screaming, "Get him the fuck out of here!"

'In the summer of 1966 I'd be surprised if *Datebook* was selling 80,000 copies, but at this time the Monkees were enormous, so *16* was up to 1.2 million. It was a very powerful publication, so she had a lot of power over record company bosses and TV stations. Gloria could take a show off air by instituting a postcard campaign. Each copy of the magazine, they figured, got passed around to five or six girls, so that could be seven million letters to CBS.'

'Gloria helped *American Bandstand* and the show helped *16*,' agreed TV host and producer Dick Clark. 'It was a two-way street. We kept track of the kids and who was popular. She would publish stories about them; we would have them on as guests. It was a snowball effect, one augmenting the other.'

During his brief spell at *Datebook*, Fields encountered other female journalists who were to have an impact. Lillian Roxon – covering pop music as New York correspondent for the *Sydney Morning Herald* – made an impression on him at a press conference for the Cyrkle, a group managed by Brian Epstein: 'Lillian asked him, in that Australian accent of hers, "Mr Epstein, are you a millionaire?" I thought that was ballsy.'

Part of Australia's left-wing intellectual movement in the 1950s, the Sydney Push, Roxon had become the country's first female foreign correspondent when she moved to Manhattan in the early 1960s. A hard-working feminist in an all-male environment, she carved a niche as a no-nonsense writer with her finger on the pulse, earning the patronising soubriquet 'the mother of rock'. This reputation was sealed by the fact that Roxon, though ten years older than those with whom she socialized, frequented such hives of activity as the Park Avenue South nightclub Max's Kansas City. There she befriended many in Andy Warhol's circle, including the artist himself.

'Lillian was my best friend, so fabulous,' said writer Lisa Robinson, later a chronicler of American music for British and US titles and *Vanity Fair*'s music correspondent. 'She had been part of a very cool scene in Sydney with a bunch of beatniks, which included [*Oz* editor] Richard Neville, and had a gossip column in the *New York Daily News* while also writing for the *Herald*. She'd always drag these Australians to Max's for us to meet: "This is Australia's leading gynaecologist and this is Australia's leading writer." That would be Germaine Greer before anyone had heard of her.'[10]

Such was Roxon's standing that she was commissioned by American publisher Grosset & Dunlap to write the first formal pop music compendium. Published in 1969, *Lillian Roxon's Rock Encyclopedia* is an important document of the form in flux. 'It's infused with her individual takes,' said Lisa Robinson, 'full of witticisms.'

During his *Datebook* days, Danny Fields encountered young photographer Linda Eastman – later to marry Paul McCartney – after he failed to join a boat party on the Hudson for the Rolling Stones: 'On the way there my fucking photographer was out of film, so he made the taxi stop at 34th Street and 6th – the worst place – to buy film. That took so much time that, when we got there, the boat was sailing away. I told the photographer, "Fuck off. Get out of here. You're fired." So I was standing on the banks of the Hudson with Gloria Stavers, who had also missed it, and some guy with a rowing boat offered to take us out to it for twenty dollars. I said, "Gloria, you want to split it?" She said, "Fuck it, the Rolling Stones aren't worth ten dollars," got into her limousine and drove off.'

Fields waited two hours for the party to return, learned that Lillian Roxon and Linda Eastman had made the trip, and cajoled the latter to drop her commitment to supply photographs to teen rival *Hullabaloo*. 'She gave them to us, Lillian wrote the story and we became friends. As a result of those pictures, Linda's career as a photographer was launched.'

Booted from *Datebook*, Fields lit out for Los Angeles. There he worked with publicist Derek Taylor, whose client list had blossomed after he represented the Beatles. 'Derek had the best publicity roster in town and was a wonderful man,' said Fields. 'He had the Mamas and the Papas, the Byrds [and] Paul Revere, and was trying to get the Stones. There was no furniture in his office at 9000 Sunset apart from a desk surrounded by sacks of unopened fan mail to all those bands.'

Despite a gentlemanly demeanour, Taylor was driven: he ghost-wrote close to 175,000 words on behalf of Paul Revere for such titles as *Flip*, *Teen Life*, *Teen Scene*, *Teen Set*, *Tiger Beat* and *16*. 'I took up well-paid offers of columns for all sorts of magazines, providing snippets of news and forecasts,' he recalled. 'Clean, honest opinions and views made up the bulk of it. In this way, I was able to drop in the names of clients who weren't making waves with their music.'[11]

* * *

On the West Coast, the fan culture that had surrounded science fiction since the 1950s proved fertile for music titles. 'I first published myself in fanzines,' recalled Greg Shaw, the San Franciscan who helped launch the mimeographed *Mojo-Navigator Rock and Roll News* and went on to found *Who Put the Bomp* magazine and its companion Bomp! label. 'A4, run off on a little machine with a crank and stapled together. They had science fiction names but

NOVEMBER, 1967

THE TeenSeT IND

35c

Exclusive: Beatles pix! Monkee Pinups!
Poems to Peter! Poems to Dylan!
Buffalo/Raiders Doors Herman Association

Teen Set, November 1967

weren't about SF; they were talking about what was interesting to you, within this community that also liked science fiction.

'My idea was to look at music from the point of view of the fan. I was part of the generation that was looking for a more subjective approach: not just talking about the facts and who these people are, but understanding the music and why it makes us feel the way we do. A lot of people who later turned up in the rock press started out in this context, so they had the fan-ish approach. This is a science fiction concept that spread out to general culture, just as the word "fanzine" did.'[12]

Paul Williams, a freshman sci-fi fan at Pennsylvania's Swarthmore College, launched *Crawdaddy!* in 1966, billing it as 'a magazine of rock 'n' roll criticisms'. The first issue consisted of ten pages of his own copy. 'Williams wrote about the music he loved in essays that were like letters to his friends,' wrote Jim DeRogatis, 'and before long his hand-stapled fanzine began to attract other aspiring rock critics. Jon Landau was a clerk at the Briggs & Briggs record store in Harvard Square, Sandy Pearlman studied at the State University of New York at Sony Brook and Pearlman's pal Richard Meltzer was about to be thrown out of graduate studies in philosophy at Yale.'[13]

Meltzer contributed a lengthy – and, noted DeRogatis, 'sometimes inscrutable' – treatise entitled 'The aesthetic of rock' to issue eight of *Crawdaddy!* This lit the touchpaper for a cerebral strand of music criticism that was to play out – particularly in the American press – for decades. Its principal exponent was Greil Marcus, then a political science student in San Francisco. 'In 1966 bedazzled college students like myself were helplessly dumping quotes from Plato on Beatles hits and Dylan albums,' he wrote, 'attempting to talk about the world the music seemed to be changing.'[14]

Lenny Kaye – later a rock critic and Patti Smith's guitarist – described *Crawdaddy!* as 'a revelation: the first time I'd seen writing about music with depth. It wasn't just likes/dislikes. The writers took music writing to a level which matched the creativity of the works they analysed.'[15]

The tone was set for US music journalism. 'I always thought of rock criticism as a masculine venture, with all of its hierarchical implications of being male-centric: the competitiveness, the pissing contests, and all the rest,' said Richard Goldstein. 'The obsession with detail, the over-reverential approach ... all of these things I think of as masculine values, and there's definitely a place for all that, but it shouldn't be the whole.'

Aspects of this male-dominated milieu were tiresome enough at the time but are downright objectionable from a 21st-century perspective, such was the attitudinizing, macho posturing and excess that accompanied the over-intellectualizing of their subject matter. 'It had to do with the claiming of turf,' said Goldstein. 'Somehow these things become like temples after a while – you're guarding the gates – and I find that to be kind of repugnant, actually. It's not like I don't like male rock critics; it's that they shouldn't be claiming the whole territory. Theirs is just one approach. The whole Hunter Thompson, Charles Bukowski style of rock criticism is really great, but it shouldn't be the dominant voice.'[16]

Other male writers were puffed up on self-importance and their dominance of the discourse surrounding popular music. 'For starters, I invented this shit, rock writing,' boasted Richard Meltzer. 'I was first. Well, maybe not literal first; just one of the first two, three, four. Probably the first to take the ball and run with the fucker. Certainly the sole early man-jack you're still reading now. Because writing was fairly easy for me, and then there was the music, it made the most sense to write about what was still rather meaningful and magnificent. In the process, I – along with two or three others – essentially invented the rock-write genre.'[17]

This confidence bolstered *Crawdaddy!*, infused as it was with the spirit of the 'New Journalism' pioneered by cultural commentator Tom Wolfe. 'Whether it was Paul Williams writing about Brian Wilson or Richard Meltzer writing about anything, they weren't trying to be cool,' says Lenny Kaye. 'As soon as I got an inkling from *Crawdaddy!* that writing about music was possible, I started working on the school paper. My first attempt was a review of the Fugs at the Village Theatre in 1966.'

Crawdaddy! stood out, noted author Robert Draper, because 'Williams and his fellow writers weren't interested in competing against the trade industry papers or the teenybopper magazines. They wanted to put out a magazine that took rock seriously as a cultural phenomenon. In no time at all, *Crawdaddy!* was the talk of the music world.'[18] Paul Simon was sufficiently impressed by a review of *Sounds of Silence* – 'never committing the Dylanesque crime of ten-minute songs full of everything but the kitchen sink' – that he called the writer to thank him for the first 'intelligent' account of his and Art Garfunkel's music.

Circulation rose to 20,000, but the magazine's ascent was interrupted when Williams joined a commune in San Francisco in 1967. It later re-emerged under the editorship of Peter Noble, minus the exclamation mark and dedicated to showcasing specialist writers as well as the likes of novelists Joseph Heller and Tim O'Brien and the libertarian political observer PJ O'Rourke.

Do-it-yourself efforts blossomed in the Bay Area. *Oracle of the City of San Francisco* featured the psychedelic graphics of artist Rick Griffin and the beat writing of Lawrence Ferlinghetti. But editor Allan Cohen was in his late thirties, and *Oracle* lacked the energy of *Mojo-Navigator*, published by teenagers David Harris and Greg Shaw. The first of thirteen issues had appeared in the summer of 1966, with the Grateful Dead – then San Francisco's hottest group – on the cover. Alongside other local heroes such as Country Joe and the Fish and Big Brother and the Holding Company, *Mojo-Navigator* covered the British blues boom, New York's Simon and Garfunkel and LA's the Doors.

Jim Morrison and his bandmates appeared in the final edition, published in August 1967. 'We got circulation up to around 2,000, but ... as your circulation grows, so does your print bill, and you're not getting paid by anybody,' recalled Shaw. 'The popularity puts you out of business. In 1967, the third offset issue had advance orders of about 3,000, so we decided to try and print 5,000 and sell the back issues. The printer says, "Great. That'll be two thousand dollars in advance." *Two thousand dollars?* I was living by selling acid, making one hundred dollars a month. My rent was eighty-five dollars a month. It became impossible.'

* * *

The homemade nature of *Crawdaddy!* and *Mojo-Navigator* chimed with the anticorporate spirit of the age. It also intrigued the man who would create the most corporate of music magazines. Jann Wenner – 'an inveterate social climber whom friends found so cocky as to be overbearing,' according to biographer Joe Hagan[19] – was a twenty-one-year-old Berkeley University dropout with journalistic ambitions propelled by his mentor, *San Francisco Chronicle* music critic Ralph J. Gleason. More than twice Wenner's age, Gleason had been an editor at *DownBeat*, a newspaper journalist and a producer of jazz documentaries for TV.

Wenner's entrée into print was a column in the Berkeley campus paper the *Daily Californian* modelled on Gleason's in the *Chronicle*. The older man vouched for the kid when he visited London at the height of its 'swinging' era, securing him an introduction to *Melody Maker*'s Max Jones.

Wenner pitched a review of the Beach Boys' *Pet Sounds* to *Melody Maker*, but was rejected. However, the paper made its mark: 'He was astonished to see a working newsroom populated with reporters smoking cigarettes and talking shop,' wrote Joe Hagan. Gleason recalled that on Wenner's return to the US, he suggested, 'How about a magazine like *Melody Maker* and *New Musical Express* but an American one, which would be different and better and cover not just the records and the music but the whole culture?'[20]

On Gleason's recommendation, Wenner scored a job as entertainments editor of *Sunday Ramparts*, an offshoot of San Francisco's muckraking literary/political paper *Ramparts*. But when that closed in May 1967, Wenner was again out on a limb. 'Jann had been a frustrated wannabe,' recalled journalist David Weir, 'one of the guys jumping around the margins of the action, handing out fliers, hanging outside the doors of the stars.'[21]

Wenner also checked out indie magazine publishers. 'He got together with me and asked a lot of questions,' said *Crawdaddy!*'s Paul Williams. At *Mojo-Navigator*, Greg Shaw had the same experience: 'Jann Wenner used to come over to my flat and sit there, watching me turn the crank and asking questions: "Why do you do this? How does this work? How do you know to put interviews in the front and record reviews in the back?" I gave him a basic course in putting out magazines.'

Wenner was also drawn to a proposed countercultural magazine – to be called *Straight Arrow* – led by Chet Helms, manager and promoter at San Francisco's Avalon Ballroom. But Wenner felt that targeting hippies who had already tuned in, turned on and dropped out was too limiting. Instead, his vision for what would become *Rolling Stone* came into focus. '"Fuck the tribes," Jann thought,' wrote Robert Draper in his history of the publication. 'Kids communicated through music.' Wenner's biographer Joe Hagan observed: 'He had an intuitive grasp of the most significant quality of the new rock audience: unlike the one that fuelled the British Invasion, it was largely male. For marketers, this new youth culture was uncharted territory, and Wenner was the pioneer. Until 1966, the primary outlets in America for the Beatles and the Rolling Stones were *16* and *Tiger Beat*: New York-based magazines for teenage girls which fetishized Paul and John and Mick and Keith as objects of romance and trivia. Wenner made it safe for boys to ogle their male idols as rapturously as any girl might by adding a healthy dose of intellectual pretense.'[22]

Wenner was determined that his new venture not emulate the fervid tone of *Crawdaddy!*, which he had condemned in a *Sunday Ramparts* review. 'He did not believe rock journalism had to be so forbidding,' wrote Robert Draper. 'The distinctly British, and at times terrifically boring, *Melody Maker* had made quite an impression on him. Here was a weekly which stayed on top of the scene – indeed, was supportive of and supported by (in the form of advertisements) the scene.'[23]

With Gleason on board and $7,500 in funding from friends, parents and in-laws, Wenner planned a professional-looking fortnightly that took its graphic cues from the elegant *Sunday Ramparts*. John Williams, that magazine's production director, handled layouts, photographer Baron Wolman cannily worked in exchange for stock in the business, and Jon Landau was lured by the promise that *Rolling Stone*, unlike *Crawdaddy!*, would pay for his work. *Newsweek* reporter Michael Lydon accepted the gig as managing editor while his wife Susan, an experienced journalist, provided copy. According to Robert Draper, she was forced into the role of receptionist at the paper's offices in a disreputable semi-industrial district because Wenner believed 'the phone should always be answered by a feminine voice'.

The brazen entrepreneur lifted from Chet Helms the name for his trading company – Straight Arrow – and blagged his mailing list from radio station KFRC-AM. This pulled the rug from under Helms and left the field wide open.

'The editorial concept came directly out of Jann's own music-crazed soul,' wrote David Weir. 'Instead of the puff pieces expected from a trade magazine, *Rolling Stone* would cover rock 'n' roll for what it was: the most powerful cultural and political force in a time of widespread social tumult. The magazine would take risks and run stories no one else was willing to cover. Jann recognized that a new social order was forming, with music as its binding energy.'[24]

Wenner hired Max Jones's son Nick to provide a column from London and commissioned a masthead from designer Rick Griffin. With 'All the news that fits' beneath, that masthead was juxtaposed to great effect with the paper's formal layout. Joe Hagan believes *Rolling Stone*'s 'radical conventionality was Jann Wenner's most important innovation ... [With] Griffin's curled ligatures and looping serifs unmistakeable signifiers of dope-peddling head shops on Haight-Ashbury, Wenner instantly legitimized and mainstreamed the underground.'

The first issue – 9 November 1967 – set out Wenner's mission: 'We have begun a new publication reflecting what we see are the changes in rock 'n' roll and the changes related to rock 'n' roll. Because the trade papers have become so inaccurate and irrelevant, and because the fan magazines are an anachronism, fashioned in the mould of myth and nonsense, we hope that we have something here for the artists and the industry, and every person who "believes in the magic that can set you free".'

The front page featured John Lennon in army gear on the set of the movie *How I Won the War*, and an investigation into a possibly criminal appropriation of funds from the Monterey pop festival. 'That was a statement of intent,' said Wenner. 'We were showing we weren't another fanzine; we were professional with good reportorial skills. Something like that, anyway. That first night we went to print remains one of my most treasured memories. We bought champagne, found some plastic glasses, and went downstairs to watch it roll off the press. I felt such elation. I remember thinking, "We can't get better than this. We've already topped out."'[25]

Only 6,000 of the 40,000 copies of the first issue sold, but the stage was set. Wenner brought on board serious-minded writers such as Greil Marcus, who became reviews editor. 'In 1967,' noted Joe Hagan, 'it was still a radical idea to publish college-educated intellectuals such as Jon Landau and Greil Marcus opining on James Brown and the Jefferson Airplane as if it was serious art, like jazz.'

'*Rolling Stone* marked the real sea change,' said *NME* writer Nick Kent, then a schoolboy in Wales. 'There's rock journalism before it arrived and rock journalism afterwards. It set the bar way, way higher.'[26] But for all his lofty ambition, Wenner wasn't averse to gimmicks, such as enticing readers to subscribe with the promise of roach clips to hold their joints. And a survey of the world of groupies, with sympathetic portraits by Baron Wolman, aced mainstream press titles such as *Newsweek* and grabbed national coverage.

Male rock stars – especially John Lennon, Pete Townshend and Mick Jagger – quickly became *Rolling Stone* staples. Rambling interviews, often conducted by Wenner himself, ran to several pages as they expounded on youth culture and beyond. 'Though he didn't invent serious pop criticism, Jann was the one who popularized it,' Jagger told Joe Hagan. 'There were magazines before, and criticism before, but the magazines were a bit fly-by-night and weren't taken seriously.'[27]

Ben Fong-Torres, a student soon to offer his services to Wenner, enthused: 'It was a bracing find, a new high, and it jumped around from one set of hands to another. It came from San Francisco but, with correspondents in London, New York and Los Angeles, it was clearly out to be a national publication. It didn't appear to be either a newspaper or a magazine but a hybrid. The first issues didn't even open like a magazine: it was quarter-folded – that is, folded twice. It didn't have a cover but a newspaper-style front page with several stories, about rock 'n' roll, written in a style that was knowing, critical, good humoured and hip –neither fawning like teen and fan magazines, nor crude and condescending like so much of the mainstream press when it deigned to cover rock 'n' roll. This was the most effectively targeted new publication since Hugh Hefner founded *Playboy*.

'After assigning me a profile of Dino Valente (of Quicksilver Messenger Service), Jann called me into his office. "Don't just ask him questions," he said, the certainty in his voice belying his twenty-one years. He turned to his antique oak desk and grabbed a couple of magazines. They were issues of *The New Yorker*. "Lookit these," he said, handing them over. "This is the kind of detail, description and reporting I want in our profiles."'[28]

Fong-Torres was one of the talented young writers – mostly male – who flocked to the new title. Another was David Dalton, later to win a Columbia Journalism School award for an interview with Charles Manson conducted with fellow *Rolling Stone* contributor David Felton. 'I saw the first issue and started calling up Jann Wenner,' said Dalton. 'I came close to getting busted and thought it a good idea to go to England for a while. I started sending Jann photos. Jann said, "We need stories to go with these pictures." The captions started getting longer and longer, *viz*, "You'll never guess what happened thirty seconds before I took this picture." I lost my Pentax in an airport and thus began my long, blessed and oft-cursed career as a rock writer: first as a journalist and then as rock-dog-on-the-road anecdotalist – "Ah yes, I well remember the time Janis and I were kidnapped in Kansas City."'

Dalton saw himself as a 'rock evangelist': 'This sounds more than a little pretentious, but that was the way it felt to me then. Rock was the very plasma that held the counterculture together. Everything was plugged into it – everything *I* cared about, anyway. I don't think I ever used the word "I" writing for *Rolling Stone*. "We" maybe. But essentially I saw myself as a chronicler, a fan who managed to enter this or that sanctum sanctorum and bring back the glad tidings, the revelations, and thus spake every word uttered by our idols.'[29]

An appeal for readers to submit reviews lured twenty-year-old Californian Leslie 'Lester' Bangs. A rabid sci-fi, comic book and music fan with enthusiastic drink and drug habits, he scorned the still formulating critical approaches of his contemporaries: 'I long ago gave up on giving the other fellow's taste the benefit of the doubt. It led to too many shitty, phony albums rhapsodized over by the influential sycophants serving as rock journalists in the absence of anyone with more style, taste and insight.' *Rolling Stone*, he grumbled, was 'crammed with the most predictable portraits of uninteresting people. In fact the literature of the counterculture could well be the most boring of all.'[30]

His crackling copy was welcomed by Greil Marcus, whose first issue as reviews editor included Bangs hailing Captain Beefheart as 'the only true Dadaist in rock' and lambasting the debut of the drippy *It's A Beautiful Day*: 'I hate this album not only because I wasted my money on it but for what it represents: an utterly phony, arty approach to music that we will not soon escape.'[31]

Amid the impressive editorial lineup, photographer Annie Leibovitz was a rare female presence. 'A gangly, bespectacled twenty-year-old dropout from the San Francisco Art Institute,' noted Robert Draper. 'An Air Force brat who showed up with a handful of prints at the offices and was quickly put to work.' Within six months of her arrival in 1970, Leibovitz shot striking cover portraits of Rod Stewart and Grace Slick, and impressed the cost-conscious Wenner by flying youth fare to New York to photograph John Lennon.

Rolling Stone's highest profile contributor was the gonzo writer Hunter S. Thompson. Having published a book about riding with Hell's Angels and profiled the deterioration of the Haight-Ashbury hippie dream for the *New York Times*, he turned up at the magazine's offices with a six-pack of beer and successfully pitched a story about his campaign to elect a biker as mayor of Aspen, Colorado.

While Thompson's excesses became the stuff of legend, Ben Fong-Torres preferred to hail less extrovert *Rolling Stone* staffers: 'David Felton was a brilliant writer, a funny guy and a smart editor. Annie Leibovitz used her charm and naked honesty, which resulted in a relaxed subject. John Burks had a casual, jazzy approach to prose, while Dave Marsh has a true fan's passion for the music. Then there's Chet Flippo, Tim Cahill, Charles Perry and Judith Sims, all excellent reporters and natural writers.'[32]

Wenner allowed these talents freedom, but he could be capricious. 'He knew not only how to develop and exploit talent but also when and how to dump it,' said David Weir. 'Every *Rolling Stone* writer and editor, photographer and designer has a bucketful of Jann tales – how the outbursts, the abuse, the breakup, the firings came down. When Jann turned heartless on you, he played that part better than anyone else.'

Rolling Stone, said Joe Hagan, was 'a man's magazine, though women read it; it was a white magazine, though African Americans were fetishized in it; it was a left-wing magazine, though it was tempered by Wenner's devotion to the establishment. If Jann Wenner had only one great idea, it was an idea with staying power: that the 1960s – "the Sixties" – was a mythic time that would be endlessly glorified and fetishized by his generation in records and books, TV shows and films, T-shirts and posters, for years to come, for ever and ever, amen. The 1960s, with all its passion and idealism, was, at its sacred core, a business.'[33]

5
‘They didn’t realise it was a men’s club’

Taking on Macho Critics

As pop fans reeled from ambitious works like *Revolver*, *Blonde on Blonde* and the Byrds' *Fifth Dimension*, and Jann Wenner consolidated his plans for *Rolling Stone*, Danny Fields returned to New York. There he became editor of *Hullabaloo*, the teen title for which Linda Eastman photographed the Rolling Stones' 1966 boat party before Fields persuaded her to give the shots to *DateBook*.

'The first issue I did was full of the Lovin' Spoonful, the Mamas and the Papas and all the underground stuff I loved,' Fields said of *Hullabaloo*, 'but they hit me in the head with this plan to do an entire issue on Herman's Hermits. I said, "Okay, I'll do it. I've learned how to be an editor."' Fields's model was the Paris-based *Salut les copains*, which used photo stories and graphics to capture the style and vitality of young French performers, film stars and celebrities: '*Copains* had this thing – "Tout tout tout," "Everything everything everything" – where they spent twenty-four hours a day with people like [singers] Jacques Dutronc and Sylvie Vartan. Or they would have seven pictures of them by seven different photographers. It was gorgeous to approach one artist from so many different angles – and, to do it properly for *Hullabaloo*, I needed to go hang out with [Hermits front man] Peter Noone and the guys for a while in LA.'

When *Hullabaloo*'s publisher balked at the expense of this venture, Fields found himself once more on the job market. Brian Epstein and fellow manager Robert Stigwood duly paid him 500 dollars to publicize Cream's US debut – an Easter pageant in 1967: 'I got *Hit Parader* and Lillian Roxon to interview them but nobody was really interested. I'd say, "You know, in London, Eric Clapton is God," but the only way I could get people to come was, guess what, "Meet Brian Epstein." I organised a special press conference at Max's Kansas City and, though [Epstein] was getting on a plane at noon, said, "Brian, I can't get this band arrested, but the press will come if you're going to be there." So he made time and, of course, everyone came. That was all very nice, but we still didn't get coverage.'

Fields subsequently became a publicist for the West Coast label Elektra, whose roster included Tim Buckley and the Doors. His involvement with the latter, and their charismatic and troublesome front man Jim Morrison, tested the limits of his job description – notably when Elektra promotions director Steve Harris set his sights on getting Morrison into Gloria Stavers's magazine: 'Steve was convinced Jim Morrison would play in *16* and sent her roses and champagne, everything, to persuade her. My part was to get a phone interview between them from the Elektra office on Sunset, to Gloria in New York: give the phone to him, have him mumble and her do whatever she did, hand the phone back to me and hang up. Then Jim and Gloria became lovers. But that's how I sold my acts.'

Morrison and Stavers's affair was intense: 'They would go on mystical adventures and she would tell me he would dematerialize – if only he would! She couldn't wait for him to get to New York. Once he called her and said he was staying at the Chelsea and that he would leave his room door open. She went up there but he wasn't in the bedroom or the bathroom. She was calling out, "Jim? Jim?" – scared and alone in a weird hotel room. So she's out of there, in a taxi. When she got home, the phone was ringing. It was Jim, chuckling. She said, "Where. The. Fuck. Were. You?" And he said, "You didn't look under the bed." What a chivalrous guy.'

Fields had experienced Morrison's unpleasantness when he introduced the singer to the Velvet Underground's doomy chanteuse Nico. The publicist was staying in a 'strange haunted house, all overgrown, with a mossy pool' in the Hollywood Hills, shared with Nico and Andy Warhol's tragic 'Factory girl' Edie Sedgwick. Fields instructed Morrison to follow him in his car, up the winding and sometimes vertiginous lanes. 'It was tricky, but keeping track of another car in your rear-view mirror, driven by a nasty demon son-of-a-bitch motherfucker who was out to taunt and make miserable everyone in his immediate radius, was another thing. He'd disappear from view, so I'd wait, and then he'd be back behind me, making sure I knew he was in control. I'm from New York so didn't drive that much. It was perplexing and horrible.'

Upon arrival, Nico and Sedgwick retired to a room to take drugs, while Morrison consumed Fields's supplies of acid, pot and alcohol. 'I thought, "Uh-oh, he's going to get so drunk he'll get in the car and drive off a cliff and I'm going to get fired." So I snuck down and hid his car keys under the doormat. I went to bed and was woken by sobbing. Nico was standing in the mock-Spanish courtyard crying and he was naked apart from a crenellated cassock-type robe, leaping from one turret to another. She came flying into my room shouting, "He's going to kill me!" I said, "He's not going to kill anyone. Leave me alone, I'm trying to sleep." There were screams later. They were in the courtyard, him pulling her around by her hair. It was like the cover of a Gothic bodice-ripper.'

After two days, Morrison's irate bandmates tracked the singer to the mansion. 'We got back from an afternoon swimming in someone else's pool and all the dining chairs were on top of the twenty-foot table,' said Fields. 'That was strange. Also on the table was a publicity still of Nico and Andy Warhol from *Chelsea Girls*. Written on the back was a message from the guys in the band and his manager: "Jim, your fucking ass is fired. Call immediately. Grow up! Okay, you've had it."'

Morrison didn't leave the group, and blamed Fields for 'kidnapping' him. 'Jim wanted me fired from that moment on, but Elektra pacified him. There were lots of incidents I won't go into. The vomiting – ugh!'

Meanwhile, the ranks of female critics finally began to swell. Journalism major Patricia Kennealy – Kennealy-Morrison after she married the Doors singer in a non-legally-binding Celtic spiritual ceremony – was appointed editor-in-chief of *Jazz & Pop*, launched in 1962 as simply *Jazz*. 'Patricia was a really interesting person and so was the magazine,' said contributor Lenny Kaye. 'It had started out in jazz and spun into pop. You look at a group like the MC5: they were covering songs by Pharoah Saunders and John Coltrane. It was a style I liked because I believe in free music. When you get into an improvisational situation, all the genre forms break down. *Jazz & Pop* was a good place to discover that.'

Kaye's first assignment was a review of the Small Faces' psychedelic *Ogden's Nut Gone Flake*, followed by the likes of Nico's *The Marble Index* and the Velvet Underground's self-titled third album. His first fully fledged feature was a survey of the a capella/doo-wop scene in the Tri-State area. 'When that came out,' he remembered, 'I was called by someone I peripherally knew from around New York: Patti Smith. She was very moved by that article and we became friends. Later she asked me to play guitar for a reading she was doing at St Mark's Church.'

As essayed in her memoir *Just Kids*, Smith was scuffling around the edges of New York's avant-garde scene and submitting occasional pieces to *Circus*, the monthly that editor Gerry Rothenberg conjured from the embers of his teen title *Hullabaloo*. 'She wasn't a music writer, she was a Patti writer,' said Kaye. 'She wrote about music the same way she wrote about art and literature. If rock writers moved from the music outwards, she was out from the start. I like to think that some of our early stuff – where she would do a poem that would segue into a song – was a form of rock writing. We would do "Hey Joe" and tie it into the Patty Hearst saga. It was commentary using rock music.'

Alongside his contributions to *Jazz & Pop*, Kaye honed his craft with the Boston-based underground monthly *Fusion*, for whom he wrote another doo-wop piece, on Little Anthony and the Imperials. Founded in 1967 by editor Ted Scourtis, *Fusion*'s highbrow approach took in interviewees such as Frank Zappa. Contributors included Michael Lydon, Greg Shaw and Bostonian student Loyd Grossman, who became a celebrity cook and broadcaster in Britain. He filed pieces on Irish hard rockers Taste, blues master Albert King, George Harrison and British bands Blodwyn Pig, the Nice, Ten Years After and Yes ('Emotionally intense and imaginatively conceived', he enthused of the latter's 1969 debut album).

'I was then, as I am now, a failed guitar-player, and *Fusion* seemed to be the place where I should advertise an upcoming gig,' recalled Grossman. 'I went to the offices to place an ad and talked to the publisher, who was for some reason extraordinarily impressed with my rock knowledge and said, "Why don't you write for us? And, by the way, the ad will be ten dollars."

'So I started writing for *Fusion* and, although we never got paid, we were given endless free tickets. And I met a lot of very interesting rock journalists – one of whom, Jon Landau, encouraged me to write for *Rolling Stone*. We were all trying to be Tom Wolfe and obsessed with the New Journalism, which meant that you spent the first 250 to 500 words of any piece riffing about what happened to you on the way to the gig, which kind of platform boots you were going to wear – that kind of self-indulgent bollocks. Then, as you got close to the last paragraph, you wrote, "Oh yeah, I went to see Fleetwood Mac; they were actually quite good."'[1]

Most dazzling of this East Coast generation was Ellen Willis, invited to be *The New Yorker*'s first pop critic after contributing a lengthy exposition on Bob Dylan to the left-leaning monthly *Commentary.* This was picked up by writer and graphic artist Jules Siegel for his short-lived youth culture journal *Cheetah*. 'I remember when she passed my office,' recalled *The New Yorker*'s Karen Durbin. 'I was wildly curious and dying of envy. I saw this girl with long wild hair and, as I recall it, jeans. Women were forbidden to wear trousers at the magazine then. But Ellen didn't know that and, if she had, I very much doubt she would have run home to change.'[2]

Willis's Dylan article observed, 'His masks hidden by other masks, Dylan is the celebrity stalker's ultimate antagonist.' As American broadcaster Ken Tucker remarked, the piece revealed 'assertions about her subject that no one had ventured before, yet which afterward became common wisdom', as well as Willis's ability to 'combine close listening to songs, adding everything she knew about the subject's public image and private life, to arrive at a critical position'.[3]

Willis remained *The New Yorker*'s pop expert until 1975, inspiring other female writers such as Lisa Robinson, who described her as 'a serious critic – capital S, capital C'. As Evelyn McDonnell pointed out, Willis 'broke critical ground' by filing 'deeply original commentary on the music that defined a generation. She wrote about landmark figures and events in prescient, unpredictable ways. She wasn't so much cranky – others pioneered that rock-crit stereotype – as she was rhapsodic, a fan who could be vociferously vexed by self-indulgent albums and overpriced shows.' Of *Ziggy Stardust*, she grumbled, 'The idea of a pop star from outer space ... just doesn't make it, except maybe as a spoof.' Joni Mitchell's *Blue*, however, she acclaimed as the album on which 'the freaky voice had found its purpose'.

Out of the Vinyl Deeps – a posthumous collection of Willis's work (she died of cancer in 2006) – shows her as, in McDonnell's words, 'strictly an analyst; there are no interviews or features. She tended to describe the settings and audience of concerts as much as the music, highlighting the fan's perspective as well as the artist's. That attention to detail keeps thirty-year-old reviews from dry obsolescence.'

Sasha Frere-Jones, music critic at *The New Yorker* in the 21st century, identified the magazine's 475,000 circulation – at a time when *Rolling Stone* was selling, at most, 75,000 – as a signifier of Willis's authority. 'At the dawn of pop criticism, when the field was barely a field, a woman wrote seven years' worth of politically engaged pieces about pop for a national magazine,' he noted in his foreword to *Out of the Vinyl Deeps*. 'Her writing on pop was a model for music criticism. Her work is striated with details of personal struggles as well as clear and calm examinations of the day's icons. Her piece about Elvis in Vegas refuses to make fun of Elvis and Vegas (a move most writers at the magazine would go for in a heartbeat, especially now) while also holding them both to the coals. The piece on Woodstock debunks the specifics of an overhyped festival without forsaking the ideals ostensibly embodied by it.'[4]

Unlike her male confreres, there is a liberated air to Willis's texts – her copy has hips. 'Ellen was that wondrous creature: an intellectual who deeply valued sensuality,' says Karen Durbin. 'She respected the sensual; in a fundamentally puritanical culture, she honoured it. She saw how it could be a path to transcendence and liberation – especially for women, who, when we came out into the world in the early to mid-sixties, were relentlessly sexualised and just as relentlessly shamed. Rock 'n' roll broke that chain: it was the place where we could be sexual and ecstatic.'[5] There are photographs of Willis dancing with abandon in front of a mirror: her preferred way of engaging with a record she was reviewing. It is hard to picture the earnest American male critics of the period doing the same. If they danced, it was rarely, if ever, conveyed by their copy.

From 1966 to 1969, Willis's partner was fellow critic Robert Christgau, who wrote what he described as a 'secular' column for *Esquire* before becoming one of the most prolific music writers of his or any other generation. 'Ellen Willis had a tremendous influence on my thoughts,' he said.[6] Her piece about Dylan remains, he declared, 'one of the richest things ever written about the artist or the sixties, even though it was formulated without historical perspective'.

Yet Christgau is clear-eyed about Willis's copy – 'Because she was writing so early, her concepts are sometimes crude and her facts under-researched' – and notes her focus on familiar names: 'She writes a whole hell of a lot about the usual suspects: Dylan, Stones, Beatles, Who and Creedence (whom she considered dance music). Inconveniently for a radical feminist, all are men. Nevertheless, she didn't miss many major women artists, either – Grace Slick I guess, [Bonnie] Raitt and/or [Linda] Ronstadt, and Gladys Knight, whom she namechecked but never tackled. Knight's absence is especially unfortunate, because beyond an imaginative Stevie Wonder report and a halting Aretha Franklin review, too much crucial Black music does get missed. More perplexing omissions than the generally neglected James Brown are failed hippie Sly Stone and politico-sexual obsessive Marvin Gaye, and I could go on (AlGreenAlGreenAlGreen).'[7]

'She believed that for any leftist agenda to succeed it had to be based on pleasure,' noted Richard Goldstein. 'Ellen would surely agree that we won't see a revival of revolutionary sentiment until we make it fun.'[8] 'Even with her tendency to use big words and big ideas, Willis always knew at heart that music was a gas, gas, gas,' agreed McDonnell. 'She celebrated the seriousness of pleasure and relished the pleasure of thinking seriously, followed in the footsteps of *New Yorker* critics Dorothy Parker and Pauline Kael, and elbowed her way into the men's club of music criticism. Maybe she didn't even realize it was a men's club – Willis seemed fiercely independent that way.'[9]

In the 1990s, by which time she was a journalism professor at NYU, Willis described her work for *The New Yorker* as 'part of this general larger atmosphere of revolt against authority, very much to do with extending pop culture and mass culture as something that was aesthetically interesting in its own right, and not something that was inherently inferior to high art'.

Willis, believes Evelyn McDonnell, 'saw through the sexual politics of rock 'n' roll in ways that were nothing short of visionary.

Her criticism was openly and avidly informed by her gender.' But by celebrating an overly macho strand of music, female writers risked identifying with male ideology. Willis's response was to articulate the sense of freedom that women could attain by listening to the likes of the Rolling Stones. 'I had the filter of feminist analysis through which I saw everything,' she told McDonnell. 'There was the whole question of the paradox of why, despite the music being sexist, I nevertheless felt it was liberating for me both as a person and as a woman. There was a complex set of mediations involved there. It has to do with the idea that a liberating form can transcend its regressive content.'[10]

6
‘The first time a critic topped the artist’

Oz, *IT* and *Friends* Reflect the Counterculture

'The first time a critic topped the artist'

As freewheeling critical thinking took hold in the US, Britain's music press remained markedly less groovy. The country's stifling 'light entertainment' industry threatened to co-opt new groups and the youth movements from which they emerged. Corporate teen magazines such as *Rave* and *Fabulous* featured high street versions of hippie kaftans and ran scaremongering editorials about the dangers of drugs. And the four weeklies – whose editorial teams remained almost entirely male and White – struggled to maintain editorial balance in an age when musicians were likely to express opinions on anything from political conflicts to spirituality. *Disc & Music Echo*, *Record Mirror* and *New Musical Express* essentially peddled pop fodder. *Melody Maker* was for fans of folk, jazz, blues and the music soon to be dubbed 'progressive'. It congratulated *The Times* for defending Mick Jagger and Keith Richards after a 1967 drug bust and presented Jimi Hendrix in a cartoon strip drawn by the Bonzo Dog Doo-Dah Band's Vivian Stanshall, yet ran showbiz stories such as identifying a hotel where the Monkees were staying and announcing a residency at the London Palladium by the Supremes.

'In the mid-sixties I had been very much a pop writer, interviewing people like PJ Proby,' said staffer Chris Welch. 'Then I started to follow bands who played live a lot, such as the Yardbirds and the Spencer Davis Group. When they broke up, they formed new groups, like Traffic and Cream. As all the underground groups popped up, most included people who had been in bands I'd known previously. So, when Jimmy Page formed Led Zeppelin, he came to see me at the office and showed me how to spell "Led". He liked the fact that I had given a favourable review of an unknown band he had been in years before and invited me to see Led Zeppelin. I was flabbergasted.'

Meanwhile, Richard Williams attracted attention for his elegant turn of phrase and openness to outré music. Writer Ian MacDonald described him as 'the model, I think, for many of us who came later: the way he covered all the bases, from Lennon to [Laura] Nyro to avant-garde jazz'.[1] Williams copresented the BBC's *Old Grey Whistle Test* and was an early champion of Bruce Springsteen and Bob Marley. And even when committing a faux pas, he received praise. Sent a preview copy of John Lennon and Yoko

Ono's experimental *Wedding Album* as two one-sided discs, Williams reviewed it on *Melody Maker*'s front page as a double album, and particularly praised the blank sides, which consisted of test signals: 'Constant listening reveals a curious point: the pitch of the tones alters frequency, but only by microtones or, at most, a semitone. This oscillation produces an almost subliminal, uneven "beat" which maintains interest. On a more basic level, you could have a ball by improvising your own raga, plainsong or even Gaelic mouth music against the drone.'[2]

Lennon responded by telegram: 'dear richard thank you for your fantastic review on our wedding album including c-and-d sides. we are considering it for our next release. maybe you are right in saying that they are the best sides stop we both feel that this is the first time a critic topped the artist. we are not joking. love and peace stop john and yoko lennon.'[3]

'Richard impressed everybody because he is very courteous, intelligent and knowledgeable, all things which are unusual in a journalist,' said Welch. 'He took on music I tended to neglect – people who were more cerebral. And his tastes divided between, say, Miles Davis and Ornette Coleman and Phil Spector and the origins of rock 'n' roll and blues. Richard had a historical perspective, whereas I was more into watching bands every night and not seeing the broader picture.'

When British politican Enoch Powell delivered his infamous 'rivers of blood' speech, calling for an end to mass immigration, *Melody Maker* interviewed Black musicians about their experiences of racism and condemned Powell's speech as offensive to a business 'where racial harmony has long been a byword'.[4] It also gave space to such non-pop fare as Keith Richards's belief that UFOs were landing in the garden of his Sussex home.[5]

Neither generationally nor musically inclined to the new sounds, editor Jack Hutton – who had been at the paper since the early 1950s – was nevertheless encouraging. 'He was a nice, old-fashioned gentleman journalist,' said Richard Williams. 'He played the cornet in a band on Tuesday nights in Crouch End and was a good boss. *Melody Maker* was on the rise and starting to reap the benefit of being a little bit more intelligent, so musicians respected it more. Musicianship was becoming an issue, and *MM* was more in tune with the fiddly bits. Mind you, the story I had to do on my first Monday morning was about the BBC banning [Serge Gainsbourg and Jane Birkin's 1969 hit] "Je t'aime ... moi non plus".'

The publication's emphasis on skill provided the edge, said Charlie Gillett: 'The reason *Melody Maker* got in on Cream and all of those bands that appeared at the Marquee [club] in the late sixties was because it had always been interested in individual performance rather than the packaged pop format.'

'*Melody Maker* was thrashing *NME*, which had stuck rigidly to the pop-picking formula of early British entertainment media,' noted Tony Tyler. '*MM* catered for a more student-y readership, which didn't want to know what a particular star had for breakfast or what their fave colours were. They wanted views on Vietnam, Tolkien and the [Hindu scripture] *Bhagavad Gita*.'

'Chris Welch was the guy to meet,' observed publicist Glen Colson, who represented acts on Tony Stratton-Smith's Charisma roster. 'I became very friendly with him and he'd put me in "The Raver" column every week. The acts became furious, because I was getting more press than them. He was very influential: if he liked your band, that was it. *Melody Maker* was *the* paper. You couldn't break a band through radio or the national press, so the *MM* was the one.'[6]

'*MM* seemed to be the one paper dealing with music in-depth and had some personality,' said Allan Jones, who joined the staff in the 1970s. 'It was the first one to build up the journalists, with pictures of Chris. He in particular came across as someone you knew, with a convivial, chatty style. And, fuck me, he seemed to know everybody from the Beatles to the Stones and Jimi Hendrix. It was incredible. I came from Port Talbot, a small town in Wales, and it opened a new world for me.'[7]

Welch welcomed a new generation of contributors: 'Lots of younger people started to come on board. Photographer Barrie Wentzell joined in 1967 and we went off to cover the Magical Mystery Tour. We weren't invited, so followed the bus in a car. Our presence was tolerated and it became a bit of a scoop. And when new people came along, they discovered new bands for us – people like Jerry Gilbert, who was championing Genesis in the early days. There was the Monday morning thing: "I saw this great band at the weekend ..."'

Jerry Gilbert had fallen under *Melody Maker*'s spell as a student, when a visit to his college by the paper's Bob Houston opened him up to the possibilities of music journalism. He replaced Tony Wilson as the paper's folk correspondent, Wilson having left after his socializing on the London music scene informed a thinly disguised character in Jenny Fabian's prurient novel *Groupie*. Not that Gilbert was averse to a convivial relationship with his interviewees: 'Acts would cheerfully come along to meet us in the pub, which has long since gone, in Red Lion Court, Fleet Street. I'd be interviewing Marc Bolan back-to-back with Chris [Welch], who'd be interviewing Keith Emerson. It was incredibly laid-back. No PRs involved, happily, and we did it all in shorthand. It was very old school. The ethos was that, a week later, it would be wrapping cod and chips.'[8]

* * *

Twenty-year-old Nick Logan had long been a pop culture fan, having spent his teenage years combing the pages of *Record Mirror* and *Beat Instrumental*: 'There'd be an offstage posed pic of the Stones where you could study their haircuts, Cuban heels, leather coats ...' His youth and skill won him a pop column on the *West Essex Gazette*, although he downplayed this first brush with celebrity: 'I might have interviewed the Small Faces, who lived locally, or the drummer of the Nashville Teens, but it was all minor stuff.'

In 1967, he was turned down for a job on *Melody Maker* – Logan believes he fell foul of Hutton's insistence that editorial staff read music – and approached *NME* editor Andy Gray. 'Surprisingly,' he said, 'this distinguished-looking, grey-haired gentleman took me on.'

Logan discovered that the paper's founder was still filing his Alley Cat gossip column: 'They were completely out of touch. Maurice Kinn was an absolutely fearsome character: this grand man talking about Frank Sinatra and Sammy Davis Jr. One of my jobs was to handle the corrections when Maurice phoned them through to the printers. God forbid you didn't show the right degree of respect and get it right. I don't remember ever being slaughtered for anything, but you knew it was the worst crime you could commit.'

The policy of focusing on artists in the charts – and thus missing out a huge variety of new acts – proved frustrating. 'There'd be a review of the singles charts,' sighed Logan, 'and we'd be expected to start from the top with the Beatles or whoever. Articles would be allotted, working our way through reporting on the same groups by rote.'[9]

This infuriated staff. 'Andy Gray would come into the newsroom every Wednesday morning and read through the charts,' recalled Keith Altham. '"The Animals are in at twenty-eight; who knows the Animals?" And one of the writers would put their hand up. One week he actually said, "Here's a newie: Otis Redding. Who knows her?"'[10]

The policy also caused reporters to be territorial. 'Some of the senior guys were incredibly protective of their turf,' recalled Logan. 'I was very much the new kid on the block. There was no way I was going to write about the Stones or the Small Faces, because Keith covered them, while Alan Smith was even worse with the Beatles. There again, Norrie Drummond had Herman's Hermits and the dross! Prog rock became my area because everything else was sewn up.' He created memorable verdicts on Jethro Tull's Ian Anderson ('an easy person to dislike'), King Crimson ('helplessly staggering from one misfortune to the next') and Pink Floyd ('Are we to presume from *Atom Heart Mother* that the Floyd are concerning themselves with man's eternal conflict with machines, and of the contrasts and gulf between the extremes of the two, or is it just that it makes a funky title?')

Logan was desperate to write about Black music, 'but there was a problem. Most of the artists weren't in the country and you couldn't get the material ... I think about the stories I could have got from James Brown, but I couldn't get close to him. So I ended up with Cream, Fleetwood Mac, Family, Jethro Tull. I liked the lifestyle and recognized they were good copy – that was my territory – but the whole culture of the paper was wrong.'[11]

Meanwhile, there was competition for readers and advertising from *Record Mirror* and *Disc & Music Echo*. The former – having stumbled through name changes to *Record & Show Mirror* and *New Record Mirror* – benefited from four-colour printing. An innovation in the world of the so-called 'inkies', this helped raise the circulation under editor Peter Jones. Already connected to the biggest groups – he recommended the Rolling Stones to their manager Andrew Loog Oldham – Jones was an early champion of Jimi Hendrix, Dusty Springfield and the Motown stable. And, unlike the rest of the music press, *Record Mirror* was a reliable source of information on Black music from across the Atlantic.

Its reputation was bolstered by writer Norman Jopling and club culture pioneer James Hamilton. The latter was the first to tailor his copy to the growing army of DJs playing parties, clubs and discotheques. 'People like Jopling and Hamilton were interested in reaching their audience,' said Charlie Gillett. 'It was absolutely dedicated to the kind of person I felt I was: somebody who was interested in records, particularly Black music.'

Record Mirror sold between 60,000 and 70,000 copies a week throughout the 1960s. That circulation was sometimes matched by *Disc*, which used colour more frequently than the market leaders and was edited by Ray Coleman, chanelling the tenacity he had displayed as *Melody Maker*'s news editor.

An admirably gender-blind recruitment policy was evinced by Caroline Boucher and Judy Noakes joining Penny Valentine as reporters. However, in the office and in encounters with musicians, women were forced to run the gauntlet. 'Female music journalists became inventive in dealing with sexual discrimination,' said writer Ines Punessen. 'Their strategies ranged from being flirty to denying their gender to being feminist and finding support in fellow victims. Caroline Boucher says, "We were running around in short skirts. I suppose we flirted a bit, flirted quite a lot, but, you know, it was fine." Boucher denies any experience of discrimination during her time at the magazine, which suggests different levels of discrimination between music titles. However, one of her comments makes one listen attentively. She says, "If Mick Jagger wanted to be interviewed with his head on my lap, which has happened quite often, go for it.

It was fun!" It shows that the times and nature of social interaction were very different back then. What was accepted in the 1970s would not necessarily be accepted in the twenty-first century.'[12]

* * *

Music was just one element of Britain's underground press – a ramshackle strand of independent publishing – though it was vital to its wellbeing. Record company advertising and occasional handouts from the likes of Mick Jagger and Paul McCartney bailed out the perpetually hand-to-mouth titles. But the market for them had been brought home by two sell-out events at London's Royal Albert Hall: the International Poetry Incarnation in 1965, which featured beat poets and writers such as Lawrence Ferlinghetti and Allen Ginsberg, and Bob Dylan's appearance a year later, showcasing his electric evolution, with rambunctious backing from the Band. 'That's 7,000 people each time,' said Mick Farren, who fast became a countercultural mainstay. 'Everyone was fucking amazed at the amount of people who showed up. There was an instinctive feeling that an underground press was needed. You didn't really read the music press for information at that time. The source was the grapevine, which was incredibly efficient, because it was based on a different marketing model to corporate distribution. The news came with dope.'

With a masthead interpreted as *International Times*, *Intergalactic Times*, *Intravenous Times*, *Interminable Times* and even *Insanity Times*, *IT* (pl. 2) emerged from London's alternative bookshop and art gallery Indica. This was funded by Peter Asher – the brother of Paul McCartney's actress girlfriend Jane – and run by his friend John Dunbar and the writer Barry Miles (known by his surname alone). 'Miles was a compassionate and dignified man,' says Farren, 'simultaneously neat and fashionable, erudite and alarmingly well-informed.'

Describing Indica's magazine rack as 'a revelation', Farren discovered that US underground newspapers were 'springing up like mushrooms. Copies of the *San Francisco Oracle*, *Village Voice* and *East Village Other* out of New York, the *Fifth Estate* from Detroit and the *LA Free Press*, featuring Harlan Ellison's TV reviews, were displayed as one great newsprint temptation'.[13]

With John 'Hoppy' Hopkins, the photographer whose encouragement had benefited young creatives including Val Wilmer, Miles published the literary magazine *Long Hair*. But he was enamoured of the *East Village Other* (*EVO*), a radical New York newspaper launched in 1965 by British journalist John Wilcock, who had been instrumental in founding the city's premier arts publication, *The Village Voice*, a decade previously. 'The style that *EVO* had was the one I particularly picked up on,' said Miles. 'It was the unedited, extended interview. No one had ever done it in Britain or America.'

'*EVO*, partly in reaction to the *Voice*, partly the result of its staff's predilections, had rapidly settled into the acid freak end of the underground and away from the politicos of the American new left,' wrote Nigel Fountain in his study *Underground*, which noted *EVO*'s adoption of inexpensive offset litho printing: 'Offset was freedom. New on the market were IBM electric golf ball typewriters. Once typed on special paper, the copy could be pasted on to boards and, with no need for hot metal or skilled printers, was camera-ready.'[14]

This lay in the future when Miles and Hopkins midwifed *IT* into being in October 1966. The magazine was launched with a wild, acid-laced party at the Roundhouse in London, featuring Pink Floyd and Soft Machine. The Floyd, wrote Nick Jones in *Melody Maker*'s review of the event, 'need to write more of their own material – "psychedelic" versions of "Louie Louie" won't come off. But if they can incorporate their electronic prowess with some melodic and lyrical songs ... they could well score in the near future.'

Tilted towards the international avant-garde, the first issue of *IT* included a preview of Yoko Ono's exhibition at Indica, which was attended by John Lennon and led to their relationship. The sole musical feature – a clunky gossip column headed 'Pop ... Pop ... Ouch' – reviewed the Rolling Stones at the Albert Hall, grumbled that *Fabulous* had been 'disconcertingly prejudiced' about drug consumption by musicians and gratuitously plugged a new single by Peter Asher and his brother.

Miles claimed the first issue sold 10,000 copies; his wife and *IT* staffer Sue Miles said it was closer to 750. And music was slow to be part of the mix: a short piece on the Paul Butterfield Blues Band here, a tiny mention of Pink Floyd there. 'One day,' recalled Miles, 'I was complaining to Paul [McCartney] about how little advertising we were getting and he said, "You should interview me. Then you'll be able to get record company ads." So I went over to his place and taped a conversation with no pre-thought questions and ran a Q&A, like Andy Warhol's *Interview* did a little later on. Paul was right: EMI took an ad. So I did one with George Harrison next and we got more ads. Then I did Graham Nash and so on.'[15]

With a cover portrait of the Beatle in a cowboy hat and rolling a joint, the interview – sample quote: 'Pot is just pot' – fed a media frenzy about young people's growing taste for mind-altering substances. Indica was among the alternative venues raided by police, with copies of *IT* impounded because authorities believed it championed drug use. 'This was all part of the fun,' declared British underground chronicler Jonathon Green. 'Wasn't *all* publicity good publicity? What mattered, as it would to any young publication, was that *IT* knew it had a constituency ready and waiting for the product. Its very existence made it a success and that first sale began climbing until, sometime in 1968, it would peak at around 44,000 copies a fortnight. As Miles noted, *IT* somehow managed to get it right. A mix that fell somewhere between the portentousness of *The Village Voice* and the stoned craziness of *EVO*, it was right for London.'[16]

Not all readers were delighted. 'I was a punter for about three issues of *IT* and then complained to Miles about the lack of Jimi Hendrix and, apart from his Beatles interviews, why weren't we getting more about the Who or the Move?' grumbled Mick Farren, who briefly held the post of music editor. 'I had no journalistic experience, so I was perfectly qualified. I didn't stay music editor for very long because about two weeks later we were busted [by the police, for alleged obscenity] and a rift was already in place.'

That rift arose from a divide between writers such as Jeff Nuttall, a veteran of anti-nuclear and beat movements of the 1950s, and upstarts such as Farren, who was reared on rock 'n' roll and pop culture. 'That fight between the Bohemian/anti-rock people and the ex-rocker/ex-mod/acid-taking contingent ran throughout the life of the paper,' observed Farren, who suggested the obscenity raid served time on older contributors and cleared the way for him to become editor. Under Farren's command, *IT* became a more rocking proposition, built on a foundation of female staff. 'Women had been on the paper since the beginning, with Maureen McGrath as news editor, and it had been women who provided the typesetting, the listings, the ad selling,' wrote Nigel Fountain. However, assistant editor Dave Robins admitted, 'Women were just "chicks". The attitude to women's rights, to equality, to a bit of *space* was at best indifference. There was a lot of downright exploitation. Yet people like [writer] Jane Nicholson were doing the really important things.'[17]

Farren was often absent, engaged in his rabble-rousing role as front man of proto-punk group the Deviants: 'I was off on the road, so the Bohemian academics took control again, publishing Anaïs Nin and all kinds of godawful crap. A kind of compromise was reached because the record company advertising started rolling in, which was bizarre in itself. CBS was running ads saying, "The Man can't bust our music." Yeah, right!'

But *IT*'s true Achilles heel was its chaotic 'What's happening' listings. Farren is among those who later confessed to a major error of judgment when Tony Elliott and Bob Harris, who had become interested in counterculture publishing at Keele University, offered to produce a readable and error-free version of the section as a standalone magazine: 'I gave away the listings to Tony Elliott through complete stupidity. Everybody hated compiling "What's happening" – it always ended up with loads of mistakes and was like punishment detail, being up to your eyes in cow gum. So I said, "Tony, if you can make that work, wonderful." I am not a very intelligent businessman.'

'We looked down our noses at this pair of student hicks,' admits Dave Robins. 'But Elliott was shrewd. He realized that listings were what people liked about *IT*. That was very smart.'[18] Elliott said the reaction made him and Harris even more determined: 'I was extremely interested in theatre and all kinds of performance, about which there was very little information at that time. I had also sold loads of copies of *IT* at Keele so knew that there was potential because students were always asking for hard facts – where, when, who, etc. – beyond the long-winded articles and wild layouts. When the *IT* crowd were cool about it, that made us even more keen on progressing the idea.'[19]

That idea became one of the most successful projects to emerge from the British underground and a brand recognized around the world: *Time Out*. The weekly's coverage ranged from social activism to experimental theatre, with a hefty emphasis on new and adventurous music: early cover stars included folk singer Bridget St John and Peter Green's Fleetwood Mac, while listings for clubs such as Middle Earth gave early exposure to Marc Bolan's Tyrannosaurus Rex and the Incredible String Band.

Elliott and Harris – who would leave within a year to become DJ and *Old Grey Whistle Test* presenter 'Whispering' Bob Harris – handled their own distribution. That, wrote Nigel Fountain, 'meant that cash flow – an almost unknown concept in the underground – was immediately instituted, and through street sales they gained an instant feedback, instant market research on the product. Such was the success that Elliott took on an ad manager, John Leaver, then contemplating a nebulous publishing project with another newcomer, Felix Dennis. Leaver joined the staff. *Time Out* had effectively sealed *IT*'s fate.'[20]

IT remained notable, however, for Miles's long-form features. 'He was doing major, in-depth, *Rolling Stone*-style interviews – in which rock stars were allowed to wank on, basically, long before anyone else,' said Jonathon Green. 'But the most important role the underground press played for the music industry was as a place to advertise.'[21]

This tension – was the countercultural media essentially interested in music beyond its role as a source of income? – played out as other alternative titles surfaced in *IT*'s wake. Principal among them was *Oz* (pl. 3), launched by Australian Richard Neville in 1967 on a platform of sex, drugs and rock 'n' roll. 'The most memorable experiences underground,' he wrote in the first issue, 'are when you commit to the music, to the light show, happening and movie simultaneously, while being stoned and fucking all the time – swathed in stereo headphones, of course.'[22]

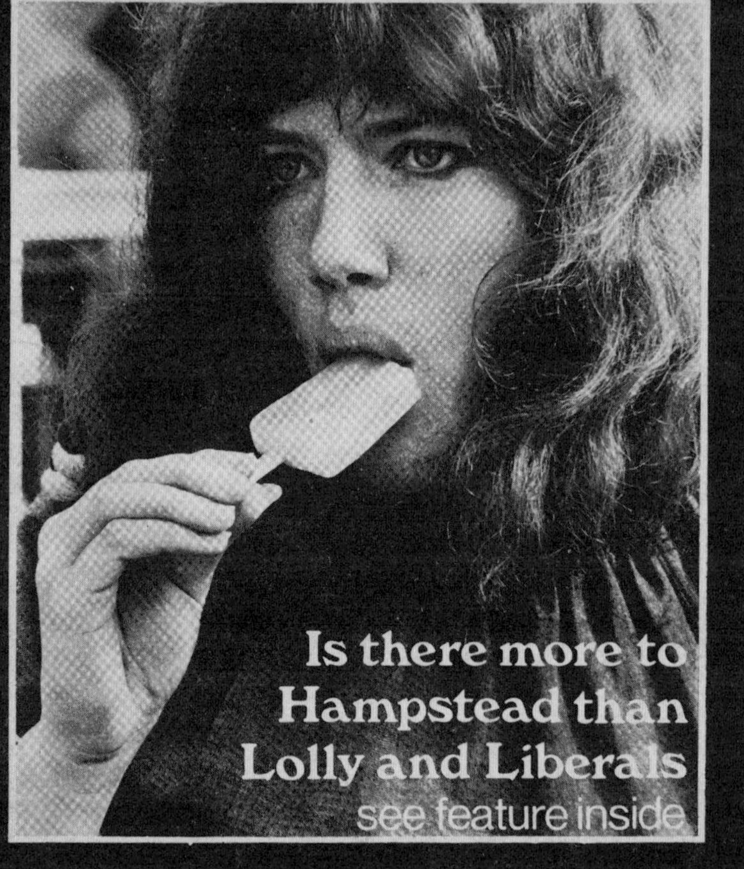

Time Out, 18 April–2 May 1970

'I don't think Neville was particularly interested in music,' suggested Jonathon Green. 'He'd come out of this relatively radical student magazine in Australia called *Tharunka* and changed it to *Oz* and gone through a trial because they'd portrayed people urinating, so came here and started *Oz* again, but wasn't into music any more than the average punter.'

Felix Dennis, a young Londoner who had scuffled around the R&B circuit as a drummer, was *Oz*'s most successful street-seller. 'His enthusiasm for the mag was unbounded,' wrote Neville in his memoir *Hippie Hippie Shake*. 'He tried his hand at record reviews, sweating over each paragraph for hours. At his suggestion, the music coverage was enlarged and separated into a supplement, *Mozic*. Felix had "contacts" in the music biz, he said, who had lucrative budgets, so I appointed him ad manager.'

Briefcase in hand, Dennis set about schmoozing Elektra and MGM, retailer Musicland and other shops specializing in imported music. 'Felix raved on about a new group, Led Zeppelin – a "turning point in rock", he insisted, "just like Dylan and *Sgt Pepper*" – and hit the phone to line up an interview with Jimmy Page,' recalled Neville.[23]

Oz was consciously chaotic. Long reports from the hippie trail and political musings by David Widgery were often illegible – secondary to the colourful overlays and experimental type.

And the magazine drew on the era's best graphic talents. Neville's fellow Aussie Martin Sharp – who created cover art for his friend Eric Clapton's group Cream, and cowrote their 'Tales of Brave Ulysses' – produced a defining poster of the era: an exploding portrait of Bob Dylan, printed on silver foil, entitled *Mister Tambourine Man*.

Graphic artist Barney Bubbles – born Colin Fulcher, but rechristened after creating psychedelic displays for hippie venues such as UFO – was commissioned to produce issue twelve in 1968. He came up with two double-sided posters, forming twenty-four pages, with board games, symbols, codes, cut-out postcards, astrology, rock 'n' roll and eastern spirituality: all the counterculture preoccupations in one package. A diagram tracing the Beatles' musical heritage was mixed with references to Chuck Berry, Cream, Bob Dylan and Elvis Presley. The back cover featured a multiple Xerox of a bleached-out naked woman advertising an *Oz* benefit concert, its attractions including the 'Sexy Barney Bubbles Light Show', operated while Pink Floyd, Soft Machine and the Pretty Things performed.

Bubbles's odyssey would last until he took his own life in 1983: record sleeves, advertising, logos, stage sets, posters and videos for clients from sonic warriors Hawkwind to the Damned, Elvis Costello and Ian Dury.

In 1969 Richard Neville was summoned to a soirée in London convened by Jann Wenner and Mick Jagger. The pair announced to the throng, which included representatives from *IT* and *Time Out*, their intention to launch a British version of *Rolling Stone*. 'I'm about to muscle in on your territory like the mafia,' Wenner told the surprised editors. 'You're not our rivals. We're here to knock off the music mags. They're dumb and out of touch.' Jagger added: 'If there's gonna be a fuck'n mag in London called *Rolling Stone*, I want a piece of it.'[24]

Excitedly announced as 'The first British issue!!', the UK edition – dated 14 June 1969 – wrapped the body of the American issue in four spreads of locally generated copy, such as an interview with Pete Townshend and drawings by Rolling Stones drummer Charlie Watts. Editor Jane Nicholson and music editor Mark Williams came from *IT*. They and their contributors were based initially at the Stones' management offices in Mayfair.

'*Rolling Stone* was much more a rock 'n' roll paper than *IT*,' Williams told Jonathon Green for his definitive history of the British underground, *Days in the Life*. 'Wenner was greedy and ultimately brutish. He was also a fucking groupie for Jagger, always was and still is, as far as I'm aware. I was hired on the understanding that we were going to produce a British edition and it went downhill very quickly.'

Green himself worked for the publication, for twenty pounds a week, 'which I don't believe I ever got paid. I was terribly naive.' His first piece was a feature on music managers, though the Small Faces' Steve Marriott refused to talk about the bullying Don Arden 'because he was so shit-scared of him. You'd get all these freebies and write nice things about people. It was incredibly corrupt in a way. I had this nagging feeling I should be more investigative.'

With Wenner back on the West Coast, the increasingly resentful British staff took liberties. 'He would send over directives all the time, just like the king,' said art director Jon Goodchild, formerly of *Oz*. 'So our first reaction was to say, "Who do you think you are?" After a while we began to take it over. He would send the negatives of his magazine and we were to take out eight pages and put ours in. We would take sixteen instead. Then we got to the point where we changed the whole thing.'[25]

Advertising manager Alan Marcuson took over from Jane Nicholson as editor and, according to Green, was soon 'trying to pull it away from pure rock 'n' roll. I think that was one of the reasons Wenner didn't like it: that we weren't mimicking *Rolling Stone* 110 per cent. No doubt he also thought we weren't as good as his guys, which may well have been true.'

This was indeed the case. Wenner's West Coast team commissioned from the Brits a long-form piece about 1969's Isle of Wight festival – featuring Free, the Who, the Band and Bob Dylan – but rejected it as too poorly written for publication. 'Wenner was fuming,' admitted Marcuson. 'For most of the time he was really uptight and, to be honest, we weren't truly professional. I remember one article on Bob Dylan where, throughout, Dylan was spelt "Dillon", which was wonderful ammunition for Wenner to say what an incompetent bunch of shits we were. He got mad, really mad.'[26]

Amid this discontent, new headquarters were found in Hanover Square. A party to celebrate the move turned disastrous when it was discovered – too late – that the drinks had been spiked. 'Marc Bolan had an overdose,' says Green. 'We were all spiked with some very bad acid. And it wasn't just Bolan; there were a lot of record company people completely fucked up.' Wenner was not impressed with this display of British fecklessness: 'He was saying to staff, "Come on, get out and about, and ask questions. We're not here just to drink Mick Jagger's wine." Apparently Jagger said, "Oh yes you are."'

Push came to shove a week after the party. 'We waltzed in to find the locks had been changed by people from Jagger's office,' says Green. 'They said, "Wenner told us to shut you down." But we had all the copy, including all sorts of shit like an essay by William Burroughs, so we decided to call the next issue *Friends of Rolling Stone*.'

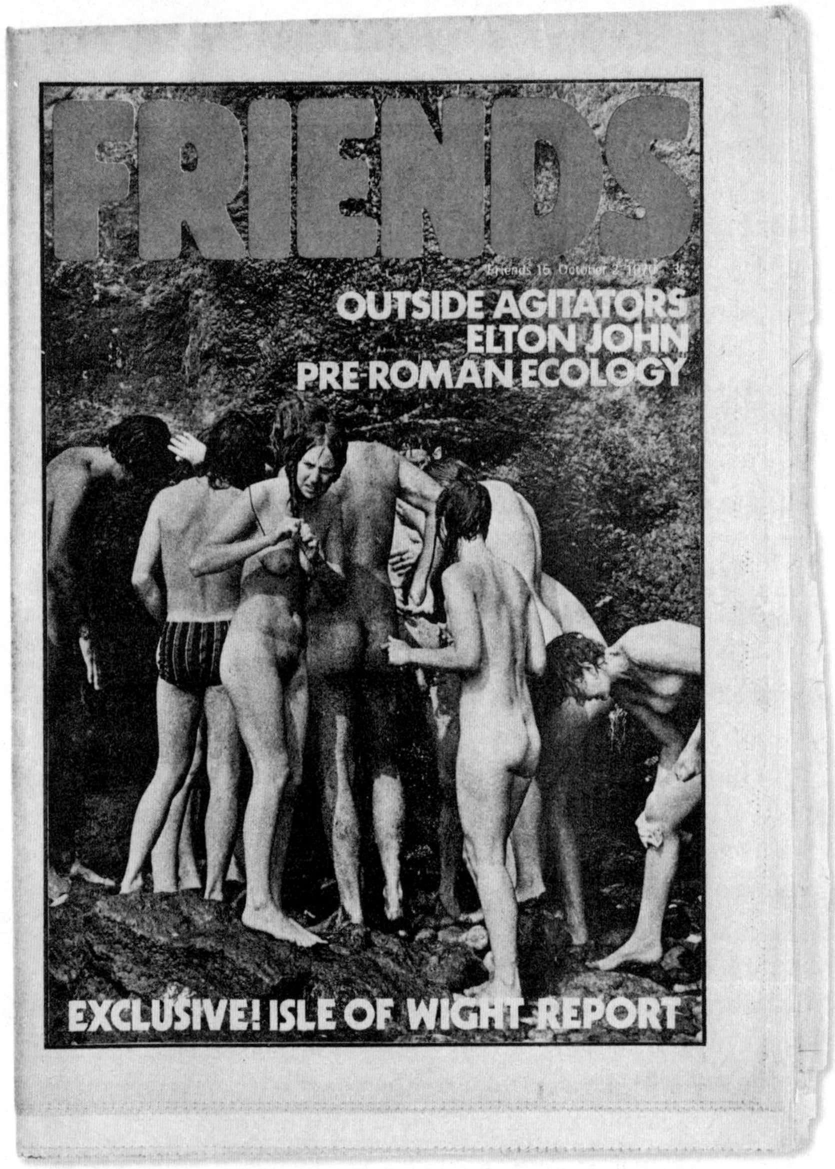

Friends, no. 15, 2 October 1970

Advertising helped. 'Many advertisers,' wrote Nigel Fountain, 'fearful of too close a relationship with *Oz* and *IT*, dismissive – or completely ignorant – of *Time Out*, but wishing for a way into the market that the then flagging *Melody Maker* and *NME* were failing to tap, seemed optimistic about the prospects for a new alternative British music paper.'[27]

Among those drafted to work on a new incarnation of the fortnightly was Pearce Marchbank, art director of *Architectural Design*. He was to consolidate his reputation as one of the greatest British magazine designers of his generation at *Time Out*, but his tenure at *Friends of Rolling Stone* lasted for the single edition published as the decade drew to a close. After an injunction from Wenner, the name was condensed to *Friends*, which was to become – in terms of music coverage – the most successful of all underground magazines.

Jagger was no longer involved. The Rolling Stones' performance at December 1969's Altamont free concert, which descended into crowd violence and the murder of an attendee by Hells Angels, made manifest the end of the optimism that had informed 1960s pop culture, not least the music press. A harder-edged approach was soon reflected in papers on both sides of the Atlantic.

7
Boy Howdy!

Creem Unleashes Lester Bangs and *Blues & Soul* Champions Black Music

Boy Howdy!

'Hi, motherfucker. You're an asshole!' This greeting, to friends and strangers alike, was a hallmark of Barry Kramer, the publisher of a Detroit-based underground tabloid whose name was a nod to his favourite band: *Creem* (pl. 9). Less than a year after the magazine's launch in March 1969, the departure of British editor Tony Reay gave Kramer the chance to shape it in his own image. Cartoonist Robert Crumb conjured two cartoon characters that appeared in its pages, on T-shirts and even on drinks: Mr Dream Whip, an animated cream topping canister, and Boy Howdy!, a cheery beer bottle. Spiky copy exuding Motor City toughness and vicious wit was in line with the scuzzy sound of hometown heroes – such as Alice Cooper, the Amboy Dukes, the MC5, the Stooges, and Mitch Ryder and the Detroit Wheels – and with the hardline politics that had produced the local White Panthers. Their leader, MC5 manager John Sinclair, became a target for the city's police: jailed on trumped-up marijuana possession and dealing charges, he was also among those indicted for the bombing of a CIA office in Michigan. Detroit and its surrounds bristled with a tough countercultural energy unrivalled in the western world.

At *Creem*, Kramer appointed twenty-year-old Dave Marsh as editor – although, as writer Jim DeRogatis pointed out, 'in the egalitarian spirit of the time, nobody at the magazine had a formal job title'.[1] A subsequent editorial declared: 'Detroit is such a unique hotbed of rock 'n' roll because the kids are so deeply involved in it: rock 'n' roll is their whole lifestyle and they know no other. Our bands are people's bands; similarly we think of ourselves as a people's magazine. We want to be "professional" only in terms of our access to information and our efficiency in putting out our magazine. We do not want to be another *Rolling Stone*. We are a rock 'n' roll magazine with all that implies. Our culture is rock 'n' roll culture. We are rock 'n' roll people.'[2] The *Creem* logo was duly appended with, 'America's only rock 'n' roll magazine'.

Among the readers who fell under its spell was Danny Sugerman, the young manager of the Doors in their final phase. Sugerman was particularly taken with Marsh's copy: 'Dave's column Looney Tunes picked a theme each month – Sly Stone's new album or whatever he felt strongly about. He had a lot of heart. I really connected with that, responded to his passion.'[3]

Jim Morrison used his pull for Sugerman to become a contributor, culminating in him filing six pages about the singer's departure for Paris (where he died in the summer of 1971). 'Jim gave me what would become his last official statement to the press,' recalled Sugerman. 'He said, "For me, it was never an act or so-called performance; it was a life and death thing, an attempt to involve many people in a private world of thought. I no longer feel I can do this through concerts. The belief isn't there." At the time, I was in total denial, expecting him to come back from Paris and tour *LA Woman*. That was the last piece I wrote for *Creem*.'

Meanwhile, Marsh coined the phrase 'punk rock' in his May 1971 Looney Tunes entry about the Michigan band ? and the Mysterians, and 'Metal' Mike Saunders – having pioneered the term 'heavy metal' in a *Rolling Stone* review of Humble Pie's *As Safe as Yesterday Is* – repeated the phrase in a write-up of the New York power trio Sir Lord Baltimore.

One of the few females at *Creem*, Jaan Uhelski met the team while operating a soda fountain at Detroit's Grande Ballroom: 'I offered to sell their T-shirts at the boutique I was managing by day without taking a cut, and that got my foot in the door. I was hired not for my writing prowess but for my entrepreneurial skills, so was given the job of "subscription kid", then circulation manager. I had to do my writing on the sly during the dead of night.'

The environment at *Creem*, says Uhelski, was 'as close as one could get to a mental care facility. We were all wildly dysfunctional. Who else would work for $22.75 a week just to get published? When Barry Kramer was displeased with someone or something, he'd hurl a typewriter through the window or slam a phone through a light table, but he wasn't the only one. We all worked at fever pitch, with little sleep – especially during the monthly deadlines – and confrontations were more the norm than not. Fistfights often broke out among the staff. We would get into it over something as benign as cover lines. The madness was channelled into the writing, which was as bombastic as our behaviour.'[4]

The magazine's reputation for untamed editorializing was sealed by Marsh's commissioning of highly extemporized submissions from Lester Bangs. One, entitled 'Psychotic reactions and carburetor

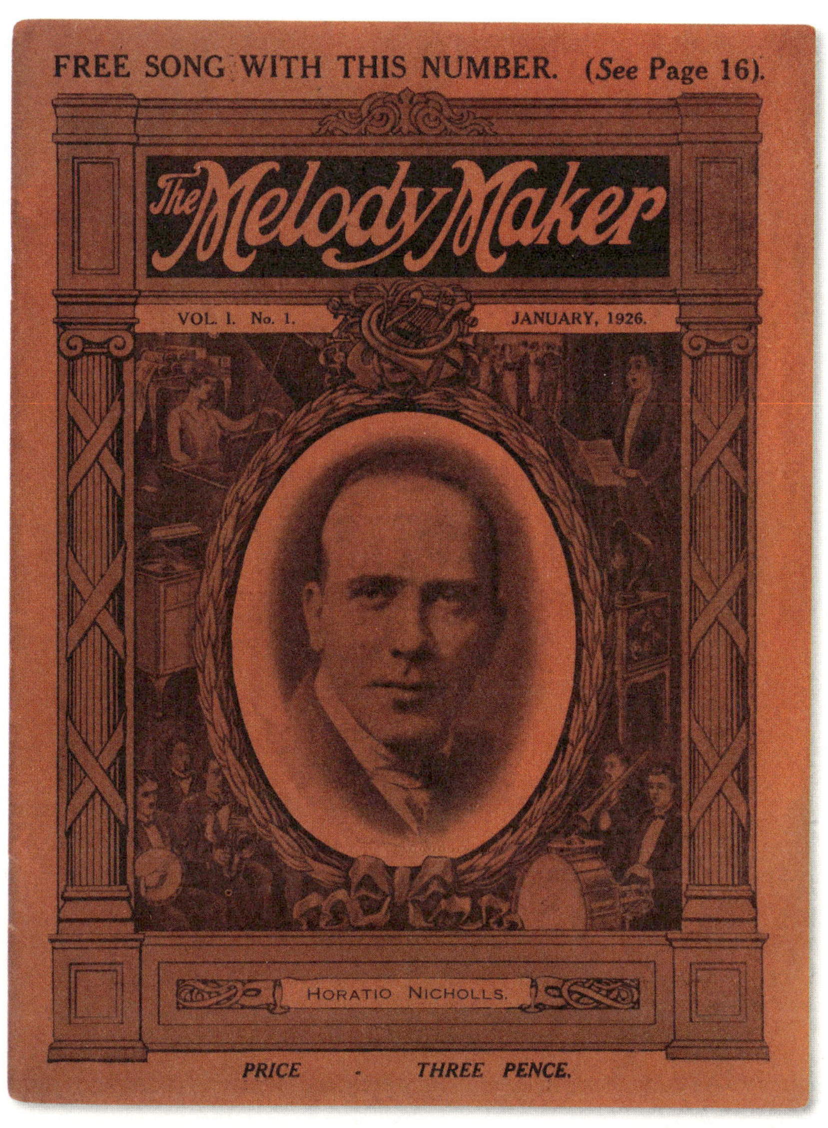

1. *The Melody Maker*, vol. 1, no. 1, January 1926

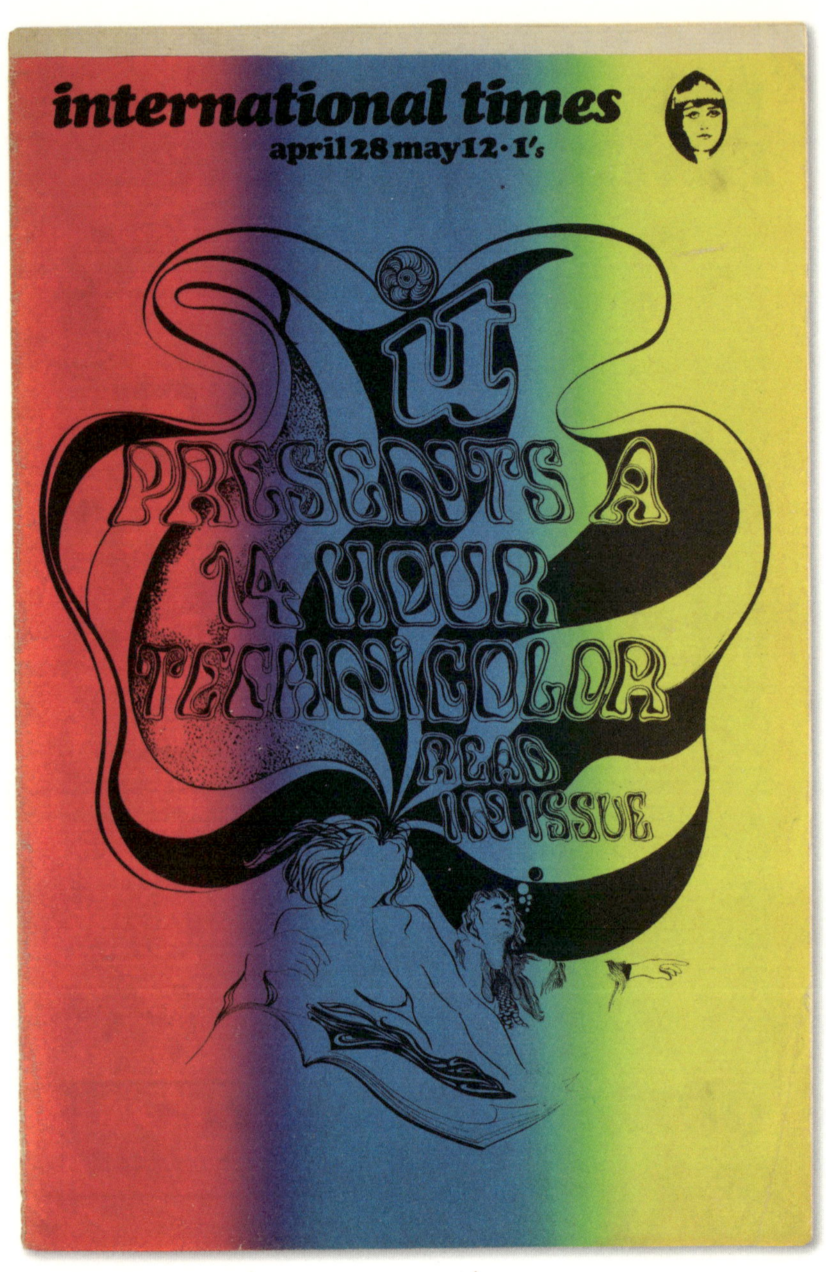

2. *International Times*, 28 April–12 May 1967

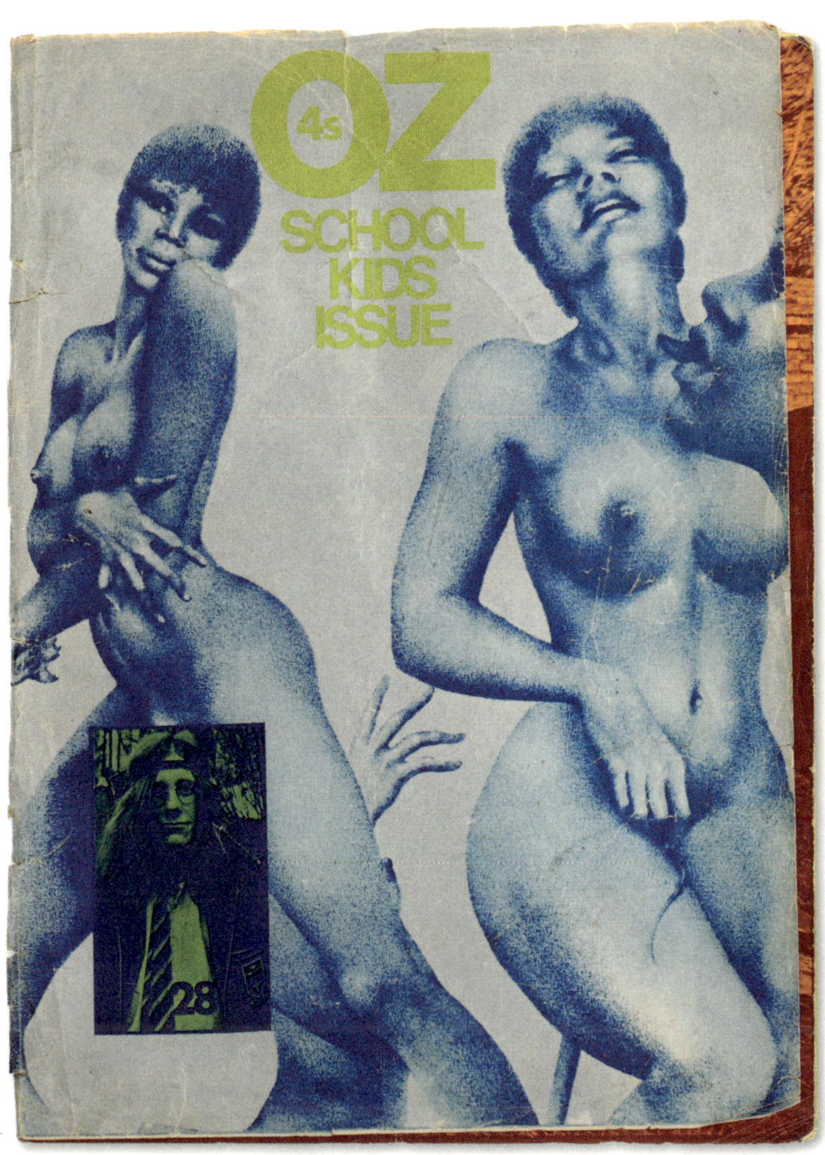

3. *Oz*, June 1970

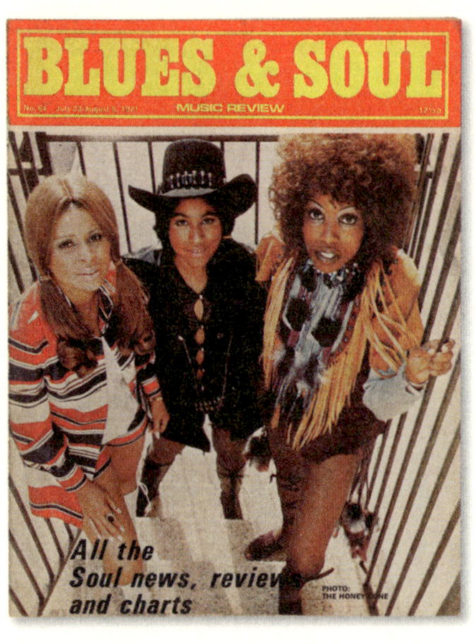

4. *Blues & Soul*, 23 July–5 August 1971

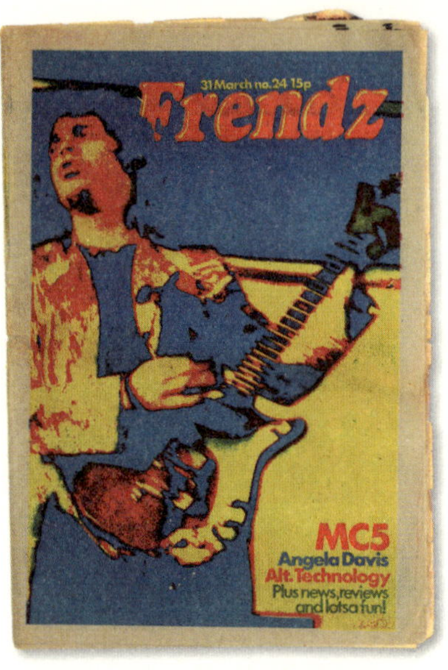

5. *Frendz*, no. 24, 31 March 1972

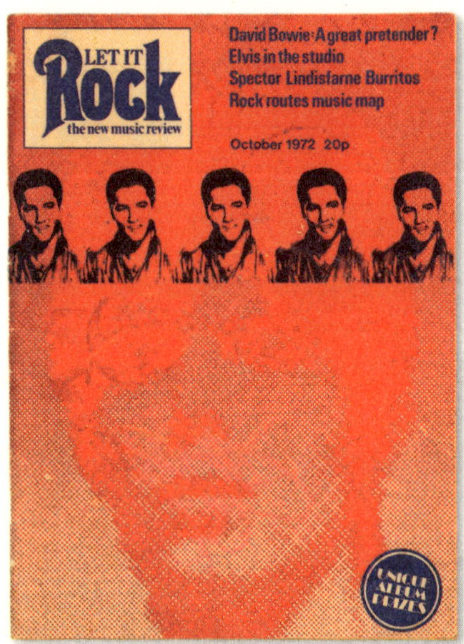

6. *Let it Rock*, October 1972

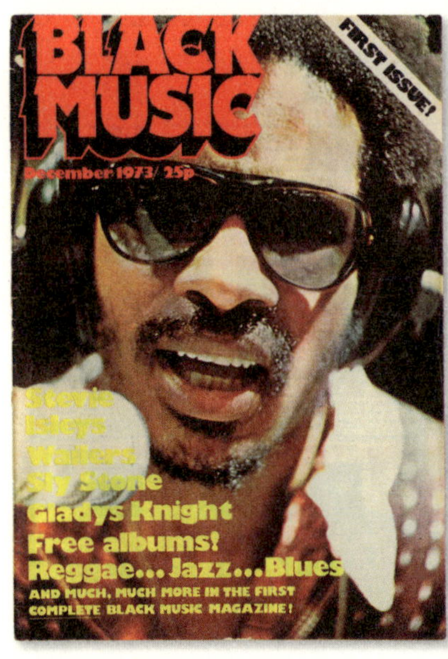

7. *Black Music*, December 1973

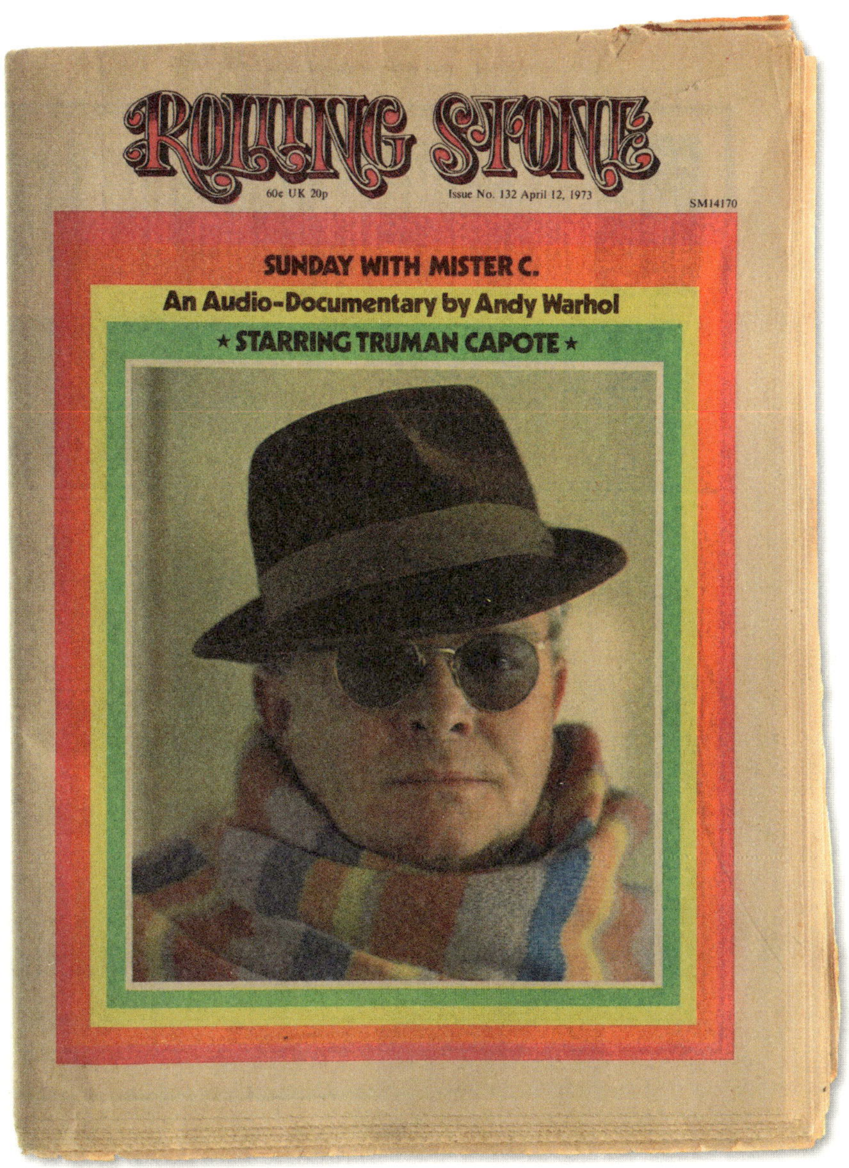

8. *Rolling Stone*, no. 132, 12 April 1973

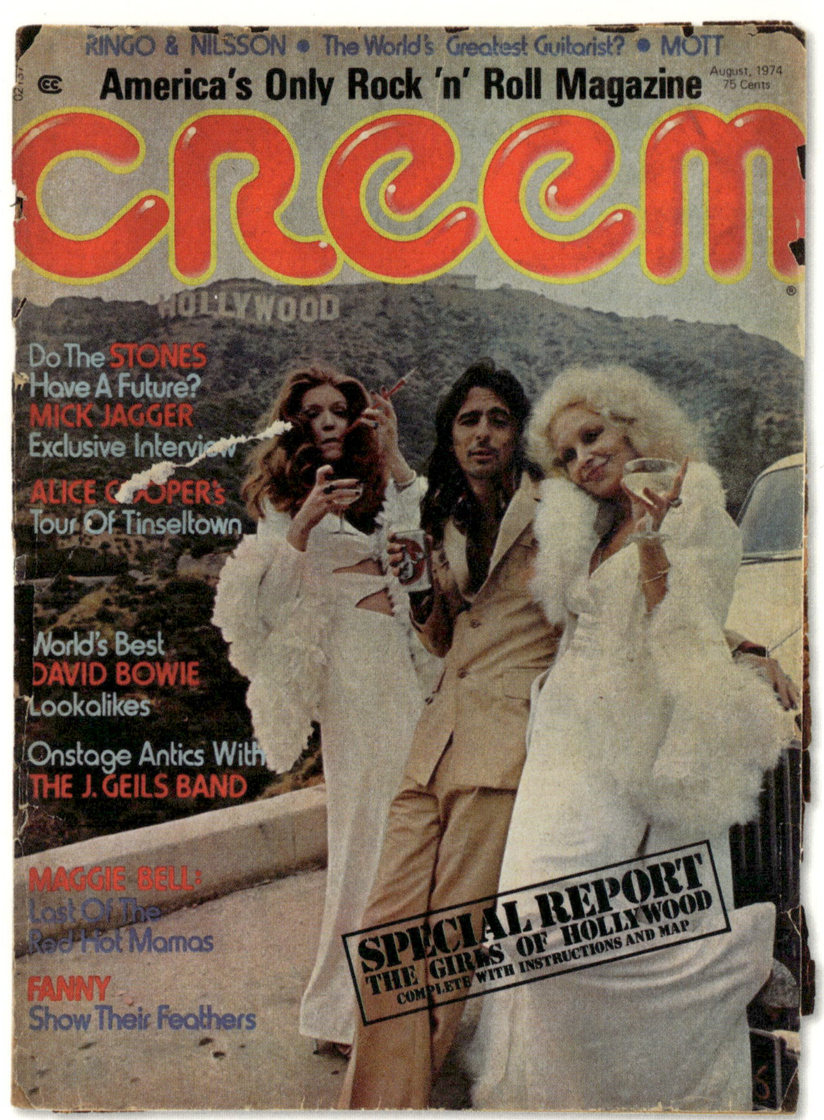

9. *Creem*, August 1974

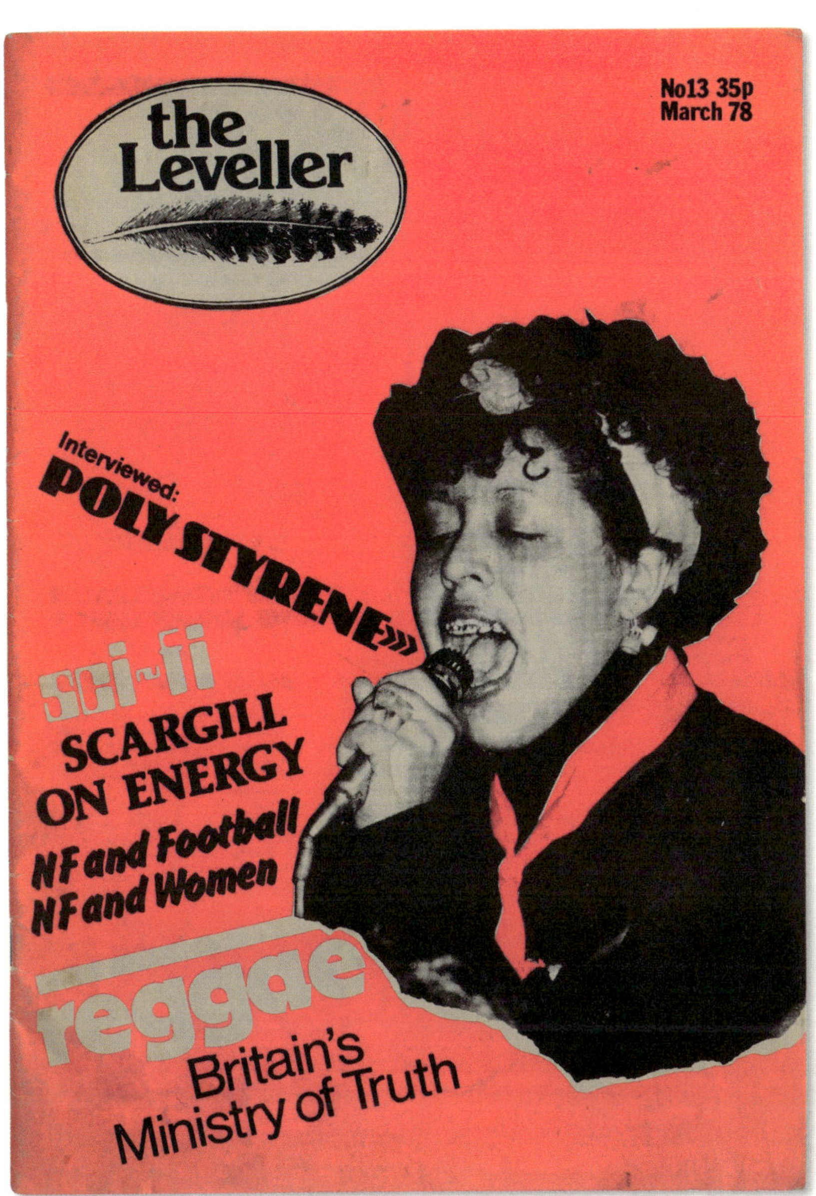

10. *The Leveller*, no. 13, March 1978

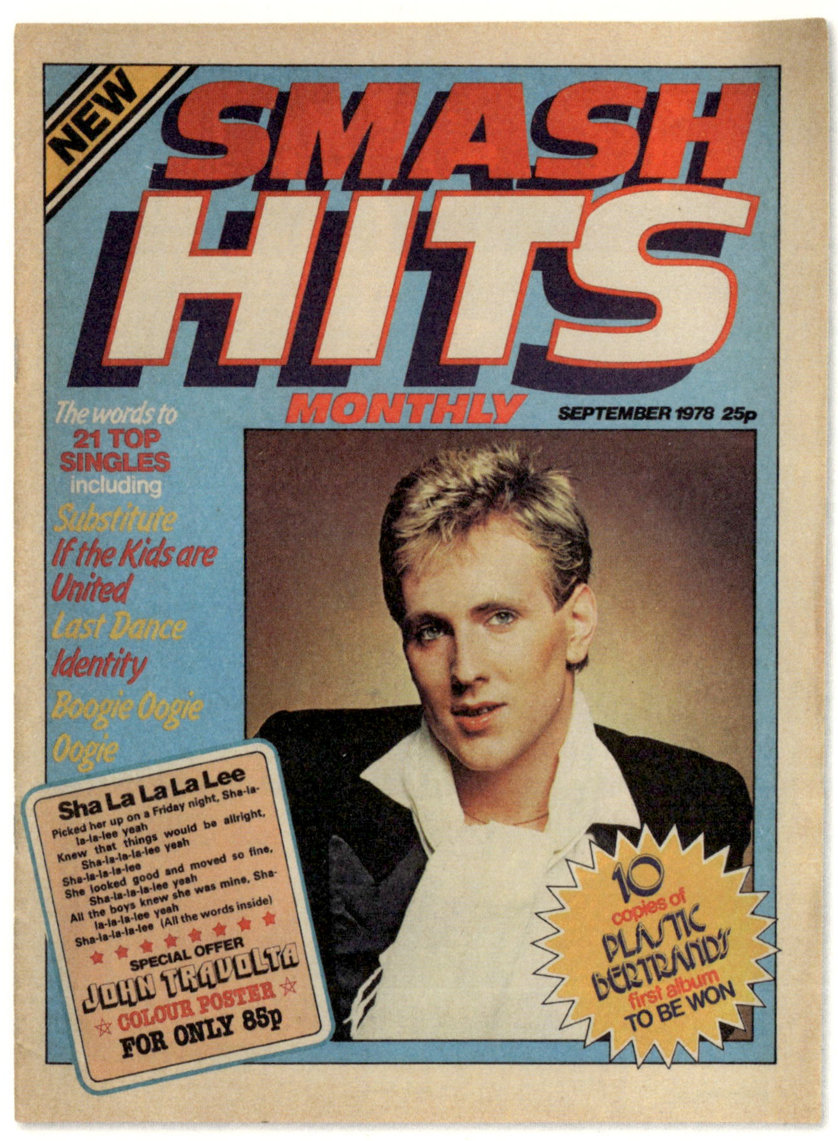

11. *Smash Hits*, September 1978

dung: a tale of these times', celebrated largely forgotten 1960s garage-rockers the Seeds. Another, a tribute to Iggy Pop's band, was headed 'Of Pop and pies and fun: a program for mass liberation in the form of a Stooges review, or, Who's the fool?' And an attack on the early-seventies trend for singer-songwriters made its position clear with the headline 'James Taylor marked for death'.

Invited to Detroit to interview Alice Cooper, Bangs accepted Barry Kramer's offer to be assistant editor, over Dave Marsh's objections: 'I wanted to keep my distance, because that's my way of dealing with competition. [Bangs] had the most raw writing talent I've ever seen in a young writer.'[5]

Bangs's pugnaciousness was evident in his call-out for readers' submissions that appeared each month: 'NOBODY WHO WRITES FOR THIS RAG'S GOT ANYTHING YOU AIN'T GOT, at least in the way of credentials. There's no reason why you shouldn't be sending us your stuff, fiction, reviews, features, cartoons, stuff about film, ecology, books or whatever you have in mind that we might be able to use. Sure, we don't pay much but then who else do ya know who'll publish you? We really will ... Ask any of our dozens of satisfied customers. Just bop it along to us and see what comes back ... Whaddya got to lose? Whaddya got?'

Among the respondents was Charlie Gillett, whose reputation as a cool assessor of Black music at *Record Mirror* was compounded by his book *The Sound of the City*. *Creem* – which published his reviews of soul stars Smokey Robinson, Eddie Floyd and Johnny Adams – was, he said, 'as close to the ideal as a rock 'n' roll writer could wish – lots of pages, but a small, overworked staff who welcome a good contribution from outside because it relieves the pressure on them to fill the space. But it doesn't get distributed in Britain, so you wouldn't get the thrill of having your friends see what you've written, and you might find it disconcerting to write for an audience you don't know. Trouble is, when you start looking at the alternatives in Britain, there's nothing as encouraging to the unconfident amateur, or the aspiring semi-pro.'[6]

Soon after Bangs's arrival, Kramer joined the White flight of businesses from Detroit's increasingly dangerous centre and purchased a 120-acre farm. He and *Creem* art director Charlie Auringer lived in one house on the property with their partners while another hosted the magazine staff. Bangs and Marsh even roomed together. But this rural setting did not free Kramer and his staff from the attentions of the authorities. Late 1990s freedom-of-information requests, reported DeRogatis, revealed the farm was monitored by the FBI as a potential safe house for the radical anti-Vietnam War group the Weather Underground.

This febrile political climate lent the title edge. 'I edited *Creem* magazine for five years and we had, like, hundreds of thousands of readers who really dug it that we were telling Dylan and the Stones and all these people to go jump in a lake,' said Bangs. 'They weren't idiots that swallowed any hype that was shoveled to them. I hate that everybody thinks that fans are just morons that'll just swallow any garbage, 'cause I think the kids are really sharp.'[7]

Among the writers Bangs commissioned was the New York-based Nick Tosches, who had contributed to *Fusion* and *Rolling Stone*: 'I was hacking out a living as a paste-up man for the Loveable Underwear Company at 200 Madison Avenue, and writing on the side. He called me one night and asked me to write for *Creem*. We had a few things in common: neither of us had college degrees to fall back on, and we were both drunks.

'But in more ways we were oil and water. My buddy Richard Meltzer and I spent a lot of time trying to shake the hayseeds out of Lester's head. One night, at a White Rose bar on Broadway, I picked Lester's pocket and then lent him his own money for cab fare. One morning, the hayseeds were literal. He showed up at my door after waking up on a subway car not knowing where he had been all night, and there were strands of actual hay sticking out of his hair.'[8]

Tosches added his distinctive voice to *Creem* with a report on an album by a commune called The Brotherhood of Spirit. Headlined 'Spirit in flesh: God-crazed hippies reap boffo BO', it featured slang – 'scuzzy', 'bizarro' – that would dominate rock criticism across the Atlantic in a couple of years. And the pay-off to Tosches's piece encapsulated *Creem*'s fuck-you attitude: 'What we've got here is a cross between Jesus Christ and Florence Foster Jenkins and everybody knows Jesus sucks.'[9]

Drugs and alcohol meant Bangs was all over the place as a reviews editor. '*Creem* was disorganized and unprofessional beyond description during his time,' said Mike Saunders. 'He chronically assigned things that didn't run and never saw print. It was a big mess. I kinda had the minority opinion that *Creem* was great for about a year, mid-1970 to mid-1971, then had to sell out to commercial considerations when they went to a slick cover in fall 1971. For me, as a reader, the magazine pretty much sucked after that.'[10]

As demonstrated by the 2019 documentary *Creem: America's Only Rock 'n' Roll Magazine*, the publication continued to blaze a trail through the 1970s and into the '80s. 'I would wait eagerly for the next issue and run down to the local liquor store to check out the much publicized, first-ever photos of Kiss without their makeup – only to be foiled when they turned out to be photos of the backs of their heads!' said US fanzine writer Karrin Vanderwal, while the MC5's Wayne Kramer summarized *Creem* as 'our Facebook, our social media'.

* * *

As Barry Kramer and Dave Marsh honed *Creem*, the launch of a vibrant weekly called *Sounds* (pl. 12) in the autumn of 1970 rattled the old guard in Britain. The surprise was magnified by it being engineered by one of their own: editor Jack Hutton quit *Melody Maker* in May 1970, with advertising manager Peter Wilkinson and directors John Thompson and Joe Sahl, to set up *Sounds*' independent publisher Spotlight. Financial backing came from a company owned by Rupert Murdoch, the Australian who had purchased *News of the World* and *The Sun*, beginning his mission to drag newspapers into the gutter for decades to come.

Even *Melody Maker*'s office tea-lady joined the exodus. 'Maisie was amazing,' remembered Chris Welch. 'She used to serve tea to all the visiting musicians, asking Ornette Coleman or Ringo Starr, "Whatcha want dear?"' Welch himself was tempted by *Sounds* but persuaded to stay by new *Melody Maker* editor Ray Coleman, the hard-nosed reporter who had switched to edit *Disc* in the mid-1960s. 'Ray offered me a pay rise and said the opportunities would open up for me. Then he said he'd make me features editor and gave me another pay rise. By the end of the day, he'd given me a third pay rise to stay where I was.'

Richard Williams had a similar experience: 'In two weeks I went from junior reporter to features editor, and the next week I was assistant editor. Jack told me that *Sounds* was going to be "a left-wing *Melody Maker*". I thought the better thing to do would be to make *Melody Maker* left-wing. I liked Jack but it was *Melody Maker* I'd come to work for, not him.'

'There was a strange atmosphere,' said reporter Jerry Gilbert, soon to fly the coop. 'I don't think everyone was 100 per cent happy about Ray being reinstated; he tried to cross-match journalists with areas outside their expertise. I was covering blues at the time, but for some reason he wanted Richard Williams to do that. Ray could be very abrasive. It wasn't a comfortable situation because there was an instant personality clash between us.' The final straw was Coleman's insistence that Gilbert write about James Taylor, after he met actress Jane Asher – sister of Taylor's manager Peter Asher – at a social event. 'Although I was well into Taylor, I didn't like the manipulation,' recalled Gilbert, 'so I decided to go to *Sounds*, for a drop in salary.'

The new weekly published its first issue on 10 October 1970. Under editor Billy Walker were writer Penny Valentine, who had left *Disc*, and Steve Peacock, who established himself as an authority on acts who attracted mainly male fans to the paper: Fairport Convention, the Incredible String Band, King Crimson, Van Morrison and Soft Machine. '*Sounds* was very much based around reportage – loads of research and quite in-depth, but also designed to be disposable,' said Gilbert, who interviewed blues legends Son House and Bukka White as well as British folk artists Bert Jansch and John Renbourne.

Writers enjoyed the largesse of labels profiting from rising album sales. 'Record companies were sponsoring journalists to go to the States,' recalled Gilbert. On one trip he accompanied Scottish hard-nuts Nazareth and prog-rockers Genesis on their first American dates: 'I said to *Sounds*, "If I'm going to New York, I may as well stay there a bit longer and tap out Warner's to see what acts they've got." That way I could build a fund of interviews. Everyone did this.

You didn't take the piss. You arrived in New York and CBS, say, were happy to put you up in a decent hotel for four or five nights and cram you out with interviews. There would be some turkeys but then they'd roll out Paul Simon.'

* * *

As *Sounds* emerged, so did the shorter-lived fortnightly *Strange Days*, steered by *IT* music editor Mark Williams. Described by Williams as 'quasi-underground', it called itself 'the rock paper that cares'. In visuals and content, *Strange Days* was an outlier and even ahead of its time. The cover stars of the first issue, in September 1970, were a gold-suited Elvis Presley, in his 1950s heyday, and his wily manager Colonel Tom Parker. Inside were features on the MC5, Frank Zappa, the Isle of Wight festival and even British soccer stars.

Motorcycle-obsessed Williams – who launched *Bike* magazine the following year – ran ads for '*Strange Days* despatch riders', offering to 'collect or deliver photographs, artwork, general print matter or anything else in the London area at really spiffy rates'. But despite such diverse business planning, the magazine folded in less than two months. *IT* accused Williams of 'a substantial lack of responsibility both to his backers and, more important, to his staff of ten who are on a month's notice'. Williams himself confessed: 'We're broke.'

Nonetheless, *Strange Days* was a brave attempt by an independent to shake up music publishing. 'At the beginning was an idea that an alternative to the mass of pop media could successfully appeal to Joe Public,' Williams wrote. 'It was worked out we'd have lottsa "in-depth" articles about rock music and a whole bunch of things that you don't usually get in a music paper, but which perhaps belonged there nevertheless.'[11]

With *Strange Days* out of the way, *Sounds* consolidated its position as the new kid on the block, chipping away at the ad revenues and circulations of *Disc*, *Record Mirror* and *NME*. But the schism at *Melody Maker* sparked a reinvention of the market leader.

* * *

'We viewed *Sounds* as a serious rival,' said Richard Williams. 'We didn't think it was as good as us, but it had two or three very good writers and was doing progressive stuff. But it wasn't as broad as we were. What I loved about *Melody Maker* at the time was that you could write about anything. If you liked a daft pop record, you could interview the person about it. *Sounds* couldn't do that; it had to be credible. *Melody Maker* was already credible, so we could take risks.'

In the aftermath of the defections to *Sounds*, 'the offices felt empty,' recalled Chris Welch, 'with wind blowing through'. Soon, however, fresh talents gravitated to the decades-old *Melody Maker* and, with Welch and Williams, came to define a new era of music writing. Among them were future book publishing supremo Chris Charlesworth, who recalled: 'Cigarette smoke hung in the air, as it did in every newspaper office I'd worked in. It was dimly lit with a scuffed parquet floor, dented bottle-green filing cabinets on two sides, old wooden desks, rickety chairs and black manual typewriters that looked to have seen service for a decade or more. The phones were also black and made from heavy Bakelite and the walls were covered in a random assortment of torn and faded posters. Richard Williams had written out some Dylan lyrics and stuck them to the walls. I sat opposite a sign that read, "You don't need a weatherman to know which way the wind blows," and to my right were the words, "Don't follow leaders, watch the parking meters." Behind Richard's chair were pictures of Italian footballers, and next to him sat Alan Lewis, the chief subeditor, whose humour was often drier than the Sahara.'[12]

Lewis divided his time between subediting and championing Black music. 'Richard started giving me soul records to review and I also started doing the odd feature,' he recalled. 'I had the amazing luck to interview people like James Brown, Curtis Mayfield, Stevie Wonder, Tina Turner, Ben E. King ... You'd get amazing access to people, but it would end up as a half-page feature. [*Melody Maker*] used to try to cram a lot in.'[13]

Another new recruit was Michael Watts. 'Many of us on the *MM* had worked on local newspapers,' he observes. 'We were professional journalists compared with the kindergarten wunderkinds who would soon start writing for *NME*. When I was on the *Walsall*

Observer, the Midlands heaved with exciting new acts such as the Move, Spencer Davis Group, the 'N Betweens, who became Slade, Robert Plant and his Band of Joy, and the Moody Blues ... I talked to every musician who came through the area – so, when Ginger Baker's Airforce played Birmingham Town Hall, I interviewed George Harrison and Eric Clapton. Then there were the profusion of local bands: I interviewed people like Black Sabbath at the local Methodists' hall, and the Edgar Broughton Band, whose manager was memorably not only their mother but also their roadie.'

Watts's work attracted the attention of Ray Coleman. 'He was slim and trim, balding with oversize glasses,' the writer recalls. 'He looked like the showbiz editor of a national tabloid. Ray was beguilingly old-fashioned, which was reassuring. It was also timely. I was on the verge of leaving the *Walsall Observer* after returning to the offices one night in a drunken mood and trashing it, throwing a metal trashcan through a window.'

Within an hour of arriving at *Melody Maker*, Watts was interviewing Diana Ross, then on the eve of releasing her debut solo album: 'I had no preparation. Suddenly I was sat in a dimly-lit room at EMI or wherever and Diana Ross literally breathed glamour. I remember her amazing hands, with what looked like sugared almonds on the tips of her fingers. This was tremendously impressive. I left the interview thinking, "Hey, I've arrived. I'm in the big time."'[14]

'Mick was a terrific writer,' said Williams. 'His writing had the kind of maturity that none of the rest of us possessed at the time. This is apart from the fact that he got those really big scoops.' Among those was David Bowie's January 1972 declaration, 'I'm gay and always have been' – a landmark on the road to Ziggy Stardust. 'I felt lucky,' remembered Watts. 'He'd almost spilled the beans to *Jeremy* magazine three years before. Laws on homosexuality had been reformed only five years previously. After Bowie came *le déluge*. He had shrewdly calculated the consequences, however. Busting taboos stokes the star-maker machinery.'[15] 'It was *Melody Maker* that made me,' Bowie agreed. 'It was that piece by Mick Watts. I became a performer after that.'[16]

Others drafted in by Ray Coleman in 1970 included news editor Laurie Henshaw. A *Melody Maker* veteran of the 1950s who had defected to *Disc*, Henshaw was described by Chris Charlesworth as 'urbane, middle-aged, a veteran of the swing era and reputedly something of a ladies' man'. But neither he nor another member of the old guard, Max Jones, had associations with the publication as deep as those of Chris Hayes, who now ran a readers' queries column. To the new young staff, Hayes struck an anachronistic chord; he had joined in 1929, three years after *Melody Maker*'s launch. 'With the bleak countenance of someone who'd just returned from the funeral of a dearly-loved relative, Chris was a man of lugubrious, melancholy, detached temperament, with levity reserved only for special occasions that seldom occurred,' recalled Charlesworth. 'I thought he might be distantly related to the Addams Family.'

Hayes was 'brilliant', according to Williams: 'He made no value judgments: a query about Victor Silvester was the same as one about Marc Bolan. He got answers to these incredible questions from extremely famous, busy people.' 'He was unusually fastidious,' agreed Charlesworth. '"Tell me Eric, old boy (Chris always, but always, called everybody 'old boy'), there's a reader from Leicester here ... writes in and wants to know what sort of guitar you use these days?" I was not so much bemused by the fact that Chris was evidently talking to Eric Clapton (at 10.30 in the morning), as much as the casual manner in which he addressed him. "Fender Stratocaster, old boy? How do you spell that? S... T... R... A... T... O... C... A... S... T... E... R. Thanks. And what sort of amp do you use these days? Marshall? Does that have two Ls?"

'Another call. "Pete, old boy, there's a reader from Brighton wants to know what sort of wah-wah you use." (This to Pete Townshend.) What, you don't use a wah-wah? But how do you spell wah-wah anyway? W... A... H... W... A... H. Sounds bloody silly to me, old boy. Best of luck with all that *Tommy* business." And so it went on, with Chris talking on the phone to the great and not so great. He became quite exasperated when a PR person refused to immediately connect him with the rock star to whom he wished to speak – "Well, can't you wake him up?"'[17]

The team was rounded out by twenty-one-year-old Roy Hollingworth, who had worked alongside Richard Williams in local news in the mid-1960s. Williams describes his colleague as one of *Melody Maker*'s 'most distinctive and influential contributors', his talents enhanced by a rock-star charisma that came into full effect when Hollingworth moved to New York and performed with his band Roy and the Rams at haunts such as the Mercer Arts Center. 'An instinctive affinity for a life of hanging out until the early hours at the Speakeasy or the Revolution and of going on the road with bands across Europe and America eased his entry into London's rock society,' wrote Williams of Hollingworth, who died aged fifty-two in 2002. 'For a while, he and the *MM*'s gifted photographer Barrie Wentzell shared a flat above a Soho pizza restaurant. Their convivial instincts and the flat's location, a few steps away from such musicians' hangouts as the Nellie Dean, the Ship, La Chasse and the Marquee, meant that it became a rendezvous for a bunch of rock eccentrics, notably Viv Stanshall and Legs Larry Smith of the Bonzo Dog Doo-Dah Band.'[18] Even John Lennon recognized Hollingworth's potential, advising him, 'Cut ya hair and get a record deal, Roy!'

'He loved to champion the underdog as well as writing about famous faces,' wrote Charlesworth. 'There was a real sense of adventure in his writing and there might not have been the likes of Nick Kent if Roy hadn't opened the door to this fearless style of music writing.'[19]

Melody Maker's venues for interviews were decidedly unglamorous: the Fleet Street branch of the cheap fast food chain the Golden Egg or an adjacent pub, the Red Lion. The latter was run by, Charlesworth recalled, 'a huge gay man called Wally who was always dressed in a black Russian tunic'.[20] This was the venue for an encounter between Chris Welch and David Bowie, who wore the Mr Fish dress he sported on the cover of *The Man Who Sold the World*. 'I think David was trying to get through to me that I should be writing about his new look and attitude,' says Welch. 'He was sort of coming out, but I wasn't taking the bait. So, foolishly, I tried to cover it up in the piece by pretending he wasn't being camp: "Don't be silly, David; put that dress away!" I didn't take it seriously because I'd known David from the Marquee days when he was in the Buzz. I rather missed the point.'

Circulation soared to more than 200,000 as *Melody Maker* became the go-to for fans eager for news of Marc Bolan, David Bowie, Genesis and Led Zeppelin. And its role as an arbiter of taste was confirmed when Richard Williams proved instrumental in the rise of Roxy Music. Singer Bryan Ferry left a demo at Williams's home in the summer of 1971. Intrigued by its retro-futuristic blend of honking 1950s rock 'n' roll, systems music and 1940s-style crooning, Williams interviewed Ferry and filed a piece on the unsigned group: 'Roxy or whatever they eventually decide to call themselves have a whole gang of potential, and the first manager/agent/record company to realise it will have got themselves something really worthwhile.'[21]

'We had a page devoted to absolutely new people,' he recalled. 'Nobody had done that before. You could cover bands before they were part of the process. Nowadays they've already sorted out their market at that stage. And one could possibly blame Bryan Ferry for that.' Williams continued to champion Roxy, even attending auditions they held for management: 'The Famous Manager said he'd call them. He'd be crazy not to. PS: He did. Last Friday, David Enthoven of ELP and King Crimson fame signed them for management. Now you can't avoid them. Great.'[22]

Signed by Island, Roxy issued their ground-breaking debut in 1972, confirming *Melody Maker*'s prescience and pre-eminence. Editor Ray Coleman was key: 'Sometimes we used to laugh behind his back, because he seemed rather strict,' admits Williams. 'But he knew the value of a good story and wanted to broaden things out. He didn't want Pete Townshend talking about chord changes; he wanted him talking about Vietnam. At the time we were a little sceptical but, to give him credit, Ray saw what *Rolling Stone* was doing. While we read its record review pages, Ray read *Rolling Stone*'s political stuff.'

Meanwhile *Melody Maker*'s musicians' ads – the basis of its income for forty-odd years –were pounced upon by amateur and professional players every week. Closing in on its golden jubilee, *Melody Maker* looked unassailable.

* * *

Melody Maker drew on Black American music of its past – jazz, blues, folk – while reporting from the frontline of White progressive rock: a balancing act enabled by having Max Jones and Chris Hayes alongside their younger counterparts. However, neither camp was well disposed to soul, funk, reggae or out-and-out pop, and an air of stodginess was evinced by a dismissive attitude towards singles. Reviews of these were, at best, patronizing; as if albums – particularly those by White male rock acts who emphasised virtuosity over grit – were the only format worthy of serious consideration. This created a vacuum into which new magazines trickled, but one renegade was already well established: *Blues & Soul* (pl. 4).

Founded as *Home of the Blues* in 1966 by travel agent and Black music fan John Abbey, its name change the following year reflected the prominence of the genre that was to dominate in forms such as funk and disco. Abbey went on to open the Contempo mail order and import record shop in London and launch a companion label that licensed hits like Tami Lynn's 'I'm Gonna Run Away from You'.

Abbey's most forward-thinking contributor was fellow soul proselytizer Dave Godin. He attended the same school as Mick Jagger and is credited with turning the singer on to Black American music. Godin's interest, nurtured by *Record Mirror*'s Norman Jopling, spurred him to spend two years in America collecting records and connecting with labels such as Tamla Motown, for whom he ran a British appreciation society. Back in Britain, Godin worked as a consultant for Tamla for five years, securing slots for Marvin Gaye and Stevie Wonder on the influential TV show *Ready Steady Go!* (though a Motown package tour of the UK that he organized was sparsely attended). And in 1967 he founded the London record shop Soul City.

Godin's *Blues & Soul* column in 1970 was the first to feature the term 'Northern Soul', describing often obscure 1960s tracks popular in Britain's provincial clubs. 'Northern football fans who were in London to follow their team were coming into the store to buy records but weren't interested in the latest developments in the Black American chart,' he recalled. 'I devised the name as a shorthand sales term: "If you've got customers from the north, don't waste time playing them records currently in the US Black chart: just play them what they like – Northern Soul.'[23] Godin also conjured the term 'deep soul' for a groove-driven strand that he defined as 'very stylised and mannered, very gospel-rooted but totally secular. Very "mind music" – the words are very important'.[24]

Godin's influence was, as Richard Williams noted, 'out of all proportion both to the limited fame and the rewards he received as a journalist, record company adviser, record shop owner and, even, briefly owner of his own labels devoted to the African American music he considered the pinnacle of twentieth century culture'. His *Blues & Soul* column was imbued, Williams said, 'with the flavour of true obsession, whether unearthing obscure waxings, exposing frauds or simply namechecking ordinary fans'.[25]

Other magazines contributed to an appreciation of Black artists in the UK. *Soul Beat* was founded by schoolboy Pete Wingfield, later to produce and play with a bewildering range of acts, from Paul McCartney and the Everly Brothers to Van Morrison and Dexys Midnight Runners. When he departed for university, Wingfield handed the reins to a friend, Mick Brown. 'I was monomaniacal about R&B,' said the latter. 'I sat in my bedroom hacking away at an old typewriter and using my mother's Roneo machine to print this thing.' Brown sold *Soul Beat* via his Saturday job at a London record shop, and by mail order.

'It was a wonderful education,' he reminisced, 'because I'd write to American R&B labels – Duke, Stax, Atlantic – and every now and again a care package would arrive, with priceless 45s and beautiful 8x10 inch photos. People in Britain at that time were largely unaware of this music, which has come to be regarded as legendary.

'There was a place in south London, the Orchid Ballroom in Purley, where I saw Stevie Wonder, Ike and Tina Turner, Clarence "Frogman" Henry, the Orlons, Garnett Mimms ... For a generation of white kids, this was a consciousness-raising exercise. When I read that people who were my heroes – Smokey Robinson and the Miracles, say – couldn't eat in the same restaurants or stay in the same hotels as white people when they toured in the South, that was my first exposure to the iniquities of segregation.'[26]

Blues & Soul thrived into the digital age like few other music magazines of the 1960s, largely due to its acceptance of newer forms such as hip-hop. But it was a long time before Black writers, let alone women, were allowed access to publishing their views on soul and its relatives.

The offbeat furrow ploughed by another independent British magazine was indicated by its title: *ZigZag*. Debuting in the spring of 1969, the sporadic publication took its name from Captain Beefheart's 'Zig Zag Wanderer' and from a brand of rolling papers, reflecting the interests of Pete Frame, a music-mad insurance surveyor who launched what was essentially a fanzine from his cottage in Buckinghamshire. 'My interest in rock music was overwhelming,' he noted. 'I went to as many gigs as I could. All around me, the sixties were reaching a crescendo and I knew I had to "drop out and do my own thing, *man*". There were no publications dealing with the music I loved, so I decided to start one. I had no training as a journalist and just relied on enthusiasm to carry me through.'[27]

Frame and his colleague John Tobler tracked down underground artists whose work they felt was undervalued by the weekly inkies – among them Beefheart, Frank Zappa and King Crimson's Robert Fripp. *ZigZag*, said Frame, 'was the first "serious" independent UK music magazine: the template for *Mojo*, etc.'[28] The timing played in Frame's favour: 'When I started *ZigZag*, even the biggest bands travelled in vans and played smallish venues. But as the audience grew, so did the scale of the rock business: private planes, massive venues, chains of record shops, big business. Records used to come out, then get deleted; they were rare and precious, and not many people knew about them. Now a huge slice of the market is based on back catalogue. I always knew that rock music was an important part of popular culture, and so it has proved.' The 1999 death of the troubled Moby Grape founder Skip Spence, he noted, 'was covered by every quality newspaper in Britain, but none of them ever wrote about him when he was alive. But *ZigZag* did.'[29]

Spence was one of a wave of new American groups and singer-songwriters emanating from the West Coast in the late 1960s and early '70s who were of interest. '*ZigZag* was much more purist than the other magazines about the music it covered – "Laurel Canyon dogshit," as Lenny Bruce put it,' said writer and rocksbackpages.com mainman Barney Hoskyns. 'I had a foot in that camp because I had a big West Coast phase, so I bought *ZigZag*.'[30]

Charlie Gillett hailed *ZigZag* as 'a rare combination of very subjective responses to music and related events [and] interviews with musicians not widely covered in the weekly papers'.[31] A third element became Frame's hallmark: the 'rock family trees' introduced in the magazine's third year. 'When I interviewed musicians,' he said, 'they were always amazed that I knew so much – that I wanted to find out so many details. And they tended to open up because I was so enthusiastic.' Frame initiated the spidery maps after interviewing Al Kooper, who founded Blood, Sweat & Tears and worked with Bob Dylan and the Rolling Stones: 'I was finding it difficult to write about all the personnel changes and connections between other groups. I just thought it would be easier if I drew out his musical history in a family tree design. It was very primitive but I started doing more and more family trees – Jack Bruce, [California blues rockers] Stoneground, Fairport Convention – and made them more and more detailed.'[32] These sustained *ZigZag*, though its lack of formal distribution meant it never threatened the mainstream music press.

More formal was *Cream*, launched by *Melody Maker*'s production editor Bob Houston and targeting a maturing demographic that no longer wished to wade through the weeklies but wanted coverage of its favourite music. Having worked on newspapers such as *The Observer*, Houston appropriated the tropes of their Sunday supplements: concise layouts, use of colour and quality paper stock. At *Melody Maker*, he had edited the companion monthly *Music Maker*, featuring illustrations by artist and satirist Barry Fantoni. This too provided a template of sorts for the monthly *Cream*, which launched in May 1971 with a cover story questioning Mick Jagger's relevance. The end of 1960s optimism was made plain in an early cover line: 'Lennon: the acid dream is over.' Instead, *Cream* championed artists who characterized the early 1970s, including Alice Cooper (cover star of three of its twenty-seven issues), David Bowie, Led Zeppelin and Slade, as well as leftfield artists such as saxophonist Lol Coxhill.

Cream also keyed into the growing assessment of those who had ascended over the previous decade, such as the Beatles and the Who. In this way it prefigured later legacy titles *Q* and *Mojo*. There was also an interest in wider popular culture – another staple of 1980s lifestyle magazines. One *Cream* cover story cast a critical eye at Tony Blackburn, then Britain's most popular DJ, while novelist Harold Robbins was considered alongside pieces on Rastafarianism, heroin and soccer.

'I knew there was a market for *Cream* but I wasn't sure that there were enough writers to provide copy that was up to scratch,' Houston admitted. 'I shouldn't have worried.'[33] Among those to whom he provided breaks was roots music fan Tony Russell, who said *Cream* 'had been inspired by university cultural studies courses and American magazines such as *Rolling Stone* to think and write about popular music as if it had things to say worth hearing, possessed cultural weight, *mattered*'.[34]

Australian cultural critic Clive James filed several stories for *Cream*, including an examination of rock lyrics from a poet's perspective. Charlie Gillett joined as reviews editor and fielded a request from his counterpart Lester Bangs: 'How about trading subscriptions, *Creem* for *Cream*? And did the guys that put that mag together have heard (uh, duhh, grammuh ...) of *Creem* when they named it?'

'*Melody Maker*, *NME* and the rest were overground and *Oz* and *IT* were underground,' observed Charles Shaar Murray. '*Cream* was ground-level, and it drew on writers from both factions.' Murray wrote for the magazine after being one of the youthful editorial team for *Oz*'s notorious 1970 'school kids' issue. The use of students alongside the magazine's near-the-knuckle imagery – not least one of the schoolgirls being labelled 'Jailbait of the month' – led to obscenity charges being levelled against *Oz*'s editors.

Murray described Bob Houston – 'a big Scottish guy who looked like an unmade bed' – as a sympathetic editor: 'He commissioned long pieces from me, 5,000-worders, and sent me out to do things I would never have dreamed of, like interviewing Tony Blackburn. He was the first really rigorous editor I'd ever had.'

Cream writers split into two ranks, said Gillett: 'One willing to consume and report on the music industry's product; the other more interested in covering music that was not necessarily being pushed by the publicists. *Cream* veered towards the first school, although its regular coverage of jazz reflected the editor's personal musical preference ... As a platform and launching pad for writers with little or no previous exposure, *Cream* was a gift from the gods.' However, Gillett lasted just six months as reviews editor: 'I never really came to grips with the paradoxical problem that a useful review needed to be several hundred words long, yet there were far too many records to cover at such length, and how did I decide which records needn't be reviewed?'[35]

Another issue was the magazine's position in the marketplace. '*Cream*'s biggest problem was that it couldn't get advertising outside of the music industry,' notes Gillett. 'The labels wanted to advertise Genesis or Yes or whatever were their big-selling records, but there wasn't anybody on the staff that genuinely liked that stuff. They liked the Byrds or Gram Parsons, which is now perceived as an important strand of music, and was already covered in *ZigZag*, but in an absolutely intense, fanzine kind of way.'

Houston's erratic leadership didn't help. 'Some of Bob's contributors had mixed feelings about his editing style,' recalled writer Dave Laing. 'He had a habit of mislaying copy, sometimes claiming that it had been blown out of the window of a taxi.'[36]

An occasional contributor was Cambridge graduate Ian MacDonald, who defined the early 1970s as 'the first era of post-modernism in pop. Music started to be conscious of itself and look back and begin to make syntheses and style references and be ironic.' That could be readily identified in the likes of Roxy Music and David Bowie, and in fashion, notably Malcolm McLaren's London boutique Let It Rock, which opened at the beginning of 1972 as a Teddy Boy emporium-cum-environmental installation.

Cream's death knell was sounded by a new magazine, coincidentally also called *Let It Rock* (pl. 6). Launched by *Cream* writers led by Dave Laing, and including Simon Frith and Charlie Gillett, its thoughtful approach to pop was executed with more discipline. Within a year, Houston was forced to close his title.

Based in the offices of Hanover Books (also responsible for *Jazz & Blues*, *Country* and *Folk Review*), *Let It Rock* dubbed itself

'The world's best rock read', signalling an intention to rival its American inspirations *Crawdaddy*, *Fusion* and *Rolling Stone*. Laing promised *Let It Rock* would 'seriously review the idea of a rock tradition, stretching from the earliest days of rock 'n' roll to now. This means regarding the music of the fifties and sixties not just as material for nostalgia, but realising the sources of today's rock lies there.'[37] The debut issue hammered the point with a glossy cover that combined a portrait of 1972's most exciting British star, David Bowie, with a Warhol-style repeat image of Elvis Presley. An accompanying feature traced the King's career through interviews with his session musicians, the Memphis Mafia.

Like Gillett, Laing had written a treatise on popular music. *The Sound of Our Time*, published when he was a student, was informed by the theories of philosophers Herbert Marcuse and Theodor Adorno. *Let It Rock* writer Michael Gray rated Laing 'a terrific editor ... very agreeable, easygoing and civilised towards contributors, with an engaging, quiet wit'.[38] Others were ambivalent towards a magazine that tended towards the eggheaded. 'I liked the people but *Let It Rock* was a bit rigorous in its manifesto,' says contributor Chris Salewicz. 'It was a lot of people from Sussex University, International Socialist members, that lot. Then there was Charlie Gillett, who at the time was known as the man who'd walked out of a Velvet Underground gig.'

The Velvets legend was disputed by Gillett. Studying in New York in the mid-1960s, he chanced upon a gig by the group: 'It was one of their first ever, at The Dom [on St Mark's Place]. I didn't walk out. I was hypnotised and fascinated but sort of appalled. But I remember I definitely stayed until the end.' Nonetheless, this type of story compounded the magazine's po-faced reputation. 'I read *Let It Rock* but everyone talks about this period like it was the golden age of music journalism,' said DJ John Peel. 'Ultimately what the reviewers were doing was reviewing themselves. Although it may have been terrifically interesting from a sociological point of view, if you wanted to know what records were actually like, you had to go somewhere else.'[39]

Still, a loyal audience sustained *Let It Rock*'s three-year run. 'It was the first time I came across intelligent discussion of pop, rock and other genres,' says Barney Hoskyns. 'It also featured American writers like Lester Bangs, and I liked the Top Ten lists submitted by readers. There was such eclecticism – Todd Rundgren and Curtis Mayfield – it broadened my horizons in a big way.' David Hepworth, the writer and editor who launched titles in the 1980s and '90s, described *Let It Rock* as 'probably the greatest influence on *Q* and *Mojo*. Interestingly, *Mojo* covers a lot of the music *Let It Rock* championed in the early seventies: obscure American funk and old country records that have never gone away, the likes of Bobby Charles. You think to yourself, "These records can't have sold more than fifty copies ever," and, "How come I know all fifty people that bought them?!"'

Even as independent voices such as *Let It Rock* shook up music publishing, Britain slid into the economic doldrums. *Melody Maker* remained top dog, bolstered by record label and musician advertising, but other titles were hit hard – none more so than *NME*. Under missing-in-action editor Andy Gray, standards had slipped and it was haemorrhaging readers. 'The hands of the *NME* clock were at five to midnight,' said news editor Alan Smith. 'Unless something was done within months to arrest the decline in sales, the magazine would be shut down.'[40]

8
'We're happy to stick pretension where it belongs'

NME Makes a Deathbed Recovery

'We used to laugh at *NME*,' confessed *Melody Maker*'s Chris Welch. 'They had these terrible front page headlines like, "Controversy! Beach Boys never to tour England again!" – really weak stories – whereas we had powerful stuff: interviews with John Lennon and Led Zeppelin. *MM*'s circulation was racing up to 200,000 a week and we'd look at *NME* in disbelief. One week we cut out an entire issue and stuck the pages on the wall, as examples of poor layout and terrible coverage.'

'We knew what was wrong,' said Nick Logan, who had been offered a job at *Sounds* but decided to stay and try to turn the ship around. 'It was not a good-looking magazine, not well written, not pertinent and completely outclassed by rivals.'

With an editorial style rooted in early 1960s showbiz-style reporting – evinced by Maurice Kinn's hoary yet ongoing 'Alley Cat' column – and an AWOL editor in the perma-golfing Andy Gray, *NME* had failed to keep step with the pop scene. Weekly sales fell below 60,000 – a quarter of the market leader's.

News editor Alan Smith came up with a management-backed action plan: a total makeover, with improved design, better photography and a cull of the editor and writers whose style dated back to the beat boom: 'I assembled a team of subversives such as Nick and Roy [Carr], who jumped to supply me with contraband material: the real stuff they wanted to write in the main paper but weren't allowed to. I was more at ease with the three-minute thrill of a good single and wanted to bring in passion, irreverence and jokes.'[1] His own lack of reverence was well established: he'd reviewed the Beatles' 'Revolution 9' as 'a pretentious piece of old codswallop' and written of a Plastic Ono Band show, 'It gave me the biggest headache since I-don't-know-when.' And he would later become the nemesis of Cockney Rebel's Steve Harley, after a vicious review of their album *The Human Menagerie* that concluded, 'By the way, Steve – when you're finished with it, David Bowie would like his voice back, and Bryan Ferry his vibrato. You can keep the clothes.'

Alan Smith road-tested the new-look *NME* in a January 1972 edition published only in London and the UK's south-east. The front page featured readers' poll winners who reflected the tastes and style of the old regime: Cilla Black, Elvis Presley and Cliff Richard, with a token nod to the new age in the form of T. Rex. But the inside back page featured an in-house ad that came to be known as 'the new week box'. This heralded more meaty fare under the heading, 'We're freaking out at *New Musical Express*,' and included Marc Bolan swearing, 'I don't give a fuck as long as I can boogie.'

Nick Logan became assistant editor and produced concert listings in the style of *Time Out*, Tony Elliott's weekly that had sprung from the counterculture. These attracted new readers and revenue-providing concert promoters, and Alan Smith was given the go-ahead to helm the national edition. Andy Gray was kicked upstairs and out of sight as managing editor and his deputy John Wells was appointed editor of *Rave*. Maurice Kinn was granted a reprieve, although Alley Cat was retired.

The 5 February 1972 issue introduced nationwide readers to the new *NME*, complete with the Marc Bolan interview and its expletive-laden headline (albeit in expurgated form). Smith reassurred readers, 'We're happy to stick pretension where it belongs,' and declared the 'intelligent' paper would cater to those with catholic tastes from 'rock 'n' roll in the charts' to [folk-rockers] Steeleye Span, Jethro Tull, Captain Beefheart, Cat Stevens 'and much, much more'.

Smith underlined the new team's credentials, pointing out that Roy Carr – a *Jazz News* veteran, but a playful character with deep musical knowledge – had performed with Jethro Tull bassist Glenn Cornick and that former *Sounds* contributor Danny Holloway had, as a ponytailed Californian, 'rock 'n' rolled in the States'. Reporter Tony Tyler – previously a publicist for prog-rock trio Emerson, Lake & Palmer – had 'played in Hamburg and sold pianos in Miami'. Smith, said Tyler, 'was in hiring mode and, as I was the first semiliterate hack to come his way, he hired me.' And staffer James Johnson, who had started at *NME* a couple of years previously but survived the cull, had racked up musical experience 'busking on the streets of Paris'.[2]

Fred Dellar was among the freelancers, having attracted Smith's attention by telling him *NME* needed a column dedicated to import LPs. He was also the in-house specialist on the growing market for cassettes, and interviewed staff and and musicians working in recording studios. These meat-and-potatoes sections proved appealing to readers and advertisers alike. 'They started doing strong lead stories and overnight it was transformed,' said *Melody Maker*'s Chris Welch. 'Within a few weeks, they were a threat to us.'

Fiona Foulgar was the sole female presence. Despite her talent, she was relegated to duties such as compiling the weekly charts and would have to wait a couple of years before being joined on the writing team by Julie Webb. An old-school remainer was Derek Johnson, who had joined *NME* in the 1950s and maintained an iron grip on the news pages until the mid-1980s. 'Derek was the best news editor anyone ever worked with,' enthused Fred Dellar. 'He always got the stories no one else had.'

Reporters who flourished under the new regime included Tony Stewart, who had freelanced for *Sounds*. 'When I got my job on *NME*, it was very much a mishmash of showbiz,' he remembered. 'I just thought, "This ain't very rock 'n' roll."'[3] But now Alan Smith actively sought that status, working with Roy Carr on promotions to attract new readers. These included flexidiscs trailing tracks from the Rolling Stones' *Exile on Main Street*, Alice Cooper's *Billion Dollar Babies* and ELP's *Brain Salad Surgery*.

A second wave of recruits included Charles Shaar Murray. 'I was a bit underground about it at first,' he recalls. '"Oh no, man, selling out!" But I'd had a pair of trousers at the dry-cleaner's for six weeks and a pair of boots at the mender's for five because I couldn't afford to pay for them, so I signed on ... I brought along [photographer] Joe Stevens, who was an American lefty I'd met via the underground connection – we'd done an MC5 piece for *Cream* together – and my buddy Nick Kent, who brought in Pennie Smith.' The latter's crisp, reportage-style photography was a cool counterpoint to the sometimes over-amped copy. 'Pennie was as important to *NME* as Nick and Charlie,' said Richard Williams. 'The strength of the pictures and what they said about the world meant so much.'

These new recruits had little time for the editorial silos of the old guard. After writing about Scottish rockers Stone The Crows, Murray crossed swords with James Johnson: 'James ambled up and said, "Awfully sorry old man, but Stone The Crows are one of my bands." I was like, "What? Are you fucking joking?" The

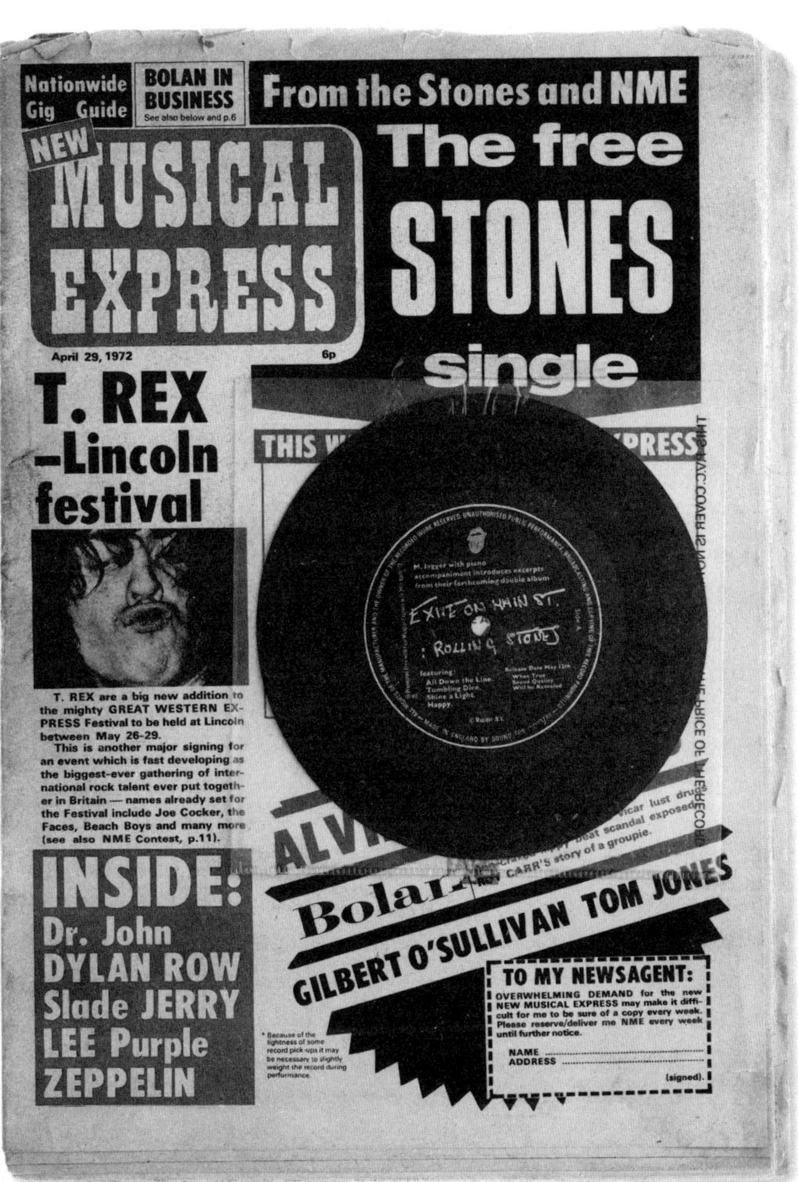

Nationwide Gig Guide

BOLAN IN BUSINESS
See also below and p.6

From the Stones and NME

NEW MUSICAL EXPRESS

April 29, 1972 6p

The free STONES single

T. REX –Lincoln festival

T. REX are a big new addition to the mighty GREAT WESTERN EXPRESS Festival to be held at Lincoln between May 26-29.

This is another major signing for an event which is fast developing as the biggest-ever gathering of international rock talent ever put together in Britain — names already set for the Festival include Joe Cocker, the Faces, Beach Boys and many more (see also NME Contest, p.11).

INSIDE:
Dr. John
DYLAN ROW
Slade JERRY
LEE Purple
ZEPPELIN

M. Jagger with piano accompaniment introduces excerpts from their forthcoming double album

EXILE ON MAIN ST.
: ROLLING STONES

featuring:
All Down the Line.
Tumbling Dice.
Shine a Light.
Happy.

MADE IN ENGLAND BY SOUND

vicar lust drug
beat scandal exposed
CARR'S story of a groupie.

Bolan

GILBERT O'SULLIVAN TOM JONES

* Because of the lightness of some record pick-ups it may be necessary to slightly weight the record during performance.

TO MY NEWSAGENT:
OVERWHELMING DEMAND for the new NEW MUSICAL EXPRESS may make it difficult for me to be sure of a copy every week. Please reserve/deliver me NME every week until further notice.

NAME ....
ADDRESS ....
(signed).

119

New Musical Express, 29 April 1972

old system was like that, where one writer staked out special turf and monopolised coverage of specific acts. Well, we broke *that* shit down.'

The rapidly strengthening team also included Ian MacDonald and Chris Salewicz, who had both contributed to *Cream*. MacDonald's zany sense of humour led to punning headlines and captions, and Monty Python-style worldplay. 'My first tries at layout were a bit stumbling but then I got the hang of it and started to introduce elements of things that made me laugh,' he recalled. 'I was a fan of *Mad* magazine, so I stole a lot of that style and speed. We gradually loosened the paper up, introducing new ideas and formats, playing with headlines and captions and speech bubbles. I wanted *NME* to reflect the life of the staff, which was funny and energetic.'

Salewicz's first commission was 'a baptism of fire': reviewing a performance by the bloodless proggers Camel at Wandsworth Prison. 'The route into the music press was live gigs no one else wanted to go to, then it was features nobody wanted to do,' he says. '[Tony] Tyler was quickly on the phone asking if I wanted to interview Uriah Heep. Actually, that sort of thing was quite good fun, because there was plenty of opportunity for jokes.' An interview with the band's organist Ken Hensley was headlined, 'So tell me, Ken, why is it Uriah Heep drive rock critics to suicide?' and cited a *Rolling Stone* writer who had threatened to kill herself if the band were successful. 'We're still waiting for her to do it,' Hensley observed.

Editor Alan Smith 'was a merciless critic', said Tony Tyler, who remembered run-throughs of the latest issue every Wednesday as 'often rather cruel affairs for the week's offenders'. Fred Dellar was on the receiving end of one tirade: 'A Dory Previn album was rather bizarre and nightmarish, so I reviewed it in pretty much the same style and Alan caught me out. He said, "We don't do those sorts of reviews here." I felt quite proud, being called outlandish compared to some of the other writers.'

'The first important piece I wrote was a review of T. Rex at Wembley ... Alan praised the piece to the skies, rewrote it and plastered it all over the front cover,' said Tyler. 'With the advent of Charles, Ian and Nick Kent, I rather fell into the second rank of featured writers and concentrated more on production, which I liked since you didn't have to meet rock stars.' This wasn't without its pitfalls: Tyler allowed into print a reference to music writer Ray Connolly as a 'hack' – a term deemed libellous at the time – in a book review by Murray. 'Not knowing any better, I also used the same word in the headline and Connolly collected £900,' he recalled. 'Not my finest hour.'

Notwithstanding such glitches, the new editorial mix reinvigorated the title. As cultural commentator Peter York observed, '*NME*'s class of '72 introduced the rock-writer superstar. [They were] personalities, musicians who wrote, and obviously part of the culture.' Keith Altham – already supplementing his *NME* income by freelancing for BBC radio – realized his time was up: 'Alan was a contemporary of mine, a Liverpudlian: tough, shrewd and easy to underestimate. With his right-hand man Nick Logan, they took on a whole bunch of people who were much more serious than us: writing about a culture, not just bands. I wasn't into that because a) I was older and b) I never did – and don't to this day – think that pop music is that important.' Altham shifted into PR and became one of Britain's most powerful publicists, representing the Who and the Rolling Stones.

NME's post-glam insouciance was embodied by Nick Kent, an epicene figure favouring leather trousers, mascara, stack-heeled boots, women's blouses and narcotics. Influenced by Tom Wolfe, Truman Capote and James Joyce (which explains his copy's tendency to meander), Kent had established his taste for the hard rock of Alice Cooper, the MC5 and Iggy and the Stooges at *Frendz* (pl. 5). 'He was late hippie *fleurs du mal* to the power of *n* and he looked like he'd crawled out of a Lou Reed song,' noted Peter York. 'Talk about decadent. Charles Shaar Murray was complementary to Kent, being altogether less of an aesthete. A stocky, Jewish guy from Reading with a *Time Out* afro, he'd come out of the underground press with a lot of ideas; this very vigorous, logic-chopping style and this new vocabulary, which was at a premium on *NME*. Between them, *NME* was quite unbeatable.'[4]

This played well with artists of the era. In 1973, *Melody Maker*'s Chris Welch suggested reporters be sent to Paris to greet David

Bowie off the Trans-Siberian Express. 'When we arrived,' said Welch, 'Charles Shaar Murray was already there.'

That individuals such as Murray were given free rein is testament to Alan Smith's leadership of *NME*. From the wreck of an old-fashioned publication, he created a hybrid that combined *Creem*'s sass, *Rolling Stone*'s individualism and a distinctly British satirical edge. Meanwhile, the sidelined Maurice Kinn departed the publication he had saved two decades previously to run a flower shop in Mayfair. Attendees at his spring 1973 leaving party illustrated the schism that had occurred: Slade's Noddy Holder and the Who's John Entwistle raised their glasses alongside Vera Lynn and Max Bygraves. 'My old friend Tony Bennett was in the country at the time,' recalled Kinn, 'so even he came along.'

Kinn's departure marked a decisive break with the past. By the summer of 1973, the elements of *NME*'s golden phase were in place: mocking headlines ('What's this? Michael Philip feeling the pinch?' above Mick Jagger celebrating his thirtieth birthday), one-liners in the Thrills and Teasers sections, oddball cartoons of music biz types by Tony Benyon (creator of the cynical Th' Lone Groover), witty responses to readers on the Gasbag page and regular photo bylines for Charles Shaar Murray, Nick Kent, Andrew Tyler (a recruit from *Disc & Music Echo* and no relation to Tony), Ian MacDonald and Charlie Gillett.

The latter – now dividing his time between *Let it Rock*, *NME* and a burgeoning broadcasting career – was keen to champion the vibrant soul scene, then being boosted by the maturing of 1960s stars Curtis Mayfield, Stevie Wonder and Marvin Gaye. Black music now inhabited space previously dominated by White rock, and was documented by Roger St Pierre – who had worked at *Blues & Soul* and contributed to *Record Mirror* and *Sounds* as 'Peter Kent' – and Henderson Dalrymple. The latter, of Afro-Carribean descent, covered the emergence of dub in Jamaica and Afrobeat in Nigeria.

Still, bum notes were struck. An interview with Bob Ezrin by Nick Kent contrasted the producer's schoolmasterly nature with that of his outré clients Alice Cooper and Lou Reed under the headline, 'The square and the faggots'. But such provocations didn't deter the mainly adolescent male readership. As newsstand purchases

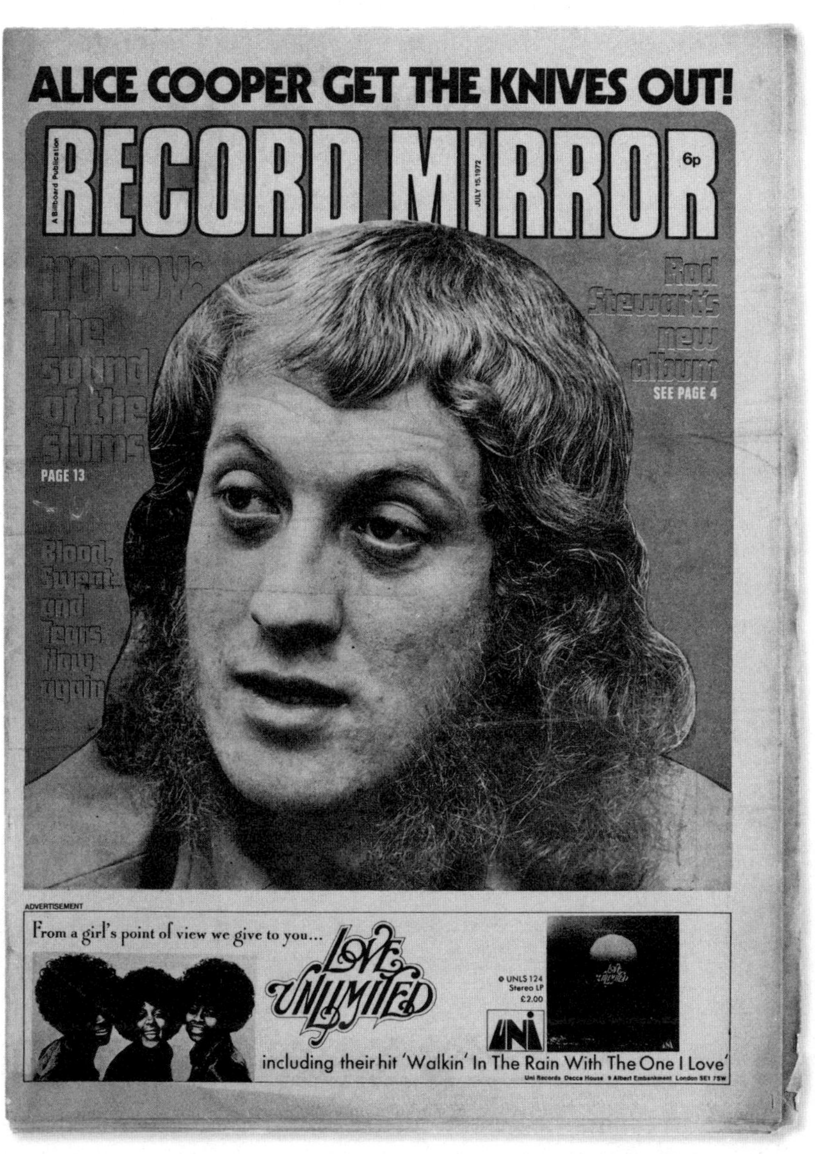

Record Mirror, 15 July 1972

surpassed *Melody Maker*, Smith inserted a new subtitle beneath the masthead: 'World's largest selling weekly music paper'. '*MM* was losing its edge,' said writer Richard Williams, who flew the coop in 1973 to become head of A&R at Island Records. 'We had too much faith in the traditional journalistic approach, whereas *NME* was obviously picking up the pace.'

Nonetheless, publishers IPC grumbled at its rock 'n' roll charges, particularly over their use of profanity without the asterisks of the past. 'The word "cunt" had lately cropped up in one feature and the higher-ups were mortified, threatening to shut the paper down if further obscenities were committed to print,' recalled Nick Kent. 'A compromise was duly arrived at. We could use "fuck" in moderation, as well as "asshole" and "bugger". But any slang word for genitalia – male or female – was strictly out of bounds.'[5] Editor Alan Smith, said Nick Logan, 'took on a lot of conservative forces [and] overcame them. He cleared a lot of deadwood for me to take over.'

This had been the plan ever since Smith began steering the ship; by the autumn of 1973, he had laboured at the paper for a decade and was increasingly focused on his property development business. 'Alan told me he only wanted to do it for eighteen months and then he would pass it on to me,' said Logan. In his memoir *Apathy for the Devil*, Nick Kent (who repeatedly refers to Smith as Alan Lewis, another journalist who rose through the ranks at IPC) described the editorial handover: '[Smith] had been a canny opportunist but Nick had the ideal mixture of sensibility and creative instinct to take us to the next level ... His first act as the journal's captain was most inspired; he persuaded Ian MacDonald to take over as assistant editor. Ian wasted no time in bringing all his daunting intellect, boundless intensity and unshakeable thirst for excellence to the role.'[6]

Logan had long believed that music alone was not enough: that the context, especially the visual culture, from which it sprang was important. An interview with Rod Stewart in 1971 was conducted as the fastidious front man tried on shoes in fashionable West End footwear outlet Anello & Davide, while writers posed in Teddy Boy gear outside Malcolm McLaren's boutique Let It Rock for the review of a rock 'n' roll revival show in 1972. 'Any kind of writing was a chore for me,' Logan admitted. 'I was that kind of writer who'd spend hours on the opening paragraphs, then have to rush the rest to meet a deadline, so I was happy to gravitate towards editing. I loved working with good writers, much better writers than me, doing layouts and working with photographers, fine-tuning the flat-plan: all the unseen stuff that goes into creating the look and feel of a publication.'[7]

* * *

NME still had a way to go to rival the evolution of the music press's biggest name. 'As *Rolling Stone* became more successful, and also as we moved out of the utopian and naive sixties, cynicism reigned, radicalism was mocked, the more extreme projects of social change became clearly unattainable,' said sometime editor David Dalton. 'We grew older, got married and went into rehab, and rock became part of the entertainment industry again. Of course, it always had been, but the illusion that it functioned as an independent engine of change was a powerful motivator. The Radical Jann [Wenner] was unceremoniously dumped over the side of the ship one night by the now hugely successful captain of industry Citizen Jann.'[8]

Nonetheless, Wenner's magazine took readers outside their comfort zones. In 1973, cover stories ranged from an interview with waspish writer Truman Capote (pl. 8) to Tom Wolfe's first drafts for his book about the space race, *The Right Stuff*. There were the usual suspects – Paul and Linda, James and Carly, Elton, Rod, Mick and Keith – but the magazine also determinedly followed the Watergate scandal, investigated the evangelical Jesus Army, interviewed Daniel Ellsberg, who leaked papers from the Pentagon about the Vietnam war, and gave space to Hunter S. Thompson's honing of his so-called gonzo style.

Jon Landau – later the man who championed, then managed, Bruce Springsteen – had written for Wenner since the first issue. 'Landau was the preeminent rock critic of the time, the word of God,' said Danny Fields, who signed the MC5 to Elektra and arranged for Landau to provide his thoughts on the group after witnessing a show in Detroit. 'One way of co-opting the press was getting Jon Landau to write an analysis of this band. When the rest of them saw that was happening, their ears pricked up. He wrote a twenty-page report for [Elektra boss] Jac Holzman about how the band should be recorded and which songs they should have on the album. It was incredible.'

On the jailing of the MC5's manager John Sinclair, Landau agreed to co-manage the group with Fields and produce their second album, all while continuing to operate as a journalist. 'Everyone was all over the place then,' explained Fields. 'It was much more fluid.'

Few *Rolling Stone* contributors epitomized Californian rock as quintessentially as Cameron Crowe. At just fifteen, his first interview – with the Eagles – had appeared in underground paper *The San Diego Door*. 'I went into the *RS* offices in San Francisco for the first time in 1973,' he noted. 'Before this I'd been a freelance journalist working on the end of the phone to music editor Ben Fong-Torres. I'd done my first piece for them in January that year: an interview with Poco. They paid me $350 for it. A few months later Jann Wenner wrote me, saying, "You may turn out to be the youngest *Rolling Stone* man ever."' Crowe chronicled this era of his life in his 2000 movie *Almost Famous*. 'I felt like I had a place in the world,' he said. 'I could write about this thing I loved so much.'

Crowe related a 1990s encounter with singer-songwriter Stephen Stills: 'He introduced me to his wife: "This is Cameron. He was a fan who always got caught in the middle between wanting to be friends with us and wanting to please *Rolling Stone*, who didn't like us as much as he did." I thought, "Wow. What happened to the power and mystery of journalism and writing?" That was the role I played: the fan who had several masters to serve, one of which was me.'[9]

Charles Shaar Murray remembered the teenage Crowe as 'the very soul of amiability, relaxed and confident beyond his years; as well he might have been, given that he was a top writer for a major publication and made considerably more money than the rest of us. Despite his considerable talents he was essentially a fan-boy who rarely upset the apple cart by expressing a controversial opinion. He had the kind of presence which relaxed his subjects, made them feel protective towards him, encouraged them to open up ... and it paid off big-time'.

Crowe's contributions to *Rolling Stone*, *Creem* and *Circus* earned him entry to an event that symbolized the excess and rampant self-regard of the era's critics: the First Annual National Association of Rock Writers Convention, held in Memphis over the Memorial Day weekend in May 1973. It was organized by eighteen-year-old journalist Jon Tiven and John King, a publicist for the city's record label Ardent, which was distributed by Stax. Tiven had given a rave review to an Ardent release – Big Star's *#1 Record* – and he and King drew on Stax funds to stage this 'wonderful opportunity' to promote the label's artists to the press.

British group Skin Alley, a new Stax signing, were flown out (along with a troupe of UK writers) to perform alongside Big Star between the receptions and loosely organized panels.

Lester Bangs and Richard Meltzer attended, as did Simon Frith of *Let It Rock* and Pete Frame of *ZigZag*. But with the exception of *Creem*'s Jaan Uhelski and Warhol protégée and publicist Susan Blond, the conventioneers were male, hence drunken boorishness on visits to a local brewery and Elvis Presley's home Graceland. Meltzer introduced Big Star with, 'Well, puke on your momma's pussy ...' and he and Bangs urinated through Graceland's gates when their party was barred from entry.

However, Crowe – described by Meltzer as 'a goony-goofy gosh-oh-gee kid, blowing on a goddam kazoo. Or maybe an ocarina' – recalled the occasion warmly: 'The mood was fun, with rock writers allowed to act like rock stars in an all-expenses-paid sanctuary. It was an opportunity for many of them to live out their own version of the stories we'd been writing – out-of-control rock stars on the road. It was a noble effort, revelatory in the level of camaraderie that developed between people who'd only been bylines to each other.'[10]

So convivial was Crowe's reputation that Jimmy Page requested he write *Rolling Stone*'s sole cover story on Led Zeppelin during the group's existence. In 1973, as press agent Danny Goldberg told Zep biographer Jon Bream, 'They had already given *Houses of the Holy* another horrible review, calling the album a "limp blimp". But now, as they hear all the publicity about how big the band is, *Rolling Stone* wants to do a cover story. So I talk to the band about it and they say, "No fucking way. Fuck them. They hate us." I said, "Alright, cool. We'll tell everyone you turned down *Rolling Stone* for the cover. That's a PR angle: you're so big, you don't need *Rolling Stone*."' Approached again two years later, the band agreed, provided Crowe write the story. The resulting interview with Page and Robert Plant, said Goldberg, 'was the turning point in getting respect from the critics'.

Crowe's wide-eyed enthusiasm meshed with hard-hitting – and, in Hunter S. Thompson's case, earth-scorching – journalism to elevate *Rolling Stone*'s standing. *Publishers Weekly* hailed the magazine as 'one of the most influential journals of the day', the *New York Times* praised its 'integrity and courage' and the *Columbia Journalism Review* testified, 'In a very real sense, it has spoken for – and to – an entire generation of young Americans.'[11]

* * *

Rolling Stone was but the most prominent in a fertile sector. Husband and wife Greg and Suzy Shaw's *Who Put the Bomp* – launched in 1970 as a successor to *Mojo-Navigator* – focused on punk and garage rock from the 1950s onwards, championing unfashionable acts such as Iggy Pop. Greg Shaw had served time as editor of the United Artists label's in-house *Phonograph Record Magazine*, which blurred the lines between editorial independence and promotion. 'We took ads from other record companies,' Shaw recalled. 'It also had a larger circulation than *Creem* – almost as much as *Rolling Stone* – but we didn't have to sell a copy, so I could pretty much hire my friends to write whatever they wanted and get paid well for it.'

Richard Riegel, later a bosom buddy of Lester Bangs at *Creem*, got his break at *Phonograph Record* with what he described as 'a sarcastic review of an Allman Brothers/Wet Willie concert in a March 1973 issue. At the time *PRM* had the folded-newspaper format of *Rolling Stone* but the writing was far more adventurous. Bangs, Meltzer and other *Creem*sters appeared regularly; ironic in view of the fact that *PRM* was published by UA as a kind of hippie-run promo tool.'[12]

'Everybody who was writing in the early seventies was writing for us,' claimed Shaw. 'It was complete freedom and lasted for a couple of years and then the powers-that-be at UA came to us and said, "Look guys, you've got to make up your minds. Do you want to be in the record business or the magazine business?" Marty [Cerf, publisher] and I walked away with ownership of a magazine worth hundreds of thousands of dollars, the subscription list – basically all of it for nothing. I stayed for a year and then split to focus on my own magazine, plus I wanted to get into releasing records.' Thus was born *Who Put the Bomp*'s companion label Bomp!, which issued the Modern Lovers, Iggy Pop, Devo and the Dead Boys.

On the East Coast, a 1973 launch by another husband-and-wife team was a more glamorous proposition. *Rock Scene* hired female writers and photographers, covered diverse music including disco and soul, and was preoccupied with the ways in which visual style interacted with pop. Co-founder Richard Robinson had hosted a show on the progressive rock station WNEW FM (which dedicated fifteen months in the mid-sixties to employing only female presenters) and produced Lou Reed's debut solo album. He was also an adviser to Neil Bogart, the wild head of Buddah Records, whose roster ranged from Captain Beefheart to folk singer Melanie. Meanwhile, Lisa Robinson – later *Vanity Fair*'s music editor – filed stories for *Hit Parader* and was US correspondent for *Disc*.

The pair met in 1969. 'I was listening to WNEW and heard this DJ who had a great voice and played the Velvet Underground, the Stooges, Ike and Tina Turner, Otis Redding,' said Lisa Robinson, then a teacher. 'He got fired three times, once for playing Jimi Hendrix's version of "The Star Spangled Banner", which the bosses there claimed was unpatriotic, and another time for playing what they called "unfamiliar" music, which meant Black music. The last time he was so pissed off he flushed a toilet on air and walked out. I was a fan and thought he was adorable and knew somebody in the music business who knew him, so got them to call him and ask if he needed any filing done.'

Working at Richard Robinson's office next to Grand Central Station in the afternoons after teaching at a school in Harlem sealed the relationship. 'Three months later I gave up my teaching job and two months after that we were married,' said Lisa Robinson. 'One

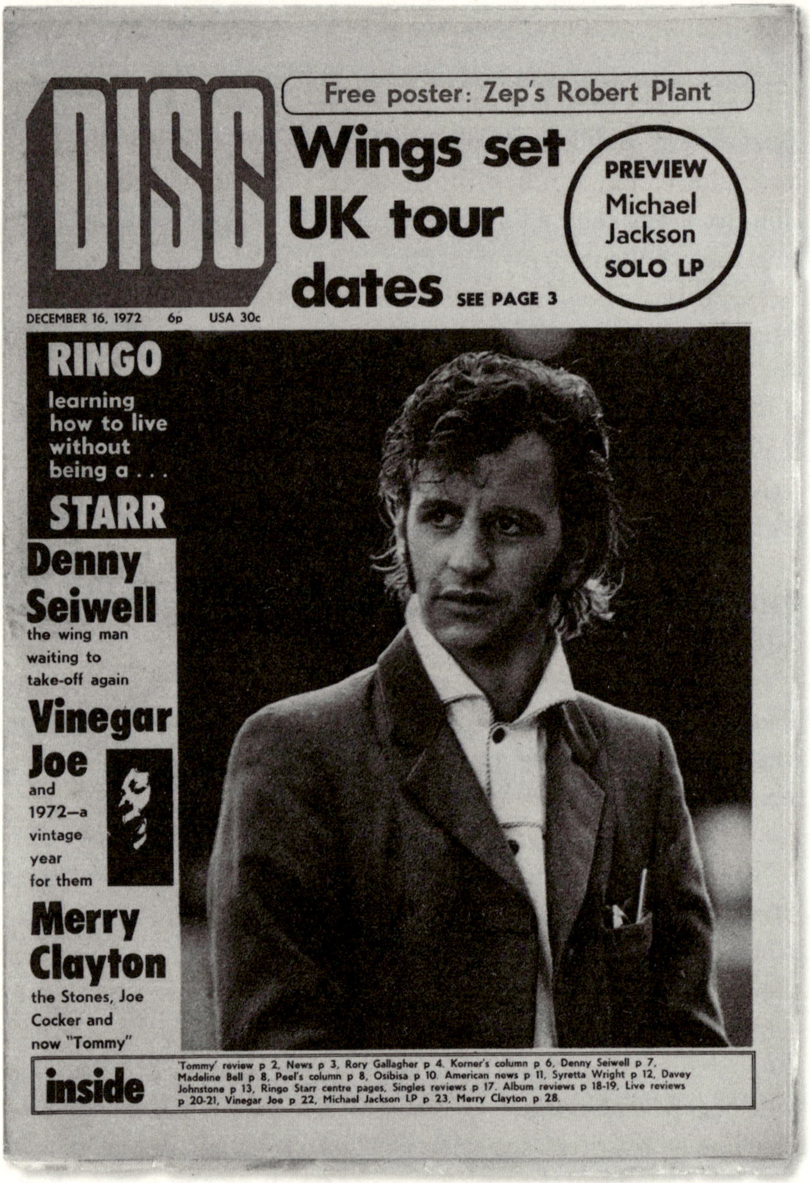

DISC

Free poster: Zep's Robert Plant

Wings set UK tour dates SEE PAGE 3

PREVIEW Michael Jackson SOLO LP

DECEMBER 16, 1972 6p USA 30c

RINGO learning how to live without being a . . . STARR

Denny Seiwell the wing man waiting to take-off again

Vinegar Joe and 1972—a vintage year for them

Merry Clayton the Stones, Joe Cocker and now "Tommy"

inside

'Tommy' review p 2, News p 3, Rory Gallagher p 4. Korner's column p 6, Denny Seiwell p 7, Madeline Bell p 8, Peel's column p 8, Osibisa p 10. American news p 11, Syretta Wright p 12, Davey Johnstone p 13, Ringo Starr centre pages, Singles reviews p 17. Album reviews p 18-19, Live reviews p 20-21, Vinegar Joe p 22, Michael Jackson LP p 23, Merry Clayton p 28.

Disc, 16 December 1972

of his jobs was writing a weekly column for *Disc & Music Echo*; he was friendly with people there like Penny Valentine. Eventually Richard became too busy and turned the column over to me. Simultaneously I started writing this mimeographed gossip sheet about the music industry called *Pop Wire*. We put it out ourselves and I mailed it. Then we started meeting a lot of the other journalists and press agents in New York: Vince Aletti, Lenny Kaye, Lillian Roxon and Gloria Stavers. Danny Fields was so unbelievably flattering to me about writing the *Disc* column. It was really through him I met everyone else.'[13]

In her memoir *There Goes Gravity*, Robinson wrote: 'By 1972, there were maybe twenty-five people in New York, Los Angeles, San Francisco and London who were writing about rock and roll. Some people took it very seriously. Some of us – who thought it was supposed to be about fun and sex and the thing that got us out of our parents' house and changed our lives – did not.'[14]

So tightknit was their world that the New Yorkers formed a group called Collective Conscience. Its members included Lillian Roxon, gay rights activist Jim Fourrat – later to found the Danceteria club – and Danny Goldberg, then an editor at *Circus* and latterly manager of Nirvana. 'It was mostly meeting up at the Robinsons, and having lots of fun and chuckles over the state of the music business,' recalled Lenny Kaye. 'And we'd meet the rock journalists from all over the US, while the British press had their own people here like [*Melody Maker*'s New York editor] Roy Hollingworth and, later, Chris Charlesworth.'

These soirees were funded by Richard Robinson's Buddah expense account. 'Some of [the group] didn't live in New York so they'd stay with us,' said Lisa Robinson. 'Dave Marsh stayed for quite a while once. Richard Meltzer was there too. And Lenny was there to the point that one August he asked me, "Are we going to have a Christmas tree this year?"'

Meltzer interpreted the couple's hospitality as social climbing. Invited to dinner with Lou Reed, he recalled, 'I look around; I'm not sure what gives. So Lisa pulls me aside, informs me I'm Lou's entertainment: "He really respects you." Uh, great. What gives is Richard's itching to produce the guy – a feather for his wighat, considering all he's done is Hackamore Brick and the Flamin' Groovies. At an opportune moment, Richard hands him an acoustic guitar. He plays rudimentary versions of "Walk on the Wild Side" and the other, whatever the title, with "They're taking her children away" [*Berlin*'s "The Kids"]. Invited, I sing harmony. Lisa videotapes, presumably for posterity. After songs, jokes. Lou goes first and I decided to spoil the ending and Lou is pissed. The Robinsons, too, like maybe I've killed the golden goose.'

Meltzer subsequently panned Reed's Richard Robinson-produced album: 'I don't spout the party line, whatever that was supposed to be, and am not forgiven.' And when Meltzer wrote lyrics for the proto-metal group Blue Oyster Cult, Reed reportedly accused him of plagiarism: 'It seems to him I couldn't have written diddleyrot without having sat at his feet and basked in his omnipoetic brilliance.'

'I guess he's a bitter guy,' shrugged Lisa Robinson. 'I remember when we were still friends and still think he's brilliant. This whole scene has been so badly reported to the point where it enrages me. In Victor Bockris's book about Lou Reed, he says I had this salon and Richard and I ruled New York society, which is utter bullshit. I was just married. It was fun to have all these people hanging out, but after a while it got a bit much.'

'Richard had this great sense of, "You can write for six magazines a month. Don't get precious about your work, and have fun with it,"' enthuses Lenny Kaye. 'They seemed to have an incredible amount of energy. He was working for record companies and doing radio shows six days a week and they were publishing this and that magazine.' One of the couple's gigs was as co-editors of *Hit Parader*. 'It was a chart magazine but we got a lot of stuff in there,' recalled Lisa. 'Interviews with John Lennon, Lou Reed and, later on, Patti Smith.'

When David Bowie arrived in town in 1971, Richard – working for Bowie's label RCA – and Lisa took him to the Midtown brewhouse the Ginger Man. Over dinner, Bowie expressed a wish to meet Iggy Pop, who was living in Manhattan with Danny Fields. 'Danny swears we went to Max's [Kansas City] and met him there,' noted Lisa, 'but I remember Iggy coming to the Ginger Man. Whatever. Iggy moved into the Warwick Hotel with David the next day. David started immediately to take care of him. That's how they got involved. They all came to our house two days later. Lenny Kaye was there, a lot of people. This was the first real convergence, to my mind, of this Warhol/rock press/glam rock situation.'

Out of this milieu came *Rock Scene*. The launch issue featured a glossy Bowie cover and newsprint pages that covered Ray Davies of the Kinks, Lindisfarne, Van Morrison, Marc Bolan and Rod Stewart. There was a fashion section – 'High-heeled shoes are back in style, dear' – and photographs of Curtis Mayfield and Black Sabbath with sassy captions by Leee Black Childers (who had worked with Warhol and Bowie). Retrospectives on Jimi Hendrix and psychedelia, and articles about glam-soul star Sylvester and 1950s revivalists Sha Na Na, were also photo-heavy, the latter captured in their gold Lurex glory by a new photographer on the scene, Bob Gruen.

In his introductory editorial, Richard Robinson wrote that the magazine was 'the alternative to the alternatives. *Rock Scene* has lots of elements to it, sort of a grafting of *Rolling Stone*, *Hit Parader*, *Popular Mechanics* and *Women's Wear Daily*. It probably doesn't read like any of those prestigious magazines, but they've all influenced this one into existence, partly for the things they're doing right, admittedly because we think there are some things they're doing wrong'.

In attitude and substance, *Rock Scene*'s challenge to the macho music press was boosted by associate editor Loraine Alterman. She had been the *Detroit Free Press*'s teen editor in the mid-1960s, covering Motown hitmakers, underground rock groups and jazz artists. Subsequently she was a stringer for *Billboard*, wrote for *Melody Maker*, ran *Rolling Stone*'s New York office and was a music correspondent for the *New York Times*.

'We thought we could do anything we wanted, because we didn't think anyone saw *Rock Scene*,' said Lisa Robinson, who also edited its sister title *Rock and Soul*. 'It had all these cheesy ads: "Buy this stone and have everything you desire" and "Are you too skinny on the beach?" Really laughable stuff. The ink came off on your hands. We made very little money, not even enough to pay people $10 each for their stories.'

But the circles in which the Robinsons moved meant *Rock Scene* readers received regular updates on big figures of the music press. The first issue noted that *Melody Maker*'s Roy Hollingworth had taken to singing self-written material at New York's Mercer Arts Center ('It's quite possible he'll become the first rock writer turned performer') and that Lenny Kaye – having compiled Elektra's cult classic *Nuggets: Original Artyfacts from the First Psychedelic Era, 1965–1968* – was producing a group called the Sidewinders (the alma mater of producer Andy Paley and guitarist Billy Squier). Lillian Roxon contributed a food column and Lester Bangs featured in a 'Know your rock critic' spot. Bangs recounted typing a review onstage while the J. Geils Band played, having complained that journalists couldn't get groupies because they didn't perform in front of audiences.

Others profiled in the series included *NME*'s Charles Shaar Murray (sporting *Aladdin Sane* makeup) and Nick Kent: 'His dishy pieces have made for some of the most memorable moments in journalism ... He is usually covered with an unparalleled assortment of scarves, belts, vests, jewels (including a pendant actually given him by Keith!).'[15]

'They were puff pieces so people would know who they were,' said Lisa Robinson, who described *Rock Scene* as the 'house magazine' for demi-monde nightspots Max's Kansas City and CBGB. 'One issue had me grinning backstage with David Bowie, another had "At home with David and Cyrinda" [a parody of a gossip magazine photostory featuring New York Dolls singer David Johansen and his partner Cyrinda Foxe]. This was stuff you couldn't possibly see anywhere else. *Rolling Stone* couldn't give a shit about any of these people, and they were always way after the fact anyway.'

The New York Dolls, featured extensively in *Rock Scene*, embodied its qualities: provocative, glamorous, decadent and downright fun. And the appointment of Wayne (latterly Jayne) County as an advice columnist drove the point home. 'Another use for ladies' hose,' wrote County. 'First cut the feet out. Then cut a round hole where the crotch is ... big enough to put your head through ... Either wear as a halter top or wear under short-sleeved blouses. Gives a fabulous effect on the arms, particularly if they're fishnets.'[16]

Rock Scene ploughed its lighthearted, photo-heavy furrow even after the Robinsons exited, running out of road only in the 1980s. 'People kept on telling me how much they loved it: Billy Corgan, Thurston Moore, Chrissie Hynde, Nick Rhodes, Michael Stipe,' recounted Lisa Robinson. 'It had a very camp sensibility and a very New York sensibility, and it evidently linked these guys who loved to wear makeup: "Oh God, there are other people out there into the same things! I want to go to New York and meet Andy Warhol!" We never took it seriously. In fact, we thought it was hilarious, but, as it turns out, it influenced a lot of people.'

9
‘You would call it blatant misogyny’

Caroline Coon Upsets the *Melody Maker* Applecart while *Black Music* Champions Carl Gayle

'You would call it blatant misogyny'

When Nick Logan took *NME*'s reins in the late autumn of 1973, he was twenty-six, and the youngest editor of a national paper. 'There were still remnants of the Maurice Kinn era,' he observed. 'I was working closely with Percy Dickins, who was thirty years my senior.'

Logan's accession coincided with turmoil in Britain, exacerbated by 1973's oil crisis. Middle Eastern exporters announced an embargo on countries supporting Israel in the so-called Yom Kippur War, which raged for nearly three weeks in the Golan Heights and around the Suez Canal. With British prime minister Ted Heath's government in its terminal phase, the crisis plunged the country into recession. The National Union of Mineworkers announced a work-to-rule and Heath decreed businesses adopt a three-day week to limit energy usage. Simultaneously, a years-long battle between the government and the Trades Union Congress came to a head. The 7,000 members of the print workers' union called strikes at production sites, impacting titles including *NME* (*Melody Maker*'s print workers did not join the action).

Consequently, Logan's name appeared at the top of the staff list once, in November 1973, before strike action stopped *NME* reaching newsstands for two and a half months. 'We couldn't shift the job to another printer, because that would have meant sympathy strikes,' he said. 'Although copy was spiked and frustration built, the staff began to gel.'

'It could have been intensely demoralizing – we were just hitting our stride – but in fact it did nothing but good,' said Tony Tyler, by now *NME*'s features editor. 'We accumulated a huge stockpile of quality items ready for "the day", but at the same time the atmosphere was almost carnival-like. It was intensely enjoyable in terms of personal relationships. A lot of friendships were formed.'

'HELLO HELLO we're back again' declared *NME*'s first post-strike issue, in January 1974. 'There was such a rush of energy in that issue, it was exhilarating,' Logan remembered. 'If it hadn't have been for the interruption of the strike, I don't think it would have happened.' He cemented the paper's rebirth by ridding the front page of extraneous material and filling it with a moody Pennie Smith portrait of Bryan Ferry. This challenged the reliance on concert photographs. 'I didn't want to see Roger Daltrey's tonsils,' Logan explained. 'His jacket was far more interesting to me.' Accompanying text set the tone for the magazine's pre-punk attitude to stars accustomed to slavish and flattering copy, billing the Roxy man as 'Byron Ferrari: prince of sleaze'.

'We despised the record industry,' observed Charles Shaar Murray, 'gave not even two hoots for the sensitivities of our publisher or the profits of their shareholders, and relentlessly satirised favourite musicians like Ferry, whose ludicrous clothes and fragile ego inspired us to seek endlessly new ways to misspell his name; the most memorable including not just Byron Ferrari but also Brian Fury, Biryani Ferret, Brown Furry and Brawn Fairy.'

'We were reinventing the idea of the music weekly as we went along and not only was it working, it was tremendous fun,' Tyler reminisced. 'We went to work in the mornings with a sense of pleased anticipation. I've never had a job like it before or since. We were flying.'

'I miss that spirit of collective transgression,' mourned Murray. 'We wanted to sin mightily. I used to write 2,000 to 3,000-word features on an acoustic typewriter at a desk in the middle of a crowded room with people taking drugs all over the place, fights, screams, three different records playing. I would almost do it as a party piece, writing amid all that chaos. I was reading an awful lot, writing an awful lot and doing terrifying amounts of speed: biker sulph, like snorting razor blades off a toilet floor. Cheap, but it worked.'

Chris Salewicz accepted that drugs – mainly pot and speed – 'probably unhinged certain fragile personalities', but said Logan ran a tight ship: 'Editorial meetings were quite serious and businesslike. People would be given a hard time about things they'd done ... smoking spliffs in the record review room, that sort of thing. He obviously disapproved, although was reasonably cool about it.'

The spring of 1974 established *NME* as Britain's most exciting youth culture read: a landmark piece by Nick Kent, about a debauched New York Dolls trip to Paris, appeared alongside Charles Shaar Murray and Elton John discussing the latter's weight problem. The gender-fluid Jobriath was cruelly dismissed as 'the fag-end of glam rock' and Brian Eno was confronted by a new addition to the staff, Chrissie Hynde. The American expat was introduced to the

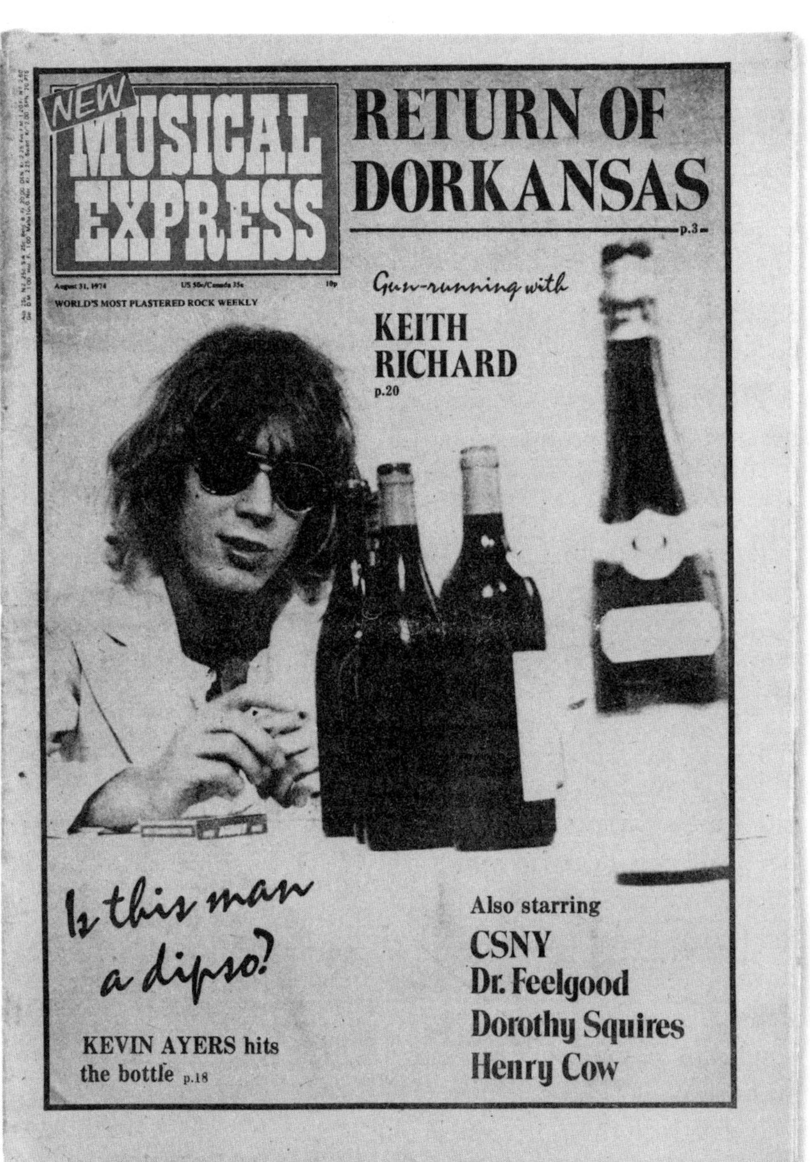

New Musical Express, 31 August 1974

editorial team by Kent, with whom she had bonded at a party over a love of Iggy Pop. He prevailed upon her to type his copy, which was previously delivered to long-suffering secretaries in spidery handwriting on any material he had to hand, including torn cereal boxes. 'One day he brought in immaculately typed copy, saying, "Hey! I've been practicing,"' recalled Murray. 'Then we found out Chrissie had typed it. I remember [assistant editor] Ian MacDonald telling Nick, "Well, what do we need you for? She's got plenty of attitude and she can type."'

MacDonald duly commissioned pieces directly from Hynde 'because she was so obviously so full of talent. I wasn't surprised she made it big-time a few years later.' 'A true visionary and humanitarian,' was Hynde's verdict on MacDonald. 'But he was wrong this time: I really couldn't write. He didn't care. He wasn't looking for quality. They were looking for sex. They wanted a pimple-faced loudmouth to push the male staff around and make them crawl.'[1]

But Hynde – credited as 'Hynd', to disguise herself from authorities because she didn't have the right to work in the UK – was more than a match for her seasoned colleagues, with a no-nonsense style that won favour with the predominantly male readers. 'It was with a certain apprehensive curiosity that I first noticed the brown lace-up shoes,' began her interview with Brian Eno. 'He displayed a normalcy that I just couldn't trust. After all, I'd seen his photos and I knew I was dealing with no ordinary deviant. Yet the toned-down reserve, the limp handshake (handshake?) and the nice-guy inoffensiveness had me baffled. He just didn't come on like someone who keeps an extensive collection of breast bondage literature in the bathroom.'[2]

In fetish clothing from Malcolm McLaren and Vivienne Westwood's boutique (rechristened Sex in 1974), Hynde cut an impressive figure, particularly in tandem with the similarly leather-clad Kent, and earned bylines on encounters with Melanie, Roxy Music's Andy Mackay and fellow American Suzi Quatro. There were also well-received pieces on the doomed Tim Buckley and pop pinup David Cassidy, with a female perspective alien to the rest of the editorial team. 'What a face!!' she wrote of Cassidy. 'He just can't take a bad photo, and his combination of features are *unbeatable* on the Teen Scale. Try to see this through the eyes of a bored, disillusioned, frustrated sixteen-year-old female. You want something you can hold like a cuddly dog, but that can seduce you at the same time. Now if you're a normal (sic) kid, a dog won't fulfill both purposes, but David will – at least in theory, if not practice. A girl could spend hours gazing into those gorgeous puppy-dog eyes, without being threatened by anything overtly sexual. That "please love me" vibe fills the bill every time.'[3] As Tony Stewart confirmed, 'We saw Cassidy in a completely different light after she went on the road with him.'[4]

But the itch Hynde was determined to scratch lay in making music, not writing about it. In the autumn of 1974, her response to a request that she write a Velvet Underground retrospective was to instead throw in her lot as a sales assistant for McLaren and Westwood. 'I thought, "Why always looking back? Working in this shop seems so much more happening than looking back at the past." So I left.'[5] But her tenure at Sex was cut short within days by Kent. Incensed at a perceived infidelity, he appeared at the shop and attempted to beat Hynde with his belt, only to be punched to the ground by another assistant. According to Hynde, McLaren said her presence at the store was 'too confusing'. She quit the UK for Paris and began her journey to becoming a professional musician.

That left reporter Julie Webb to tamp down the male posturing. She was another adept interviewer; just seven years after the relaxation of laws pertaining to homosexuality, Freddie Mercury told Webb he was 'as gay as a daffodil, dear'.[6] And she was among the first to recognize that the wheels were coming off the Marc Bolan bandwagon, describing a T. Rex show at the Glasgow Apollo as 'a dire musical experience ... Never have so many screamed for so little.'[7]

Kate Phillips also made her mark. Toiling at a women's magazine owned by *NME*'s publisher IPC, she contacted features editor Tony Tyler on the off-chance that there was room for another writer. 'She did a few freelance pieces very well,' he remarked, 'so Nick Logan told me to take her out for lunch and offer her a job.' Only then did Phillips reveal that her father was IPC's managing director. 'We all really respected the way she'd kept that in the dark until she was offered the gig on her own merits,' said Tyler. They married and were together until his death in 2006.

Meanwhile, Mick Farren became part of the pack after an approach from Charles Shaar Murray: 'Charlie said, "You really ought to come to *NME* because making a living is fun. Come down and see Ian MacDonald. You're a fool to yourself." I didn't want to work for IPC but he pointed out, "What else are you going to do? You going to be Bruce Springsteen next week?" I said, "No, that doesn't seem to be on the cards."' Irreverence proved the making of Farren: 'Why bother to write about the new ELO album on the day *The Godfather* comes out?' he ranted to Ian MacDonald.

'I turned in a piece of copy about *Star Trek* and the Trekkie cult and wrote about Evel Knievel,' Farren recalled. 'Then I discovered record companies, trips to America and free coke, and I did start writing about music. They were totally unscrupulous in the seventies, so our attitude was, "Yeah, why the fuck not?" It was a wonderful time to be a music journalist. Record companies treated you like God. Everything was on offer but cash money and hookers. Unfortunately you couldn't get anything to wear from the waist down: T-shirts, jackets, hats, but nobody sent you a pair of Johnny Cash cowboy boots or tour jeans.'

Farren summarized the dilemma facing *NME*: 'Did we put out a kind of high-school magazine about everything that might be interesting to a bunch of people pulled together for their liking of music, or did we put out a purely music magazine? I mean, how could you write about Bob Marley without at least giving an insight into colonialism or the politics of Trenchtown? Nick Logan kind of sat on the fence.'

Of the contributors, Farren was the most overtly concerned with the wider world, and filed state-of-the-nation diatribes in 1974. Written with fellow underground émigré Chris Rowley, a piece about the ongoing recession was headed 'Inflation, gloom, depression, dread; fear and loathing, lack of bread (If it's back to the 1920s, what price triple LPs?)'. 'A lack of cash could force the music to become cheap, gaudy, vital and energetic,' concluded Farren and Rowley, unwittingly prophesying punk, '[and] could be the boost rock needs to bail itself out of the stagnation that seems currently to be sucking it down to the level of boredom.'[8]

Farren was the antithesis of the neat and scrupulous Logan: 'I scared him, as this combination of a yeti and Dracula hanging around the office, but we all scared him a bit. He was a working class, mod geezer who'd come up the hard way, and us flash cunts didn't go to college – or, if we did, we'd got thrown out. He'd take an awful lot of valium some days, but he had a hard job. The management were breathing down his neck all the time over the language. We'd have meetings about headlines, such as "Bryan Ferry screws up" because we'd already rejected "Bryan Ferry fucks up".'

Logan's patience was also tested by another new staffer, Pete Erskine. This blond bookend to Nick Kent joined from *Disc* and was instantly on the offensive, describing Eno's early ambient explorations as 'smacking of the bogus'. And in 1974, a joint Erskine and Kent feature so spectacularly demolished Pink Floyd that Dave Gilmour called the former to say he was 'very angry about it'. Ironically, Farren's verdict on Erskine, who died in 1984, was that 'he was too androgynously cute for anyone to take him seriously': 'He was very nervous, tenuous, ghostly. Kent and him were leaving one day and I was heard to remark, "There's Verlaine and Rimbaud clocking out."'

'Kate Phillips was reviewing the singles in this black-draped, gothic cubicle we maintained for the purpose,' remembered Ian MacDonald. 'We were chatting while some dumb record was playing when the door opened and Pete Erskine leant in with an air rifle, said, "What's that ridiculous crap?" and shot the stylus off the record. Perfect aim. I'd say that was pretty characteristic.'

While Henderson Dalrymple plugged away with reggae, *NME* remained dominated by rock. 'They needed to do something about Black music,' said Neil Spencer, poached from *Beat International*. 'Nobody on *NME* was interested. Roger St Pierre knew everything about the subject but was not a writer in the same way *NME* had writers. That was my entrée to write about soul: Johnny Bristol, the Philadelphia Sound, TK Records, George McCrae. I did pieces on Smokey [Robinson], Stevie [Wonder], Curtis [Mayfield], Al Green. There was a lot of derision. [Cartoonist] Tony Benyon was always taking the piss out of the Chi-Lites and people like that because they wore the wrong clothes.'

Spencer, who would become editor within four years, felt himself an outsider, 'not only because our musical interests were different but also because of the lifestyles which went with the musical interest. I thought the music and the people Nick Kent was interested in were completely dull. I thought Lou Reed was a complete twat. The fixation on people like Mott the Hoople and 10cc was laughable. And the dress sense! The leather trousers and promotional T-shirts and Warner Brothers satin jackets. For their part, they were bemused by me, because I used to come to the office in Doc Martens and barathea trousers. They were impractical as people and had no social skills that I could see. Nobody drove a car. Nobody danced, and anybody who couldn't dance was beyond the pale for me at that time. I was a dancing fool: going down soul clubs and starting to hang around the reggae scene.'

He was aided by Chris Salewicz, whose penchant for Jamaican music earned him the soubriquet 'the Rasta Pole' from Mick Farren. Salewicz attended the Wailers' four-day residency at London rock haunt the Speakeasy, which is credited with having introduced

reggae to the London audience, and would go on to write the definitive biography of Marley.

Meanwhile, Andrew Tyler fulfilled Logan's ambitions for expanding *NME*'s remit. A trip to Las Vegas to witness performances by 1974's biggest group – Mormon boy band the Osmonds – resulted in a tour-de-force about Sin City: 'Five cents gets you a coffee, a donut and free air-conditioning; for forty-nine cents, twenty-four hours a day, there's a Lady Luck breakfast special comprising a cup of coffee, two fried eggs fashioned out of formica resin and candle grease, two sticks of crinkly ranch-fed deep-fry bacon made from antimatter and rearranged molecularly inside a sanitised microwave oven, and a couple of slices of toast so light you have to hold your breath when you're near them.'[9] 'Andrew was the most human of our writers, the most grown-up, thoughtful and quiet, more interested in people than music,' said Tony Tyler, noting that his near-namesake – who died in 2017 – became a powerful advocate for animal rights as director of Animal Aid.

NME's audacity often drew fire from its subjects and readers. One issue alone in October 1974 featured missives from producer

Mike Batt (mastermind of the Wombles' hits), former Fleetwood Mac maestro Peter Green, and author and satirist Francis Wheen (who signed his letter "Frank" and weighed in on a debate about whether public-school-educated musicians could make authentic rock). The Strawbs, King Crimson's Pete Sinfield and Henry Cow's Chris Cutler, Roxy Music publicist Simon Puxley and Brian Eno also used the letters page to grumble about their treatment. One of the latter's communications prompted Logan and MacDonald to run a mock advert: '"I find it incredibly boring – Eno." Yes, well-known pop personality Eno thinks that *New Musical Express* is simply a rancid collection of middle class moralists. Here's what he says: "None of them has yet come up with a good reason for my existence. All they do is put people down. I just don't take bad photos. I guess I'm lucky with my bones. Take my advice – read Porno World instead."' This was juxtaposed with the paper's masthead and the slogan, 'The one that offends all the right people.'[10]

Meanwhile, mission statements beneath the front-page logo changed each week. 'The world's most mobile weekly' appeared when paraplegic performer Robert Wyatt's band posed in wheelchairs alongside their leader and 'The world's most plastered weekly' when hard-drinking songwriter Kevin Ayers presented a wine guide. Continuing the catering theme, Man guitarist Deke Leonard provided a guide to the motorway cafés that serviced bands on tour (one, he grumbled, was 'designed by a comedian', while its shop was 'terrible' and its food 'vile').

Nick Kent's interviews got star billing, with insolent headlines: 'Wizard. Or silly sod?' (Todd Rundgren); 'I was a hausfrau from Hamburg until I discovered heroin' (Nico); 'Crazed, crippled or convicted?' (John Cale); 'Speak up ya creep' (John Sebastian). Before hard drugs took hold, Kent filed hundreds of pieces about the acts that fascinated him and, often, became part of their stories. 'An unlikely, ungainly figure,' noted Iggy Pop of the writer, 'well over six feet tall, unsteadily negotiating the sidewalks of London and LA like a great palsied mantis, dressed in the same tattered black leather and velvet guitar-slinger garb, regardless of season or the passing of time, hospital-thin with a perpetually dripping bright red nose caused by an equally perpetual drug shortage, all brought to life by a wrist-waving, head-flung-back Keith Richards effect and an abiding interest in all dirt.'[11] 'Kent never dressed for the weather,' confirmed Nick Logan. 'If it was minus twenty-three, Nick would have the arse hanging out the back of his trousers. In summer he'd have a leather coat with the collar up. But none of that mattered. He wrote fantastically.'

'Loud music by self-destructive white boys was what I wanted to write about – the Stones, the Stooges, the New York Dolls – so I wasn't interested in temperance,' declared Kent. 'I was devoured by rock 'n' roll.'[12] He is particularly remembered for longform, multipart features on such missing-in action artists as Pink Floyd founder Syd Barrett, the Beach Boys' Brian Wilson and folk singer Nick Drake. 'Those articles about then-forgotten geniuses forced us all to reappraise where music had got to,' said Logan. 'I'm so proud I was editor when they came out. I think they are among the best pieces of journalism in any genre.'

'I wasn't a great writer – I was more a work-in-progress,' Kent reflected. 'But I had the energy, passion and drive to go out and find that fucking story. Of all of them at *NME*, I was the one going, "Let's do investigative journalism. Let's not just be as good as *Melody Maker* but let's be better than the best, *Rolling Stone*." Those Syd Barrett and Brian Wilson pieces were my attempt at that.'[13]

Notoriously, Kent wangled an all-expenses trip to Los Angeles for a cover story on Jethro Tull. Legend has it that he promptly hooked up with Iggy Pop, then ploughing a hopeless furrow in the town he labeled 'Kill City'. The pair acquired expensive luggage from the hotel shop on the room tab, then sold it to buy drugs. On his return, Kent filed stories about his time on the West Coast, featuring Alice Cooper, Bob Dylan, the Faces, Lou Reed, Elton John's manager John Reid and Bobby Womack. He had also completed his research for the Brian Wilson feature. When Kent arrived for an interview, Wilson is said to have exclaimed, 'Man, you look more like a rock star than me!'

Kent's writing on Iggy described his reduced circumstances: 'After two solid years of misfortune, mismanagement to total non-management, a kind of tragic-comic collapse incorporating the Stooges' very own stupifyingly bloated gamut of self abuse/destruct mechanisms is guaranteed to destroy every shred of glory just as victory is within mauling distance. It's almost as though a hex has been placed on everything the Ig has striven towards ever since he made that conscious brain-belled decision to transform himself from simple Jim Osterberg, the academic whiz-kid from Ann Arbor, into a brilliant monster called Iggy who would stand over the Michigan freeways, flying on acid, entertaining all manner of godforsaken visions.'[14] The louche Kent, recalled Danny Sugerman, 'OD'd at [Sugerman's Laurel Canyon residence] Wonderland Avenue when he came over with Iggy one time. He collapsed in the bathroom. We found him in there in these little pink underpants and had to rush him to hospital just wearing those.'

'I never had to change a word of his copy,' observed Ian MacDonald, 'but he had this neurotic compulsion to get insanely close to deadlines before he started writing: usually sitting in the office, with me standing over him, telling him through gritted teeth that he'd only got minutes left. He almost always managed to finish the last sentence about ten seconds before copy was collected for the printers.'

Tony Tyler recalled suspending Kent for a couple of weeks over his 'deadline-busting antics, as a way of saying, "Shape up." I don't think he ever really forgave me for that'. 'When I became a rock journalist,' said Jon Savage, 'I discovered I really disliked Kent's MO, which was to hang around groups and then print stuff which was off-the-record.' And Julie Burchill, whose arrival at *NME* consigned Kent to the old order, described him as 'a middle-class wanker and a junkie and a freak to boot. Rumour has it that Keith Richards was once copiously sick on his jacket after a prolonged smack binge and Kent never washed it again.'[15]

But his heavily stylized copy drew plaudits from *NME*'s peers across the Atlantic. 'He's a no-bullshit interviewer and he has ACTUAL LITERARY STYLE,' marvelled *Fusion*'s 'Metal' Mike Saunders. 'No kidding: the first rock writer in newspaper format whose writings can be identified by technique rather than overbearing nature, obnoxiousness or overbearing notoriety.' Saunders compared Kent to the Victorian art critic John Ruskin, and described Charles Shaar Murray as 'the most demented journalist I've ever had the pleasure to listen to'. His observations reappeared a few weeks later in *NME*, which noted, '*Fusion* went out of business right after that issue came out.'[16]

Latterly, Kent paid tribute to pop culture observer Nik Cohn, whose disenchantment with pop was expressed eloquently in his turn-of-the-decade tome *Awopbopaloobop Alopbamboom: The Golden Age of Rock*. 'MacDonald, Murray and I were hugely influenced by that book,' Kent confessed in 2021. 'I read it again three or four years ago and was bedazzled by how much I'd taken from it. It was like, "I thought I'd invented that, but that son of a bitch Cohn had already done it before me and I'd just taken it!"'[17]

Although *NME* was top dog, certain elements – including the above-cited homophobic dismissal of Jobriath – jarred even at the time, let alone in hindsight. Foremost was the decoration of the Nationwide Gig Guide with pictures of bare-breasted film starlets. Occasional criticism from female readers was summarily dismissed on the letters page. Despite this casual sexism, racial stereotyping and homophobia characteristic of most of Britain's media of the period, it is hard to refute Ian MacDonald's claim that *NME* had 'most of the best writers and photographers, the best layouts, a sense of style and humour and feeling of real adventure'. Such was its power that Roy Carr could drop in on a Phil Spector session in 1975, where he took the opportunity to introduce the producer to his companion, Bruce Springsteen. 'Phil turned round jokingly at one point,' Carr recalled, 'and said, "Hey, doesn't that make *Born to Run* suck?" And Bruce just laughed and put his arms round him.'

'We also set out to beat *Melody Maker* on its strong suit: being the serious, responsible journal of record,' Ian MacDonald said. 'We did Looking Back and Consumer Guide features that beat the competition out of sight, and we did this not just to surpass our rivals but because we reckoned rock had finished its first wind around 1969/70 and deserved to be treated as history, as a canon of work.'

Bob Geldof was among the irregular contributors. During a period of globetrotting, he had contributed to Vancouver's underground music paper *The Georgia Straight* and San Francisco's *Berkeley Barb*. Back in Dublin in 1975, before his band the Boomtown Rats

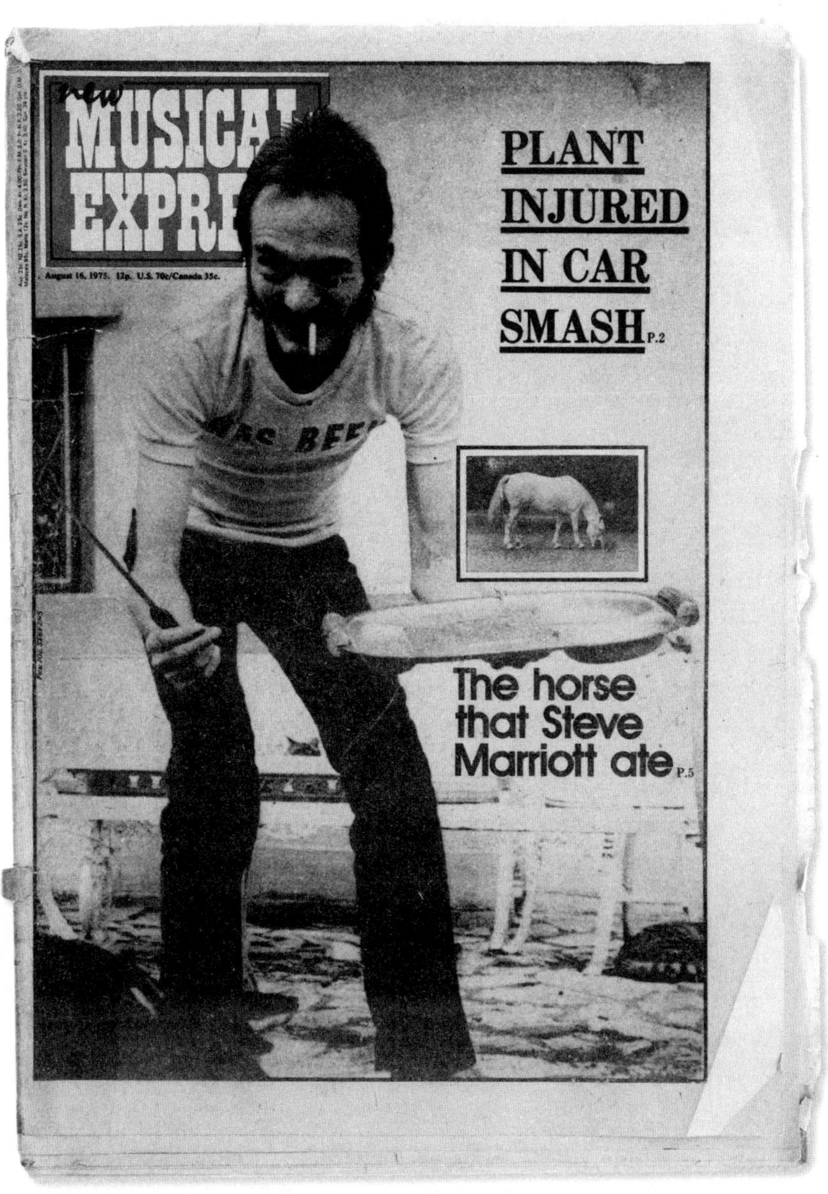

New Musical Express, 16 August 1975

became a gigging concern, Geldof – as 'Rob Geldof' – filed features for *NME*. These included a profile of Eric Clapton, then residing in a castle in rural Ireland.

'*NME* had an incredible pass-on rate,' noted Mick Farren. 'We could claim 900,000 readers at its peak. This was a massive attraction, but a bit like the thing about starting out as Che Guevara and ending up as a mercenary. That's probably why I drank so much. The pride was in getting really good at it – also, not running with the worst scumbags.'

* * *

While *NME* blazed, *Melody Maker* plodded. '*MM* went back to the twenties, was founded upon jazz and became the mouthpiece of the music industry,' observed star writer Michael Watts. 'That worked totally against it because *NME* was all about punk, rebellion and overthrowing everything we stood for. Unfortunately, at some point *Melody Maker* had become the mouthpiece for prog rock. In fact, apart from Chris Welch, none of us liked it. But it sold tons of records. Ray Coleman followed the album charts religiously, so whoever was in the top five was regularly in *MM*.'

Nick Logan's visual sensibilities also left *MM* for dust. Watts characterizes his own paper's typeface as 'two-point unreadable' (nine-point or above being the readable minimum). 'The layouts were poor,' he added, 'with the exception of the front pages, which were classic tabloid style and amazingly powerful. Whoever we put on the front page sold their records and live tickets.'[18]

'We had become victims of our success,' suggested Welch. 'There were powerful advertisers booking large amounts of ads, which meant we had a lot of space to fill. It wasn't very well laid out and we had acres and acres of verbiage, which made the paper look dull.'

But Ray Coleman can take credit for promoting diversity: when chief subeditor Alan Lewis pleaded for a Black American music platform, he agreed to launch the monthly *Black Music* (pl. 7). 'I don't think he had any great interest in black music, but he saw it might have some potential,' said Lewis. 'Perhaps he felt there was no risk – and also, perhaps more importantly, launching magazines in those days was a very cheap business. There wasn't much money at stake. It was brave of IPC, but to be honest it was dead cheap, because we had a staff of three.'[19]

Those three were Lewis, Tony Cummings, from *Shout*, and Carl Gayle, whose exemplary journalism – particularly on the potency of reggae – was key. Gayle is Black, and his first published music piece was a *Let It Rock* feature on the Wailers that put the group's music in the context of day-to-day existence in the Caribbean: 'Life in Kingston, Jamaica can be very hard. Stories of guys as young as twelve robbing and killing for just a few cents are commonplace. The anguish and anger of the music of the Wailers is a product of their concrete jungle and the unfair and corrupt dealings of the big Jamaican studios.'[20]

Gayle used patois and slang in his copy, which proved a hit with readers. His writing also exposed the patronizing tone of most coverage of Jamaican street culture in the White rock press; even the liberal-leaning *NME*, in an early interview, described Marley as incomprehensible.

With a cover story on Stevie Wonder, then riding high with his masterpiece *Innervisions*, *Black Music* hit the ground running in December 1973. It showcased artists who, like Wonder, were crossing over: the Isley Brothers, whose *3+3* mixed funk and rock, and the Wailers, whose *Catch a Fire* and *Burnin'* set them on the path to acceptance by a White audience. And the magazine's title was politically informed. 'We'd seen soul music develop as part of the Black movement in America,' Lewis noted. 'For most people it would still be called soul or R&B. But the use of the word "Black" had become very powerful in America for several years through the Civil Rights movement. And it began to get a harder edge, with people like James Brown embracing Black music as Black Power. So it seemed appropriate to call it *Black Music*, to show a seriousness of intent ... A lot of it was superficial, to do with fashion as much as anything else: the Afros, the style of dress, the style of talk. But politics was bound up in there.'[21]

With colour covers of stars such as Marvin Gaye, Barry White and Curtis Mayfield, *Black Music* sold around 25,000 copies a month: a fraction of the inkies' weekly sales but proof of a profitable niche. It was bolstered by Davitt Sigerson, later a distinguished novelist.

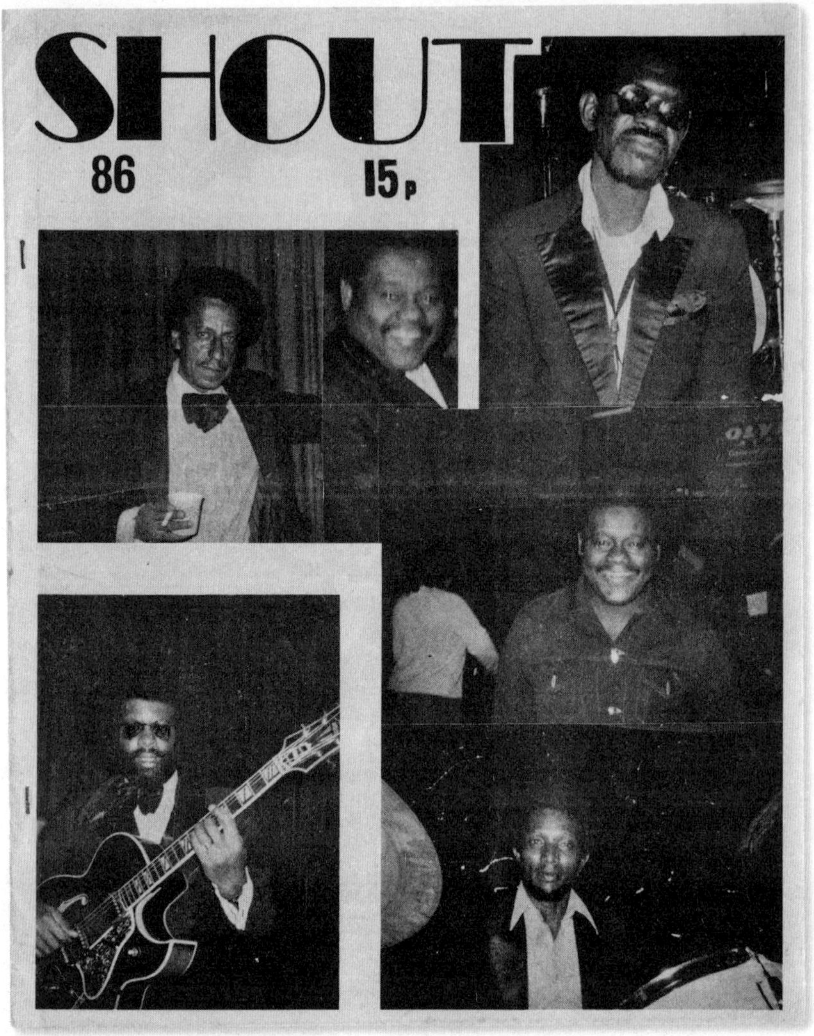

Shout, no. 86, 1973

Among Sigerson's finest articles was a look at producer and disco remix pioneer Tom Moulton: 'His name has appeared on the credits of discs by Gloria Gaynor, B.T. Express, Bobby Moore, Al Downing, People's Choice, South Shore Commission and many others. Yet Moulton's vital contributions to the hits of a dozen soul acts is in a manner new to an industry increasingly immersed in the complexities of a technological age.'[22] Returning to the US, Sigerson became *Melody Maker*'s New York correspondent and recorded two albums for the independent label Ze, before producing acts including the Bangles and Tori Amos.

'We weren't on any particular crusade,' Alan Lewis reflected. 'We had an early front cover that said, 'Do Black musicians get a fair deal?' The politics arose from the music; I can't claim that we were trying to impose anything on it.'[23]

Carl Gayle set the benchmark for writing about reggae's big names, such as King Tubby and Lee 'Scratch' Perry. His two-parter on the latter ran across the first issues of 1975, years before Perry's wayward genius was recognized by the White media. 'The partnership between Lee and Bob Marley was as important to the Wailers' music from '69 to '71 as any other factor,' he wrote. 'That partnership established the groundwork, the musical direction, that the Wailers took with *Catch a Fire*. And the partnership was Marley's inspirational source for the work he does today.'[24]

A year later, Gayle appeared to be ruing Marley's mainstream breakthrough: 'Even if Bob does greet you from the cover of our worthy magazine every time him step off de plane, it doesn't mean we (well, me at least) wouldn't rather have Junior Byles or Yabby U or Leroy Smart or Jacob Miller or Big Youth or Peter [Tosh] and Bunny [Wailer] laughing, grinning or screw-facing in glorious colour.'[25] He subsequently launched *Jahugliman*, a Kingston-based fanzine that covered Rastafarianism and Jamaican politics, before trading writing for farming.

Gayle set the stage for other writers to consider Black music more seriously. Penny Reel – pseudonym of former mod Peter Simons – graduated from *International Times* and *Let It Rock* to *NME*, while Idris Walters wrote for *Let It Rock* and *Sounds*. Among other contributors to *Black Music* was the poet and former British

Black Panther Linton Kwesi Johnson, a Jamaican-born Brit who would tap his political fire as a recording artist. Alan Lewis, however, found his own status as editor of a Black music magazine under fire from broadcaster and activist Darcus Howe: 'He said, "You're a cultural imperialist," and I could see what he was driving at. I knew there was a weird illogicality that I was editing a magazine called *Black Music*. I tried to point out that I felt I knew quite a bit about it and, if we could find more young black writers, we'd be using more of them. But in London at that time there were virtually none.'[26]

* * *

'*Melody Maker* needs a bullet in the arse – and I'm the one to pull the trigger.'[27] So said Allan Jones when Ray Coleman – inspired by Nick Logan's overhaul of *NME* – advertised in *Time Out* for 'highly opinionated' writers aged twenty-one and under. 'I was hired to be the equivalent of Charlie Murray or Nick Kent,' he recalled. 'Unfortunately, they were much better writers with much better contacts. There was this vague notion of, "Do the same sort of thing." I decided to do everything that was offered me.' In his first few weeks, that meant interviewing Bryan Ferry, Leonard Cohen and 1950s revivalists Showaddywaddy. 'I was on an absolute pittance – something like twelve pounds a week,' he recalled. 'I was spending more money on getting to gigs than I was earning. Mick [Watts, assistant editor] explained the arcane business of claiming expenses and introduced me to Max Jones, who gave me a crash course in creative accounting.'

A more adventurous recruit was freelancer Caroline Coon: a visual artist and activist whose role in the drugs charity Release had positioned her at the forefront of the 1960s counterculture. 'We're deeply in need of funds,' she told *Melody Maker* at the time. 'The reason we continued in the past was because of the help of George Harrison and Eric Clapton. George and Eric were fantastic. I'd like all pop stars to think of their debt to the kids. Actually, I asked Mick Jagger not long ago but he said he was broke.'[28]

By the 1970s, she said, 'We at the vanguard of the underground movement had been targeted by the authorities. *Oz* had been busted for the school kids issue, free festivals were being banned and rock 'n' roll had become corporate.'[29] Coon was knowledgeable about music, highly opinionated and forthright about sex and sexuality. She was also posh, which – in class-ridden Britain – meant she rubbed against the beery grain of *Melody Maker*.

'We were pretty sexist,' admitted Michael Watts. 'Caroline had a difficult job asserting herself by writing about music which frankly most of the people absolutely hated. And the subs hated her because she's dyslexic and they had a problem dealing with her prose. It did change, but we have to hold our hands up. We were a boys' club.'

By design or serendipity, the appointment of Coon was forward-thinking, and not just in the context of the music press. In national newspapers, women tended to be relegated to columnists or agony aunts; only the liberal *Guardian* positioned female journalists on a par with their male counterparts. But Coon took her cue from those women who had made their mark in music writing, hailing Penny Valentine as 'an enabling image. I knew I could write about pop because I had read her'.

Coon was not interested in revisiting the 1960s gods who remained the focus of her colleagues. Instead she investigated artists who resonated with pop's younger fans: Alice Cooper, Mud, Slik and the Bay City Rollers. The latter were huge in 1975, with 'Rollermania' evoking the frenzied heyday of Beatles fandom. Yet the music press largely ignored or derided the phenomenon; *NME* ran a picture of a band member signing an autograph with the caption, 'How do you spell X?'

'We were a gang of girls having fun together, able to identify each other by tartan scarves and badges,' said Rollers fan Sheryl Garratt, later an editor of *The Face*. 'I hardly remember the gigs themselves, the songs or even what the Rollers looked like. What I do remember are the bus rides, running home from school together to get to someone's house in time to watch [the band's TV show] *Shang-a-Lang*, dancing in lines at the school disco and sitting in each other's bedrooms discussing our fantasies and compiling our scrapbooks. Our real obsession was with ourselves; in the end, the men behind the posters had very little to do with it.'[30]

A sympathetic piece by Coon, published in September 1975, explained the Rollers' appeal: 'Teenagers had made do with pop stars, like Gary Glitter and Alvin Stardust, masquerading as their peers behind thick pancake make-up. The Rollers captivated an audience starved of the genuine article. Teenagers now had real teenage idols. Many people believe the ballyhoo and the talk of Rollermania [is] "hyped" and "manufactured." Nothing could be further from the truth. They are successful not because thousands of pounds have been poured into their image – the record company was reluctant to spend any money on them at all – but because they project a convincingly youthful optimism for life, an unjaded dedication to the process of entertainment, and they sing distinguished pop anthems which applaud, endorse and pay homage to the teenage state of being.'[31]

'I didn't want to write about big bands like the Rolling Stones or Yes,' Coon declared. 'I wanted to write about women in music and loved the camp kind of pop.' She examined largely dismissed female performers such as Dana Gillespie, Lyndsey de Paul and Kiki Dee, while a commission to compare and contrast the fortunes of Australian hit-maker Olivia Newton-John and the US-born Suzi Quatro enabled her to dig beneath stardom's surface: 'Suzi's press might have led you to believe that zipped inside her rough and tough exterior there beats a heart of solid granite. But the picture painted of Suzi as a machine-made libbing [*sic*] doll is inaccurate. At least two layers beneath her leather epidermis lives a sensitive and intelligently thoughtful person. The music industry seems reluctant to give Suzi Quatro any credit for having a creative mind of her own ... As the girl bass player and lead singer of a rock band she's making a really extraordinary contribution.'[32]

None of this earned Coon the respect of her colleagues: 'I think you would call it blatant misogyny. The minute I walked into the office there would be howls, catcalls, jeers. It needed a tremendous amount of bottle and courage when I wanted to put forward ideas and participate in editorial meetings.'

'For Coon, walking into the *Melody Maker* office meant facing a barrage of "not allowed" tactics,' Ines Punessen observed in her study of misogyny in the music press. 'Women journalists were an alien concept to their male colleagues whose social attitudes were groomed by older men. They grew up in a patriarchal society, which subordinated females.'[33] However, as Coon notes, 'My class protected me. My manner and my Queen's English stopped the bucketsful of macho bullshit aimed my way. One would put on one's Princess Margaret hauteur to get it to back off. It worked.' A glamorous image further undermined her critics: 'I was quite upfront about being a feminist but was confusing because I wore lipstick and was determined to be decorative for its own sake. I loved champagne [and] I loved fucking.

'One of the ways male journalists diminished me was [to say] that I was too beautiful and too sexy. Part of the feminist movement at that time said that our sexuality was dangerous, because men will want to rape and kill us, so we will get rid of our decorativeness and female attributes, wear no makeup and boiler suits ... My tactic was: I'm going to deal with this flak. I'm not going to change my position and eventually, because I am right, men will have to deal with it.'[34]

Coon outmanoeuvred the *Melody Maker* men by joining their booze-fuelled outings: 'I thought that, if you were going out drinking and partying, part of it was to surveil the scene and get laid. I always imagined that, when the guys came into the office with dreadful hangovers, they were having a good time. But when I went out with them, I was the only one who got laid. The more drunk they got, the less attractive they became.'

Coon recalled one particular star and his PR man organizing a champagne-soaked interview in a chauffeur-driven Rolls-Royce from London to Stonehenge and back: 'I love champagne, I love Rolls-Royces, I love driving through the countryside, but it was such a set-up. That artist spent the whole drive trying it on between answering questions. I could never have written about it. There was a double standard that, to maintain your professional standing, you didn't fuck or look pretty.' Of the paper's only other high-profile female of the period, Val Wilmer, Coon said: 'Val is a brilliant and wonderfully attractive woman, but she wasn't seen by the men on *Melody Maker* to be stereotypically pretty, so she could just get on and write her stuff.'

Brave attempts to burst the macho bubble awoke the dark forces that controlled it. 'I always wanted to write Barry Manilow's real story, get under the skin and talk about his sexuality and his days playing [Manhattan's] bath-houses,' said Coon, who seized on a chance to see Manilow play in Amsterdam. Before the show, a powerful publicist arrived at her hotel room: 'He closed the door and said, "You're not leaving here until I've fucked you." I knew immediately that he didn't fancy me: that this was a rape scenario. In fact, he was gay – one of a group of men on that pop scene who were closet gays. So I became Princess Anne, talked myself out of it and covered the gig.' Back in London, she told her editor about the attempted assault: 'He said, "Oh my God, don't worry. Just drop it." There would have been a view then: "What do you expect when you send a bird on the story? PRs behave like that." We weren't socially advanced enough to handle it. So, to a certain extent, there was a lot of stuff you couldn't write about.'

10
'I felt I could conquer'

Street Life, *Black Echoes*, *Pressure Drop*, *Punk* and *Temporary Hoarding*

While Caroline Coon fought to be heard at *Melody Maker*, the writer she hailed as her 'enabling image', Penny Valentine, worked as a publicist for Elton John's Rocket Records, then the Anchor label. 'You had to "nanny" people,' she groaned. 'You had to make sure everyone was comfortable, to make sure they all had drinks at receptions, that they had everything they wanted. And if they phoned up whinging about how to get there, you'd order a car. It was just like running a kindergarten, except that the people you were dealing with weren't as nice as kids.'[1]

Valentine's hope of using the role to attain an executive position was stifled by sexism. 'Men I knew with equivalent writing status and the same "ambition" had had no trouble getting into A&R departments,' she wrote in the mid-1970s. 'I spent two years trapped in a press office. At the moment this is the highest position a woman can hope for in British record companies. There are generally no openings for them to move further. However competently they do their job, however much of an asset they would be if many of their talents were used as resources by record companies, the result is still the same ... My case simply highlighted the problems I had known existed in the industry and yet, for some strangely optimistic reason that had little to do with logic, I felt I could conquer. Not so. I have never been particularly ambitious yet at both companies I was obviously viewed as incapable of holding down a job a man with less experience than myself could easily cope with.'[2]

Based in New York, Valentine resumed writing for *Sounds*, profiling Minnie Riperton, Gladys Knight and LaBelle. She returned to London in the autumn of 1975 to a senior post with *Street Life*, the British media's most serious attempt thus far to emulate *Rolling Stone*. It was founded by Billy Walker and Andrew Sheehan, who had jumped ship from *Sounds* to forge a more thoughtful offer. Walker had been at *Melody Maker* prior to *Sounds*, and *Street Life* benefited from distribution by Condé Nast, publisher of *The New Yorker* and *Vogue*.

Among the staffers were Angus Mackinnon, New York correspondent Chuck Pulin, underground veteran Nigel Fountain, and *Let It Rock* and *Sounds* refugees Simon Frith and Idris Walters. Richard Williams also contributed, after leaving *Melody Maker* for

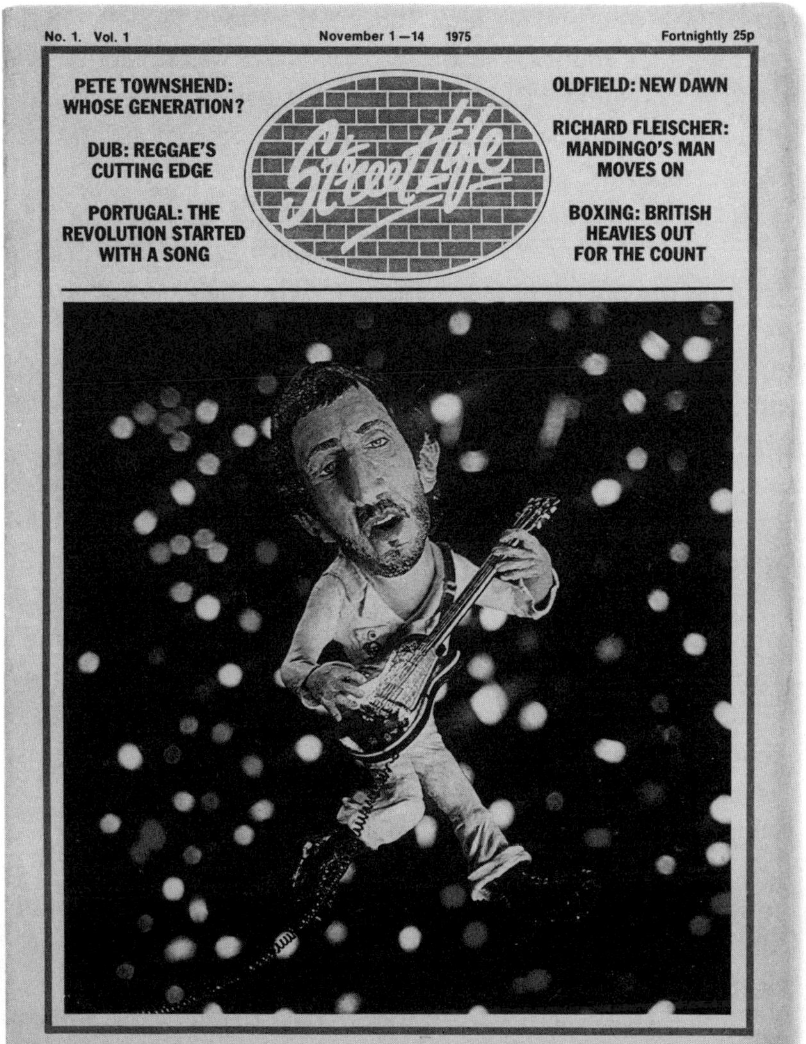

No. 1. Vol. 1 November 1—14 1975 Fortnightly 25p

Street Life

PETE TOWNSHEND: WHOSE GENERATION?

DUB: REGGAE'S CUTTING EDGE

PORTUGAL: THE REVOLUTION STARTED WITH A SONG

OLDFIELD: NEW DAWN

RICHARD FLEISCHER: MANDINGO'S MAN MOVES ON

BOXING: BRITISH HEAVIES OUT FOR THE COUNT

Street Life, vol. 1, no. 1, 1–14 November 1975

an A&R post at Island Records. Indeed, the Island connection was so strong that Fountain suspected *Street Life* was in fact funded by the label's founder Chris Blackwell: 'One piece of investigative journalism none of us ever carried out was to find out exactly who put the money up, but we did initially have a lot.'[3]

This first issue earned plaudits from British TV's only serious rock show, *The Old Grey Whistle Test*, which particularly praised its survey of reggae's potent subgenre, dub. 'Right now, dub is at the cutting edge,' wrote Idris Walters. 'Jamaica (bless her) has finally come up with a music, an alarming, Dada music comparable (for impact) with that of John Cage (almost), John Lennon (his Primal Majesty), John Fahey (as regards its evocation of the inner logics), BB King (his Minimal Majesty) ... and so on. Dub is probably Jamaica's most substantial contribution to The Evolving Twentieth Century Music Show. Thus far.'[4]

A willingness to allow writers agency distinguished *Street Life* from the papers locked to a weekly cycle. Penny Valentine framed a story on the Who around her Italian family roots in London and an introduction by a boyfriend to the group at mod hangout the Scene in the early 1960s: 'We shared Soho, Tolliday and I, as we shared everything else. He stood – a kid in his Rolling Stones T-shirt, hands spread pseudo-Italian gangster style on his skinny hips, mobile knobbly face poised for an act, bending his Cockney accent round the unfamiliar words. Up against the window of Del Monico's: "Eh – whata you wan? You wanna de bowl a spaghetti?" Losing the "t" on the last word so it became "spageii". Punching each other with familiar grins, lighting up Players No. 6, moving on into the night.'[5]

Street Life attempted to take on *Time Out* with listings for films, TV and gigs, alongside ambitious material such as a report on the Troubles in Northern Ireland and an examination of social revolution in Portugal after the fall of its authoritarian government. Closer to home, the magazine looked at pub rock band manager Dave Robinson – shortly to found the Stiff record label – and the London music venue the Hope & Anchor. Later issues focused on roots music, including country singer Emmlyou Harris and salsa exponents Fania All-Stars, and shone new light on Bobby Womack and Gil Scott-Heron.

Valentine covered newcomers Bruce Springsteen and Nils Lofgren, but used the magazine to launch further broadsides against music industry misogyny: 'Musicians, in the main, treat all women the same – which is not a good thing since musicians by and large treat women badly. It is no accident there are groupies, a natural by-product of the male musician's attitude to his role. The attraction to some men of standing onstage is, in part, the prospect of getting an easy and convenient lay once they're offstage. The perks, you could say, of the job.'

Gay men didn't escape her ire: 'It became increasingly clear that even gay men, whose path in the industry has been very smooth compared to most other job opportunities open to them, were determined not to stick their necks out to help the situation. They are just as wary as everyone else of women holding any important post or competitive position – a situation I find equally depressing.'[6]

Valentine hammered her point in a feature that profiled singer-songwriter Joan Armatrading and soul singer Linda Lewis: 'The number of women working in British music is pitifully small. You can count them on one hand. Why? In America the field is vast. Easily equivalent to the number of important male artists. [Bonnie] Raitt, [Maria] Muldaur, [Emmylou] Harris, [Linda] Ronstadt, [Janis] Ian, [Dory] Previn, [Laura] Nyro, [Patti] Smith, [Dolly] Parton, [Tammy] Wynette, [Helen] Reddy, [Rita] Coolidge, [Carly] Simon, [Carole] King, [Joni] Mitchell, [Judy] Collins, [Joan] Baez – latest additions the McGarrigles and Scarlet Rivera. Here, the story is depressingly reversed and the numbers of girls pushing out for individual recognition is limited to a few survivors.'[7]

Beyond these home truths, *Street Life* sought to steer musicians away from interview staples and towards their personal interests. 'I spent a civilised morning discussing pop art with Bryan Ferry at his palatial London residence, complete with maid service,' recalled Nigel Fountain. 'Bryan had been taught by [painter] Richard Hamilton, and maintained a keen interest in contemporary developments in art. The piece was printed with faux-Hockney-style illustrations, and I was looking forward to approaching Jeff Beck to talk about hot-rodding.'[8]

Street Life can also claim to have been at punk's ground zero: it interviewed Malcolm McLaren in the early spring of 1976, when his charges the Sex Pistols were still finding their feet. 'Kids have a hankering to be part of a movement like the Teddy Boys of the fifities and the mods of the sixties,' McLaren declared. 'They want to be the same, to associate with a movement that's hard and tough and in the open.'[9]

Yet for all the prescience of its copy and excellence of its writers, *Street Life* failed to challenge the inkies. The last issue was produced in June 1976, just as music papers geared up for the movement McLaren had outlined. 'Who knows why *Street Life* didn't take?' mused Richard Williams. 'Maybe people in this country who wanted to read that kind of thing were already getting what they wanted from *Rolling Stone*.'

* * *

Two months after the first issue of *Street Life* hit the racks, a more enduring specialist title appeared. *Black Echoes*, which is online these days and returned to physical publishing as a monthly in 2020, capitalized on a growing British interest in blues, disco, soul and reggae: a fast-moving scene with fresh artists, independent labels, promoters and venues. Co-founders John Thomson and Alan Walsh were White; as were, initially, *Black Echoes*' contributors. These included Robin Katz, an American who had written for *Disc* and *Sounds*, toured with Bruce Springsteen for *Street Life* and contributed a weekly page to *Record Mirror* about the Jackson 5, featuring news, contests, and poems and artwork by fans. Katz used the pseudonym Tamara Jermott for some of her submissions, which included reviews of the Fatback Band and interviews with Black Americans Gladys Knight and Gloria Jones, the latter popular with Northern Soul fans and married to Marc Bolan.

Echoes, as the magazine eventually became known, also benefited from Roger St Pierre, who had soldiered alone covering soul at *NME*, and from idiosyncratic copy credited to 'Penny Reel'. This – the title of an early ska hit – masked the identity of a writer who was neither Black nor a woman, Peter Simons. Having written about reggae for *International Times*, he shifted to *Let It Rock*, where his voice

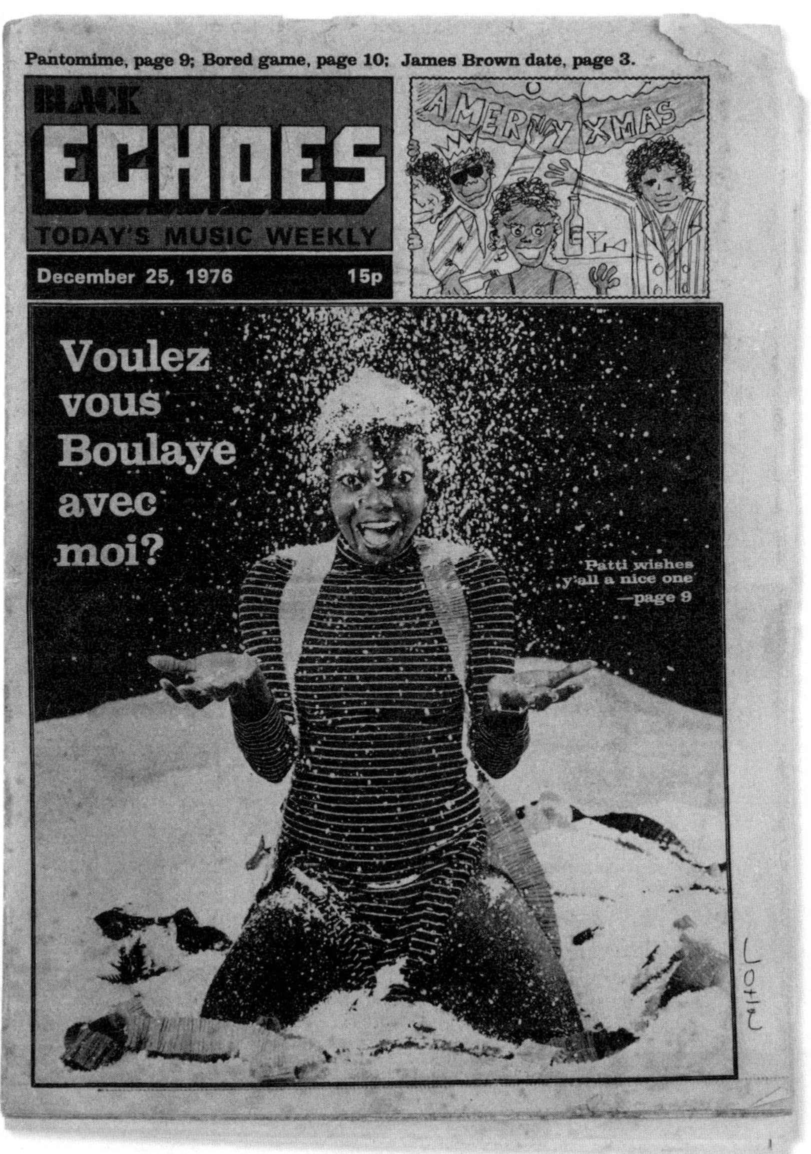
Pantomime, page 9; Bored game, page 10; James Brown date, page 3.
BLACK ECHOES
TODAY'S MUSIC WEEKLY
December 25, 1976
15p
A MERRY XMAS
Voulez vous Boulaye avec moi?
'Patti wishes y'all a nice one'
—page 9

Black Echoes, 25 December 1976

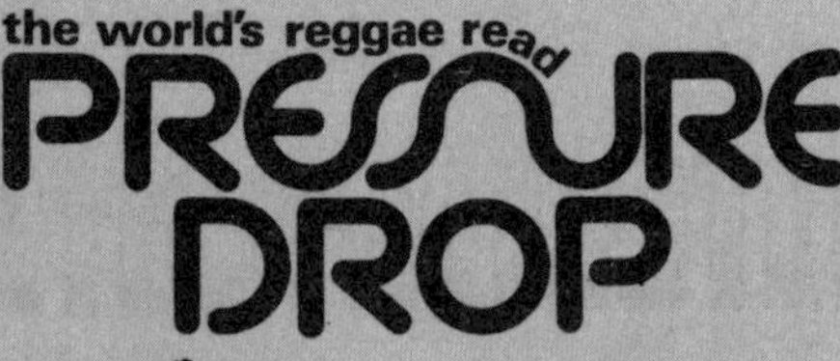

40p

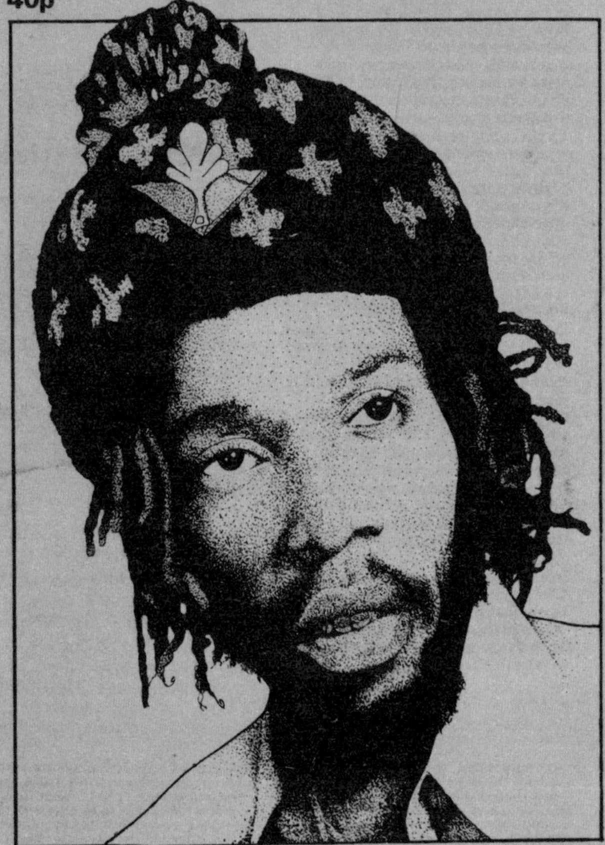

BIG YOUTH

Studio One • Glen Brown • Starlite listing • and more

Pressure Drop, 1977

drew on an upbringing in working-class London neighbourhoods in the 1950s and '60s. His reputation was boosted by participation in *Pressure Drop*, the reggae fanzine launched in autumn 1975. Its founder Nick Kimberley – who worked at London's leading alternative bookshop, Compendium, and had been at its 1960s forerunner Indica – edited the short-lived radical poetry magazine *Big Venus* and was *Time Out*'s reggae correspondent.

Pressure Drop debuted with Toots and the Maytals on its cover and, inside, histories of Tapper Zukie, Delroy Wilson and Niney the Observer. 'Full of deeply researched material about backstory and record releases and labels and context, and very engagingly written, the abiding tone is a trust in its own seriousness,' concluded music press expert Mark Sinker. 'There's no melodrama, no hyped-up justification – it absolutely believed in the self-motivated curiosity of its readers. And it was breakthrough-important because of this diligent care. The music was beginning to be covered in the weeklies, yes, but there was a tart editorial note: "Superficial knowledge has been allowed to pose as authoritative."'[10]

Contributor Chris Lane, who had written for *Blues & Soul* and *Black Music*, notes that the first issue contained an uncredited article: 'It turned out to have been [by] Carl Gayle, but there was nothing on it because they found it in an office somewhere.' Lane himself had considerable experience and contacts, having interviewed Lee 'Scratch' Perry for *Blues & Soul* in Jamaica, where he made long-lasting connections with producers Bunny Lee and King Tubby, singer Keith Hudson and Bob Marley and the Wailers, whose recording sessions he attended.

Pressure Drop was well received: the second issue, featuring a cover portrait of Big Youth, appeared among a selection of 'little magazines' in a *Harper's & Queen* survey by style guru Peter York. A planned third edition would have focused on a year in which they agreed reggae had reached a pinnacle of excellence. 'We were going to write it all as though it was 1972: "Look at this great record from Glen Brown, Merry Up. It's like nothing you've ever heard before,"' said Lane. 'Of course, we never got round to it.'[11] Diverted by a publishing contract for a book about reggae, they went their separate ways, with Lane becoming a producer, engineer and record label owner.

Reel's *Black Echoes* news and reviews column was mandatory reading for reggae fans. And he took a lead from Gayle by peppering his text with patois; as historian Paul Gilroy noted, Reel and Gayle's 'writing in the poetic registers of Jamaican speech that were being refined and polished by the Sound System toasters'[12] was followed by Black writers such as Trinidad's Sebastian Clarke (now Amon Saba Saakana) and St Kitts-born Imruh Ceasar (also Imruh Bakara) contributing to *Black Echoes* and *Time Out*.

Inevitably, it was the White Reel who crossed over to *NME*. And his first piece, about Junior Byles, set the tone: 'In a previous incarnation, manifest as a dread, dread one-eye man, Junior Byles urged all *sufferers*, youth and rasta bretheren [*sic*] to overwhelm Babylon the wicked and slaughter its iniquitous disciples. More recently, his resentment has been self-directed; his music, drained of vanity, an anguish; his personal life, a bleak confusion.'[13]

* * *

As *NME*'s reggae correspondent, Penny Reel introduced readers to Dr Alimantado, the Mighty Diamonds and the Twinkle Brothers. But these did not steer the ship away from rock made by White men. A spring 1976 issue containing an interview with Toots Hibbert also featured a live review by Neil Spencer signalling the future of pop and the press. Its heading: 'Don't look over your shoulder but the Sex Pistols are coming.'

Spencer had been alerted to the band by fellow *NME* writer Kate Phillips and her partner, deputy editor Tony Tyler, who encountered the young punks at an end-of-term party at London's Queen Elizabeth College. 'The Sex Pistols were huddled against a far wall of the dance floor,' Phillips wrote. 'They are all about twelve years old. Or maybe about nineteen, but you could be fooled. They're going to be the Next Big Thing. Or maybe the Next Big Thing After That.'[14]

Spencer reviewed a Pistols show at London's Marquee in February 1976. 'When we arrived,' he recalled, 'the doorman said, "You'd better get in there quick: they're busting the place up." I opened the door and a chair sailed across the room and crash-landed. There were only about twenty people there, but it was immediately obvious that something fantastic was going on.'

Enlivened by a Mick Rock closeup of the spiky-haired Johnny Rotten, Spencer's piece sat awkwardly in an issue that featured reverential treatment of cover star Patti Smith by US correspondent Lisa Robinson, and features on post-Peter Gabriel Genesis, jazz label ECM's founder Manfred Eicher and fast-fading pop star David Cassidy. Spencer's review ended with the prescient words of guitarist Steve Jones: 'We're not into music. We're into chaos.'[15]

Punk was nurtured and mediated in the pages of the music press until the national media took over towards the end of 1976. This was dictated in part by the geography of Britain, where the five weekly papers were able to bang the drum. In America, punk was to remain a marginal, bicoastal movement for another decade – even though the genre's name had been adopted by a colourful and chaotic US magazine that debuted in January 1976, nearly a year before the form was recognizable to the UK masses.

Punk was founded by friends John Holmstrom, Ged Dunn and 'Legs' McNeil. Having moved from Connecticut to Manhattan, they had become fans of groups such as the Ramones, Blondie and Richard Hell and the Voidoids emerging from the tight-knit scene around the Bowery club CBGB. Holmstrom wanted to name the publication after an unreleased New York Dolls track, 'Teenage News'. 'I was like, "That's stupid, John!"' protested McNeil. 'Why don't we call it *Punk*!?'[16]

Holmstrom had studied at New York's School of Visual Arts under *Mad* magazine founder Harvey Kurtzman and cartoonist Will Eisner, creator of the comic series *The Spirit*. *Punk*'s editorial flavour was conveyed by his horror magazine masthead and cartoonish portraits that adorned covers of the fifteen issues the trio produced over the next few years. Holmstrom also insisted on hand-lettering all the text and, with McNeil, posted flyers that declared '*Punk* is coming!' 'We thought, here comes another shitty group with an even shittier name,' remembered Debbie Harry, 'but when we went out to the newsstand one day, there was this new comic rock mag that everyone loved immediately.'

Into this goofy atmosphere were thrust photographers Frances Pelzman and Roberta Bayley, whose work defined the east coast phenomenon, and Mary Harron, a Canadian who, while studying at

Britain's Oxford University, had dated future prime minister Tony Blair. 'I was living in New York after leaving college, working as a cook in this crazy film commune in exchange for room and board,' said Harron, later director of the movie *American Psycho*. 'I met Legs there and told him I wanted to be a writer. I thought [*Punk*] was a brilliant title but had no idea what type of magazine it was going to be. Legs and John dragged me to CBGB to see the Ramones. I'd never heard of them, but then neither had the rest of the world. That night we met Lou Reed, who I *had* heard of, and they asked me to interview the Ramones.'[17]

In the first issue – the cover of which featured Holmstrom's depiction of a leather-jacketed Reed – Harron wrote: 'This is an outsider's view. I just want to make that clear. I knew that I was an outsider from the moment I walked into CBGBs because I kept falling over my high-heeled boots. People who knew were wearing sneakers. One of the *Punk* magazine editors explained: "We don't believe in love or any of that shit. We believe in making money and getting drunk."'[18]

Meanwhile, the editorial made clear *Punk*'s opposition to the other new sound of the era: 'Kill yourself. Jump off a fuckin' cliff. Drive nails into your head. Become a robot and join the staff of Disneyland. OD. Anything. Just don't listen to disco shit. I've seen that canned crap take real live people and turn them into dogs! And vice versa. The epitome of all that's wrong with western civilisation is disco. Edducate [*sic*] yourself. Get into it. Read *Punk*.'[19]

This stance earned 2,500 subscriptions and 20,000 sales of each issue. 'It was distributed at 7-Elevens, so we were actually out there,' said McNeil. 'People were just so shocked when they saw it. The 7-Elevens didn't know whether to sell it as a comic book or a rock 'n' roll magazine. And if we kept our production schedule, we actually made lots of money, instead of having all the fun in the world.'[20] Holmstrom also struck upon a solution to filling the letters pages: 'John just put in everything that came in, including a letter from his mother complaining about his dad, one from the gas company, a jealous letter from a girlfriend, a rejection from a distributor and an offer of life insurance,' recalled Harron. 'I thought that was very punk.'

The magazine mapped out the area occupied by the still-forming movement. 'The key word – to me, anyway – in the punk definition was, "A beginner, an inexperienced hand,"' wrote Holmstrom. 'Any kid can pick up a guitar and become a rock 'n' roll star, despite or because of his lack of ability, talent, intelligence, limitations and/or potential, and usually does so out of frustration, hostility, a lot of nerve and a need for ego fulfillment ... It takes a lot of sophistication – or better, none at all – to appreciate punk rock at its best – or worst. (Not much difference.) Punk has become a catchword for a lot of critics to describe N.Y. underground rock, most of which is not punk rock.'[21]

Lester Bangs moved to New York in the mid-1970s and made a natural move from the knockabout *Creem* to the shambolic *Punk*: 'He showed up in our office,' Holmstrom recalled. 'I think he was probably doing speed and drinking, and sat down and banged something out on the typewriter. It was this rambling, crazy thing that was unpublishable. I think I edited it and ended up with about four usable sentences.'[22]

The so-called '*Punk* Dump' office at 10th Avenue and 30th Street was, recalled Harron, 'a fun place to hang out: it had a loose, underground feel. Fran Pelzman and I used to deposit Legs on the doorstep when he got too drunk to make it home alone. For a while, John Holmstrom put Roberta Bayley and I on salary, literally $25 a week, and we would hang out and do the filing, but then John couldn't pay us any more.'

Punk, wrote Debbie Harry, 'was always funny, very hip, and had lots of good pictures ... It was the most interesting magazine in the world when it came out. It was very cool to be in it, too.'

* * *

Back in the UK in the spring of 1976, Mary Harron interviewed the Sex Pistols for *Punk*. But in the months that her write-up took to appear, the group and those who followed in their wake gained ground in the inkies. *NME* should have been the genre's natural constituency: former contributor Chrissie Hynde was part of Malcolm McLaren and Vivienne Westwood's inner circle, and her erstwhile paramour Nick Kent had briefly rehearsed with the nascent Pistols the previous summer. But apart from sporadic mentions, the paper that most mirrored the Pistols' worldview – note 'I use the *NME*!' in their clarion call 'Anarchy in the UK' – ignored punk's progress for months.

This was surprising, given that it provided a forum for reggae – a favourite of scene leaders like Johnny Rotten and Paul Simonon – and bemoaned the dominance of dinosaur rockers. One cover story posited that, at thirty, many acts were past their sell-by date and asked, 'Is rock 'n' roll an old man's game?'[23] A year earlier, in the spring of 1975, Mick Farren had complained: 'There are times when it really appears that over the last ten years we have produced a new strain of executive fat cat who is just as conservative as the old Tin Pan Alley breed who did their best to stop the flood of creativity during the early sixties. What once were maverick outfits have turned into big money operations with the big money reluctance to trust their technology and finance to a bunch of raw, ignorant punks from out of nowhere.'[24]

Farren stuck to his guns in 1976, bemoaning White rock's absorption into 'the turgid masterstream of traditional establishment showbiz', comparing Mick Jagger to sixty-year-old Hollywood celebrity Zsa Zsa Gabor and likening promoter Harvey Goldsmith to the old-school entertainment entrepreneur Lew Grade. Headed 'The Titanic sails at dawn', Farren's piece took its cue from mega-gigs by the Rolling Stones and the Who: 'Letter after letter repeats the same thing. You all seem to have had it with the Who, and Liz Taylor, Rod and the Queen, Jagger and Princess Margaret, paying three quid to be bent, mutilated, crushed or seated behind a pillar or a PA stack, all in the name of modern seventies-style super rock ... The time seems to be right for original thinking and new inventive concepts, not only in the music but in the way that it is staged and promoted. It may be difficult in the current economic climate, and it may be a question of taking rock back to street level and starting all over again ... Putting the Beatles back together isn't going to be the salvation of rock and roll. Four kids playing to their contemporaries in a dirty cellar club might.'[25]

As Farren later acknowledged, he was pushing at an open door. 'Punk was already well established among the pogo cognoscenti long before I put pen to paper,' he wrote in his memoir *Give the*

Anarchist a Cigarette. 'If the *NME* rant contributed anything, it was to spread the ripples a little wider.'[26]

But Farren's diatribe made no direct mention of punk or the Pistols. *NME*'s reticence also arose from Nick Kent's antipathy to the Pistols' clique after the debacle at Sex when he attacked Hynde, a year or so previously. This was compounded by a reprisal from then-group follower Sid Vicious, who whipped Kent with a bicycle chain at a Pistols gig the night before Farren's Titanic piece appeared.

'A lot of people at *NME* didn't like punk,' Chris Salewicz admitted. 'There was an attitude that only people who were articulate and literate were intelligent.' *Sounds* and *Melody Maker*, however, championed the growing cult. Malcolm McLaren found his charges a rehearsal space via the *Maker*'s classifieds, and posted an ad for a second guitarist when there were concerns about Steve Jones's competence (such was his speedy progress that none was required). Caroline Coon's reaction to the band was, she said, 'Immediate recognition: seeing these nineteen-year-olds deconstruct pub rock and take rock 'n' roll back to its basics, but with a genuine anger. Standing at the back – as you do, as a journalist – you could see the pub audience turn their noses up but the kids in the crowd knew what was going on. I couldn't go to a gig at that point without the manager of the band wetting his knickers. So, afterwards, Malcolm McLaren introduced himself and I thought, "Interesting." At the next gig, Bernie Rhodes came up and said, "I've got a band too," because the Clash were rehearsing. And within about three weeks I'd seen the Damned and pretty much knew what was going to happen.

'I went into *Melody Maker*'s next editorial meeting and said, "I want to do a story on what's happening on the streets. There's this band called the Sex Pistols who are part of a new movement." All I got was sneer, sneer, sneer from Mick Watts, Allan Jones, all of them. Had I been male, they would have said, "Really? Okay, go and find out more." All the journalists that ran the music scene at that time were like men in aspic. They had spent years socializing with the people they'd championed, so they'd lost journalistic distance.'

But it was Allan Jones, not Coon, who filed *Melody Maker*'s first Pistols live review: 'The novelty of this retarded spectacle was soon erased by their tiresome repetition of punk clichés. They do as much for music as World War Two did for the cause of peace. I hope we shall hear from them no more.'[27] 'Looking back,' he confessed twenty-five years later, 'I'd been infected by a complacent, patrician attitude about the young punks: "It'll all blow over; we'll be fine."'

The first to achieve substantial coverage of the Pistols and punk was John Ingham, a sharp-witted Australian who had grown up in North America and styled his first name with the punk-like misspelling 'Jonh'. Having studied under Robert Christgau at the California Institute of the Arts and been published in *Creem*, *Phonograph Recorder*, *Rolling Stone* and *Who Put the Bomp*, Ingham arrived in Britain to attend film school. Alert to trends and street style, he contributed to *NME* before joining *Sounds* in the summer of 1975.

The following spring he became aware of the Pistols and was encouraged by Alan Lewis, who had graduated from *Black Music* to become editor of *Sounds*. 'He was constantly looking for angles that the other papers were ignoring,' Ingham recalled. 'One of the writers was Geoff Barton, who was really into metal and hard rock, so *Sounds* was giving big coverage to Deep Purple, Kiss and Budgie when they were largely ignored in the other papers. Both *MM* and *NME* had already dismissed the Sex Pistols – so, when I talked to him after seeing them for the first time, he made me interview them long before I would normally have done. I was telling him about the gig and he was looking more and more amused. I couldn't figure out why, and when he said to do a story I protested that it was much too soon ... He replied, "How long have you been talking about them?" Turned out I'd been going on for about ten minutes.'[28]

Lewis was displaying the qualities that had led him from *Melody Maker*'s subs desk and would propel his innovations over the ensuing decades. He bolstered *Sounds* with two women: Barbara Charone, a Chicagoan who had cut her teeth at *NME* and freelanced for *Rolling Stone*, and Vivien Goldman, a Londoner who had worked as a publicist at Island, where she helped turn Bob Marley and the Wailers into stars. 'Dub was my sound because of postcolonial movements,' said Goldman, the daughter of German Jewish refugees. 'I grew up in it. I bathed in it. I breathed it. So why shouldn't it be mine?'[29] At *Sounds*, Goldman's byline became associated with the genre, to the dismay of young Black contributor Paul Gilroy: 'My unsuccessful attempt at begging for work from Vivien Goldman at *Sounds* in the mid-seventies taught me ... how to cope with being told, oh so very politely, to go away and fuck myself. That memorable experience confirmed an early lesson in how easily many white self-appointed custodians of these musical archives could become threatened and defensive when faced even with polite requests to be minimally accountable for the way they used the music and its increasingly audible rebel ontologies.'[30]

Goldman's interests contrasted with Charone's focus on headline acts the Stones, the Eagles, the Faces, Genesis and the Who. 'This was immediately pre-punk,' Goldman observed. 'People like Barbara Charone were firmly of the old school: unreconstructed. She worshipped those people, elevated them as gods.'[31]

However, Charone had an essential asset: access. Her first assignment for *Sounds* was a piece on the Stones in New York, for which she interviewed Keith Richards and Mick Taylor. 'I was crushed that it wasn't Mick Jagger,' she confessed, 'but that was the best thing that could have happened because I wrote, "When Keith walked into the room, rock 'n' roll walked into the room." That led to me getting my foot in the door with the Stones and not having that door shut, ever.'[32] Charone published the first biography of Richards, in 1982.

Meanwhile, *Sounds*' ranks had also been swelled by Giovanni Dadomo, whose angular presence and fascination for such acts as the Stooges and their pharmaceutical pursuits marked him out as a Nick Kent in the making. Dadomo's lively copy and interest in grass-roots music coincided with those of Goldman and Ingham, whose small live review of the Pistols in an April 1976 issue of *Sounds* was followed by a six-page feature two weeks later. This noted Malcolm McLaren's desire for 'a rumbling, anarchic, noisy, energetic rock scene, the likes of which haven't been seen in this country since the mid-1960s'.[33]

A couple of weeks later *NME* belatedly broke its omerta, printing a letter from future Pet Shop Boy Neil Tennant about a fight at a Pistols gig as a news story, complete with a photograph of McLaren and the group duking it out with audience members. Describing Johnny Rotten as 'a real live dementoid', Tennant – then an editor at the UK branch of Marvel Comics – highlighted the front man: 'While the reaction of the rest of the band is a little confused, Mr Rotten joins in the fight and has a few kicks at the victim. He cackles, he leers, the amps are turned up. He's pleased. The Pistols finish another unforgettable act.'[34]

Caroline Coon opened a door for punk at *Melody Maker* with a review of Eddie and the Hot Rods. Though not strictly aligned with the movement, they were at least high energy. However, when Coon and Mary Harron visited the Hot Rods backstage, they were 'literally pounced on by the band. They physically attacked us and ripped our clothes off. We were standing there with our notebooks in our hands and our T-shirts round our waists. We just got our quotes and walked off'. Equally offensively, the Stranglers B-side 'London Lady' accused Coon of being stupid and committing the ultimate female crime: talking too much. That this behaviour was not censured speaks volumes about the period. It also explains why female journalists bonded. 'Me and Caroline really hit it off,' said Vivien Goldman. 'There wasn't a sisterhood of us women writers as such, but she made me aware of some of the pitfalls that could occur.'

Coon finally documented the Pistols in the summer of 1976, in a story illustrated with a photograph from the fight witnessed by Neil Tennant: 'It's no coincidence that the week the Stones were at Earls Court, the Sex Pistols were playing to their ever-increasing following at London's 100 Club. The Pistols are the personification of the emerging British punk rock scene, a positive reaction to the complex equipment, technological sophistication and jaded alienation which has formed a barrier between fans and stars.'[35]

After that, punk was off to the races, albeit with a stumble or two. At *Melody Maker*, Allan Jones filed a diatribe that he claims was 'mucked about and came out anti-punk. The connection I was trying to make was to people like [British singer-songwriter] Kevin Coyne but it was a huge stitch-up'. Meanwhile, Michael Watts produced a negative thinkpiece headed 'So shock me punks'. And in an *NME* review of the Clash, Charles Shaar Murray sniffed: 'They are the kind of garage band who should be speedily returned to their garage, preferably with the motor running, which would undoubtedly be more of a loss to their friends and family than to either rock or roll.'[36]

* * *

'Attention hip young gunslingers. The *NME* has a vacancy for a STAFF WRITER. Previous experience in either journalism or the music business is not essential, but a good knowledge of rock and enthusiasm are, together with the ability to write lively and incisive prose. All applications must be accompanied by a sample 5–600-word review of any album of the applicant's choice.' This job ad, written by Charles Shaar Murray, prompted hundreds of applications. Among them were Neil Tennant and future novelists Jonathan Coe, then a teenage schoolboy, and Sebastian Faulks, then a teacher.

Too in awe of *NME*'s reputation to apply was author Nick Hornby, then studying at Cambridge. 'There was a time in British music writing where the journalists were bigger than the artists themselves,' he observed. 'The idea of walking into this office at the age of nineteen and having to deal with these people ... I thought, "Well, I'm not even going to try."'[37] Jon Savage, a Pistols fan who was to launch a punk fanzine a few months later, said: 'I always found it funny Hornby et al would have killed to work in the music press in the late seventies but they weren't good enough, or they refused to enter – in any way, small or great – into the maelstrom. Because that's what it was to me, at least: a risk.'

Among braver hopefuls were student Ian Cranna, bookshop assistant Paul Morley and graduate Paul Du Noyer, all of whom would ultimately make names for themselves in the music press. 'I sent in a review of Kilburn and the High Roads' album *Handsome* written in biro,' said Du Noyer. 'Tony Tyler said that, even if I didn't get the staff job, they would like me as a contributor, so I started freelancing and then went on staff in 1980. Initially, I got the stories no one else wanted – [pub rock survivor] Bram Tchaikovsky live in Sweden.'[38]

The triumphant applicants were the seventeen-year-old Julie Burchill and twenty-three-year-old Tony Parsons. But Burchill's initial response to Murray's text was repulsion: 'I thought, "Ewww, macho cowboy imagery. They must be really sexually inadequate up there,"' notes her memoir *I Knew I Was Right*. 'Then I thought,

I can do that. I am singularly thin and pale and profoundly, lividly young. My youth stands out on me like welts, stinging, and I wear my zits like medals. I'm young, young, young, and I'm going to milk the cash cow for all it's, all I'm, worth.'[39]

Burchill reviewed Patti Smith's *Horses* – 'on bad school notepaper, torn and jagged, just like me, a word or two deliberately misspelled' – while Parsons sent his recently published novel *The Kids*. 'I don't know why it never occurred to me earlier that I could write for *NME*,' he said. 'Yet I had written a novel, got an agent and a publisher. It wasn't a good book – juvenilia really. It's amazing to me that I did all that but it never crossed my mind to review Dr Feelgood in Canvey Island. I'd already seen a lot of the bands I knew they'd want covered.

'It wasn't really a job interview, more an audition. You had to look right. That's why the standard of writing on the paper went down, because it was more about, "What do these kids look like?" They were impressed because I was really young to have had a novel out, even if it was crap. At the second interview, Nick Logan said,

"You've got one of the jobs. The other will go to either a girl from Bristol or a boy from Manchester."'[40] The latter was Paul Morley, who was instead tasked with reporting on Manchester's punk scene.

Burchill grew to like Charles Shaar Murray and Mick Farren – 'They were genuinely nice fellows' – but was less impressed with the rest of the staff, starting at the top. Nick Logan, she said, 'God help him, probably smelled like me: skinny, rattled, scum-surfing.'

She and Parsons promptly made their mark. 'They can write, they are a team and they are totally uncontrollable,' noted Peter York. 'Julie said Bryan Ferry was a worthless person – think of it, a worthless person. I hadn't heard that kind of language in years – because of the social climbing and because he'd deserted the kids who made him. Bowie was "a toothless piece of old burnt meat ... a dead man's brain floundering around the stage" because he'd gone esoteric.'[41]

The duo's reputation was burnished by tales of Burchill pulling a switchblade during an interview with former Hawkwind singer Robert Calvert and Parsons spiking Iggy Pop's drink with laxative just before a concert. *NME*'s editorial team became increasingly wary, particularly those who had been considered *enfants terribles* just a few years previously. 'They wanted to kick over the statues, which is a healthy impulse,' observed Murray. 'I was a bit mortified to find that I'd become a statue. For fuck's sake, Parsons was only four years younger than me.'

But the cultural divide was wide. 'They did tend to call each other "man", which grates if you're a girlie,' wrote Burchill. 'And one's working class credentials made them a little chippy. "Stop flexing your roots, man!" one of them said to me when I cracked open a tasty tin of Tizer.'[42] 'We were told off for fighting in the office and for taking drugs,' confirmed Parsons. 'They were quite frightened, because it was a different pace – speed, mostly. Smoking dope wasn't considered drugs there. Bob Marley did it, so it must be alright.'

The legend was capped by the couple's 'kinderbunker': a merging of their desks, which Burchill claims were decorated with door jambs, barbed wire, broken glass and a noose. 'I don't remember any barbed wire,' Logan rebutted. 'They took a little space in the middle of the office, which no-one else wanted. It had little privacy, and was basically just a walkthrough, so they put up an incongruous curtain of plastic strips, like you'd find in shops' back doorways ... There were certain people who wouldn't walk through it: probably those who were less impressed by them. I ran the risk.'

A fling between Burchill and Farren brought matters to a crescendo. 'Mickey seemed both dangerous and attractive because he appeared genuinely to despair in life while never, ever whining about it,' wrote Burchill. 'I really, really admired the way he abused his big old burned-out body, and I wanted to be the same. When somebody told me that, as well as being a radical hero, he was a sexual sadist, there was no stopping me.'[43] One Monday morning, Chris Salewicz dropped into the room where staff reviewed records: 'Farren had blood pouring from his mouth. Parsons had come and whacked him a few times.'

'I must have carpeted Tony for hitting Mick Farren,' said Logan, 'but I can't remember the details. There was a lot of stuff going on. It was miserable and not just about Julie and Tony. We were all unhappy.'

The root of this despondency was publisher IPC's relocating of *NME*'s offices to King's Reach Tower, a brutalist block in south London. Freedoms enjoyed at the previous Covent Garden premises were curtailed. Alongside *Horse and Hounds* and *Titbits*, and in full view of the executives who controlled their wages, the *NME* renegades were expected to knuckle down. This obliged Logan, long the buffer between staff and management, to field objections to profanity, and sex and drug references, while allowing the writers to express themselves – even if, as it often did, this antagonized record label advertisers.

'It was a disaster waiting to happen, trying to protect the likes of Charlie, Tony, Julie and Mick from the suits,' said Logan. 'I was under incredible pressure. In retrospect it was a mistake to put so much distance between the two. I should have made everyone aware: "These are the people you work for. We can make it work within this."' Ian MacDonald described the offices as 'an open-plan nightmare' while Logan suffered a nervous breakdown and had to take a six-week absence: 'I couldn't cope any more. IPC was kicking my arse over petty stuff while the paper was earning them millions because it cost nothing to put out.'

On his return, Logan negotiated a way out. New offices were found in Soho's former Swinging London epicentre Carnaby Street, and *NME* began to benefit from a music sales boom in the immediate post-punk period.

* * *

Mancunian teenager Steven Morrissey plagued the music papers with letters that rarely missed an opportunity to pay tribute to his heroes, the then-unfashionable New York Dolls. One such missive accused American hard rockers Aerosmith of being 'as original as a bar of soap' and offering as much to seventies rock as the elderly *Coronation Street* soap opera character Ena Sharples. 'Thanks but no thanks Aerosmith,' wrote the future Smiths leader to *Melody Maker*. 'I'll stick with the New York Dolls for my rock 'n' thrills.'[44]

As punk came to the fore, Morrissey reported from the frontlines: 'I pen this epistle after witnessing the infamous Sex Pistols in concert at the Manchester Lesser Free Trade Hall. The bumptious Pistols in jumble sale attire had those few that attended dancing in the aisles despite their discordant music and barely audible lyrics ... The Sex Pistols are very New York and it's nice to see that the British have produced a band capable of producing atmosphere created by the New York Dolls and their many imitators, even though it may be too late. I'd love to see the Pistols make it. Maybe they will be able to afford some clothes which don't look as though they've been slept in.'[45]

Music press correspondence was also the genesis of the pro-diversity group Rock Against Racism. In the summer of 1976, not long after the Pistols played the Lesser Free Trade Hall, Eric Clapton – having traded heroin for alcohol – interrupted a concert at the Birmingham Odeon to slur his support for politician Enoch Powell. In 1968, Powell had condemned the Race Relations Act, which made illegal the barring of people of colour from housing or employment on grounds of ethnicity. At a venue opposite the Odeon, he had given a speech predicting 'rivers of blood' flowing from race wars sparked by immigration. Eight years later, the hard right movement the National Front had taken up the cudgels on Powell's behalf and so had Clapton. 'Stop Britain from becoming a black colony,' exclaimed the man whose career relied on emulating music made by African Americans and who had topped the US chart with a version of Bob Marley's 'I Shot the Sheriff'. 'Get the foreigners out,' he ranted. 'Get the wogs out. Get the coons out. Keep Britain white.'

A couple of weeks later, the letters pages of *NME*, *Melody Maker* and *Sounds* featured a response from activists including Roger Huddle and photographer Red Saunders: 'What's going on Eric? You've got a touch of brain damage. Own up: half your music is black. You're rock music's biggest colonialist. You're a good musician but where would you be without the blues and R&B? You've got to fight the racist poison, otherwise you degenerate into the sewer with the rats and all the money men who ripped off rock culture with their chequebooks and plastic crap. We want to organize a rank-and-file movement against the racist poison in rock music – we urge support – all those interested please write to ROCK AGAINST

RACISM, Box M, 8 Cotton Gardens, London E2 8DN. PS: Who shot the sheriff, Eric? It sure as hell wasn't you.'[46]

'This was when David Bowie was prattling on about Adolf Hitler being the "first superstar" and Rod Stewart deciding Britain had become too overcrowded for him,' said Saunders. 'It made me sick with disappointment, then fucking pissed off. I was an activist on the left and [had] been involved in Vietnam solidarity and street demonstrations. [The letter to the music press] was a letter of anger.'[47]

At least one of the weeklies ran a lame excuse from Clapton: 'I'd had a few [drinks] before I went on and one foreigner had pinched my missus's bum ... I think Enoch is the only politician mad enough to run this country.'[48] Meanwhile, as Huddle wrote, 'We received hundreds of replies. The founders of Rock Against Racism were all soul fans, but what really propelled it into what became a mass movement was the explosion of punk. Our slogans were "Reggae, soul, rock 'n' roll, jazz, funk, punk – our music" and "NF = No Fun".'[49]

The establishment of the Anti-Nazi League in 1977 provided Rock Against Racism with a political context and helped attract huge crowds to anti-racist carnivals: 85,000 in London's Victoria Park to listen to the Clash, the Tom Robinson Band and Misty in Roots, 25,000 in Manchester's Alexandra Park (the Buzzcocks and Steel Pulse) and 100,000 in London's Brockwell Park (Elvis Costello and the Attractions and Aswad). Attendees were mobilized by the fanzine *Temporary Hoarding*, summarized by musician-turned-author Daniel Rachel as 'a mixture of eye-catching graphics influenced by the punk do-it-yourself cut-and-paste style and prewar montage techniques, addressing not only the threat of the National Front but also broader issues such as British troops in Northern Ireland and international concerns in Zimbabwe and South Africa'.[50]

Temporary Hoarding was aligned with other left-wing, progressive agitprop publications of the period such as *The Leveller*, which was established as a monthly in 1976 and, in the main, published investigative and campaigning articles; it also targeted the music industry with exposés on its rampant sexism. Eye-catching front covers included a fluoro-pink backdrop for featured interviewee Poly Styrene (pl. 10), while *Temporary Hoarding*, folded to A4 or A3, opened out into posters for readers to hang on their walls.

Both titles benefited from technological developments: offset litho had replaced letterpress as the dominant publishing method, and was relatively cheap to produce at a professional level. This was 'as liberating to designers as Apple Macs were to be a decade later', according to photographer Syd Shelton, who was part of the *Temporary Hoarding* collective including Ruth Gregory and Carol Tulloch. Gregory and Shelton had gravitated to Rock Against Racism via the Socialist Workers Party print shop, where the zine was produced alongside badges and posters. 'Ruth was one of the great graphic designers,' said Huddle. 'She understood the punk sensibility. Her fastidiousness and patience [was applied] to cut little dots from a Letraset sheet and build up layers without technology; it was all hand-cut.'[51]

'Putting together *Temporary Hoarding* almost always involved at least one all-night session,' said Shelton, 'sometimes with people dropping into the studio with a few beers or to put their two bobs' worth into the artwork.'[52] The first issue benefited from David King's Rock Against Racism logo: a red, five-pointed star encircled in black. The cover text declared: 'We want rebel music, street music. Music breaks down people's fear of one another. Crisis music. Now music. Music that knows who the real enemy is. Rock against racism. Love music. Hate racism.'[53]

'It gave me a platform to write about feminist ideas to an audience who were probably not familiar with them,' said Lucy Whitman, who – having produced her own 'feminist, anti-racist, anti-fascist' 'zine *Jolt* – contributed as 'Lucy Toothpaste'. 'People would come along to the gigs because they wanted to hear Buzzcocks or the Ruts or whoever. They weren't necessarily committed anti-racists. That was why we had to do the paper, because we wanted to give them something to take home and read and think about. *Temporary Hoarding* reflected the energy of the gigs. It was educational agitprop.'[54]

'Some of the best contributions were the letters from supporters from all over the country and from other countries,' she said. 'These showed young people "thinking aloud" about the menace of racism and fascism and how best to challenge it in their everyday lives.'[55]

The co-option of punk by the record business was attacked by a contributor credited simply as 'Sharon': 'We are being exploited left, right and centre when we used to be SO AWARE! Got your Destroy T-shirt, Punk Rock Monthly and the rest of the shit they are throwing in your face? A lot of ordinary rock bands are changing their images, taking advantage of the fact that it is so easy to get a record contract. At the moment "New" Wave is the latest get rich kwick [*sic*] scheme. Every man and his dog is making money out of it and none of us seem to be trying to stop them. It can and has to be done. IF WE DON'T BUY THEY CAN'T SELL!!!'[56]

Temporary Hoarding's aim, said writer David Widgery, was 'to rescue the energy of Russian revolutionary art, surrealism and rock and roll from the galleries, the advertising agencies and the record companies and use them to change reality, as had always been intended. And have a party in the process'. Day-Glo T-shirts and 'Nazis are no fun' pin badges were modelled by teenagers, while one in-house ad offered a badge with the slogan 'Skateboards against Nazis'.

By issue four, the editors announced Rock Against Racism had organized 200 live events and sold 12,000 badges. 'The music press loved it,' said Rock Against Racism organizer John Dennis, who nonetheless regretted the fanzine's weak distribution: 'A lot of energy went into the process of making it and, by the time it came off the press, there was no energy left.'[57]

Still, Ruth Gregory believes *Temporary Hoarding* 'challenged the cultural status quo in music, writing and design. We did not see ourselves as some kind of artisan élite, but as part of a conversation'.[58] And it was published under circumstances not faced by run-of-the-mill punk zines: the White nationalist group Column 88 attempted an arson attack on the Socialist Workers Party premises that provided its mailing address.

Temporary Hoarding's revolutionary zeal attracted young Black writers Linton Kwesi Johnson and Paul Gilroy, still smarting from rejection at *Sounds*. 'I could publish things in *Temporary Hoarding* or whatever,' said Gilroy, 'in the space that they made much more readily at Rock Against Racism.'[59]

The fanzines that greeted punk revolved around replacing one mode of White rock with another. *Temporary Hoarding* was entirely different, as it demonstrated over fifteen issues between 1976 and 1981. Years later, Gilroy located the distinction, paraphrasing the Pistols' 'God Save the Queen': 'The insubordinate spirit of emergent punk-dom discovered common cause with the rising generation of young, Black people who had learned by a different route that they too had no future in England's pathological dreams of greatness restored.'[60]

11
'I didn't want to write anything *literary*'

Savage, Goldman and Suck at *Sounds* as Nick Logan Launches *Smash Hits*

'The "punk rock" movement of the early seventies was something of a damp squib,' wrote Nick Kent in a review of the Ramones' debut album. 'It never made any real indentation on the national rock front as upheld by the likes of *Cashbox* and *Billboard*. Now, some three years later, after the New York Dolls' pratfall, after the likes of Iggy and Jonathan Richman have been rejected for being the real rock visionaries they are, the coast may be clear for the new wave punks.'[1]

Disaffected music fan and bank clerk Mark Perry was impressed. He was also inspired by *Bam Balam*, a fanzine painstakingly researched by 1960s musicologist Brian Hogg. The music weeklies, said Hogg, 'saw the stuff made by the big groups ten years previously as juvenilia, particularly since people like the Kinks and the Who were still big in the seventies. Now we look upon it as the opposite. So *Bam Balam* was my way of bringing this stuff to the fore.'

A particular issue of Greg Shaw's *Who Put the Bomp*, dedicated to British Invasion bands of the 1960s, 'was a major inspiration', said Hogg, who used his archive of music papers to research releases, reviews and concerts. His sparse and meticulous writing marked out *Bam Balam* for critic Jon Savage, who likened it to 'haiku in its simplicity and elegance'.[2]

Mark Perry bought *Bam Balam* from the London record stall Rock On, which stocked new wave records and other media such as *Punk*. After witnessing the Ramones' London debut at the Roundhouse in July 1976, he asked a stall-holder if there were any other magazines covering the genre: 'He suggested I start one up myself; I think more as a joke than anything. I obviously took his idea seriously, because I went straight home and typed *Sniffin' Glue and Other Rock 'n' Roll Habits*.'[3]

Sniffin' Glue was the punk do-it-yourself ethos in full effect. The first issue's stapled pages of scrawled text were produced during Perry's lunch hour on the photocopier of the bank where he worked. Sold at gigs and by indie record retailers, it was snapped up by members of the media investing in punk. The editor, now known as 'Mark P', was invited to a Sex Pistols gig by Caroline Coon as he and contributor Danny Baker – who had forged connections by working in a specialist record shop – became faces on the rapidly expanding scene. Coon and Jonh Ingham, said Baker, 'were older and seemed more worldly-wise, very art school. They knew about anarchy. We didn't fucking know what anarchy was. I think they invested in us a lot more credibility than we had.'[4] The *Sniffin' Glue* attitude was summed up by another fanzine, *Sideburns*, which ran a diagram of three chords annotated with 'This is a chord – this is another – this is a third – now form a band'.

That challenge was taken up not only by musicians but also by a host of mainly male wannabe publishers. In Scotland, Lindsay Hutton had fallen under the spell of American garage rock and lionized Lester Bangs. He was also inspired by John Holmstrom's hand-rendered text for *Punk*, and adopted it for his 'zine *The Next Big Thing*, the first edition of which appeared within a couple of months of Mark P's publication. 'The staple in the corner of *Sniffin' Glue* heralded the age of folding and collating not being necessary anymore,' said Hutton, who continued to issue *The Next Big Thing* into the 21st century. 'Praise the lord and pass me that wee stapler! There was a pilot issue with Eddie and the Hot Rods on the cover in September 1976, and the first proper issue came out on 1 April 1977, the day [before] the Damned came to Stirling University.'[5]

In Sheffield, *Gun Rubber* was published by 'Ronny Clocks' – also known as Paul Bower, later a Labour Party activist. In Manchester, *City Fun* was founded by a group of young men but taken over by Cath Carroll and Liz Naylor, who brought front-line news from the city's vibrant music scene to 2,000 readers. Carroll later graduated to *NME*, while Naylor worked with alternative labels such as Blast First.

Jon Savage, then law student Jonathan Sage, was similarly motivated: 'I self-published a fanzine called *London's Outrage* in December 1976. It was very much stimulated by *Sniffin' Glue*, but then Mark [Perry] had been inspired by much the same sources, like *Who Put the Bomp* and *Bam Balam*. The whole fanzine idea, as Mark would freely admit, came from those two funny little magazines that wrote about rock history.'

Savage was an interesting study when viewed through the prism of punk. Born in central London, he attended top boarding school Rugby (setting of the Victorian novel *Tom Brown's Schooldays*) before studying classics at Cambridge University's Magdalene

College. Subsequently Savage undertook a law degree, but exposure to the rambunctious new genre persuaded him to alter the course of his life and repudiate his background: 'I had an urge to start writing, but didn't have a great urge to write something "literary" because of the kind of people I'd been educated with, who I realized I despised.' He sold copies of the first *London's Outrage* through record shop Rough Trade, prompting an invitation from art editor and writer Dave Fudger to join the staff of *Sounds*. 'My first task was to work pretty much all night with Vivien Goldman, Giovanni Dadomo and Dave on something called "Images of the new wave". That became the cover story, with a picture of Shane MacGowan rolling around the floor.' 'We stayed up all night taking speed,' remembered Goldman, 'and turning the magazine into a fanzine, because Jon had come out of fanzines and that was the look of punk.'

Savage remained affectionate about the paper that gave him a shot: 'We didn't have to hang back, and were luckier working there because the older writers – people like Vivien, Giovanni and Jonh – were very helpful and very nice to new people when they got on board. They were supportive, when I don't think [writers] on *NME* would have been.'

Sounds' assimilation of punk graphics was, says Savage, enabled by Fudger: 'Dave was a very creative designer who used things like typewriter fonts really well. *NME* had a rigid format and *Melody Maker* was hamstrung because it had to fight all the other stuff: folk, jazz, etc. Dave was the person doing all the work and overseeing *Sounds*. Alan Lewis would smile and say, "Go ahead."'

By his second issue, Savage was handling the week's biggest story: a midnight Sex Pistols performance with new bassist Sid Vicious. Recognizing that punk was already subject to the hierarchies it had sought to displace, he wrote: 'The Pistols have become symbols – us against them – the songs anthems, inviolate from criticism. Just to see them is enough – it's a bonus that they played a good set. So, ultimately, the environment was totally controlled in favour of the Pistols – no risks. I admire the media manipulation, but feel the sour taste of patronage and the exploitation of base brutality instincts. It's too easy. The eventual problem may be – who cares? They're being overtaken. Fast.'[6]

Savage, who is gay, ensured that acts from, as he described it, the 'distaff side' were afforded equal space. These included the Pauline Murray-led Penetration (whose anthem was the declamatory 'Don't Dictate'), the proudly unpolished Slits, the imperious Siouxsie Sioux and the high-voltage X-Ray Spex. The latter were fronted by one of punk's rare women of colour: Poly Styrene, born Marianne Elliot-Said to a Scottish-Irish mother and Somalian father. Friendly with Savage before she formed X-Ray Spex, she accompanied him to an early gig by the Clash, and subsequently opened a clothing stall selling customized secondhand garments. With the band, her dervish-like persona was augmented by teeth braces and twin sets. That, coupled with songs such as 'Identity' and 'Oh Bondage! Up Yours', undermined expectations of women in music. 'She looked terrific and her voice was terrific,' Savage enthused. 'It was full attack mode. No woman had done anything like that remotely before in music performance. She was a revolutionary who took the energy of the Pistols and punk and transformed it into her own thing.'[7]

Other punk fans were pulled aboard *Sounds*. Sandy Robertson, whose fanzine *White Stuff* was largely dedicated to Patti Smith, documented mavericks such as pop-punk svengali Kim Fowley and cult musician Alex Chilton, hailed Pat Benatar as 'Wonder Woman meets ZZ Top' and interviewed Frank Zappa. Punk, Zappa told Robertson, 'definitely gave the writers of the rock 'n' roll publications something to write about, which is what they always want. And since what they do with their little typewriters and pencils has little or nothing to do with music, then the punk rock phenomenon was ideally suited to their talent and craftsmanship.' In the same interview, he reiterated his oft-quoted aphorism, 'Rock journalism is people who can't write, preparing stories based on interviews with people who can't talk, in order to amuse people who can't read.'

But Robertson was, like pretty much everyone else in the music press, overshadowed by the mysterious Jane Suck (née Jackman). Another Dave Fudger recruit, the eighteen-year-old's provocative nom de plume was matched by an idiosyncratic style, as evinced by an early piece on punk club the Roxy: 'I got too drunk to remember why I was there. I did not seem to hit it off with *anyone*. What a drag: I can't wear my shades downstairs because it's too dark ... The barmen don't like me because I tell them the prices are a rip-off, the orange juice tastes funny, and later there is a shortage of wine glasses – guess who dropped their glass on the floor every time they finished a drink (just to watch it break). The records they are playing are great, but I can't stand in the middle of the floor all night ... The Ladies was THE place to be. First time I went in there I decided to play journalist. Talked to the girl who changed into her gear because her mum would not let her out of the house dressed like "that". Shared sympathies over the predicament of being called "sir" by the straights of this world.'[8]

Suck's deadpan reportage extended to interviews. Iggy Pop, she noted, was naked when they met: 'I sat in his lap. Got three kisses. Spent two whole days trying to see him again – rags. Mom threw me out for playing *Lust for Life* too loud and being as stoned as my hero.'

Pop promptly commandeered her inquiries: '"Does it surprise you that the audience seems so young?" No. "Are you aware of the dangerous power you have over people? You seemed to on your last tour and held back." I am aware of the enormous responsibility I have to myself and I was very aware of that last tour and held back. "What made you write songs like I Wanna Be Your Dog and She's Not Right? I bet you've never had trouble with gurls." Wrong! I'm very choosy ... "What kind of music do you listen to when you're on your own?" John Coltrane ... "*Raw Power* comes across as a celebration of drugs. *Fun House* is a lunatic's anthem." Answer: just ditto it. (Screws up question sheet.) *Sounds:* Is that it? Iggy: That's it, babe.'[9]

Roxy Music's 1977 *Greatest Hits* aroused Suck's ire for its break from the band's erotic iconography: 'You can't even take the cover of this to the bathroom – a photograph of a gold record and Jerry Hall's eyebrow. Big thrill!! What I'm getting at is you just *cannot* take Roxy Music songs out of context. The albums themselves were like walking a tightrope. *Greatest Hits* is just one Godalmighty safety net. My advice, dear, buy the re-released 'Virginia Plain/ Pyjamarama', hock your tuxedo and get the collected works.'[10]

Her trajectory burned bright and short until the end of 1978. 'I can't remember whether Jane had taken too much amphetamine or whether it was part of the amphetamine-abuse scenario,' said Jon Savage, 'but she'd threatened Suzi Quatro during an interview – I think in some rhetorical way. Suzi didn't mind but the publicist did and got Alan Lewis to sack her. I thought that was shoddy, because he'd exploited her talents but hadn't taken care to look after her.'

Lewis remembered it differently: 'She was totally out there. One day I came in and she had destroyed the women's toilets. The windows, washbowls, mirrors: everything was smashed to bits. [But] she was so talented that I rehired her the following week under another pseudonym.'[11] As Jane Solanas – after the Society for Cutting Up Men manifesto writer Valerie Solanas – Suck also contributed to *NME* a couple of years later. Her work suggested an outstanding raw talent, although Julie Burchill dismissed her as an imitator: 'Jane had read my adolescent ramblings, been teased by my Sapphic posturing and boy did she like what she read ... *Sounds* – which was a music paper quite like *NME*, only crap – decided they wanted one just like me, and Jane was there, on their doorstep, teenage, alienated and boasting a stupid, sexually provocative name.'[12] This is disputed by Jon Savage, who hailed Suck as 'the best of us at that time'.

More talents emerged from the fanzine realm, including Gavin Martin (publisher of *Alternative Ulster*) and Adrian Thrills (*48 Thrills*). 'Through the Mark P myth – bank clerk to media star via ten-sheet Xerox-zine – the idea of fanzine editor as star was in currency,' wrote Savage. 'At one stage, everyone was to get a fanzine/band together ... *Jolt*, *Gun Rubber*, *Flicks* and others used the lack of censorship to write *exactly* what they wanted, and, in the case of the 'zines outside London, to try and provide a focal point for areas where there weren't four punk bands playing a night.'[13]

Savage believes he and others who graduated to the inkies were 'exploited terribly, though of course we were terribly eager to get into print. There was a lack of unionization, proper payment and any kind of regulation. This became clear when I was attacked – not at all severely – by one of the Stranglers and got absolutely no support.' The band's ire was aroused by Savage's review of their *No*

More Heroes, which contained tracks such as 'Bring on the Nubiles': 'What comes off this album, with its deliberate unrelenting wallowing, is the chill of death. No life force, nothing vital. Not so that it's frightening, just dull and irritating, ultimately. And it doesn't make it as a statement, even though it's all taken so seriously ... It sounds as though everyone's intelligence is being insulted: yours, mine, and that of this record's creators.'[14]

Days after the review appeared, Savage was identified in a crowd to Stranglers bassist Jean-Jacques Burnel by *Sounds* contributor Chas de Whalley. 'I think I did it innocently,' says de Whalley, 'though maybe at the time my motives weren't all that pure.'[15] Burnel, a trained martial artist, 'hit me three or four times', recalled Savage. 'I slapped him in the face and that was that. It didn't stop me doing what I was doing. In fact, it made me more determined. I didn't have much of a sense of my gay identity at the time, nor did Jane, but it dictated our response to the increased laddism of punk, which we abhorred. There were endless arguments in *Sounds* editorial meetings about their objectification of Debbie Harry. I hated – and still do – the bully-boy aspect of punk, which began to emerge later in 1977. The Clash fell victim to it in a big way.'

Savage and Suck unleashed their disillusionment on *Sounds*' editor: 'Alan Lewis called a meeting with Viv, Jane, Sandy [Robertson], Dave Fudger and myself and said, "We've got these great pictures and we're going to run Images of the New Wave, part three." These things basically meant cheap content. This was October 1977. We all went, "Bleeeaurgh! We hate new wave and we even hate punk!" The music industry had long got involved and turned it into thirty-year-old pub rockers or, worse, the endless refried mod of the Jam. For all of us in varying degrees, the thing we'd loved about groups like Subway Sect, the Banshees and the Slits was that they were new. Punk had become a cliché and we wanted to continue that sense of newness, of discovery.'

Lewis indulged his truculent charges' desire for what Savage dubbed 'The new musick': 'Viv [Goldman] did a great piece on dub and a great interview with Siouxsie. Steven Lavers wrote about Kraftwerk. Sandy did Throbbing Gristle. I did Devo and the Residents. Jane got to explore all this in a great keynote editorial.'

Savage expounded on releases by US pioneers Pere Ubu and Devo, and more advanced British new wave acts such as Wire. These bands, he maintained in a cod computer-speak piece that introduced the term 'post-punk' into the music lexicon, rendered punk obsolete: 'Shock tactics used to gain space/attention now redundant ... Already the term redundant as new paths are charted. More overt reggae/dub influence, for starters. Also fresh energy from regional centres, where they keep the faith purer, and the USA.'[16]

* * *

Curiosity and suspicion marked the initial responses of America's music press to British punk. But while some suggested the styles and sounds of New York and Detroit had been lifted wholesale, others embraced the phenomenon. 'I loved the Pistols and really did think they were revolutionary,' enthused Greg Shaw of *Who Put the Bomp*. 'I was obviously from a different world and they were probably calling me a hippie behind my back, but I had long talks with Rotten. His agenda was that he hated rock stars, he hated the whole rock culture, which is what I hated. We had that in common.'

Bomp was the first US publication to feature the Pistols. 'I believe I was the first American to interview them,' said Shaw. 'I was at an early gig at the 100 Club [in London] – there were only about a dozen people there. This was a year or more before anybody in America knew about them.' This early access was thanks to a brief stint as manager of San Francisco power-pop outfit the Flamin' Groovies when they visited the UK in 1976: 'It was such a transitional time. Our opening band on the tour was the Damned, but they started getting more response than we did, so we kicked them off and got the Vibrators instead.'

Among those Shaw encountered was Kris Needs, a young journalist on a mission to haul Pete Frame's *ZigZag* into the punk era: 'Frame let me write a few album reviews and was propagating an unjust image of me as a pissed maniac in his editorials. As I turned twenty-two in June 1976, he took me to do my first rock interview. The victims were the Flamin' Groovies. I was a major fan but, once the tapes started rolling, I completely dried up from nerves, especially when the Thai sticks appeared.'

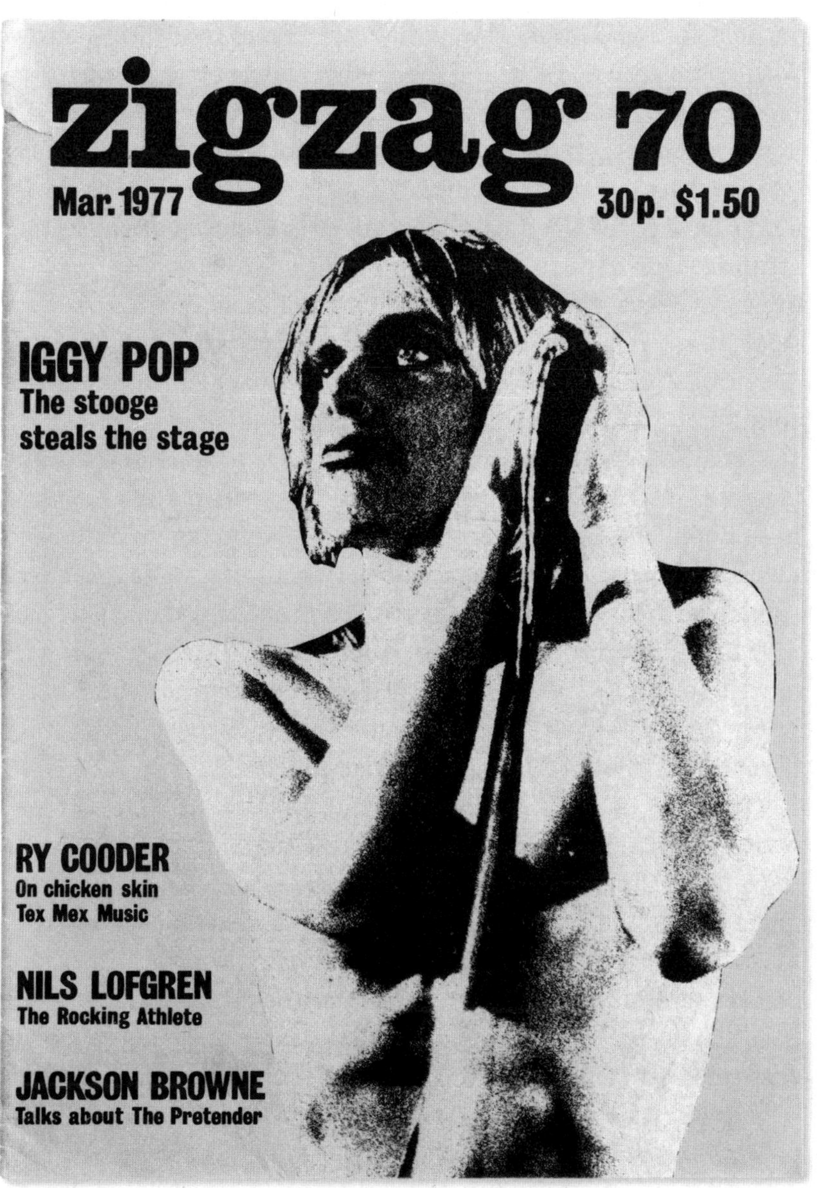

ZigZag, no. 70, March 1977

Next for Needs were the Ramones: 'It went fine with the New York cretin ambassadors and resulted in another friendship which took me around the country until the end of the seventies. By now I was *ZigZag*'s token punk and the butt of much uneasy piss-taking from the Eagles contingent. The more tolerant Frame – who might have hated the music but enjoyed the apple-cart-upsetting attitude – gave me my own supplement called *Over the Top*. On the cover I was shown tucking into an Eagles album in spike-top, safety-pinned jacket and paint-splattered shirt.'[17] Needs became editor of *ZigZag* itself, recasting the magazine with new wave content and a ripped and torn Day-Glo design.

Greg Shaw, meanwhile, fell victim to the Sex Pistols' light-fingered guitarist Steve Jones: 'When the Groovies played Dingwalls in London, the Pistols were hanging out backstage with us and nicked our bags, which had our plane tickets, everything, in them. I had to go to Malcolm to get the stuff back and ended up being pals with him.' *Bomp* promptly changed direction. 'Punk gave me a lot to write about,' Shaw observed. 'I'd go to London; I'd come back; I'd file a report on what was happening and a discography of every punk record that had been released in England.'

Other US magazines ploughed parallel furrows to the British press. The stapled 'zine *Trans-Oceanic Trouser Press*, founded in the mid-1970s, evolved into *Trouser Press*, a glossy-cover magazine influenced by *ZigZag* and *Bomp*. 'Our view of what mainstream rock magazines were overlooking,' said editor Ira Robbins, 'included history as well as obscurity, so *Trouser Press* latched onto the past – namely British Invasion bands – as well as pub rock, prog rock and assorted marginal artists few people cared about. Glam was mostly done and there was a lull in innovation and novelty, so history made us feel like we were doing something valuable.'

An exhaustive interview with Jimmy Page in June 1977 confirmed the magazine's credentials. It also revealed that, nearly seven years after the release of *Led Zeppelin III*, the guitarist was still seething about a misconception concerning the album: '*Melody Maker* said we'd decided to don our acoustic guitars because Crosby, Stills and Nash had just been over there [to Britain] ... You should read that *Melody Maker* review, though. It's absolutely classic.'

'I didn't want to write anything *literary*'

Unlike Lisa and Richard Robinson's *Rock Scene*, *Trouser Press* avoided over-praising Manhattan punk. 'I was opposed to making too much of the New York underground scene we all loved and took part in, because we didn't want to be seen as locally obsessed,' said Robbins. 'It wasn't as if bands like Blondie or Television or Talking Heads would ever escape the Bowery (as I foolishly believed) and be able to be heard by anyone outside the metropolitan New York area. Bear in mind that most CBGB/Max's groups never released any independent records, and major labels were very slow to come calling. Then came the deluge, and in retrospect we quickly found out how naive that view had been.'[18]

In contrast, *New York Rocker* – launched in February 1976, two months before the Ramones' debut album – took a mighty bite out of the Big Apple. It was helmed by Alan Betrock – who, Debbie Harry noted, 'produced our first demos [and] played an important part in shining some publicity onto the groups and keeping the whole scene exciting'.

'Betrock defined the new rock and roll,' wrote the magazine's publisher Andy Schwartz. 'His covers made stars of Patti Smith, Blondie, Television and Talking Heads before they'd even crossed the Hudson. He was a brilliant conceptualist who created board-game centrefolds ("How to become a New York rock star") and imaginary 45rpm picture sleeves for "Singles we'd like to see." He opened *NYR*'s pages to future fashion legends Anna Sui and Steven Meisel, photographers Stephanie Chernikowski and Roberta Bayley, and artist Duncan Hannah, among many others.'[19] But after eleven issues, Betrock departed to launch the label and publishing company Shake. This issued records by Richard Hell and Marshall Crenshaw and books based on his huge pop ephemera archive, including *Hitsville: The 100 Greatest Rock 'n' Roll Magazines (1954–1968)*.

On the West Coast, punk inspired San Francisco's *Search & Destroy* and LA's *Slash*. The former was launched by Vale Hamanaka, who had been in an early lineup of hard rock pioneers Blue Cheer. In 1977, he was thirty-three and working at the Bay Area beat bookstore City Lights. As 'VALE' – and, later, 'V. Vale' – he published the first *Search & Destroy* with $100 each from beat writer Allen Ginsberg and City Lights co-owner and poet Lawrence Ferlinghetti.

The result was an arty zine that owed a debt to Andy Warhol's *Interview* and was more open about sexual diversity than any other music publication of the period. The cover featured a plummeting skydiver collaged with safety pins and the slogan 'Johnny Rotten lives', while the contents included a feature on Iggy Pop and an article by local scenester 'Vermilion', headed 'Loudmouth leathergirl reveals punk finesse'.

Mixing beat and outsider figures with new groups proved *Search & Destroy*'s hallmark. William Burroughs and JG Ballard shared one issue with the Dead Kennedys. Another edition reported from the set of David Lynch's *Eraserhead* and profiled future filmmaker Penelope Spheeris, then in San Francisco band the Avengers. Jon Savage acknowledged that he distilled much of the information for his 'New Musick' *NME* article on emerging American bands from its pages: 'At that point, it was the best magazine in the world.'

Search & Destroy lasted eleven issues. 'It took two years to build up 200 hardcore people truly into punk,' Vale told the online magazine *Bomb*, 'so that they just got into it one hundred per cent and quit working full-time – most of them – and started bands, or publishing, or taking photos, or making posters, or making clothes, or whatever they did ... Our scene was different, with fabulous songs most people still don't even know; a huge amount of creativity that is under-documented and will probably remain that way.'[20] For his part, Vale later turned to specialist book publishing with the influential RE/Search imprint.

In Los Angeles, *Slash* was founded by graphic artist Steve Samiof, photographer Melanie Nissen, their friend Claude Bessy and his British partner Philomena Winstanley. 'I'd seen *Melody Maker* and *New Musical Express* talking about the Sex Pistols gobbing on their fans,' enthused Samiof. 'It sounded like something I was into! We were thinking of naming the 'zine after a Situationist term but it all got a bit pretentious, so I just said, "Let's call it Piss." Philomena responded by saying, "You know, in England, to take a slash is to take a piss." I thought, "*Slash* – perfect!"'

'We got this one ad from A&M and another from I-don't-know-where, which totally financed the first issue, which came out on May Day 1977,' recalled Bessy. 'By luck we ran into the Damned,

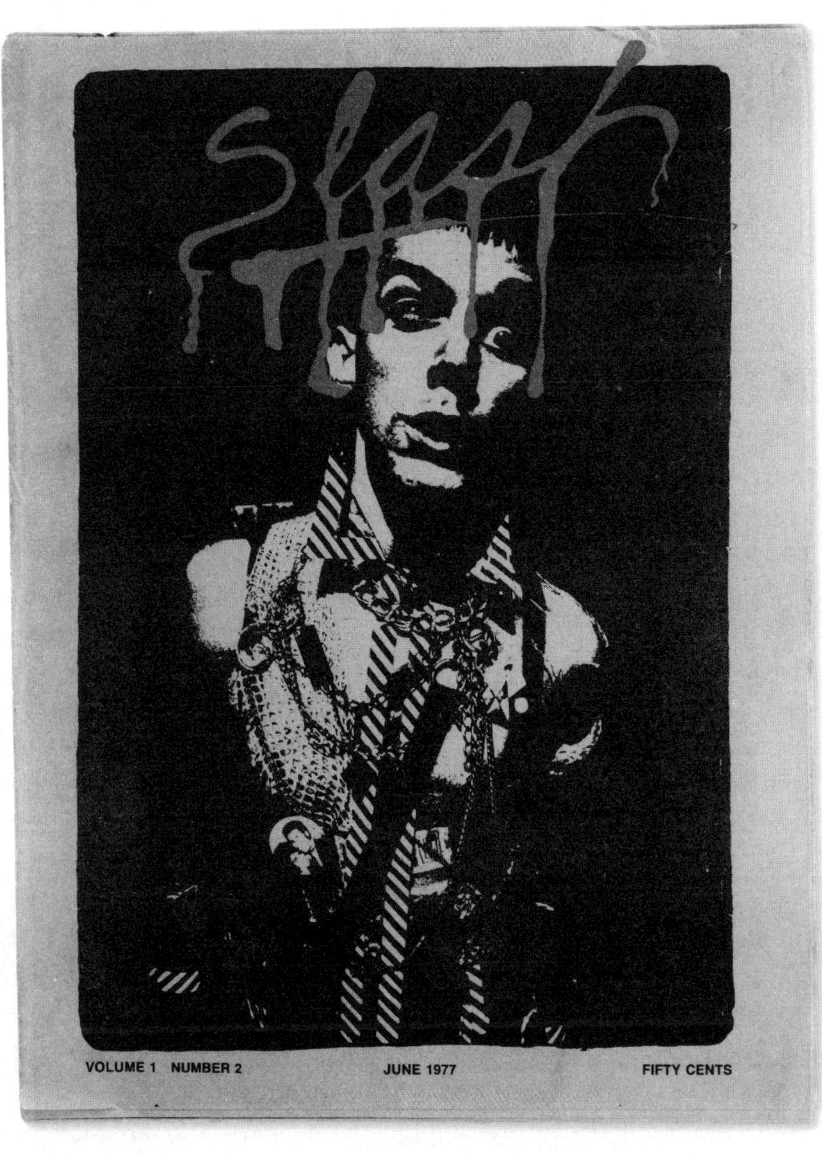

Slash, vol. 1, no. 2, June 1977

who were doing their first concert here, for an interview for that issue. For the first two or three issues, we pretended there was an LA scene when there was absolutely nothing.'

With Nissen's bleached-out portraiture and authentically jagged design by expat British designer David Allen, *Slash* provided a platform for illustrator Gary Panter and sometimes over-the-top contributors including Richard Meltzer. 'The paper started interesting some kids,' said Bessy, who was credited as 'Kickboy Face' (the title of a song by Jamaican artist Prince Jazzbo, which he encountered while running the reggae fanzine *Angeleno Dread* with Winstanley). 'Bands started forming because of the paper and we had a scene to report on; it started snowballing. The media and the artist became very connected. We featured the Screamers on looks alone and let them play the first *Slash* concert before we had heard one note of their music. And it worked. Suddenly *Slash* was indispensable.'[21]

'One of the most passionately irreverent characters I have ever met' was LA punk chronicler Brendan Mullen's verdict on Bessy. 'No one was spared his barbed wit, not even myself (and I liked to think of him as my favorite drinking crony); certainly not the major record companies who'd frequently find their full-page ads adjacent to an editorial review mercilessly trashing their record.'[22] For some, Bessy and *Slash* presented a more formidable take on independent publishing than their English counterparts. '*Slash* was punk but it was nothing like *Sniffin' Glue*,' said Greg Shaw in 2000. 'It was literary, not in a polished sense, but it had style. Mark Perry, bless his heart, he's not a writer. He was a participant in the scene and chronicling what was going on. *Slash* had an aesthetic with what they were trying to capture: a uniquely LA vision.' Richard Meltzer, who hailed Bessy as 'the greatest rock writer you never heard of', said, 'In matters punk versus no-punk, I defer to Claude.'

Dreading the co-option of the music he celebrated and the curtailing of the freedoms of the 1970s, Bessy left America for Europe when Ronald Reagan was elected president. Before he left, he recorded a statement for Penelope Spheeris's LA punk documentary *The Decline of Western Civilization*: 'I have excellent news for the world. There is no such thing as new wave. It does not exist. It's a figment of a lame cunt's imagination. There was never any such thing as new wave. It was the polite thing to say when you were trying to explain you were not into the boring old rock 'n' roll, but you didn't dare to say "punk" because you were afraid to get kicked out of the fucking party and they wouldn't give you coke anymore.'

For Jon Savage, Bessy and *Search & Destroy*'s Vale were beacons: 'I was starting to develop a relationship with them and realised, incredibly, that there were like minds several thousand miles away. They seemed far more interesting than England trying to claim punk for itself as a kind of negative version of Swinging London.'

Yet one of the period's most evocative articles on punk – Charles M. Young's 'Rock is sick and living in London' – appeared in the publication by then viewed as a corporate pariah: *Rolling Stone*. Lester Bangs's attempts to grapple with the UK punk phenomenon were more self-indulgent than insightful; his three-part *NME* account of life on the road with the Clash ('Six days on the road to the Promised Land', December 1977) is wearisome. In contrast, Young delivered to American readers a journey through London during the summer when the Pistols' 'God Save the Queen' provoked assaults on the band members and questions in the Houses of Parliament. With a cameo by sexploitation movie king Russ Meyer – lined up to direct the Pistols biopic – it detailed the group and their manager Malcolm McLaren's disdain. Interviewed on the day Elvis Presley died, McLaren told Young: 'This band hates you. It hates your culture. Why can't you lethargic, complacent hippies understand that? You need to be smashed ... This is a very horrible country, England. We invented the mackintosh, you know. We invented the flasher, the voyeur. That's what the press is about.'

The Pistols made Young question the relationship between musicians and the media and acknowledge that the music championed by his magazine was out of touch with the realities of youth: 'I can't dislike Malcolm McLaren for figuring out that reporters are vampires, lurking in the night, ready to suck out every last corpuscle of titillation, leaving the victim to spend eternity as a Media Zombie. If he were merely a manipulator, he wouldn't have chosen such genuine fuckups for the band ... Kids destroyed schools to the tune of $600 million in the U.S. last year. That's a lot of anger that the Southern-California-Cocaine-And-Unrequited-Love axis isn't capable of tapping.'[23]

* * *

'I gasped. I couldn't believe it. It was an attempt to sabotage me as a great writer.' Punk champion Caroline Coon had weathered slings and arrows at *Melody Maker*, but the final straw was a request from editor Ray Coleman that she pen a gossip column titled 'Bitch': 'I felt that I was being put down; that all the important, vanguard work I'd done was being diminished. There's an agenda in misogyny, which likes to turn one into this bitch character. A bitch can be pointed, interesting and entertaining but absolutely never authoritative and powerful.'[24] Coon noted: 'Julie Burchill played that role and was absolutely lauded and salivated over by a coterie of male journalists. So off I went.'

She landed on the other side of the fence as manager of the Clash. Acclaimed but broke, the group had tired of their Situationism-spouting manager Bernie Rhodes. Bassist Paul Simonon – Coon's partner – warned her that the band was on the verge of collapse just ahead of their first tour of the US. 'Bands get to a certain level where you're talking hundreds of thousands of dollars to record companies, and, if you're a male manager, you have to deal in quite a confident way with men who have more authority than you,' observed Coon. 'Neither Bernie Rhodes or Malcolm McLaren felt comfortable with men they perceived to have more authority. Rather than nurture them to their next level, they broke their bands up. It's very easy to do: you just have to set the band members against each other. When the Clash told me they were breaking up, I said, "You can't do it."

'I had put myself on the line as a journalist to say, "This movement is going to be the defining music for the next decade." Having said that in the press, I was bloody well not going to stand by and see the bands at the vanguard of the movement broken up by incompetent managers. So I said, "I'll do it." Despite the other political advances they may have made, the Clash were still very orthodox and the idea of a woman managing them seemed to be very sissy.

So they said, "Absolutely. Do the job. But you can't call yourself the manager."'

Coon's intervention proved the group's salvation. Buoyed by the response to their US tour and exposed to a variety of music, they returned to the UK, dispensed with Coon and set about creating *London Calling*. The following year saw them reunited with Rhodes.

Upheaval was in the air at *NME* too: after eleven years, six as editor, Nick Logan decided to leave: 'I still had something to prove. I had been written out of the story of why *NME* was so successful. That is what happens if you are always behind the scenes, but I was determined that wherever I went next would be mine. But I'm not very good at presenting a case or articulating what I want to do. Put me on a committee and I won't say a word. I'll bow to everyone else's superior judgment every time. So that forced me to go out on my own.'[25]

Logan had a head full of ideas. One was a magazine about country music; another about reggae, with *NME*'s Penny Reel. A third was a *Rolling Stone*-style 'intelligent' music paper with *NME* writer Chris Salewicz and cartoonist Tony Benyon, called *Modern Times*.
Yet another was a glossy, photo-led celebration of chart music, featuring the lyrics of hit songs.

He pitched these to *NME*'s printer East Midlands Allied Press (Emap), whose newly established magazine division boasted *Angling Times* and *Motorcycle Weekly*. 'I threw in the song lyric proposal to round out the ideas and was really surprised that that was the one they took to. It was the opposite of an intense newsprint rock weekly.' Emap suggested the title *Disco Fever*, to capitalize on the popularity of the Bee Gees and John Travolta. Logan, keen to include Elvis Costello, Ian Dury and the Clash, countered with *The Pop*. They compromised on *Smash Hits*.

'My interest was in having excellent photography, with the song lyrics as the ballast, and bringing good acts like the Jam to a young audience,' said Logan. He campaigned for quality stock; existing titles in the field such as *Disco 45* were derided for being printed on close to lavatory tissue. Serendipitously, Emap had sufficient ninety-gram glossy stock to produce the first issue in the autumn of 1978. Logan was paid to clear song lyrics and produce issues on his kitchen table, for which he initially adopted the pseudonym Chris Hall. 'I didn't want everyone knowing what I was doing,' he said, 'until I was certain it would come good.'[26]

Test-marketed in Yorkshire, the first issue (pl. 11) featured Belgian novelty punk singer Plastic Bertrand on the cover and, to Emap's dismay, a centre spread of the skinhead-approved Sham 69. But it sold tens of thousands. When it went national and fortnightly, sales soared to 100,000. Early in 1979, Logan was set up in an office in London's Carnaby Street, opposite the *NME* office he had vacated just months before. 'We could actually see Nick working away,' says *NME* writer Paul Rambali, who would reunite with him in the 1980s.[27]

Logan's nineteen-year-old sister-in-law Bev Hillier came onboard as subeditor. 'The main part of my job was transcribing the song lyrics,' she recalled. 'That's what it was at first: song lyrics and posters. [Later] Boy George, Simon Le Bon and Phil Oakey all came in with their lyrics. I was the envy of all of my friends.'[28]

NME regular Fred Dellar provided a crossword and the team was bolstered by David Hepworth. 'The first thing I did for *Smash Hits* was interview Elvis Costello,' he recalled. 'The idea was: don't talk down. Use simple language. You're not here to tell us what you think about Dr Feelgood and your place in the world. Shorter, tighter, more disciplined. The barriers between music – this is pop, this is dance, this is hip-hop – didn't exist in those days. When I was at *Smash Hits*, we were putting the same people on the cover as *NME*: the Police, the Jam, Buzzcocks, Blondie, Ian Dury. These were big pop acts liked by twenty-one-year-old Johnny Student and thirteen-year-old Tracy from Grantham. But *NME* made a conscious decision that it shouldn't be doing the same thing as *Smash Hits*, so they went and covered bands like Rip Rig + Panic who nobody gave a toss about.'

Within a year, circulation topped 166,000: just 35,000 less than *NME* and 10,000 more than *Melody Maker*. '*Smash Hits* shaped, as well as reflected, the popular music scene at the time,' British academic Stephen Hill observed. 'The house style was much more seductive than *NME* or *Melody Maker*. In part this can be attributed to the luscious colour and quality of the paper. And the addition of poster supplements and pictures to stick on bedroom walls was key to the magazine's teen appeal. The magazine reflected the rise of music video production during the 1970s and an increasingly visual portmanteau of stars from the glam rock era onwards ... The use of garish pinks and yellows alludes to the visual codes of punk and the Pop Art sensibility of Warhol. Indeed, it is this presentation of stars as consumer objects that is perhaps the key to the magazine's appeal.[29]

A more prosaic explanation was expressed by Charlie Gillett: 'There should never have been a need for *Smash Hits* to exist. It only came into being by default of *NME* and *Melody Maker* abandoning pop music. I was really glad and thought, "Serves you right."'

12
'Oh! Marvellous time!'

Danny Baker Joins *NME* and Felix Dennis Makes Mischief with *New Music News*

Turbulence and transformation followed Nick Logan's exit from *NME*. The natural choice of successor was sure-handed deputy editor Neil Spencer. Instead, publisher IPC plumped for underground press veteran Mark Williams, formerly *IT*'s music editor and a contemporary of Mick Farren. Then, before a disgruntled Spencer could hand in his notice, Williams was arrested for drug-related offences. IPC returned to Spencer and, he said, 'They were pretty shamefaced when they told me I'd got the job.' Logan also had mixed feelings: 'I had been on £4,250 a year – a ludicrous salary for dealing with all that strain. Remember it was also a fantastically successful magazine. Neil immediately got twenty per cent more than me.'

With record sales at a high, all five weeklies benefited. But *NME* led the field, regularly surpassing 200,000 a week. Keen to maintain this dominance and brand the new regime, Neil Spencer commissioned a redesign from Barney Bubbles, who had delivered startling sleeves, posters and ephemera for Elvis Costello and the Attractions, the Damned, Nick Lowe, and Ian Dury and the Blockheads. With his assistant Diana Fawcett and illustrator Andy Martin, he whipped 20th-century art and design references into a melange suited to the creatively chaotic post-punk period.

Bubbles also produced a supplement to mark the relaunch: *The NME Book of Modern Music*, available as a series of free inserts. For its A–Z format, he formulated a quirky alphabet that, enthused Spencer, 'borrowed from twenties Russia, sixties Britain and beyond. Barney was so wily technically, and conjured unexpected colours and effects.'

The paper itself now had defined sections for news, features, reviews, charts and concert listings, and placed greater emphasis on photography. The new presentation was capped by a block capital logo, based on a lighting manufacturer's signage at a warehouse near Bubbles's London studio. However, fearing readers wouldn't recognize the paper, IPC decreed the stencil-style masthead not be introduced with the redesign. Only after six weeks of back-and-forthing did the Bubbles logo appear. This, however, survived into the digital age: at the time of writing, a version is used by *NME* to brand its online presence.

Meanwhile, new editor Spencer was forced to confront an uncomfortable reality. Julie Burchill and Tony Parsons had helped re-establish the paper's credibility, but then delivered a so-called 'obituary of rock 'n' roll' in the form of their book *The Boy Looked at Johnny* and gone AWOL – while continuing to draw a wage. 'Julie and I caused a lot of trouble for Neil Spencer,' acknowledged Parsons. 'We were quite disruptive and really full of ourselves. We must have been unbearable.' Spencer concurred: 'They were holed up in the 'burbs with speed habits. They hadn't come in in six months and nothing had been done about it. So I replaced them with Max Bell and Paul Rambali and started to refurbish the staff.'

Bell had been writing smart features, particularly on American hard rock, for *NME* since the mid-1970s (of Kiss, he declared, 'I like any kind of trash music that has no pretensions to being sophisticated'). Rambali had been a UK stringer for *Trouser Press* during the punk era and was joined by Angus MacKinnon, who had shone at the short-lived *Street Life* ('Rock 'n' roll is so nauseatingly centralised and bureaucratic,' he fumed in a review of Finnish band Wigwam, 'it's no wonder it thrives on a contrived dynamic of inconsequentiality'). MacKinnon was allowed to develop what Spencer hailed as his 'fantastic, analytical but readable prose', while production editor Monty Smith's background in film editing was tapped to boost *NME*'s movie coverage.

Reggae buff Spencer also gave licence to Penny Reel to flaunt his idiosyncratic style, which by now blended Jamaican argot and London street slang, with immediacy added by Runyonesque application of the present tense. 'One night I am standing outside the Jamaican pattie shop in Portobello Road partaking of the same,' ran one 1978 piece, 'when a car pulls up on the street and from it emerge certain characters from Kilburn by the name of Militant Barrington, Tapper Zukie and Jah Lacey, which is by no means an unusual combination to see, as these are very intimate idren and frequently keep each other's company, except that now there is a fourth person with them in the rear approach, one known as King Saul ... King Saul is a guy I do not require to share an intimate relationship with whatever. Furthermore, nobody else in this town requires the immediate co-existence of King Saul, except sometimes in the capacity of bailiff or bodyguard ... [He] is known often to hold a gun on his person, which he will sometimes produce to shoot at people if, for instance, he does not like the political party they favour.'[1]

Sharing Parsons and Burchill's working-class origins, Danny Baker was the last person appointed to *NME* by Nick Logan. As a *Sniffin' Glue* contributor, he had – as Peter York noted – 'the sharpest line of chat'[2] and had been an avid *NME* reader. 'People like Tony Tyler and Charles Shaar Murray were as big as rock stars to me,' he said. 'The culture which it invented is the culture now: the way it dealt with celebrity, the breathless prose, the way it understood that the writers and the readers were more important than the celebrities. Those *NME*s from '72 and '73 tore a new culture right out of the air.'

Baker undertook occasional assignments but preferred to be the paper's rock 'n' rolling receptionist: 'I had a terrific time earning £15.58 a week on the phones. Nick Kent's mum used to ring up and say, "Can I speak to Nicholas Benedict please?" He'd sit there waving his arms, saying, "No, no," but I'd always make a point of putting her through.'[3] Eventually it became evident that Baker's talents were being wasted. 'I coaxed him onto the staff, which meant that Danny had to churn it out like the rest of us,' said Spencer. 'It was always a problem getting the words out of Baker because he's a lazy bugger. That's why it was always down to him to write [gossip column) Teasers and review the singles, because it didn't involve doing much work.'

Baker's good humour and self-evident skills eased his graduation to full-time writer. The paper's highlights included his searching and often hilarious encounters with punk-poet John Cooper Clarke, Ian Dury, Public Image Ltd and film director Mel Brooks. In certain respects, *NME* was remade in Baker's image as he pitched headlines, captions, gossip and, on the singles reviews page, an arsenal of rapid-fire gags. '*NME* was just a ball,' he enthused. 'Can you imagine? Eighteen to twenty-one, flying all over the world, reviewing records. Oh, marvellous time! Writing copy on the way to the printers, just solidly laughing and being drunk. What I brought in, perhaps, was out-and-out jokes that didn't depend on counterculture knowledge. My writing never depended on whether anyone had heard of the group. It was outrageous liberties with somebody else's craft, but that was the point.'[4]

Visiting America for the first time, Baker and inebriated friends spotted John Lennon and Yoko Ono on a Manhattan street and engaged them in an impromptu chat. Lennon asked whether *NME* still ran Maurice Kinn's Alley Cat column and gave his message to the world as, 'Rock on. Be good.' 'As soon as we sat down in the next bar,' Baker recalled, 'I wrote down everything I remembered from the giddy ninety-second exchange. *NME* ran every word with a front-page strapline saying, "Lennon speaks!" A couple of the dailies used bits too, adding that the "former Beatle looked content, well and happy" – something I'd not included in my copy but should have done.'[5]

Beatles nut Baker was also a near-obsessive fan of prog rock, Steely Dan and Black American music, making the Village People and Earth Wind & Fire as likely as Ian Dury and the Blockheads to receive his Single of the Week accolade. 'I was really pissed off with the snobbery towards disco in the music press,' noted Barney Hoskyns, then an *NME* reader and soon a staff writer. 'Danny was virtually on his own championing it. Whenever he did the singles column in *NME* and said, "These are the best singles around," I would buy them. I still remember his review of [Chic's] "Good Times" as being a classic piece, which opened my ears.' Indeed, that review was cited by Peter York as a turning point: 'Danny said how all the pale boys were knocking disco as mindless consumer fodder, all these theory boys, and how they were contemptuous of the real people's music. He meant it perfectly straight, though of course he was paying off a few scores, since here was someone who really had worked up a sweat to Johnny Bristol and the Philadelphia Sound in the mid-seventies, and knew the whole white-suited world. It was one of those pieces that made you want to send a telegram. Within a month, however, there was "the theory of disco" and the pale boys were writing about Donna Summer and Abba and the Bee Gees as if they'd been keeping tabs all along.'[6]

York's 'pale boys' – and they were all male – were a new generation of writers inspired by literary criticism as they grappled with the experimental, angular music of Cabaret Voltaire, the Fall, Gang of Four, the Human League and Joy Division. The thoughtful inspirations of such groups justified the approach: 'Pop music,' remarked critic Sasha Frere-Jones, 'needed the destructive more than the descriptive.'[7] But the liberal and sometimes seemingly indiscriminate quotes from French intellectuals Roland Barthes, Jacques Derrida and Michel Foucault became as irritating as the rock 'n' roll platitudes they replaced. Structuralism, pronounced *Sounds* writer Pete Silverton, 'did for the music press as much as it did for British academia'.

Foremost among the 'pale boys' were *NME*'s Paul Morley, the 'hip young gunslingers' alum who gave up his post as Manchester stringer to move to London, and Ian Penman, who began freelancing for the paper in 1977. Andy Gill, who had also applied for the job taken by Burchill and Parsons, was well placed as *NME*'s Sheffield correspondent: he had been friendly with members of Cabaret Voltaire and Clock DVA before they released records and covered the northern city's rich music scene.

Together, they sought to reinvent rock writing as the eighties loomed. 'Music journalists in the early seventies typically blended traditional critical virtues (objectivity, solid reporting, authoritative knowledge) with a New Journalism-influenced "rock 'n' roll" looseness and informality,' observed *Melody Maker*'s Simon Reynolds in his peerless post-punk overview *Rip It Up and Start Again*. 'This jammed-out, chatty style, juiced with "ain'ts", hep slang and sly, winking references to drugs and chicks, didn't suit post-punk.'[8]

What Reynolds identified as the 'intellectual underpinnings of this older rock criticism – notions of rebellion as male misbehaviour, genius-as-madness, the cult of street credibility and authenticity' were challenged by the new breed that abhorred music they regarded as 'rockist' (a code for worn-out White musical formulae minted by Liverpudlian singer Pete Wylie in an *NME* interview). Morley and Penman, wrote Reynolds, 'seemed to be made of the same *stuff* as the music they championed. The stark urgency and clean lines of their prose mirrored the light-metal severity of groups like Wire, the Banshees and Gang of Four. The new school of music writing merged puritanism and playfulness in a way that simultaneously undercut the casual tone of the old rock journalism while puncturing its stodgy core of certainty – hidden assumptions and taken-for-granted notions of what rock was all about.'

Chapter 12

Morley's mission hit its stride in 1979. Subjects viewed through the prism of his dense and deliberately overloaded prose included Gary Numan, Squeeze, Lou Reed, Ted Nugent and Lou Reed. And so scathing was his review of the Cure's debut album – 'More anguished young men chalking up more sanctioned and sanctimonious marks' – that, in a BBC radio session, the band reinvented their song 'Grinding Halt' as 'Desperate Journalist', incorporating Morley's words into the lyrics. 'I agreed with some of what he said,' admitted front man Robert Smith. '[But] he was saying that we were trying to do something and then not achieving it, which was obviously not true.'

A trip to the West Coast to interview Devo proved a Morley classic (helped by Pennie Smith's monochrome portraiture): 'Los Angeles is a home for many things. It's a mass of empty gestures, hopeless dreamers and holes in the ground. There are no days, no weeks, just light and dark. The name – and subsidiaries like Bel Air, Beverly Hills, Hollywood – conjure up images of a decent heaven, a cushion of leisure, a bed of golden straw on which to enjoy life and have the ego soothed. To be intensely happy and have nice days. You'll know by now that if Los Angeles was to be sliced away from the rest of America it would be the sixth richest nation in the world. All but physically it *has* been sliced away. It's ahead of its time.

'The paradise is hell and the beauty is ugly and the place is hanging in limbo and on the edge of forever. If you were to die in some parts of Los Angeles you would wake up next morning, have another nice day and forget what was supposed to have happened.'[9]

Morley proved prescient: he was among the first to grasp that Joy Division were post-punk's most substantial group, and identified U2 as world-beaters even in their days on the club circuit. And his copy quickly became an *NME* selling point: readers loved or loathed his elongated prose, and filled the letters page with reactions. 'You've got to give your new writers a go, but I was too indulgent,' admitted editor Neil Spencer. A case in point was Morley's interview with the Grateful Dead's leader Jerry Garcia: 'He wrote this stitch-up. I swear we lost about 20,000 readers that week. I shouldn't have allowed things like that. I should have stuck up more for the old guard.' Garcia – cheerfully unfazed by questions such as, 'There's been over a score of Grateful Dead LPs, none of them in any way essential. Do you have a quiet laugh at all those people who buy all those LPs?' – remarked, 'It's been surprising to me that people haven't been walking out in droves ever since we started.'[10]

Ian Penman, meanwhile, 'rattled readers with his references to Barthes and a fair amount of stone-cold nonsense,' according to Sasha Frere-Jones,[11] who admiringly cited a review of Sheffield quintet ABC at a London venue called A-Z that made no mention of their music or performance: 'So sorrowful an event. The A-Z boasts video cocktails and other code works but, sneery me, IT DOESN'T HAVE A CLOAKROOM. Just a place to faint onto a fag end. Is this the sleep end of this year's club craze? Black and smelly, cramped and SELL ME? Show me. But the other. Always other. Just ... the sort of questions ABC are basking in. Questions like: *can we step outside history by slipping into one another's arms?* And if not ... die untying the knot?'[12] Not averse to tongue-in-cheek pretentiousness themselves, ABC looted the headline of Penman's review for the title of their debut album *The Lexicon of Love*.

Naturally, the journalistic old guard were unmoved. 'Just a bunch of pretentious people,' sniffed Chris Salewicz of the pretenders to the throne. 'You wouldn't notice them apart from the fact that you wouldn't like some of their stuff, but be surprised that other people were impressed with it. It was worrying but also quite funny when pieces would start with quotes from French philosophers.'

Barney Hoskyns, who later joined *NME*, put it to Penman that the paper was 'brought down by you and Paul Morley because your writing became so abstruse and referential that nobody could understand it any more. People who'd grown up on pub rock or reviews of Eddie and the Hot Rods didn't know or want to know who Roland Barthes was.' Penman responded that he was just nineteen when he joined: 'There may have been a brief period of six months when I was unhappy and stuck it to a number of rock bands, but it was *fun*. I was young so you can be a bit glib. There was an enormous sense of pleasure and play about it. That was the point of using the quotes. It was like throwing lots of sweeties up in the air and seeing what came down ...

'One complaint was that we were these forbidding, doom-laden Joy Division types who wrote abstruse, semi-academic pieces, and the other was that we were somehow out of touch with the roots, man – apolitical, running around drinking expensive cocktails and making silly remarks. These are two things which don't go together and don't take into account the fact that I was a fairly lazy young man. If you look back at my time on *NME*, there isn't a huge amount of stuff and a lot of it is about TV and film. There wasn't much that was forbidding about my pieces about *The Rockford Files* and *Coronation Street*.'[13]

And Penman denied that he and Morley were pretentious: 'That's just another word for aspiring to something, for trying something out. Because I didn't know about rock 'n' roll history and rock 'n' roll writing, I didn't realise that you had to write in a certain way about things. In the middle of a singles column once I wrote about Marks and Spencer mayonnaise, recommending it instead of some single. It was supposed to be funny.'[14]

The post-punk era was also defined by *NME*'s stark – and necessarily monochrome – visuals. Dutch photographer Anton Corbijn was developing a wintry style that helped make icons of Joy Division and, later, Depeche Mode and U2. 'The fun we always had with Anton was rarely captured in his photographs,' Bono observed. 'Anton took pictures that looked like the music rather than the musicians.' Meanwhile, Pennie Smith had honed her craft to such an extent that even casual readers could identify her work.

A Smith portrait of the Slits, naked and covered in mud, proved a particularly memorable cover. 'The Slits turned all expectations on their head,' recalls Spencer. 'There was so much hostility towards them because they didn't play the game. Guys would shout at them, "You look ugly," and they'd reply, "We're not here to look nice for you." Were these crazy pictures of the band stripped off and covered in mud okay or not? Was this titillation, or was it something else? I think Pennie persuaded me that it was emancipation. Putting the Slits on the cover was, in itself, slightly controversial because they didn't sell records. A lot of the readers would have thought, "Oh, this is a London-centric thing," or, "This is *NME* getting carried away putting obscure people on the cover." But I always thought the Slits were an important event. The point of punk was attitude, and the Slits had attitude to spare.'

Meanwhile, *NME*'s office became, as Spencer recalls, 'a bear pit. It was forbidding to enter if you were an outsider, or even if you worked there, because there were a lot of giant egos and very sharp people. Everyone had very abrupt opinions on who should be on the cover and how many words everybody should have and who was going to write the lead review and so on. There was a lot of turf being fought over, so a big part of my job as editor was to balance the factions.'[15]

Friendly boozing eased the tension, and Ian Penman spent much time on licensed premises with Danny Baker and Monty Smith. Less impressed was Frank Zappa, who Baker and Smith interviewed after a session in a Soho pub. 'Great – drunk English guys,' sneered Zappa. 'He was rude and we were stupidly drunk,' notes Baker, whose sole question reminded Zappa of a 1971 incident when a concertgoer pushed him from a London stage, inflicting severe injuries. 'I need to leave now,' said Zappa, terminating the interview, 'and I mean right now.'[16]

Outside these cliques was one of the paper's most consistently readable contributors: Cynthia Rose. An Anglo-American who had lived in Paris in her teens, she made her first forays into journalism via *Harper's & Queen* and *Viz*. For the latter – a short-lived experiment in lifestyle publishing from the late 1970s (and not the satirical comic of the same name) – she staked out her turf by interviewing the B-52's, Robert Fripp, Iggy Pop and Patti Smith. At *NME*, she helped alleviate the boysy content with intelligent and thoughtful writing on Lene Lovich, Marianne Faithfull, Angie Bowie, the post-punk scene in Austin, Texas, and sex and romance in 1950s rock 'n' roll.

In one of her first pieces, Brian Eno discussed the impact of the new pop criticism: 'In this country everything is seen as ideologically linked ... I was responding to the [Ian Penman] review in *NME* of the Harold Budd and Jon Hassell records I've just done [1980's *Ambient 2: The Plateaux of Mirror* and *Fourth World Vol 1: Possible Musics*] and I was thinking, "Why does this piss me off?" It didn't piss me off a lot but, before those records were released, I wrote what I thought was a mock-*NME* review as a joke while I was talking to Harold. Some of it I got word for word, and I thought, Fuck me! I've been away from this country two years and I can still make accurate predictions about what's going to happen on the "fashionable" level ...

'All the papers have got involved in a fairly local ideological struggle. They've all taken new wave and punk much more seriously than any musicians I know. For the musicians it was not even a defined term as such. No one who was working in that area saw such clear boundaries and definitions and meanings as writers have. And it seems to me now they have made such a heavy emotional investment that they have to put a lot of distance between themselves and anything which does not fit into a certain area – as those two records obviously don't.'[17]

A more unsavoury element was highlighted by editor Neil Spencer: '*NME* [was] incredibly homophobic. There was a hardcore. They were always on about it, which was pretty weird, because on the other hand we had Phil [McNeill, production editor, formerly of *Gay News*] and showbusiness is, was and ever more shall be full of gay people.'

* * *

An extraordinary period at *Sounds* saw articles by Jon Savage – who helped blaze a trail for experimental writers of the period – alongside copy by Garry Bushell, who joined the team in 1978. A Londoner whose focus on working-class groups coalesced in the punk subgenre Oi, Bushell had run a 'zine that featured Sham 69. 'I did my journalism training on *Socialist Worker* and wrote the first piece in the left-wing press about the Clash in it in 1976,' he recalled. 'I showed Alan Lewis a Sham interview I'd done. I think he liked my tattoos. He asked me to show him what I could do, so I went out every night, saw bands like UK Subs and stuck the reviews through the *Sounds* office door the next day. After a week he called up and said, "You've got the job." Wallop! Straight onto the staff! I was in awe of it all; so naive I actually thought Jon Savage made sense. After a few years, some of the *Sounds* staff resented me because rowdy bands would always roll back from the pub with me. I mean, there were nine or ten people in Bad Manners.'[18]

The groups that Bushell liked sometimes attracted right-wing fans. This led to tension, particularly when he oversaw the release of the *Sounds*-backed compilation *Strength Thru Oi!* – its title a play on a Nazi slogan and its cover star the neo-Nazi activist Nicky Crane.

This was a fraught period politically, as *Sounds*' Vivien Goldman discovered when she reported undercover on a gig in aid of the far-right National Front party by the Nicky Crane-associated skinhead band Skrewdriver: 'Obviously the music was horrendous but I was chatted up by this guy in black leather drag, a Mussolini thing. He asked me to the pub, so I went along. He was ranting on about the country being over-run "by a race of coffee-coloured bastards" and saying he wanted more women in the movement. At the end he asked me for another date, and by then I'd had enough of his toxicity, so said, "You maybe won't want to do that because I'm Jewish." So he said, "Oh." Then there was a pause and he added, "Yeah, but you've got to make an exception sometimes." It was like the end of *Some Like It Hot*: "Well, nobody's perfect." When the article came out, he sent me a plaintive, angry letter saying I'd betrayed him because he'd been drummed out of the party when his cronies saw the story.'

Goldman downplays this as 'me striking my little blow against fascism' but, she says, 'The political thing at *Sounds* got worse and worse until I couldn't stand to go in. So I resigned. I will say this about Garry [Bushell]: he is very polite. I'm completely opposed to him but we never had slanging matches. It was always very civilised. I dealt with Alan [Lewis] on this, but Garry's was the face that fit rather than the spiritual, peace-and-love, reggae-ghetto vibe I was giving out.'

Goldman joined the ranks of journalists-turned-music-makers: her twelve-inch single coupling 'Launderette' – coproduced with Public Image Ltd's John Lydon and Keith Levene – and 'Private Armies' is a post-punk cult classic. The songs were, she admitted, 'pretty out there. They weren't necessarily suitable to be played on the radio. I was putting together interesting groups of people: Neneh Cherry, [steel pan player] Bubble ... and a violinist from a Hungarian restaurant. During the mix of "Launderette" we were wondering what to do with the violin and Johnny Rotten was like, "Whack it up. Distort it! Who cares?"'

Back at *Sounds*, members of the Cockney Rejects, a band supported by Bushell, attacked one of his colleagues. 'I came back from lunch a little drunk,' says Pete Silverton. 'They were sitting all over my desk and I asked them to move. Obviously I wasn't polite enough, because they beat me up. Not badly: ripped clothes and a little blood. I wasn't backed by Garry, which I hadn't expected, but I didn't get full support from the editor either. I was probably being a bit precious, but was bored by that stage and left pretty soon afterwards. I didn't respect Garry's shtick. If it was a cynical exercise, that's one thing. I can put up with cynics if what they produce deserves attention, but this wasn't interesting. There was no irony – no style about him or the music he was writing about. There were none of the things I cherished in pop music.'

More aligned with Jon Savage at *Sounds* was Dave McCullough, who had graduated from Northern Irish fanzines and favoured similarly adventurous music. His opinionated copy made fans of readers but not of all his colleagues. 'He destroyed everything that was around,' grumbled Chas de Whalley. 'The idea was that everything is there to be deconstructed, which is fine, but when the critique is based more or less on prejudice, it can do a lot of damage. That, between 1979 and 1982, became the cutting edge of journalism.'

'One of the reasons I left *Sounds* was because Alan Lewis was championing Garry Bushell and Dave McCullough,' said Savage. 'I didn't particularly like either of them, and thought, "If this is the kind of person he is going to hire, there's no place for me here." Also Dave Fudger and Vivien had left and Jane [Suck] had been sacked. We were very young and there were a lot of drugs around. By the end of 1978, cocaine and heroin started to replace speed and a few people in the music press, including one or two on *Sounds*, got messed up.'

Among these was Giovanni Dadomo, who had made hay during the punk era, even releasing a record with Fudger and others as the Snivelling Shits. 'He was one of those Lou Reed fans who should never have heard "I'm Waiting for the Man",' opined Pete Silverton. Dadomo succumbed to liver cancer in the mid-1990s.

Savage pitched up at *Melody Maker*, which, in 1979, was in a period of transition. Staff had long been disillusioned with editor Ray Coleman, a veteran of the Beatlemania era. 'It got horribly messy,' lamented Allan Jones. 'We used to make [assistant editor] Mick Watts's life a misery by moaning about the editorial direction every night in the pub. Ray seemed like my granddad. It got to the point where you thought, "What the fuck is he doing in charge?"'

New publisher John Redington agreed, and promoted Coleman to editor-in-chief. In his place as day-to-day editor came Richard Williams, who had followed his spell in A&R at Island with editing *Time Out*. The old guard was cleared, including Michael Oldfield, a production editor who, according to Allan Jones, 'would take his team to the pub for three hours at lunch time and then come back and slash your copy to ribbons.'

'I thought it was what I always wanted to do,' Williams reflected of his return. 'I'm not sure it was now. Maybe it was just a bad time, or maybe it was me.' Nonetheless, Jones enthused, 'Richard was brilliantly refreshing. He made some brave and eccentric decisions – featuring the Pop Group on the cover before they had a record out and having Chris Petit write a strange piece about searching for Kraftwerk in Europe. It was great to have an editor who was aware of what was happening.' For his part, Petit admitted to bfi.org.uk, 'I became a rather bad music journalist for *Melody Maker* with the express intention of meeting Kraftwerk. This achieved, I gave them a folder with the script for [his 1979 road movie] *Radio On*. Ralf Hütter mistook the name of the folder for the title of the film and thereafter it was referred to between us as the Digby Wallet.'

New *Melody Maker* contributors included Mary Harron, fresh from *Punk* in New York, and Vivien Goldman from *Sounds*. Harron applied with a piece about Leeds punk group the Mekons: 'Richard called me and said he loved it, which was a big thrill. I became a music writer for the next four or five years, eventually moving to *The Guardian* on Richard's recommendation, but I never felt at home in the British scene the way I did in New York ... The older I got, the less connected I felt to the culture, so I knew I had to move on. That was hard to do, because at the time no one took you seriously if you wrote about pop music. The music press was really ghettoized. A lot of people were trying to break out.'

'Mary was excellent,' says Williams, 'as was James Truman, when you could get copy out of him. One of my clearest memories of editing during that period was being woken at about 5.00 a.m. on Monday morning – when I set off for the printer in Colchester – and hearing this *tap, tap, tap* noise outside. It was James sitting in his Mini with his typewriter on his lap, and he would still only be on page three of fifteen. In those days you couldn't fire it down the line; you had to have the stuff in your hand to take to the printer.' Among Truman's victims was *Tubular Bells* mastermind Mike Oldfield – who, the *Melody Maker* man wrote, 'would be treated with the compassion and understanding he so deserves if he behaved himself and stopped making such outrageously dull records'.

Harron, Truman and Goldman were constituents of what Jon Savage described as 'an incredible roster' of writers: 'We all got on. One of the reasons is that I personally didn't have an urge to be a rock writer star. I didn't think I was good enough.'

Also on the team were Ian Birch, who had worked at *Time Out* and would become a big cheese at Emap and Hearst, Paul Tickell, who became a TV director, and Chris Bohn, who focused on new and avant-garde music. 'We always thought it was quite like *Street Life*, which we agreed had been a lost opportunity,' said Savage.

'They were determined to have somebody young,' recalled contributor Paolo Hewitt. 'I wrote this huge thing on the Jam which made loads of references to Woking [home of the band and Hewitt] and small-town life. Then I got Madness, the Specials and Dexy's Midnight Runners, but also horrible things like [second-division neo-mods] the Lambrettas.'[19]

The mission handed by publishers IPC to Richard Williams was a familiar one for *Melody Maker* editors: outdo *NME*. 'They had a certain amount of rights to punk,' acknowledged Williams. 'We were struggling to a) catch up and b) reconcile it with the rest of the coverage. In other words, [we] didn't want to drop Led Zeppelin, Genesis and all that. I went back thinking I could make it into a paper that would be better than *NME*, so I fiddled about with it for a year or so and then we got to a full-blown redesign.'

The latter was by Pearce Marchbank, veteran of *Friends of Rolling Stone* and *Time Out*. 'The redesign was great, with an ink-splattered logo and grainy pictures,' said Williams. 'I realized I was going to have to throw some things away or downplay them, but I never liked redesigns. They're an admission that something is wrong at the roots.' But the dummy issue of the paper's new format, said Allan Jones, 'looked fantastic – it would have been brilliant'. According to Jones, IPC even agreed the budget for a television advertising campaign.

Melody Maker had endured a relocation even more ignominious than that suffered by *NME* a couple of years earlier: owing to overcrowding at King's Reach Tower, the team was moved, for months, to a Nissen hut in semi-industrial wasteland next to the Thames. This naturally added to inter-office tensions. 'People started to get very competitive and aggressive,' sighed Chris Welch. 'It's inevitable, having twelve rock journalists in one room. There was less tolerance than there had been and a gradual deterioration in atmosphere because there were people like Chris Bohn, Paolo Hewitt and Jon Savage. When I joined in 1963, there were people who had been there in the thirties and we tended to look back rather fondly at the older chaps. But this time we were perceived as boring old farts.'

Meanwhile, Williams's attempts to introduce the redesign were hamstrung by editor-in-chief Ray Coleman. 'Ray had been getting on Richard's case,' said Allan Jones, 'holding him up and questioning everything at publisher's meetings.'

Then forces beyond *Melody Maker*'s control wrought havoc.
Over the preceding months, the government had passed the first of six acts to restrict industrial action by requiring pre-strike ballots. Secondary picketing was outlawed and employers were given the right to seek injunctions where there was doubt about the legality of industrial action. In 1980 alone, *Employment Gazette* calculated, there were 1,330 strikes in Britain's main industries. In the spring, print unions took up the cudgels and the National Union of Journalists called its members out in sympathy.

'When we'd completed the dummy for the new look and were ready to go, the strike happened,' said Richard Williams. 'IPC wanted me to produce what we called a 'scab issue', without any staff, which I certainly wouldn't have done.' Williams responded by handing in his notice. 'That day we had been down the pub, so I started to smash up the office,' said Allan Jones. 'I was so angry because I knew all the work Richard had done would count for nothing. I also knew that, when he went, Ray Coleman would come back in some form like the undead. I threw every typewriter I could lay my hands on through the windows, followed by the chairs. Everyone else was a bit stunned. The alarms went off and the rest smuggled me out before security got there. Word got through to the negotiating team that there was a riot going on. The workers were revolting, and fuck me if that didn't spur them on to settle the dispute.' But it was too late for Williams, who was, he said, 'pleased to go'.

* * *

IPC's pressure for a blackleg issue of *Melody Maker* was, in part, a panicked response to *New Music News*, a weekly rushed out during the strike by Dennis Publishing. This fast-growing independent was led by the buccaneering Felix Dennis, who had drummed up advertising at *Oz* a decade before and surfed on the popularity of poster magazines for fads such as kung fu. The newcomer's editor, Mark Williams, had been freelancing for *Melody Maker*. He told Dennis, '*NME* and *Melody Maker* are off the streets and are likely to be so for some time, so let's start a music weekly. Because, apart from anything else, there'll be a ton of money to be made from advertising, because the record companies have got nowhere to go.'[20]

A hotch-potch of hastily gathered material, the first issue of *New Music News*, in May 1980, featured an interview with Malcolm McLaren licensed from LA's *Slash*, plus features on Blondie and the Sex Pistols biopic *The Great Rock 'n' Roll Swindle*. According to Williams, it sold 80,000 copies.

The staff included other refugees from the underground press: designers George Snow and Michelle Mortimer, and writer Barry Miles. They joined contributors who had lost out because of the strike, including Mark Ellen, an *NME* freelancer. Ellen's future *Smash Hits* and *Q* compadre Tom Hibbert – then 'doing stuff on how to improve your home' – also contributed. His first interview was with Alex Chilton, the Memphis legend who had played in the Box Tops and Big Star in the 1960s and '70s and latterly produced the Cramps. 'I'd never done an interview before, which was very worrying,' recalled Hibbert. 'So I took a load of drugs in preparation. He'd obviously done the same, so then we did some together and got on very well.'[21]

'Tom admired very few musicians beyond Iggy Pop, Ray Davies and Jerry Garcia but filed fond, waspish and lightly mocking deconstructions of many others,' wrote Mark Ellen. 'Asked by another

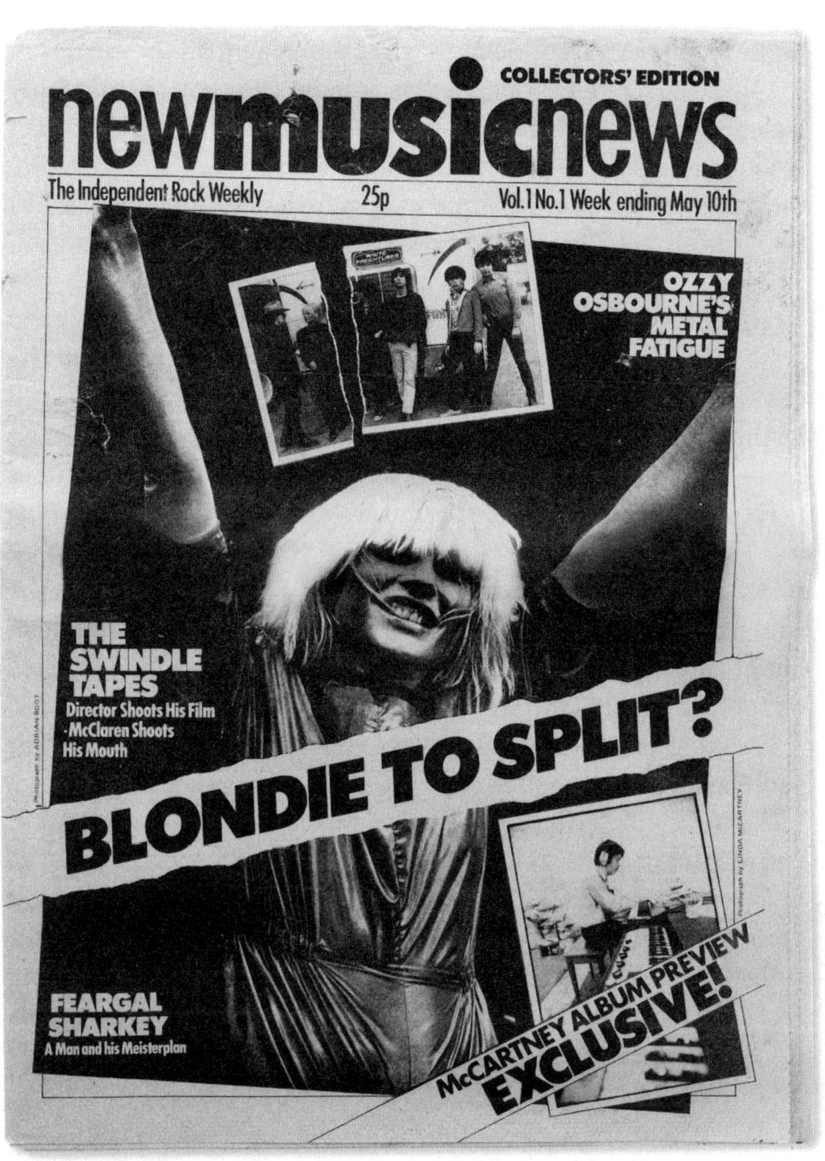

New Music News, vol. 1, no. 1, 10 May 1980

New Music News staff member why he made up all the entries in the short-lived publication's letters column, his response was flatly logical: "Because we don't have any readers."'[22] The publication itself, said Hibbert, was 'much more *Private Eye* than *NME*. We thought we were offering something more humorous and scabrous than the others. The atmosphere was barmy, psychotic. It was in a tiny office and everyone was on masses of speed.'

Hitting the weekly deadlines, said Mark Williams, was 'ridiculously hard work, because there was no structure to it and the resources were extremely limited'. Mark Ellen agreed: 'We stayed up three nights in a row bashing the whole thing together in a frantic fireball of smoke and booze, then collapsed in a heap for three days to recover. And did the same the next week. And the week after. The less I slept, the more I felt I was suffering for my art and the more rock and roll the end product. If I wrote my pieces alone and in the cold light of day, it seemed like a profession; if I hammered them out at three in the morning in a room full of skinny girls crashed out on cushions, I felt I was changing the world.'[23]

By issue six, Mark Williams had resigned, *Sounds* regular Giovanni Dadomo was editor and *New Music News* began to carve a niche for itself. 'From a frankly derivative substitute, *NMN* went on to develop some style of its own as it attempted to outlive the reappearance of the IPC weeklies,' wrote Cynthia Rose in *NME*'s year-end review. She noted that it 'scored respectable rock paper coups', including a preview of David Bowie's *Scary Monsters (and Super Creeps)*, and organized a summit of leading women Viv Albertine, Pauline Black, Debbie Harry, Chrissie Hynde, Siouxsie Sioux and Poly Styrene.

'When Felix Dennis wooed Ian Birch from the review editorship of the shrinking *Melody Maker* to reviews editor of *NMN*, he told Birch he would personally guarantee the paper for a year,' wrote Rose. 'A few weeks later Dennis announced he was folding the publication.' The stumbling block, apparently, was the non-payment of £100,000 from US investors. With the sixteenth issue ready to go to print in August 1980, Dennis offered each member of staff the opportunity to buy the title for a penny. A similar offer to Richard Branson was countered by a suggestion from the Virgin boss that

Dennis buy his London club The Venue for a far greater sum. 'The paper,' wrote Rose, 'was dead as of seven that evening.'[24]

Then the early 1980s recession bit; Neil Spencer calculates that *NME*'s circulation, formerly around 260,000, fell by 40,000. Meanwhile, a threat to the inkies' dominance had emerged. A kind of poetry lay in the fact that this was masterminded by one of the music press's architects: Nick Logan, who had begun his challenge to the weeklies' hegemony with *Smash Hits* – which had grown into a huge money-spinner – and now informed publishers Emap that he wanted to pursue new opportunities. *Melody Maker*'s Ian Cranna – who had impressed Logan in the interviews for Tony Parsons and Julie Burchill's 'hip young gunslinger' posts – was brought in to edit *Smash Hits*.

The new magazine bubbling in Logan's brain would combine the production qualities he had honed on *Smash Hits* with a more sophisticated take on music and popular culture: 'It needed to have a degree of commerciality but the idea was that it would be a good-looking general interest magazine, which documented its time. Graphically I had *Paris Match* very much in mind, and there were some Japanese rock magazines with luscious colour. I'd cut out pictures of Patti Smith from them and they looked great.'

He also drew on the London-based *Ritz* and *Boulevard*, which mixed glamour and gossip, film stars and celebrities. 'Rich people's playthings,' observed Logan. 'I thought, "They've got glossy paper and look good. Why shouldn't the common people have glossy paper?" It felt like a mission, just like *NME* had. I felt I had a lot of things to prove.'

Early in 1980 Logan presented a dummy edition to Emap, with music at its core but an expanded focus on fashion, film, clubbing and social issues. 'They said, "Maybe. Come back in six months; we've just launched [soccer magazine] *Match*." I thought, "Fuck you. You've only been able to do that with the money I made you from *Smash Hits*." It wasn't that fair of me, because six months isn't a long time, but I'm very impatient, always have been. So I talked to my wife and started making a few phone calls.'

13 ‘No focus groups’

The Face Breaks the Mould

Fusing the sounds of ska with the energy of punk, the 2 Tone genre skanked its way into the mainstream during 1979. In November, scene leaders the Specials and Madness scored hits with their debut albums, the former's self-titled classic crashing in at number four. Keen to plug into this new scene's potent visuals, social commentary and multicultural makeup, Nick Logan – still based at the *Smash Hits* office in London's Carnaby Street – conjured up his new creation. 'I wanted it to be monthly, to get me out of that weekly rut; on glossy paper so that it would look good; and with very few ads,' he said. 'At *NME* in particular, the awful shapes of ads often meant that you couldn't do what you wanted with the design.'

Logan and his wife Julie had £2,500 in savings, supplemented by £1,000 in royalties from his co-editing, with Bob Woffinden, the cumbersomely titled *The Illustrated New Musical Express Encyclopedia of Rock*. That meant they could fund the first issue of what might have been titled *Real World* had Logan not instead settled on *The Face* – harking back to a term given in his youth to the most stylish mods. Emap execs judged it too abstract and urged him to add the word 'monthly'. But, Logan observed, 'As it was my savings at risk, I felt I could call it what I liked. After all, *The Face* was to be my escape from a career where I struggled to explain myself to publishers or committees. No focus groups here: I was purely and wholeheartedly following instinct.'[1]

But this was not a promising time to be risking life savings on an untested venture. Sectarian violence in Northern Ireland was reaching a peak. The Iranian revolution was in full swing. The Afghan War had prompted Soviet intervention and the former Hollywood actor Ronald Reagan was cultivating his candidacy for US president. In the UK, the policies of Reagan's soon-to-be political partner in crime Margaret Thatcher were the source of domestic strife while the economic slump gathered pace. 'Industry figures, more at IPC than Emap, advised me that it was a bad time to go with it,' recalled Logan. 'I remember thinking, "Recession? You might worry about it, but what's that got to do with me, and with people wanting to read a decent magazine?" Essentially, I was desperate to get going. Things had been crap for so long that I could have been waiting forever if I listened to their or anybody else's advice.'

Logan banked on a projection that newsstand sales and subscriptions could fund the venture, to be published by himself under the self-mocking banner 'Feet First Productions'. He called the best photographers he had worked with – Anton Corbijn, Jill Furmanovsky, Sheila Rock and Pennie Smith – and asked them for special material, particularly colour, that had not been used in the music press and that had interesting framing and subject matter. And he struck a deal with a distributor that ensured the new title would be afforded space in newsagents around the country – 'as opposed to a publication that has as the height of its ambition a showcase at the ICA bookshop and a few glossy ads placed by fashion companies in Milan who have more money than sense'. In the event, the first issue, published in May 1980, exceeded expectations by selling 56,000 copies.

Art director Steve Bush came up with a square blue and red logo that drew on the bisected flag of 1930s anarchists in the Spanish Civil War. Of the twenty-seven listed contributors, one third were photographers. Most had *NME* and *Smash Hits* connections, although Logan, inspired by the do-it-yourself aesthetic of punk fanzines, also provided space for untested writing talent. Singer Vaughn Cotillard – using the pseudonym Vaughn Toulouse – documented his memories of following a UK tour by the Clash in 1978. His friend Gary Crowley, who had taken over from Danny Baker as receptionist at *NME* (where he sat beneath a banner proclaiming 'The world's loudest receptionist'), reviewed the film about that tour, *Rude Boy*. And Ian Dury reviewed a volume of Alfred Wertheimer's photographs of Elvis Presley in his 1950s pomp.

But it was the upbeat, inclusive 2 Tone that dominated the issue, starting with a cover photograph by *NME* regular Chalkie Davies of the Specials' tonic-suited, Bluebeat-hatted leader Jerry Dammers. 'The Specials embodied everything the magazine aspired to,' recalled Logan. 'They had a look, passion and great music, so there was never an alternative. In a sentimental way, I owed 2 Tone for the inspiration.'[2] There was also a photo-essay by Jill Furmanovsky on a trip to Manhattan by the Specials' London confreres Madness, and four pages on a King's Road boutique that sold the best of the movement's clothing. Written by moonlighting *NME* contributor

Adrian Thrills, this showcased designer Lloyd Johnson's checkerboard collection with photographs by Sheila Rock, whom Logan had commissioned at *Smash Hits*. 'Featuring Lloyd in that first issue also lent itself to the reportage feel I wanted,' Logan noted. '[And] my promotional campaign, to give it a fancy term, was based on getting copies to places like Lloyd's, where I knew appreciative people, among them hopefully some readers, would gather.'

Julie Burchill and Tony Parsons were on board from the start. 'When we quit *NME*, we realized no one had heard of us,' said Parsons. 'But Nick Logan was always there to slip us a job. The stuff I did for *The Face* was much more reflective. To find things which excited me as much as punk did, I had to look outside music.' Burchill's page, ostensibly dedicated to reviewing new singles, became a platform for her iconoclastic opinions, such as lambasting BBC pop channel Radio One and its DJs.

Such pieces struck a chord with Sheryl Garratt, who had emerged from Birmingham's 2 Tone and Rock Against Racism scenes and was contributing occasional reviews to *NME*. 'I loved it from the off,' she says. '*NME* – which was really the only other game in town – had slipped. It had not responded to the ways in which music had expanded in London, still concentrating on rock. But the music being played in the clubs or by people I knew like the Slits was so much more diverse. I'd offer them stories on a funk or reggae band and they would commission the odd piece but it felt much more restrictive. You looked at *The Face* and thought, "All the stuff I want to read and write about, there's room for it here."'[3]

Melody Maker contributor James Truman, who become *The Face*'s New York correspondent, hailed it as 'a clean break from the then-dominant music magazines. It was printed on good paper stock, had colour photography, and even in the first issues had a voice that was playful and both masculine and feminine.'[4] But the response from mainstream media was curiosity: why would an established figure venture out on a limb? London's *Evening Standard* ran a photograph of Logan brandishing copies of the first issue and asked whether the launch meant he was 'a maverick or a madman'.[5]

From the second edition (featuring Paul Weller on the cover), Logan achieved his ambition of delivering *The Face* to stores and subscribers in the final week of the month preceding the cover date. 'We worked on a very fast turnaround and would always go to the wire with copy and photos,' he says. 'That way we could be sure our readers were up to speed.'

Julie Logan, assisted by her mother and sisters, packed and addressed subscription envelopes. Nick Logan took them to his local sorting office, then drove around London, dropping off copies and picking up unsolds at Lloyd Johnson's outlets, the independent record store Rough Trade, and clothes retailers and hairdressers in Kensington, Soho, Covent Garden and Chelsea.

Assisting *The Face*'s evolution was journalist Steve Taylor, who had written for *Melody Maker* and *Time Out*. According to him, Logan defined the new magazine's audience as music press readers who 'had outgrown *NME* and were hungry for information about all sorts of other stuff, whether it be film or clothes'.[6] But *The Face* remained, for the time being, rooted in music: for seven issues from August 1980, the masthead was appended with the line 'Rock's final frontier' (pl. 13).

A youthful slant came courtesy of Deanne Pearson, who started at *Horse & Hounds* and freelanced for *NME*. She tired of male posturing at the latter – describing the office as 'an unthreatened, pampered lions' den'[7] – and crossed Carnaby Street to contribute to *Smash Hits* and *The Face*, the latter enlivened by her encounters with reggae poet Linton Kwesi Johnson and new groups Echo and the Bunnymen and Killing Joke. Pearson recalled being commissioned to accompany the Slits on tour but 'doing a runner after having put up with two days of them refusing to speak to me even though they'd agreed to an interview. Then being told I still had to deliver copy, so duly chronicling my observations and thoughts on the Slits and carefully avoiding them for a while afterwards.'[8]

Another who crossed Carnaby Street was Robert Elms, a political science graduate who had contributed three pieces to *NME*, one of which was the first published review of Spandau Ballet (whose name he had suggested; they were managed by a college friend, Steve Dagger). The quintet were spearheading a new movement whose disciples – London night-lifers and fashion students – congregated at the Blitz and Hell clubs. Elms had taken to visiting the

NME offices, proselytizing on his friends' behalf and sometimes openly scorning what he regarded as the paper's outdated content.

Eventually, editor Neil Spencer told him that his presence was no longer required; it seems Elms had raised the hackles of a staff member who felt the voluble Londoner might encroach on their turf. 'Neil told me he didn't think I was right for *NME*,' Elms recalled, 'but that I could write, and that Nick had started a new magazine, which was literally across the road. I clearly remember Neil saying that Nick liked the kinds of things that I liked – clothes and nightclubs – and that he was an old mod, so I walked into Nick's office and told him that I loved his magazine. I hadn't actually seen it.'[9] He also gave Logan a well-practised speech about sounds and styles incubating at Spandau Ballet gigs, on college fashion courses and at London club nights.

The first in the music press to acknowledge Spandau's potential was *Sounds*' Beverly Glick, formerly editor Alan Lewis's secretary, now star writer Betty Page (her stylish look hailing back to the era of the model whose name she adopted). 'Most dyed-in-the-jeans music hacks hated the idea of being bypassed by a bunch of sharp-suited upstarts,' she recalled, 'so Spandau had been dismissed as elitists, fops, dandies, upper-class twits and even fascists, because of the Nazi connotations of their name. It didn't help that the Ballet boys deemed fashion to be of equal importance to music. The fact that they were actually working-class Labour supporters from north London didn't seem to count.

'And so it was with a combination of naive enthusiasm and blind panic that I called Spandau Ballet's manager, Steve Dagger. I had no reason to believe he'd give me the time of day – the last thing he needed was another stitch-up job by an ignorant music hack. But Steve quickly realised that I was something of a blank canvas upon which he and Gary Kemp, their chief theorist and songwriter, could paint their ideas.

'As I sat down to interview the pair, Gary fished out a well-thumbed copy of George Melly's book *Revolt Into Style* and read out a passage about the true meaning of mod being a small group of young working-class boys forming a mutual admiration society "totally devoted to clothes". I carefully copied down the words without taking them in. I had to check again – was he telling me that, when the band first met, it was only about dressing up? "Yes, basically it revolved around admiration of clothes," interjected Steve before Gary could open his mouth, "and featured extreme posing." Extreme posing: words to strike fear into the heart of any rock music purist.'[10]

The resultant article in *Sounds* dubbed the group 'New Romantics', giving the scene from which they sprang its name. 'Spandau Ballet are already very suspicious of the music press due to its total ignorance of them and their ilk,' wrote Page, tracing the group's lineage to Malcolm McLaren and Vivienne Westwood's King's Road boutique that had incubated the Sex Pistols. 'This is the first time they've been asked to present their point of view, to explain their lifestyle. Instead of another revival, here's something new to come to terms with. Fashion cannot so easily be dismissed: remember the first mods, remember that outrageous scene spawned from a shop called Sex back in '76.'[11]

Robert Elms's visit to Nick Logan proved crucial. 'I could see that 2 Tone was fading,' the editor recalled, 'and he had info about this new scene, which showed how pop culture was alive.' The October 1980 issue included three pages by Elms on Spandau – still weeks away from scoring their first hit – with photographs of the group amid the Edwardian splendour of London's Waldorf Hotel. As if intent on annoying rock journalists, Elms drew parallels between Spandau and the Sex Pistols, and described their sound as a mix of early Roxy Music and Chic. 'Openly poseur, stridently elitist, their performances have been limited to six in twice as many months, each occasion "advertised" strictly by word of mouth and each attracting the capital's pretty young things,' he wrote.

On the cover were American kitsch-pop outfit the B-52s, maintaining Logan's focus on the visually interesting; other cover stars included Bryan Ferry and Siouxsie Sioux. But, six issues in, sales plateaued around the crucial break-even 50,000 mark. Logan duly appealed to readers to ensure their local newsagents were ordering sufficient copies. 'It was getting desperate,' he admitted. 'I thought I'd better put this stuff in, because we may not last.'

Nonetheless, the magazine confirmed there was substance beneath the New Romantic style. 'The entire generation of British acts who went on to become massive in America – Boy George, Spandau, Wham!, Sade, Duran Duran – would all go on to be broken by *The Face*,' observed Elms, 'and almost all of them were in Blitz on a Tuesday night.' His piece 'The cult with no name' – packed with Derek Ridgers's vérité photos of scenesters including Marilyn (née Peter Robinson) and George O'Dowd (on the cusp of becoming Boy George) – described London's nightlife as 'a colourful, exotic world which has set the styles to be copied in terms of both look and sound'.

'*The Face* was how the rest of the world got to know that the Blitz generation had arrived and the party had started,' wrote Peter York in the 1980s. 'Elms supplied insider knowledge, total user-friendliness. From "The cult with no name" onward, *The Face* became a Publishing Event. After that, the nationals took it up as a key feed and we had the first style diary of the New Age.'[12]

Underlining Logan's grasp of the zeitgeist, that issue of *The Face* appeared within weeks of another new magazine that included music but was more rooted in fashion: *i-D*, launched as a quarterly in October 1980 by the husband-and-wife team of former British *Vogue* art director Terry and Tricia Jones. In contrast to *The Face*'s sophisticated colour photography, *i-D* showcased monochrome street portraiture that Jones developed with photographer Steve Johnston. And it was avowedly fanzine-like, with typewriter text containing corrections left for readers to see, as well as scrawls and scribbles. Initial copies of the oblong title were hand-stapled, with no tangible distribution beyond Better Badges in London's Portobello Road. There were later claims that the first issue sold only fifty copies[13] and, for the first five years, *i-D* was produced at the Joneses' London home.

The Cult With No Name's ancestry was made explicit by the cover of issue seven of *The Face*: a Brian Duffy image of David Bowie, in makeup and costume, from the shoot for his 'Ashes to Ashes' video (which featured Blitz club denizens such as Steve Strange). 'The mystique is still deadly strong,' wrote Jon Savage. 'Why? Because David Bowie has entered British life as the model for every kid who says: "I wish I was ..."'

Savage had been alerted to prospects at *The Face* by Gary Crowley. 'Nick was a very laid-back, laissez-faire editor,' he recalled. 'You'd

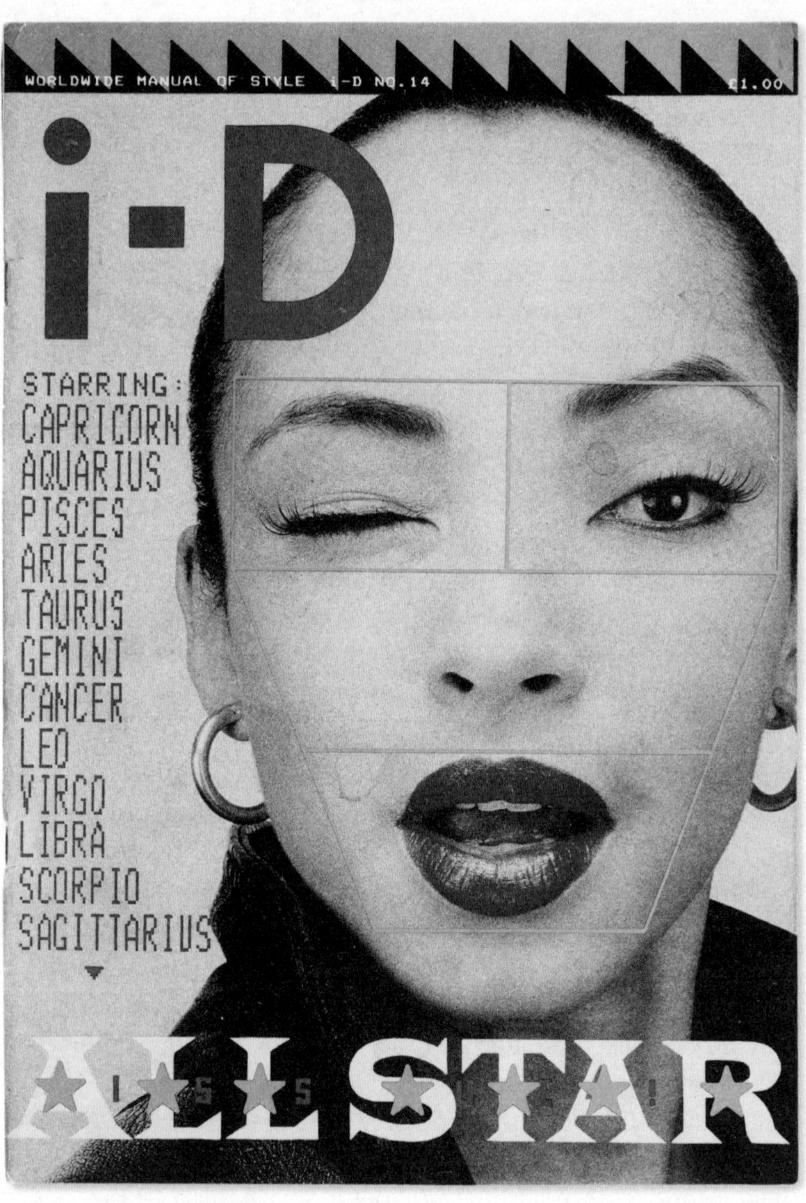
WORLDWIDE MANUAL OF STYLE i-D NO.14
£1.00
i-D
STARRING:
CAPRICORN
AQUARIUS
PISCES
ARIES
TAURUS
GEMINI
CANCER
LEO
VIRGO
LIBRA
SCORPIO
SAGITTARIUS
ALL STAR

i-D, no. 14, 1984

go into his little office and there wouldn't be any of the hassle you'd have with the music press, where everyone vied for attention. Through instinct and talent, Nick Logan and Terry Jones had captured a new, socialized pop attitude that seemed refreshing after the extravagant alienation of pop. Central to this was the idea of club culture, of group social activity and of Black music used as a metaphor for cool community and that indefinable "soul".' Savage's pieces demonstrated the ways in which *The Face* was accelerating ahead of the pack, including the first interview with Vivienne Westwood that seriously assessed her potency as a formal fashion designer and a feature on Bow Wow Wow, the group that Malcolm McLaren masterminded in the wake of the Sex Pistols.

NME veteran Chris Salewicz also threw in his lot with Logan after a bust-up with the weekly's assistant editor Phil McNeill: 'He implied I wasn't allowed to write for *The Face*, which showed they were threatened. I said, "Fuck you." I realized I had to get out of there. It was too limiting, just writing about music.' Salewicz profiled actor and singer Divine and model-turned-performer Grace Jones, documented the invasion of the formerly hippy Kensington Market by post-punk designers and wrote a cover story on John Lydon and Public Image Ltd. This appeared in the December 1980 issue that also contained Logan's first stab at the type of lists that later became a fixture of *The Face* as barometers of style and taste, that were promptly imitated in the music papers, and that remain a media staple to this day.

The magazine's year-end review of 1980 documented pop culture but also the dark shadows cast by that year's economic slump and the failure of the Left to oppose the Conservative government. A '15 dodgy concepts' list included 'Thatcher's independent [nuclear] deterrent ... the unemployed ... Cruise missiles in the UK ... [Secretary of State for Industry] Keith Joseph's policies ... recession, depression, unemployment ...' But such bleakness didn't define *The Face*. After just nine months, and with Logan having established a base at Pete Townshend's Soho office, it proclaimed itself 'The world's best dressed magazine'.

* * *

At the Emap offices vacated by Nick Logan, *Smash Hits* features editor David Hepworth – who became editor on Ian Cranna's departure in 1981 – was ringing changes that challenged the pale boys' chin-stroking approach and preoccupations. 'I have a great problem with "post-punk",' he said. 'The fact that there is the expression post-punk indicates punk's major problem, which is that it had a massively over-inflated sense of its own importance. Punk rock was just one of the things that was going on at the time. You might as well say post-disco, because actually if you're looking for the real commercial phenomenon in the mid-1970s, it was disco music.'[14]

Like disco, the pop covered by *Smash Hits* was dismissed by the music press, not least because its most visible fans were teenage girls and gay men. But the magazine turned the tables on dreary rock criticism: by 1984, *Smash Hits* was shifting 500,000 copies while *NME* sold around 120,000, *Sounds* 80,000, *Record Mirror* 70,000 and *Melody Maker* 68,000. 'We didn't look down our noses at the kids, and were genuinely interested in teen enthusiasm, even if we didn't necessarily share it ourselves,' said Hepworth. 'It helped that the stars around then were interesting people. Debbie Harry, even the likes of Duran Duran and Spandau Ballet, had lives, which made the magazine have a sort of crackle. They also had huge careers without being all over the tabloids. Debbie Harry was terribly well known but you didn't pick up *The Sun* every day expecting to see something about her. Tabloids weren't desperately focusing on this world like they are now.'

Smash Hits' stance was made clear by a circular that Hepworth sent to record company press departments: 'It is my intention to reverse the entire direction of popular music publishing in favour of trivia. Consequently we are bringing back the "Personal File". We want to know the colour of your artists' socks.' Hepworth explained: 'You had a format, which had applied to David Cassidy, being taken up by Ian Dury, [the Human League's] Phil Oakey and Debbie Harry. I'm not claiming it as the sole reason but, if you look at every magazine from *Vanity Fair* to *The Spectator*, they have something like that: bitty, capsule-size pieces of information. We lob the ball to you, you lob it back to us. We're here to play a game. It's got to be entertainment before it's anything else.'

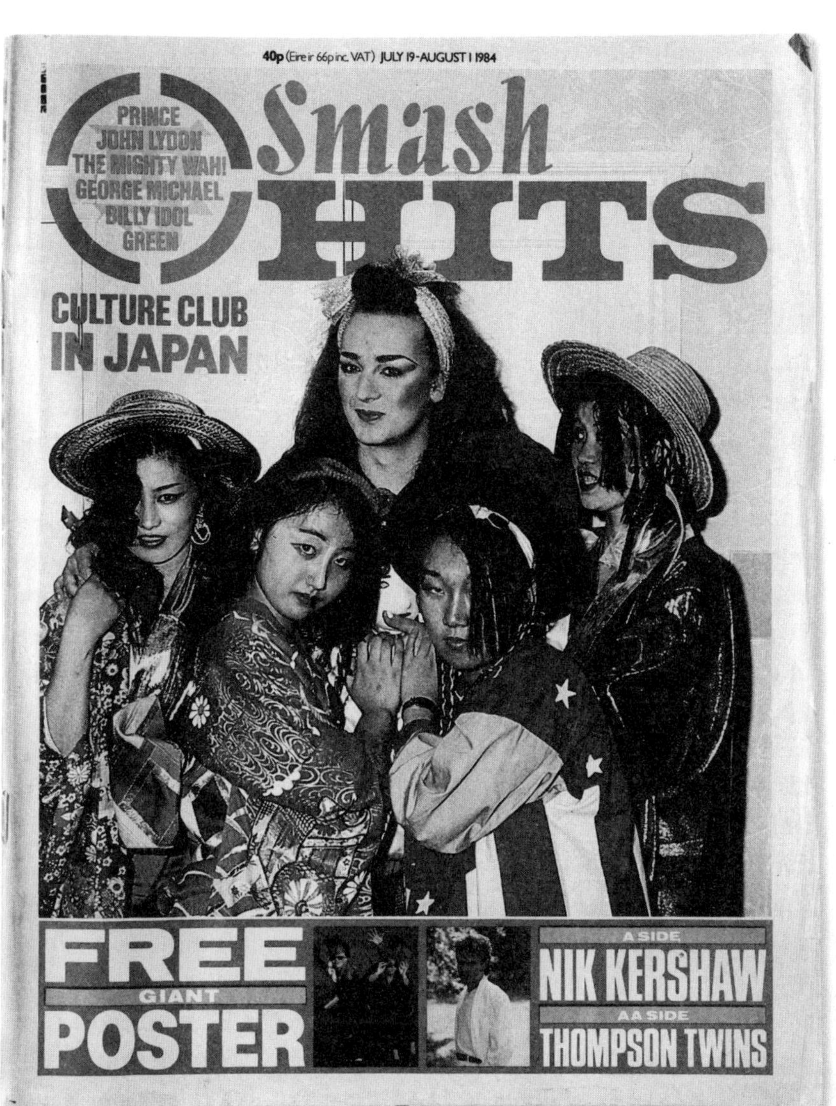

Smash Hits, 19 July–1 August 1984

The result, Hepworth observed, was 'younger, more vibrant and more female than the rest of the music press'.[15] Bob Stanley, who wrote for *NME* and *Melody Maker* in the 1980s before co-founding indie pop band St Etienne, described the magazine as 'a safe space for girls' that avoided the weeklies' tendency for captions 'which would make you wince' when attractive female performers were pictured: '*Smash Hits*' editorial stance avoided almost all of the era's sexism, knowing that it had a larger proportion of female readers than the weekly papers. Initially, it was still largely written by men, but Bev Hillier's disco column was very much a return to the uncynical breeziness of *Fabulous*, and a time before rock writing existed. What mattered most to Bev was danceability: she wasn't blind to the lyrical banality of much of the music she was reviewing, and said that she preferred instrumentals. Her presence was benign and encouraging.'[16] '*NME* was too academic for me when I was fourteen,' said star writer Sylvia Patterson. '*Smash Hits* felt like a brick through the window. The tomfoolery spoke to me like nothing else had.'[17]

Hepworth's enlistment of Mark Ellen – first as a writer, then as his successor as features editor – proved a turning point. In the wake of the collapse of *New Music News*, Ellen had freelanced for *Record Mirror* and *Time Out*, his copy displaying a mocking bent that matched Hepworth's. Shared populist sensibilities resulted in an enduring professional relationship: Hepworth and Ellen would launch the magazines *Q*, *Mojo*, *Heat* and *The Word*, cohost *The Old Grey Whistle Test* (and, consequently, the British leg of Live Aid) and establish the digital media company Word In Your Ear.

'*NME* was really vicious and really cruel,' Ellen reflected. 'It just wasn't in my nature to be like that. I didn't have the required cynicism. I was slightly sarcastic but I wasn't cynical. I think everyone else at *NME* really enjoyed laying into yesterday's news. Obviously we were keen to promote tomorrow's news, but having promoted them, for me there was a little too much pleasure in pulling the rug out from under their feet. It was a harsh environment.

'With *Smash Hits*, the idea was that you can't take pop and to an extent rock music 100 per cent seriously, because half the fun of pop music is that it can be colourful. It can be over the top. It can be shallow. And it's populated with very exotic, charismatic and often rather peculiar characters. It's good to encourage them to be like that, because that's what you want them to be.

'Also, pop is full of preposterous pretension a lot of the time. It's very easy to laugh at, but often pretension is just people trying to do something different, willing to go out on a limb. They might make themselves look ludicrous but they might succeed. I always used to think Queen were pretentious. A lot of people really liked what they did, and good luck to them. So part of the *Smash Hits* thing was that we were trying to suggest the landscape was filled with these kind of cartoon characters.'[18] A case in point was a 1981 telling of the story of the Human League's formation as a comic strip. Front man Phil Oakey was noted for his lopsided fringe, so illustrator Harry North rendered Oakey's family, including his grandmother and pet dog, with the same tonsorial arrangement.

'We thought pop stars were terrific but absurd, so we developed a way of dealing with this supposedly glamorous world in mundane style,' said Hepworth. 'Adam Ant was called "Alan Ant", Paul McCartney "Fab Macca Wacky Thumbs Aloft" and I came up with Tony "Foghorn" Hadley [for the stentorian Spandau Ballet singer]. The office was like a weird boarding school, where everyone called each other "Maaaan!" because it was the most ridiculous way to talk to someone when you're from Yorkshire or Newcastle. But magical things happened.'

Key to the magazine's lingo and mickey-taking was Tom Hibbert, brought on board by his *New Music News* colleague Mark Ellen: 'I joined and started making up ridiculous things like the "Bits" page, taking the piss out of pop stars. In the letters pages we had lots of running jokes about the groups, and the readers picked up on them. [But] strangely enough, working on *Smash Hits* could be difficult. You spent all your time flattering people and putting in little jokes to cheer yourself up and then people you never hear of any more – Howard Jones, Nik Kershaw – threatened to sue. It always turned out to be about getting the name of their wives wrong. We'd have to explain to them that this wasn't actually libellous.'

Hibbert's interview technique created an atmosphere in which subjects expressed themselves, sometimes unwisely. 'Tom was unafraid of silence,' said Mark Ellen. 'He would give his subjects the impression that, despite their obvious successes, they were still somehow shameful underachievers, and then sit back quietly with a cigarette to enjoy the panicked response.'

And his refusal to take anything seriously – in work and in life, according to Ellen – egged on the rest of the team, who came up with satirical soubriquets such as 'Dame David Bowie' and – thanks to his moustachioed likeness to a missing British aristocrat – 'Lord Frederick Lucan of Mercury'. Ellen noted, 'When given the job of writing the "trail" to flag up the contents of the next *Smash Hits*, Tom would advertise groups that existed only in his fertile imagination, such as the failed pop idol Reg "Reg" Snipton or an intriguing electronic duo, the Human Saucepans of the Orinoco.'

Hibbert's comic takes were complemented by Ian Birch, who had absconded from *Melody Maker*. 'He was as fascinated as I was by the demands of our new readers,' said Ellen. 'In his first week Ian dashed off dutifully to interview Japan when a reader announced she would leap from the Forth Bridge if rumours of the pale quintet's split weren't officially denied.'[19]

Smash Hits also offered the sometimes revelatory reportage of Dave Rimmer, who had contributed to *The Face* in its early days and was well placed to chart the rise of Japan, Heaven 17, Simple Minds and, in particular, Culture Club, with whom he toured the world. Rimmer's pieces became mandatory reading for anyone interested in music business machinations, and resulted in his mid-decade overview *Like Punk Never Happened*, a first-person account of Culture Club's position in pop. '*Smash Hits* turned into a bit of a pop star itself,' he wrote, 'a fact that was underlined as *NME*, desperately trying to work out what had gone wrong in its fall from prominence in the punk era, namechecked *Smash Hits* several times in each issue. They were usually slighting references, rather in the manner of the paper looking down from its high horse at, say, Wham!'[20]

Meanwhile, Hepworth drove the publication forward. 'He knew instinctively what appealed to the teenage viewers of [BBC chart show] *Top of the Pops*,' wrote Ellen. 'A picture of Toyah turned up, her face painted with seagulls and her hair a bright orange vertical explosion, as if she'd been connected to the electrical grid. The black and white music papers called her a histrionic harpie of no audible talent but *Smash Hits* readers thought she was the liberated sister they'd never had. Dave slapped it on the cover and it sold 150,000 copies. He decided the next issue should have two covers: Kim Wilde on the front, the Stray Cats on the back. The two half-magazines met in the middle, one printed upside down.'[21]

The readership grew in numbers and engagement. 'Every night, the thirteen- and fourteen-year-olds of Britain went to their rooms, got out their Friends Forever notepaper and multicoloured pens and wrote – actually with their hands – long letters suggesting something we'd got wrong, or somebody we ought to feature more, or somebody they liked,' said Hepworth. 'I think *Smash Hits* was more instrumental in teenage literacy than all the education in the world.'[22]

Neil Tennant – the editor and writer whose letter about a fight at a Sex Pistols gig had been published as a news story by *NME* in 1976 – was drawn into the *Smash Hits* circle by designer Steve Bush and photographer Eric Watson, with whom he worked on a book spin-off for the Madness film *Take It or Leave It*. When Hepworth commissioned a *Smash Hits* annual from Tennant, he also became the magazine's news editor. 'Mark Ellen said to me, "Welcome to the world of free records,"' Tennant recalled. 'The whole of the music press, as I found out when I became a musician, was very stab-you-in-the-back. But at *Smash Hits* we went with our enthusiasms and people you knew were a great story. The sense of humour really took over. Tom Hibbert was an amazing, baroque writer, and Mark and Dave were very, very funny. That was important because we turned pop stars into characters.'[23]

Tennant dubbed Billy Idol 'Sir William Idol' ('Our greatest living Englishman') and added 'Does your mother play golf?' to the Personal File because, according to Hepworth, 'the answer revealed if someone was posh. Most stars tolerated it because we sold hundreds of thousands of copies, and they could tell *NME* they didn't need to talk to them. Paul Weller – or "Paul Welder" as we called him – said, "It's like punk never 'appened," but he kept talking to us.'

'The readers were always taken very seriously,' recalled Tennant. 'At the editorial meetings we talked about, "What do the readers like?" There was nothing slapdash about *Smash Hits*. In fact we used to sneer at other music magazines because we thought they were a bit lazy and clichéd.'[24]

Tennant adhered to the Logan/Hepworth dictum of never patronizing the magazine's young readers, gleaned fascinating responses from playful questions such as, 'Who would you most like to have round for supper? a) Michael Parkinson; b) Sting; c) Prince Andrew; d) [French singer] FR David', and captured Malcolm McLaren predicting the coming of club culture ('Discotheques will be more vigorous and exciting than any concert on the stage of the Hammersmith Odeon. Live discotheques. I really think that'll happen').[25]

Smash Hits, Tennant told *Interview*, 'had an ideology, a belief that pop music could be really good and really popular. When it's both of those things, it's fucking great.'[26] And in his foreword to a weighty retrospective, Tennant wrote that his time at the magazine was 'the best "proper" job I ever had. This was the period when young, intelligent pop stars had learned the lessons and ideas of punk and decided to link them to the glamour of pop stardom and nightlife. A stylish, thoughtful, hedonistic pop era flourished, and *Smash Hits* was its house magazine.'[27]

Tennant's view that the first half of the 1980s was defined by 'gorgeous pop music which conquered the world' is supported by a photograph of Boy George and Annie Lennox that appeared on the front of the Christmas 1983 issue of *Smash Hits*. Within a month, a photo from the same session appeared on the cover of *Newsweek*, with the headline 'Britain rocks America – again: from the Beatles to Boy George and beyond'.

The inclusivity and openness of *Smash Hits* made the weeklies look monotonous. 'Everyone has got a look: Culture Club, Duran Duran, Spandau,' reflected Tennant. 'Frankie Goes To Hollywood come along and they're outrageous. Bronski Beat have a gay rights manifesto happily spread across two pages and the front cover of *Smash Hits*. There's a dance music thing going on with electronic music and *Smash Hits* covers it before *NME*. Me and Dave Rimmer are playing hip-hop and Euro-dance music all day long on the office record player.'

Tennant rose up the ranks while his musical talents led him into an enduring pop partnership with Chris Lowe as the Pet Shop Boys, whose recording debut was a song to advertise sticker sets given away with the magazine. 'We had no idea he was making music when he offered to do it,' said Mark Ellen. 'The song was absolutely brilliant.'[28]

Smash Hits' 'dumper box', the resting place of free promotional records, also played a part. 'It was next to my desk and I would stay after work and go through it to see if there was anything good; to my astonishment there were all these records produced by Bobby Orlando,' said Tennant, who had been introduced to the music of the American hi-NRG producer by Lowe. Meanwhile, a tourist shop in the magazine's Carnaby Street radius had taken to blasting Orlando's 'I'm So Hot for You'. 'Dave Hepworth promptly made it record of the week,' he recalled, 'comparing him to Bruce Springsteen.'

In the summer of 1983, on a visit to the US to see the Police play at Shea Stadium, Tennant took the opportunity to track down Orlando: 'I was working on the *Smash Hits* annual, which included a feature, "One Night in New York." It shows how blasé we were becoming because no-one else wanted to go.' After interviewing Sting, Tennant hooked up with Orlando and, a month later, he and Lowe were back in New York cutting 'West End Girls'. Tennant was too embarrassed to play the track to his colleagues, because he rapped on it, but designer David 'Scoffer' Bostock heard it and declared the song a hit, encouraging Tennant to pursue his music career – ultimately at the expense of becoming editor. 'It was quite a thing to turn it down, at the age of thirty-one, and decide to become a pop star.'[29]

'When Neil left to form the Pet Shop Boys, we mocked up a cover, reading: "How I left Britain's greatest pop magazine to become a pop star and then came back with my tail between my legs,"' recalled Hepworth. "Which, of course, he never did.'[30]

14
‘You could say, “I love this”’

From *i-D*, *Collusion* and *WET* to *Flexipop*, *Star Hits* and *Kerrang!*

The success of *The Face* and *Smash Hits* sparked new bids to cash in on two burgeoning markets: twentysomethings eager for coverage of cinema, music, design and fashion, and teens seeking colourful news of their favourite pop stars. The Emap executives who had hired Nick Logan made their bid with the New Romantic-themed monthly *New Sounds New Styles*. 'They'd effectively pooh-poohed my idea,' he frowned, 'made me go through a lot of heartache to get it somewhere, and then tried to muscle in.'[1]

Evidently concerned that New Romanticism might be a flash in the pan, Emap piloted a sixty-four-page version before launching the monthly run, helmed by designer Malcolm Garrett and writer Kasper de Graaf. 'I gave [de Graaf] info about the editorial direction,' recalled *The Face*'s Steve Taylor, 'and wrote a few pieces for the first issue but then didn't hear anything more.'[2] While Taylor stayed at *The Face*, Robert Elms jumped ship 'because they offered me a salary. I remember telling Nick and him just chuckling. I was rather hoping he'd say, "I'll give you some money to stay," but he didn't, so off I went for a while.'

Elms's sojourn didn't last long. Unable to gain a satisfactory hold on the market, Emap pulled the plug with the thirteenth and final *New Sounds New Styles* in July 1982. Garrett and de Graaf headed out of publishing and back into the music industry, with a design studio servicing Culture Club and Duran Duran.

Others treading the trail mapped by *The Face* were Oxford undergraduates Simon Tesler (son of a British television mogul) and Carey Labovitch (niece of government minister Michael Heseltine's partner). Just ahead of Emap's *New Sounds New Styles* test run, Tesler and Labovitch circulated the first issue of their magazine *Blitz*. A quarterly A3 fold-out, it featured a *Face*-esque mix of music, fashion and film, but with surprisingly old-school contributors: theatre columnist Sheridan Morley and film critics Quentin Falk and Alexander Walker.

The title was no coincidence: Elms had referred to 'Blitz Kids' in the 'cult with no name' feature and Steve Taylor marked the signing of Steve Strange's group Visage to Chrysalis by pronouncing 'Blitz culture is about to go public'. And it proved a more durable alternative to *The Face* than *New Sounds New Styles*, attracting contributors such as Paul Morley. Issued monthly and distributed nationally, it dropped the folded A3 format in favour of the retailer and advertiser-friendly A4. With *i-D* still published in its odd rectangular format (it finally went A4 in 1983), this posed a head-to-head challenge to *The Face*.

'We'd like to establish it as a magazine which will be launching new writers and writing about new artists,' Labovitch told *The Observer*, which noted that 'punk rock and New Romantic street journals pop up and disappear from the bookstalls like a bad case of acne'.[3] The similarity in approach, content and execution earned *Blitz* the disapproval of Logan and his staff; there are stories of false items being placed in *The Face* as bait for *Blitz*.

At Spotlight Publications, *Sounds* editor Alan Lewis came up with a bimonthly rock/pop hybrid with colour posters and song lyrics. Called *Noise!*, it was edited by Betty Page, who followed her Spandau Ballet exclusive at the start of the 1980s by showcasing Duran Duran. But the mix of acts – from Haysi Fantayzee and the Associates to Motörhead and Iron Maiden, and second-wave punks including the Anti Nowhere League – proved unappealing. *Noise!* closed after six months and Page became assistant editor of *Record Mirror*.

There were intriguing attempts to experiment with the magazine format. *SFX* (pl. 15) was a sixty-minute cassette tape of interviews with acts including Ian Dury, Madness and, discussing John Lennon's murder, Paul McCartney. Edited by former *NME* writer Max Bell, this was a brave attempt to break the mould, but its inherent clunkiness and lack of visual appeal limited newsstand sales, and it closed after nineteen issues.

Longer-lasting was *Flexipop!*, which featured cover-mounted, seven-inch flexidiscs. Exclusive tracks included Adam and the Ants spoofing the Village People's 'Y.M.C.A.' as 'A.N.T.S.', the Pretenders covering the Small Faces' 'Whatcha Gonna Do About It', and Blondie and Fab 5 Freddy reinventing 'Rapture' as 'Yuletide Throwdown'.

'The design looked as if it had been executed by a chimp,' confessed co-founder Tim Lott. 'The paper quality was poor and the contents were puerile.' His claim that the magazine represented 'the first reaction against the previous decade of music reportage, dominated by *NME*' is overcooked, given that *Smash Hits* was

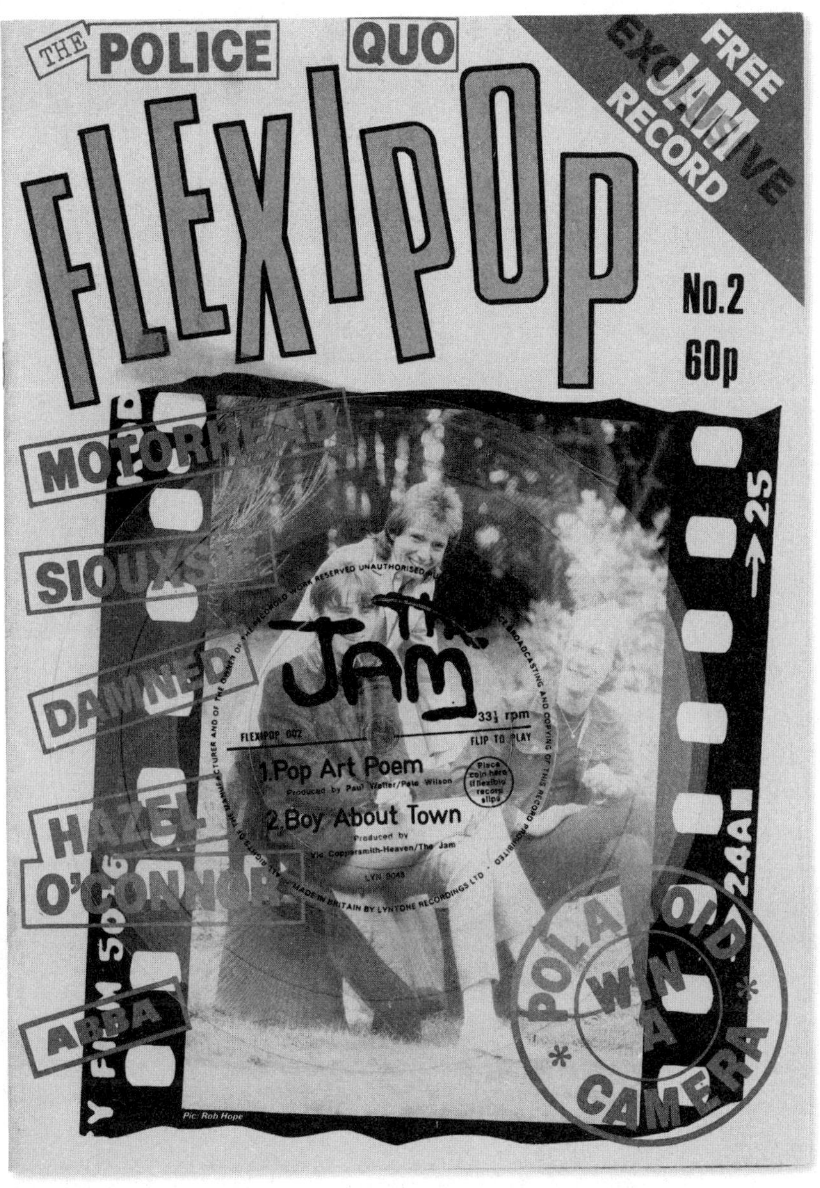

Flexipop!, no. 2, 1981

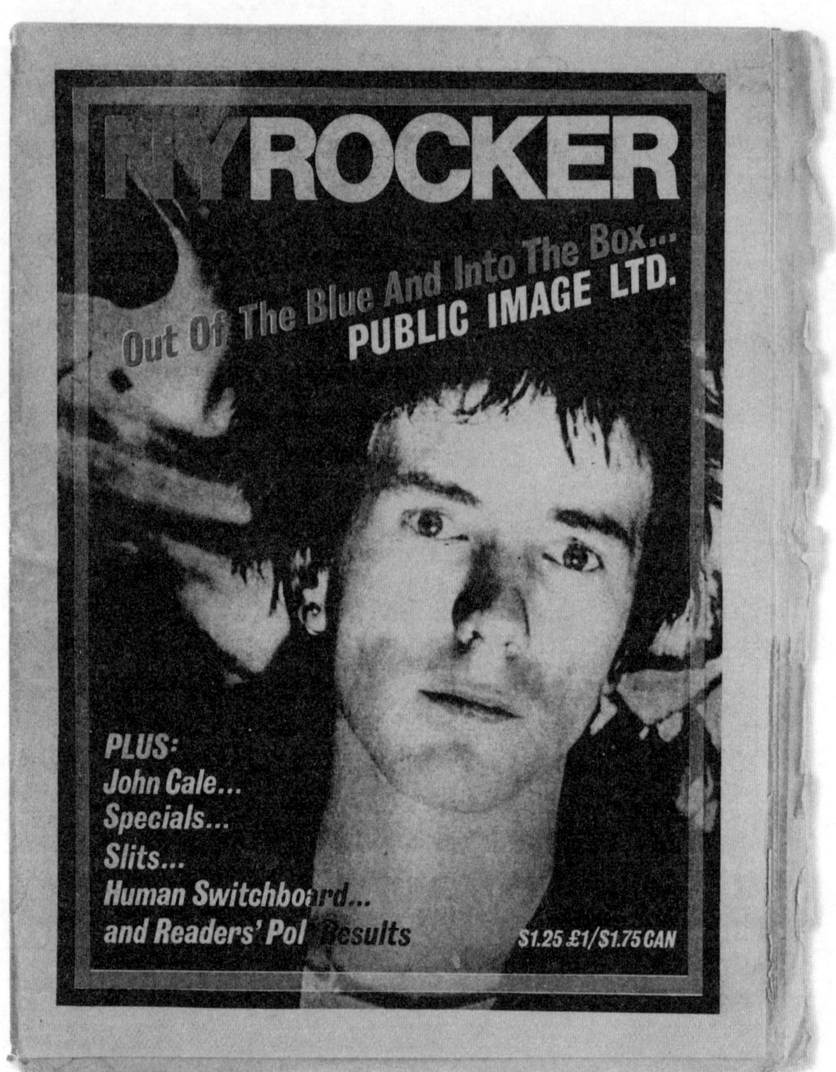

New York Rocker, no. 21, 1980

already two years old. But it certainly fulfilled Lott's belief 'that pop music should be fun again'. 'The *Flexipop!* cover was vulgar, brash and burst out at you like an explosion in a paintball factory,' he observed. 'Issue one came out the same month as *The Face* was launched. *The Face* was much better written and produced. But it was concerned with matters of high style. *Flexipop!* dealt with pop music in a pop style, taking it back to its shallow, larky roots.'[4]

The magazine ran for three years before the public tired of the flexidiscs – which, in any case, had also been given away by *Smash Hits*. However, a stronger challenge came from IPC's *No 1*, the brainchild of former *NME* deputy editor Phil McNeill. It had less colour, fewer pages and a familiar mix of lyrics, posters, charts, giveaways and questionnaires. Issued weekly, rather than fortnightly like *Smash Hits*, it encroached aggressively on the latter's territory. A heavyweight promotional campaign launched the debut issue in May 1983, and TV ads featured testimonials from Annie Lennox, Paul Weller, Bananarama and Kajagoogoo. Staffers were encouraged to attack the magazine they dubbed *Sm*shed Tw*ts*.

Although it lasted until the early 1990s, *Number One* – as it became – was never able to topple its rival. Weekly sales hovered around 100,000, compared to 500,000 for *Smash Hits*, which was also franchised in Australia and North America.

The stateside *Star Hits* was another attempt to muscle into music publishing by Felix Dennis, who licensed the rights from Emap. In late 1983, Neil Tennant and designer Kimberley Leston were drafted to the New York office to work with editor David Fricke, who had made his bones covering rock for *Circus*, *Rolling Stone* and *Trouser Press*. At the latter, a year before he threw in his lot with Felix Dennis, Fricke wrote a lengthy piece on King Crimson. 'It's just a pop group with some good ideas,' drummer Bill Bruford insisted. 'The more we remember that, the more everyone will enjoy it.'

For *Star Hits*, Fricke recruited two writers whose work he had spotted in the monthly *New York Rocker*: Mark Coleman and David Keeps. 'I read *New Musical Express* to keep up with the UK scene, but I wasn't familiar with *Smash Hits*,' Coleman told the website Mullets I Have Loved. 'There was a resistance, even hostility, among American journalists toward English groups at that point. I wrote about

New Order/Joy Division in *The Village Voice* earlier that year and other writers were like, "How can you stand that shit?" Somehow I fronted my way through a job interview with David Fricke and Neil Tennant. They gave me a test assignment and a few copies of *Smash Hits* to take home. Reading the magazine for the first time, I freaked out: this really was a teen mag, with screaming girls and everything. However, studying Neil's cover story on Kajagoogoo was a revelation. The story was brilliant: witty, sharp and observant. Instead of gushing or condescending, *Smash Hits* (and I hope *Star Hits*) gave readers a sense of what the pop-star subjects were like as *people* – as well as a peek behind the Wizard of Oz music-biz curtain.'[5]

David Keeps was already a *Smash Hits* reader, and had a background in fashion: 'I came to the interview with two recent articles I had written: one about Clare Grogan of Altered Images and the other about socks and underwear for the *Village Voice*.' The style-savvy Tennant had read and been impressed by the latter article. '"Frickers", as Neil called him, was a more traditional rock 'n' roll journalist with established contacts throughout the music industry,' noted Keeps. 'I was the devoted punk rock/New Romantic/New Wave indie music fan – tapping into teenage girl obsession with ease and abandon.'

The celebratory but sardonic attitude of the British original travelled across the Atlantic. *Star Hits* even adapted Tom Hibbert's pseudonym Black Type for droll responses from 'Bold Type' on the letters page. 'There was always an attempt to be inclusive of all pop music of the time,' said Keeps. 'We covered very early hip-hop and straight-up pop, but mostly made fun of the bands we didn't like. It was all in the photos and captions, context-setting quotes and italicized parenthetical asides.

'The first issue, dated February 1984, had Duran Duran on the cover and it was clear after a very short time – because we had a very vocal, letter-writing audience – that the core of the magazine was going to be contemporary British pop. Boy George, Thompson Twins, Billy Idol, Wham!, Depeche Mode, the Cure, Dead or Alive – if they talked or dressed funny, they were our heroes.'[6]

A flavour of the breathless style and editorial content may be found in an early Fricke editorial: 'So we meet again, right here on the best

Page Three in pop journalism. I've been asked to keep it short this time, some grief from the gang in the design dungeon about a space crunch. Not that I see that wise guy the Bold Type pulling in his belt over in Lettersland. But jealous, *moi*? I have to admit there isn't a lot of breathing space here this month. The feature call alone includes our cover cops the Police, Cyndi Lauper, synth-scientist Thomas Dolby and those bearded Monkees, ZZ Top. Hum along with Culture Club, John Cougar Mellencamp and Spandau Ballet on the song pages. And this issue is a regular pinup festival with Van Halen and Michael Jackson leading the way. Uh, oh, they're looking at me funny in the art department again. Quick! You get to interview the Stray Cats and win signed LPs in the process! Go for the Sony Videocassette give away! And dig those exclusive Duran Duran tour pix!'[7]

When Fricke left to resume his rock critic career – notably as a senior editor at *Rolling Stone* – Keeps took over as editor. Of life at *Star Hits*, he recalled, 'Lots of inane arguments. Lots of nicknames, inside jokes, stupid jokes and friendly one-upmanship. We usually lunched together and there was often a cocktail hour and a costume change before going out for the evening. Hilarity ensued at a very high volume. Until Felix Dennis or one of the more mature office-management or business types stuck their head in our door and told us to knock it off. Of course there was always some drama – a band (usually U2) refusing to do an interview or Billy Idol knocking over lights at a photo session and us getting stuck with the bill – but it was almost always, like we so proudly advertised, "A party on every page."'

However, noted deputy editor Mark Coleman, 'By late 1985 the pop landscape was changing. Duran went on hiatus, Boy George flaked out and groups like Tears For Fears, though popular, weren't charismatic enough to sell magazines. The next wave was Depeche Mode and the Cure, both of whom we loved in the office but seemed a bit edgy to our publishers. This was when Felix Dennis pushed the magazine toward covering pretty-boy TV stars named Corey who I regarded with contempt.'

Star Hits endured until 1989, but, according to staffer Steve Korté, Dennis drained the staff's writing talents into the teen magazines *Wow!*, *Hot* and *Wow Whopper*, the poodle-rock title *Metallix*, the hip-hop journal *Full Effect* and the single-issue fashion magazine *Attitude*. In its relatively brief life, *Star Hits* fulfilled Dennis's aim of translating the *Smash Hits* formula for an American audience. 'There were little daily triumphs,' recalled Keeps. 'Like writing the best caption ever: that award goes to Suzan [Colón], who captioned a photo of Madonna clutching her stomach with, "Aaaargh, that third tuna Blimpie! Why did I do it?" which got us blackballed by Madonna for a while. Over the course of the magazine, the pride comes from creating our own universe and language, from immersing ourselves and our readers in a world of wit and imagination and possibilities, and from exposing hormone-hopped-up kids to some really great music. In our own sly way, we were also social activists, treating things like gay pop stars, vegetarianism and alternative belief systems not only like they were no big deal, but that they were actually cool. And where would all the young Goths be without our coverage of Siouxsie and Bauhaus and Tones on Tail and Gene Loves Jezebel, I ask you? If you were "weird" or had "weird" taste in music and clothing, you were not only our target audience, but our friend.'[8]

* * *

Music-powered magazines of the 1980s could usually be traced back through *The Face* and *Smash Hits* to punk's do-it-yourself principles. But two utterly different British titles launched at the same time in 1981 bucked the trend and shared editorial values that resonated down the decades: the metal bible *Kerrang!* and the eclectic triannual *Collusion*.

Kerrang! appealed not to pop teens, arty sophisticates or world music fans, but to dyed-in-the-wool followers of hard rock. The brainchild of *Sounds* writer Geoff Barton, it began as a one-off supplement in that paper as a result of his championing what he dubbed 'the New Wave of British Heavy Metal'. The determined slog of scene-leaders Iron Maiden, Saxon and Def Leppard from pubs to *Top of the Pops* satisfied *Sounds* editor Alan Lewis's interest in grass-roots movements and acted as an apolitical, long-haired counterpoint to the mercifully short-lived skinhead genre Oi. 'There wasn't a publication anywhere in the world that was specifically designed to cater for us,' observed Judas Priest front man Rob Halford. 'It was so difficult to get into the other music magazines at the time and there were all these bands that needed some attention.'

Jovially impervious to fashion, *Kerrang!* thrived by incorporating fresh subgenres as they arose, although its readers' early resistance to thrash metal – not unlike prog fans' abhorrence of punk – led to the likes of Slayer and Megadeth being more sympathetically covered in the 1986–89 spin-off *Mega Metal Kerrang!* That aside, the magazine rode the waves of glam metal, grunge, nu-metal, pop-punk and emo. This versatility enabled what Metallica's James Hetfield described as 'the extremely unbiased *National Enquirer* of heavy metal' to topple *NME* as Britain's bestselling music weekly in 2002, and the print edition to survive long after *NME* shut down.

The magazine has remained true to Barton's editorial approach, which wasn't a million miles from *Smash Hits* – albeit channelling the passions of adolescent males rather than teenage girls. 'Geoff's writing and editing style was free of pretence and combined his love of hard rock and metal with a larger-than-life style drawn from his love for comic books, which is where the word "Kerrang" comes from,' said one-time editor Phil Alexander. 'Geoff's favourite band was Kiss, the personification of hard rock and comics, and he was probably the only British journalist in the mid-seventies who loved them. When he finally got to meet Kiss, the first thing he asked Gene Simmons was, "Can I feel your armour?"

'He taught me that you didn't have to make snide remarks in your reviews; instead, you could say, "I really love this," and show real passion for it. It sounds clichéd now but, in terms of rock journalism, a lot of people spend too much of their time trying to be cleverer than thou, trying to interject elements of faux intellectualism, or be as snide as possible. In a way, Geoff was the antidote to all that.'[9] 'You've got to have a laugh,' Barton observed. 'You can come at it from a fan's point of view, but you should be aware of the inherent stupidity too.'

British freelancer Sylvie Simmons, then based in LA, was early in spotting the potential of acts such as Mötley Crüe. 'Working for *Kerrang!* was an endless series of free trips and jacuzzis,' she said, 'but I never thought about being the woman in a boys' club. I suppose I had a certain novelty value, particularly on the interview circuit. It perked their ideas up, sometimes too much. There were a few who thought that women rock writers weren't necessarily there to write about them.'[10]

Kerrang!'s constituency, heavy metal, was among the genres studied by *Collusion*, launched by musicians and writers Steve Beresford, Peter Cusack, Sue Steward and David Toop. Beresford had links to the Slits and the Frank Chickens, Toop to Brian Eno – and both found traditional music journalism stultifying. 'You have to be really careful when you start talking about popularity,' Beresford told *NME* in 1982. 'Every LP the West Indian singer Tim Chandell makes sells 80,000 copies in this country – he's never mentioned. There are selling areas which aren't acknowledged by the press or anybody and equally very over-hyped areas that do commercially much less.

'Obviously "out" music has less resonance than maybe the Rolling Stones, who get enormous advertising and attention every time they put a record out. It's an ongoing thing to keep them up there. But improvised music has resonance in areas that are far more covert. It's a very good music to write about.'[11]

Part of the improvisational London Musicians' Collective with Toop, Sue Steward had worked for the Virgin label in its early, experimental years, then for Malcolm McLaren's management company Glitterbest. There, her tasks included acquiring Habitat furniture for the London apartment occupied by the doomed Nancy Spungen and Sid Vicious. 'Sue never became a victim of the male-dominated culture of that now distant era,' wrote her colleague Mark Hudson, 'but fought her way through to become a significant figure in her own right, as a writer, journalist, DJ, broadcaster and curator.'

Collusion itself, wrote Hudson, 'contained some of the first tentative articles on what would later become known as "world music". Sue could feel it in her bones that the elastic polyrhythms of hitherto unconsidered forms such as Congolese soukous, Nigerian juju music and her beloved salsa had the capacity to make a powerful impact on the western music scene. For her, opening people's minds to the sounds of the rest of the world was a political as well as an artistic objective.'[12] 'It was about diversity,' said Toop, 'particularly the way in which musical genres were atomised according to age, race,

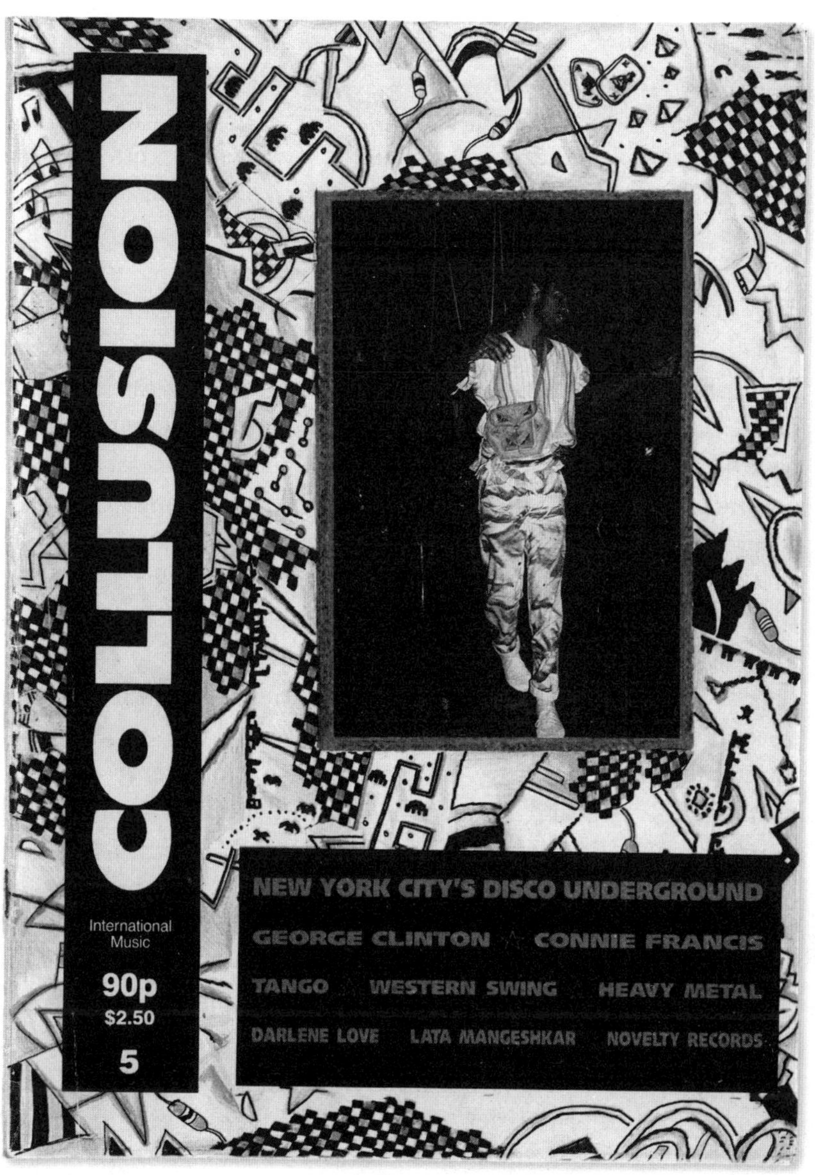

Collusion, no. 5, September 1983

class, geography, economic status, cultural and tribal allegiances, education and other demographic factors, all of which suited the selling of music as a commodity.'[13]

The magazine was distinguished by its range – from western swing to disco to hip-hop, via funk, tango and novelty records – and its approach. 'Music could be an oppositional force without being overtly political,' Toop observed. 'So we ignored the practice elsewhere of matching content to release schedules or current fashions, and either wrote about or commissioned articles on music that we liked, embracing such unfashionable topics as country music, female big bands, music enjoyed by middle-aged Jamaicans, Japanese *enka* ballads and the Bay City Rollers.'[14]

The five issues produced over two years from summer 1981 celebrated the pompadoured, mixed race, gender-blending Esquerita, the hipster slang-spouting Slim Gaillard, tortured alternadiva Diamanda Galas and the spaced-out Sun Ra and his Arkestra. They investigated the birth of New York rap, female DJs, the music of early Disney movies, the story of the Hawaiian guitar and the travails of African pop musicians in Manhattan. Writer Chris Kirk discussed records with gay subject matters, from Scott Walker's Jacques Brel covers to the work of David Bowie, Nina Hagen, Lou Reed, Pete Shelley and Gina X's 'No GDM'. Noting that *Record Mirror* included a Gay Disco chart, Kirk wrote: 'I can hardly deny that the tacky end of disco is the genre most associated with gay men. I'm becoming increasingly suspicious of that part of myself that stands for ghetto mentality.'[15]

David Toop, who invariably provided illustrations to accompany his text, wrote about the Beach Boys, exploring Dennis Wilson's links to cult leader Charles Manson and underground filmmaker Kenneth Anger. Meanwhile, Leon Thorne's 'Executive Action' page dissected EMI's finances and Pink Floyd's investment portfolio. In addition, Mary Harron searched out troubled country-pop singer Connie Francis; Nick Kimberley, co-founder of reggae fanzine *Pressure Drop*, reflected on the fluid sexuality at the heart of soul music; Stuart Cosgrove examined Northern Soul; and Sheryl Garratt filed her landmark piece about life as a Rollers fan as well as articles on such contrasting subjects as Indian film music.

New York correspondent Steven Harvey's cover story on Manhattan's 'disco underground', in the publication's fifth and final issue in summer 1983, marked one of the high points of *Collusion*'s incisive, all-encompassing approach. With photographs of clubbers at Paradise Garage and the Loft, and pioneers John 'Jellybean' Benitez, François Kevorkian, Larry Levan, David Mancuso and Shep Pettibone, Harvey's piece dissected the scene for dance music fans in Britain and made the case for 'DJs as artists': 'Disco has always revolved around the cult of the DJ and the club, and, as such, record spinners have shaped the music in a way that is unique.'[16]

By the time a version of Harvey's story appeared in *The Face*, *Collusion* had closed, unable to secure sufficient sales and advertising. Beresford, Steward and Toop continued to toil at the cross-hatches of adventurous music and journalism, with the latter becoming a regular at Nick Logan's magazine.

* * *

The peppy presentation and varied editorial angles of British magazines made an impact across the Atlantic beyond *Star Hits*. In New York, from the wreckage of the alternative newspaper *SoHo News*, staffer Annie Flanders emerged with $6,000-worth of funding. Having sold seventeen adverts at $500 a page, Flanders printed 10,000 copies of *Details*, which mixed music with art, celebrity, design, fashion and film. The first cover, in March 1982, was a black and white image of a 1920s-style female; subsequent issues featured Billy Idol, Boy George and Malcolm McLaren.

After eighteen months, as the club culture examined by *Collusion* began to break through, Flanders attracted $200,000 in backing from Gary Bogard, owner of the UK aristocrats' bible *The Tatler*. Within a couple of years, *Details* was shifting 30,000 copies an issue and ad rates had tripled to just under $1,500 a page. Key to its appeal were street and fashion photography, with sassy gossip tracking the toings and froings of the city's clubland figures. 'We are not an intellectual magazine,' Flanders declared. 'We are strictly for people who have an artistic bent, or are fun-loving people. We represent a way of life: people who really like to laugh, have a good time, go out, and care, at least some of the time, about what they wear.'[17]

On the West Coast was *WET* (pl. 14), whose subtitle, 'The magazine of gourmet bathing', hinted at its Dadaist leanings. Launched in 1976 by avant-garde writers and artists led by the architect Leonard Koren, its cover stars and interviewees included Debbie Harry, John Lydon, Mick Jagger, Brian Eno, Tom Verlaine, Elvis Costello, Steely Dan and Van Halen. It was also the first publication to grant space to work by *Simpsons* creator Matt Groening. 'The only binding principle was to give the readers something completely unexpected, tinged with absurdity,' said Koren. '*WET* was extremely focused when it came to being an incubator of novel ideas relating to publication design and editorial packaging.'[18]

WET's design-heavy influence could later be seen in *Beach Culture*, *Ray Gun* and *Wired*, although it ground to a halt in 1981 after thirty-four issues. 'The computer era hadn't yet arrived,' Koren pointed out. 'For three or four days every two months, the only thing that mattered was creating graphic magic and excitement. On all the other days, life at *WET* was a juggle between trying to make art and trying to make money. It was hard work.'[19]

The ingredients brewed by *WET* and *Details* had long been in place at Andy Warhol's *Interview*, where editor Glenn O'Brien started out covering music in Manhattan's downtown scene. 'I had the best of times,' he announced in 2000. 'Drinking Bloody Marys with Lou Reed very early in the morning. Meeting the Wailers. Smoking pot with Curtis Mayfield. Dating Grace Jones. Interviewing Ted Nugent and a really, really sleepy Ronnie Spector. Making friends with Chris Stein and Debbie Harry. Teaching Robert Fripp how to dress. Making friends with [Mudd Club co-founder] Anya Phillips and James Chance. Getting high with George Clinton. Hanging out with Grandmaster Flash at the Police Athletic Club in the South Bronx. The Go-Go's being afraid of me because they thought I was a junkie. Sitting with Anita Pallenberg and Marianne Faithfull when they made up. Meeting Tom Waits. Opening for [David Johansen's alter ego] Buster Poindexter as a comedian for a few years. This and that about Madonna ...'[20]

Meanwhile, *Rolling Stone*'s 1977 shift from San Francisco to Manhattan had improved its national distribution, aided by a bank loan that saved the overspending business from bankruptcy. But accountants began to call the shots, and cracked down hard on the budget of managing editor Harriet Fier, who was nurturing the talents of Charles M. Young – who had documented the Sex Pistols and was styling himself 'The Reverend Charles M. Young' – and Timothy White, who joined from *Crawdaddy*.

As the magazine gradually became part of the establishment, Jann Wenner was distracted by a short-lived gig editing the French publisher Daniel Filipacchi's *Look* magazine. This coincided with an exodus of prominent *Rolling Stone* writers. 'By the end of the seventies, I started to burn out on journalism,' confesssed Cameron Crowe. 'I was taking on too much and taking too long with stories. I didn't know how much further I could go.' He began to formulate the project that would become his screenwriting debut, 1982's *Fast Times at Ridgemont High*. 'Having exhausted rock journalism and kind of hit a wall, I wanted to write a book about high school and the experiences I didn't have because my mom skipped me grades. I thought it was almost more rock and roll to write about the high school experience. Ironically, I found the entire school year was about Led Zeppelin coming to town and everyone was gearing up for it. Then John Bonham died and the tour was cancelled, so it really did change lives. The original title of *Fast Times* was *Stairway to Heaven*. I was still writing about rock, but from a different perspective.'[21]

Wenner hoped Crowe would deliver the screenplay to his newly formed movie production company. When it went to his rival, the manager and producer Irving Azoff, he pressed Charles Young to produce a new treatment. The result was rejected as 'dark and desperate' and spelled the end of Young's career at *Rolling Stone*, particularly after he attacked Wenner with a bullwhip – an incident observed by an amused Hunter S. Thompson. 'I went into exile at the end of 1980,' said Young. 'I spent the next two years depressed, unwilling to write, poor and drunk. Timothy White suggested I give the editor of *Musician*, Vic Garbarini, a call. I didn't think anyone remembered who I was, but Vic had read my stuff in *Rolling Stone* and was eager to have me do what I do in *Musician*. My first assignment was with Tom Petty in 1983, and it got me back into the groove.'[22]

Another disillusioned *Rolling Stone* regular was Paul Nelson, the veteran who had begun at folk 'zine *Sing Out!* in the early 1960s, talent-spotted the New York Dolls, and spent a prolonged stint as Wenner's record reviews editor. 'I left because Jann was setting rules I did not agree with,' he explained. 'The reviews had to be short. I could never write anything short in my life. I told him he was asking us to write sonnets. He wanted twenty-two lines. That's, like, four sentences. Writers don't want to count words. Also, I didn't want to do it anymore. During my last years at *Rolling Stone*, I was losing interest in the music.'[23]

Donald Katz, author of serious pieces on non-musical subjects, also departed, noting, 'The business question facing Jann was whether to grow up with the baby-boom audience, which would entail *RS* becoming the *New Yorker* of its generation, or to go after the teenagers in the grocery stores. He chose the latter, which obviated the need for people like me.'[24]

New blood arrived in the form of Anthony DeCurtis. An English professor in Atlanta, he was commissioned to cover a B-52s concert by *Rolling Stone* editor Jim Henke: 'Jim said, "I have no idea who you are or what your writing is like, but go see the show and, if your piece is good, we'll run it." A little over five years later he hired me to work at *Rolling Stone*, taught me how to be a news reporter, and then turned me loose.'[25]

In 1981 *Rolling Stone* was relaunched with a glossy cover, and the return of such New Journalism figures as Hunter S. Thompson relegated music content, according to Robert Draper, 'to the back of the magazine'. John Belushi and Robin Williams were as likely to be cover stars as the Go-Gos – objectified in panties and skimpy tops – or Boy George, depicted at his most doll-like. 'It went all in for Madison Avenue glitz and celebrated the wealth that marked the Boomers' ascent into the establishment,' wrote former staffer Rich Cohen in a review of Wenner biography *Sticky Fingers*. 'The magazine's own "Perception/Reality" ad campaign of the eighties touted its transformation, with a bearded hippie, an old Jimi Hendrix cover and a peace symbol (perception), juxtaposed with a yuppie, a recent Bill Murray cover and a Mercedes-Benz trademark (reality).'[26]

* * *

In the UK, the inkies that once dominated pop culture discourse continued to be diminished by *The Face*, which was enhanced by the presence of young graphic artist Neville Brody. Having produced work for independent music and fashion labels, his daring typography and page designs recast early 20th-century art tropes such as those of constructivism. Applying them to a youth culture magazine created surprising results that, in turn, quickly influenced British advertising.

Brody's first *Face* cover, in June 1982, featured a Sheila Rock portrait of Haircut 100 pinup Nick Heyward. 'That's when it all started coming together,' said Nick Logan. 'Neville took the magazine to a different level. I've come to appreciate what he did more and more. The way he combined photography, type and white space was so good. Many people have tried to rip him off but they can't manage it.'[27]

The Heyward portrait illustrated a story by Lesley White. Subsequently a political interviewer at *The Sunday Times*, she was among the many hopefuls who sent unsolicited pitches and contributions to the magazine: 'I set my sights on it and sent a few pieces, based on interviews with people who played my friend's club in Brighton [mod revivalists Secret Affair and quirky post-punk performance artist Frank Tovey], to the address in the back of the magazine.'[28] Assistant editor Steve Taylor commissioned a piece on the electro-pop duo Yazoo, then topping the charts with 'Only You', followed by the Heyward cover story and encounters with Phil Oakey of the Human League and Kevin Rowland of Dexys Midnight Runners. The latter revealed the magazine's interest in fresh approaches to interviews: the opening paragraphs discussed how Rowland's conditions for an encounter with the magazine had been turned down. This and White's interrogation of Rowland's reaction to the mixed response he was receiving from the music press drew back the veil on the industry's promotional machine, humanizing him in the process.[29]

Dexys and a new wave of British popstars had become familiar faces to the wider public, featuring in the popular dailies and performing on light entertainment TV shows. As *The Face*'s Dave Rimmer pointed out, this pop wave 'didn't make sense in terms of the only criteria the music press could muster. It simply didn't look right in artily unfocused monochrome snaps. And there were few people still interested in reading tortured analytical prose.'[30]

With the magazine's circulation approaching 80,000 by 1983, Logan recruited *NME* writer Paul Rambali to oversee features, replacing Steve Taylor, who was presenting Channel 4's chaotic late night chat show *Loose Talk*. Rambali had become disenchanted with the machinations of publisher IPC, in particular its initiation of a 'management strike' to ward off industrial action by staff during annual pay negotiations (a technique repeated by Rupert Murdoch when he took on the newspaper print unions). 'This brought home to me that I worked for a big corporation, which didn't square with the punk ethic of independence we were preaching at *NME*,' says Rambali. 'Meanwhile Nick was actually doing it. I admired the fact that he had put his money where his mouth was and done something audacious. Also, because it was a glossy monthly, it seemed like the future, which of course it turned out to be.

'In his wonderful, hands-off management style, Nick provided me with the space to do what I wanted. Steve Taylor had started widening the coverage out from music to the arts, film and fashion, and the plan was to expand on this. Around that time, people were always asking me, "What *is The Face*?" because it didn't fit an accepted idea of what a magazine should be. My answer was: "What *LIFE* was to the fifties, what *Playboy* was to the sixties, what *Rolling Stone* was to the seventies, we are trying to be to the eighties."'

NME still sold around 100,000 copies but remained in the shadow of *Smash Hits*; Neil Tennant recalled the magazine's team triumphantly plastering its circulation figures in the windows of the Carnaby Street offices that overlooked those of the weekly. 'I certainly began to feel threatened by *Smash Hits*,' admitted Barney Hoskyns. 'I knew that things were changing. There was a seismic shift occurring.'

Once again the finger of blame was pointed at the 'pale boys' Paul Morley and Ian Penman. 'Their writing was impenetrable,' complained special features editor Roy Carr. 'Overnight there was a revolt among the readers. They left in their droves and never came back. And *NME* never recovered.'[31] Penman dismisses this argument: 'Maybe the reason wasn't our fireworks box but a lot of dull articles about indie bands or rather long political pieces that put people off.'

'There was a misguided policy of surrendering things we weren't keen on,' confessed writer Paul Du Noyer. 'Heavy metal, punk at the Cockney Rejects stage and hard rock to *Sounds*; pop to *Smash Hits*; and prog, jazz and folk to *Melody Maker*. [*NME*] was painting itself into a corner. Editorial meetings had something of the atmosphere of Chinese Red Army cadre get-togethers. There was a fanatical ideological purity about it. Quite admirable in a way, but commercially suicidal. There was a view that if readers didn't get it, they should just clear off. I wasn't keen on this because I was populist by inclination.'

An article by Du Noyer birthed the derogatory term 'rockism', coined by fellow Liverpudlian and singer Pete Wylie: 'He used it originally as an inversion of Rock Against Racism. Ironically, he was considered one of the most rockist acts, because he was a straight-down-the-line, guitar-heroic, sub-Springsteen character. A very good one. But there was a growing feeling at *NME* that rock – as in the classic guitar/bass/drums line-up – was a spent force. Public Image Ltd, the Gang of Four and the Pop Group all produced early records which were fundamentally new but, as it turned out, didn't lead to anything fantastically new. And, in the end, the old patterns reasserted themselves. Rockism survived.'

Meanwhile, *NME* attempted to encroach on *The Face*'s territory with features such as an extended piece by Lynn Hanna that showcased fashion stars and designers who would make names for themselves later in the decade: 'There's no doubt that British fashion '81 has seen a new vibrancy and vigour at almost every level ... Perhaps the present fashion manifestations are also providing just a little bit of a defiant poke in the eye of the grim, dim early eighties.'[32] However, the impact of Hanna's text was torpedoed by poor reproduction of Peter Anderson's photography. Colour portraits fell victim to out-of-register printing, while monochrome images were dull and fuzzy. Alongside a clunky page of cocktail recipes, it was another example of the failure of the weeklies to change with the increasingly visually sophisticated times.

Some of the staff succumbed to personal problems. 'I got very heavily into drugs,' admitted Barney Hoskyns. 'It was a horrible time to be writing about music because there was so little going on. Disco had died and what was happening in rock was so effete and timid.' The only group offering excitement, he said, was the Birthday Party – fronted by Nick Cave, whose predilection for drugs compared with that of Hoskyns. 'They were my crusade, but were regarded as a bit of a joke, just like Nick Kent and Johnny Thunders. That leather trousers/smack thing was a bit uncool. The New Romantics weren't into heroin until later!

'Apart from the fact that I had no control over it, hanging out with the Birthday Party and doing heroin was for me a revolt against the prevailing mood of the times. Nick Cave represented everything to me that was great: the Stooges, Captain Beefheart, mad, out of control, eccentric, dangerous, American avant-gardism. I went to New York with them and years later was told I was drunk and virtually unconscious all the time ... The drugs got out of hand and I ended up living in a flat in Paddington with Cave and a bunch of Australian junkies. I became unreliable and unmanageable, though I didn't go flaunting it. I would sometimes inject in the loo at *NME* and, to anyone who knew, I was very clearly opiated.'

Floundering, Hoskyns took six weeks to deliver a feature on British punk-funk outfit 23 Skidoo that should have taken a couple of days: 'So I did what we in the recovery business call "a geographical". That's when you go from A to B, and when you get to B you will feel miraculously different. I thought that if I left London my troubles would cease, so I went to San Francisco and got in touch with a photographer to work on some stuff for *NME*. Within two weeks he was a junkie. We were bang at it. I had a dark year in sunny California. I did do some work for *NME*, but not nearly as much as I could have because I was fucked up.'

Editor Neil Spencer felt he had lost control of the staff: 'It was all a bit deranged. I don't know what drugs they were all taking but I was in an unhappy phase of my personal life and overwhelmed by work.' A second print union strike added to the pressure. 'I was picketed but, because I was a member of management, I could go in to the offices. They knew I wouldn't put a paper out. Also, the music wasn't saying anything to me and there was all this talk among the staff about how we should be more like *The Face*.'

Spencer's solution was to propose a *Rolling Stone*-style format: 'It would have been slightly smaller, on better paper and heat-set so the ink didn't come off on your hands. It was to be broad church: music, movies, social stuff, books – a cultural paper centred on music. But there was this schizoid thing that had happened to pop. Kids buying Adam Ant wouldn't have been interested in that kind of paper. But if you put Adam Ant on the cover, people into the Clash wouldn't want to know. The Clash and Simple Minds – who I couldn't stand – were *NME* heartland stuff, because they would sell papers to people interested in rock, so I'd get Dave Dorrell [later a member of 'Pump Up the Volume' hitmakers M|A|R|R|S] to write up the Southern Death Cult. But the balance of the paper went wrong. It slid out of focus, for which I blame myself.'

'It was one of those events where the dream you have had for ages turns out to be horrible in reality,' sighed Paolo Hewitt, who joined from *Melody Maker* in 1983. '*NME* was directionless. Sting would be on the cover one week, Yoko Ono the next. And I was directionless because I wasn't hearing a lot of good new music. There was a long time between "White Lines" by Grandmaster Flash [1983] and the emergence of Def Jam, which made the cover in 1985.'

Meanwhile, Barney Hoskyns returned from America. Having 'hit rock bottom and then got into recovery', he found himself part of Spencer's bid to get *NME* back on track. 'The solution had been to cut back on the long stuff and toughen up,' said the editor. 'We got these good writers with good attitudes and the right focus: hard workers, not trying to skank around and pull a fast one. Barney was part of the solution.' Ditto Chris Dean, who wrote under the name X. Moore and led agitprop trio the Redskins. 'Chris may have been a bit too Socialist Workers Party for comfort,' admitted Spencer, 'but he was a good writer, a bloody good sub editor and he worked hard.'

Other recruits included Stuart Cosgrove, whose pieces for *Collusion* had marked him out as highly knowledgable and opinionated, and Hoskyns's acquaintance Mat Snow. 'I liked that nexus of Australian bands – the Go-Betweens, the Birthday Party – who I was introduced to by Barney,' said Snow. 'This was during a cheerful drug phase on my part, which lasted a year or so. The first version of my feature on the Go-Betweens was thrown back in my face by [deputy editor] Tony Stewart. I had another go and they ran it so I got associated with that movement and hung out with them.'

Snow's relationship with Nick Cave suffered when he reviewed the single 'Yü-Gung' by German group Einstürzende Neubauten, which included singer/guitarist/keyboard player Blixa Bargeld, also a member of Cave's Bad Seeds: 'I knew Blixa and Nick Cave, who had lived at my flat once for a few weeks, so we were all great chums. I wrote in the review that the track was more exciting than anything on the new Nick Cave album [the then forthcoming *The Firstborn Is Dead*], which was me saying to the *NME* readership, "Hey, I've heard this hot new record." Just boasting. About a year later Nick Cave was really weird and cold during an interview. I asked him what was up and he said, "To be perfectly honest, I hate you. I was upset by that disloyal thing you wrote. In fact, I've written a song about you called 'Scum'." It's great. The best thing he ever did; the most virulent, hate-filled record about me and Antonella Black, another journalist who had crossed his path. It's my undying claim to fame in the world of Goth.'[33] Black, the pseudonym of Australian writer Antonella Gambotto, had offended Cave in an article for *Sounds*; she had also previously contributed to *NME*, until, so she has said, her description of Cliff Richard as 'Satan' in a review for the paper resulted in a settlement with the devoutly Christian singer.

At *NME*, petty and divisive turf wars were fought over groups and genres. Paolo Hewitt – dubbed 'the cappuccino kid' by his friend Paul Weller (then leader of the Style Council) – was subjected to 'piss-taking and a bit of antagonism'. Even a piece by Hoskyns for *Mojo* in the early 2000s smarted: 'Barney was saying, "Soho soul-boys were all laughing at the Birthday Party's lyrics." We weren't laughing at their lyrics. We weren't even listening to them.' For his part, Hoskyns fumed at the born-again mods: 'It was so fucking po-faced. These people took themselves so seriously.'

Chris Bohn, who transferred from *Melody Maker* and adopted the pseudonym Biba Kopf, and jazz critic Richard Cook were more to Hoskyns's taste: 'I really respected Chris, although he was very aloof about a lot of the music I liked. At least intellectually he was interesting, unlike some people I could mention. And Richard was one of the best I have ever read on music. He was an outstanding writer but, because he wasn't an egomaniac or a druggie but grown-up and self-effacing, he has never received the dues he should have.'

In an obituary for Cook, who died at forty-nine in 2007, Hoskyns wrote: 'He came into the paper as a jazz specialist but quickly established himself as one of its true stylists, penning reviews as trenchant as they were subtle, and conducting droll, revealing interviews. He was an anomalous character at the paper's Carnaby Street offices, invariably appearing in a white mackintosh and eschewing the sex/drugs/rock 'n' roll attitude of many of his colleagues ... Before he was even thirty, Richard was an exemplary curmudgeon. "I think writing about music is one of the hardest things you can do," he told *All About Jazz*. "Describing a piece of music in a way which isn't either cliché-ridden or merely fanciful is desperately difficult. I suppose if I have any advice to offer, it's the simple truth that you have to listen properly, and hard, and ask yourself what's going on and why."'[34]

'The war on pop' – an overextended polemic devised by Barney Hoskyns and Chris Bohn – conveyed how rattled the team had become by the shifting sands in the mid-1980s. '*NME* slams the flim flam,' crowed the cover of an issue that described chart music as 'a monster comprised of a million heads, a million tongues, and no body, no nervous system, no sense of direction'.[35] Hoskyns 'wrote a rant which was anti-*Smash Hits*, anti-dumbed down teen pop' in response to a piece by *The Face*'s Steve Taylor that 'basically said that since *Smash Hits* was presenting information efficiently for teen punters, *NME*'s would-be intellectual and serious attitude was irrelevant. I was incensed'.

That *NME* no longer had the lock on music culture was evident not just to teens but to older readers exhausted by features that ran to thousands of words and involved multiple page turns. 'It was one of those in-between eras,' said David Quantick, who joined after writing to Neil Spencer about a Bob Seger album review. 'When I went in to see Neil, they were holding Danny Baker's farewell party. I remember Danny sitting on a desk drinking and telling jokes with Andy Gill and Monty Smith. I'm like, "I've missed the bus, haven't I?"'[36]

Baker's position as a lead feature writer was taken by Gavin Martin, who had graduated from operating the influential Belfast fanzine *Alternative Ulster* to become a staffer. Ploughing his own soulful, singular and sometimes quirky furrow, Martin – who died prematurely in 2022 – was alone among *NME* writers in successfully riding the changes rung at the publication from the late 1970s until well into the 1990s, when he departed to chronicle new music for the *Daily Mirror*.

Martin's Celtic roots enabled him to analyse and contextualize such performers as John Lydon, Kevin Rowland of Dexys Midnight Runners, Shane MacGowan – particularly when his post-punk group Pogue Mahone broke through as the Pogues – and U2. Martin was responsible for the latter's first *NME* cover story and, having championed them, was undeterred in issuing a takedown of their second album, *War*. Similarly, Martin's love for the music of Van Morrison did not stop him from calling out the often irascible singer's behaviour, while his passion for Black American music was evidenced by acute interviews with the likes of Marvin Gaye and James Brown.

At *NME* 'there were real factions', said Barney Hoskyns, who had begun work on his first book, about the history of soul music in the American south. The omens for *NME* weren't entirely bad, however. 'There was a new management team at IPC who were sympatico,' recalls Spencer, 'and I'd finally got a full-time designer, Joe Ewart, who was funny and lifted my spirits. Stuart Cosgrove was writing much more for us and I'd tried really hard to get women writers. But later I found out what had been going on: as fast as I recruited them, certain people alienated them with chauvinist wind-ups. Vivien [Goldman] I gave work to. Mary Harron. Cynthia Rose we employed, but people didn't like her. Cath Carroll wasn't liked because she was openly gay. Amanda Root was another one. Lynn Hanna – she didn't last long. Jane Suck. Jaswinder Bancil ...'

Bancil had benefited from Spencer's policy of hiring not just women but people of colour. She moved into broadcasting and eventually filmmaking, while Amrik Rai used his base in Sheffield to focus on northern indie groups such as A Certain Ratio and the Fall. He became a force in what became known as the Asian

Underground and a manager for Manchester funk outfit Chakk, US house group Ten City and the Asian-dub hybrid Black Star Liner.

Rai's copy for *NME* was pithy and pointed; a savage review of experimentalists Clock DVA reportedly led to a group member knocking him out. And when the Smiths surfaced, he described singer Morrissey as 'an ambitious fool, a charming idiot who would be [Paul] Morley's missing link, [ABC singer Martin] Fry's follow-up, northern hero, having a giggle, playing the fiddle while brave new pop burns in a pyre of sentimental idiocy, consumers and cretinism'.[37]

Rai was still contributing when Neil Spencer's tenure ground to a halt: 'I handed in my notice on the first working day of 1985. I'd had enough.' His replacement was Ian Pye, a senior writer at *Melody Maker*. Tony Stewart, who had expected the job, handed in his notice and pitched up at *Sounds*, where he was joined by another *NME* refugee, Richard Cook.

Pye proved even less effective than Spencer in reining in *NME*'s rampant egos. Fractures deepened between the indie rock fans and the so-called 'soulcialists' led by Stuart Cosgrove, who championed Black music in all its forms, including hip-hop. '[Appointing Pye] was a ridiculous decision,' said Paolo Hewitt. 'Here was an editor who was very malleable and Stuart, who could talk the fucking collar off your shirt.' Charles Shaar Murray agreed: 'Stuart was carving a bigger and bigger empire to the point where his pages didn't look like they were part of the same publication. He knew what he was doing: essentially showcasing himself as much as possible, as a way to getting a better gig. And of course he's had a succession of them.' Cosgrove subsequently became head of arts and regions at British TV's Channel 4.

A more positive spin was generated by Lucy O'Brien. She had written for feminist magazine *Spare Rib* about the lack of opportunities for women in the music business, illustrating how little had changed since Penny Valentine's crusading work for *Street Life* a decade earlier.

At *NME*, O'Brien locked step with Cosgrove and Hewitt in their promotion of Black music and Red Wedge, the music-based agit-prop group backed by the Labour Party in a bid to win the youth vote. 'There were independent soul singles coming through with the new hip-hop,' says Hewitt. 'It was street music ... With Cosgrove as our leader we went for it, and we also reacted against the rampant Thatcherisim. Miners were losing their jobs and families were being thrown on the scrapheap.'

According to O'Brien, she and Hewitt 'often agreed with Stuart because we were into what he was into. As the media editor, he was a very influential force on the paper when Ian Pye had trouble making up his mind. And [Pye] was a great one for that, listening to both sides before deciding, which infuriated everyone. "Come on! Make a decision! What do *you* think?!?"'[38]

O'Brien's first cover story, prompted by statistics that showed youth suicide was rising, drew links between groups such as Joy Division and the woes of young people at a time of recession, hard-line Conservative government and high unemployment. 'There was a romanticism attached by musicians to figures such as Sylvia Plath, and a connection between literature, suicide and music,' she reflected decades later. 'Songs such as Joy Division's "24 Hours", or "Asleep" by the Smiths, had a mythic status. The Samaritans had an advert featuring Pink Floyd's 'Is There Anybody Out There?' following a thirty-nine per cent increase in youth suicide in the previous decade. There was something going on that affected our core constituency that I wanted to investigate.' The issue sold poorly, but O'Brien later discovered that Kurt Cobain and Manic Street Preachers guitarist Richey Edwards acknowledged the feature's impact on them, albeit not necessarily positively: the Nirvana front man killed himself in 1994 and Edwards disappeared and is presumed to have committed suicide the following year.

Despite the weightiness of the subject, O'Brien's piece didn't automatically earn front-page status. 'It was battling it out for the cover with a profile of Lawrence from [indie band] Felt,' she recalled. 'The debates in our weekly meetings became heated, epitomizing the two factions of *NME* then: those into the indie rock canon and those of us in the other camp – the "hip-hop Hitlers", as we were known. It symbolised the fight for the territory of *NME*. We felt it was really important not just to talk about music, but youth culture and politics. It was a highly charged time politically, in that you had an incredibly right-wing Tory government with a reactionary agenda. We won in the end, although I think our mischievous art director used Lawrence from Felt's silhouette as the cover image.'[39]

Into this charged atmosphere returned Barney Hoskyns, albeit not as a writer but in editorial production: 'That meant I didn't have to be in the other room with people who weren't very nice. I did take part in some editorial meetings and felt alienated. Cosgrove was running the show.' But staffer Len Brown remembered it more rosily: 'For me, *NME* was the only place to be if you wanted to learn to write passionately, radically and poetically about popular culture.'[40]

Also coming on board in this period were Sean O'Hagan, latterly the cultural critic for *The Observer*; Danny Kelly, who would edit *Q* and *NME* itself; Steven Wells, the 'ranting poet' who performed as Seething Wells; Andrew Collins, later a film critic and broadcaster; John McCready, who would cover the emerging dance culture; Stuart Maconie, now a popular BBC presenter; and William Leith, who became a newspaper columnist and author. According to Brown, he and the other members of this editorial team 'saw ourselves as outsiders in one way or another'.[41] The fact was, however, that they were anything but: like most of their predecessors, they were white, male, had benefited from forms of tertiary education and were setting themselves on the by-now predictable career path into national media.

'I loved the fact that I could interview PD James or Robert Zemeckis and Don [Watson] would go and do JG Ballard,' remembered David Quantick. 'But Julie Burchill, always good at this sort of thing, said that *NME* in the eighties had acquired a "quiet in the library" feel. The humour had gone. I liked and was obsessed with pop and can remember a member of staff who shall remain nameless asking me, "You don't really like the Pet Shop Boys, do you David?" – suggesting I was adopting this as a pose to somehow make people look at me.'

Battlelines were drawn over *C86*, a compilation of White indie bands issued by *NME* and Rough Trade. 'I hated indie and I hated *C86*,' said Quantick. 'There was this whole thing about, "Public Enemy are okay, but the Soup Dragons? *Now* you're talking!"'[42] Barney Hoskyns was equally unmoved: '*NME* was saying, "Enough with pop and enough with Bobby Womack on the cover. We need to get back to what it was when it flew the flag for the early punk bands: an indie aesthetic championing pale white boys and girls with guitars." Christ, what a load of junk that was! Primal Scream is the only band from that tape to do anything, and their success has nothing to do with what they were doing then. The fucking Shop Assistants!'

NME's indulgence of Smiths front man Morrissey – whose appearances were thought to boost sales – began to draw fire. 'The rap, go-go and early house music lobby was rapidly growing in strength, arguing that *NME* should be more cutting-edge rather than promoting a character such as Morrissey, who they regarded as, at best, traditional and backward-looking,' wrote Len Brown. 'Already the hostile anti-Smiths letters were coming in from readers – usually variations of "Why don't you just change the name of the fucking paper to *New Morrissey Express*?" – although Smiths supporters among us suspected most of them were written by peeved soul boys within the office.'[43]

The factions did however agree that, in Brown's words, 'this once radical paper [was] gradually being brought to heel by management'. Come 1987, Stuart Cosgrove was out and Alan Lewis, fresh from his stint at *Sounds*, was in and raring to impose a more populist template. Bright, talented writers and brave editorial decisions remained, but the paper's 'golden age' – which commenced with Alan Smith and Nick Logan's rescue in 1972 – had juddered to a halt. 'There had been a fight for the identity of *NME* and IPC grabbed it back from the writers, who had developed unprecedented power,' said Lucy O'Brien. 'I was a freelance, so couldn't be sacked, but there was a combination of me not wanting to work there and a few of my pieces not getting in. So I, along with a lot of others, buggered off. *NME* changed after that to "Here's the band, here's the music".'

More interesting takes bubbled up in the margins. *ZigZag* provided an outlet for diverse writers, including Antonella Gambotto (latterly Gambotto-Burke), whose ability to skewer prominent male performers remained undiminished. Following her contretemps with Nick Cave and exit from *NME* over her Cliff Richard review, an interview with Morrissey for *Sounds* apparently brought her subject close to tears. 'Nobody told me that, in the flesh, Steven Patrick Morrissey looks like Judy Garland's understudy,' she wrote. 'Nobody informed me that Steven Patrick can't quite wrap his pretty tongue around the letter "S". Nobody unbridled the fact that my arse was to be booted out of Steven Patrick's boudoir once the interview reached a sticky consistency. Steven is celibate, yet Steven has a double bed. Steven isn't paranoid, yet he now has all interviews doubly recorded. Steven shrills long and loud about castrated cows and lambasted lambs, yet he confesses to finding leather seats "highly erotic". Steven is a funny little kettle of fish.'

Her questioning of the singer culminated with a quickfire exchange: 'If you have "erotic feelings", why don't you sleep with anyone? "Well, it just doesn't happen." Why don't you make it happen? "I don't want to anymore, I don't want to. I don't. No, I'm not going to instigate things anymore." So you're telling me that if some dark man came up behind you in the hall, pulled your Marks and Spencers down and ... "I can't grasp what you're talking about!" I'm sure you could if you tried hard enough. "I just can't grasp it, I'm sorry." Half a minute later, and the Pope of Pop is conveniently removed from my vision.'[44]

Gambotto-Burke was recruited to *ZigZag* by Mick Mercer, who had contributed in the early 1980s and was brought back as editor by the company that resuscitated the title. 'On the original *ZigZag*,' he said, 'I had always encouraged new writers, such as Marina Merosi and, through her, [future All About Eve singer] Julianne Regan, Jon Wilde – then Jonh Wilde – and especially those I was aware of in the fanzine world, like Tom Vague and Tony D. That continued at this new *ZigZag*, including involving those who worked for music papers; sometimes under assumed names – Robin Gibson of *Sounds* being Rex Garvin – and sometimes not, such as Mick Sinclair, Johnny Waller and Richard North.'

Among the talents that Mercer spotted were Barbara Ellen, who had run her own fanzine and would become a newspaper critic and columnist, future author William Shaw and designers Deborah Barker – later editor of *Homes & Gardens* – and Caroline Grimshaw. The latter's work, according to Mercer, 'would be ripped off by other designers'.[45]

But it was Mercer's publishing of work by Dele Fadele that kick-started the career of one of the more extraordinary music writers to emerge in the 1980s. As he would be now, had he not succumbed to cancer in 2018, Fadele was a rare figure: a Black rock critic. Born in London and raised in Nigeria, he studied in New York, where he created industrial music, consumed imported *NME*s and spotted new talent; friends recall Fadele raving about U2 on their first US college tour.

Back in London, freelancing for *ZigZag* led Fadele to *NME*, where he sidestepped the divisions by shifting effortlessly between guitar and Black music. Public Enemy's Chuck D recalled Fadele as the first Black British writer to interview him: 'That was amazing,' he told *The Guardian*. 'It was for our first important spread in the UK music press too. He got us.'

'He could be a combative writer,' observed *The Guardian*'s Tim Jonze. 'Courtney Love once described his review of Hole's Camden Underworld show in 1991 ("Their ability to depress in the name of entertainment is unrivalled") as the worst of her career. And Dele didn't mind a scrap in person either. During an unruly encounter with the Happy Mondays, he criticised them all for "that parochial attitude that keeps 'em locked within a three-mile radius of home". A live review of NWA begins: "Anyone who calls themselves 'Niggas With Attitude' has to be dumb, myopic and unaware of the great changes in the lives of Afro-Americans since slavery."'[46]

That argumentative style was foregrounded in the encounter with Chuck D, when Fadele observed that 'Martin Luther King got into the history books by pacifist means': 'Oh-oh, I've misjived. Chuck shouts, "Traitors!" and the rest of the interview, in the Def Jam office, is conducted at the top of our voices. Tolerance stops here. "I wouldn't call them traitors," Flavor Flav joins in. "I'd call them snakes, man. Don't set yourself up to do something and then not follow through. Be real." Dangerous talk has claimed many a life, but Public Enemy are fearless in their quest. Their first priority is to deal with the situation at home, by any means possible. One suspects they might be a front for a much more sinister organization. One could also wonder if they're conversant with Louis Farrakhan, the controversial Black Muslim leader whose speeches fetch high rates on the bootleg market – probably 'cos he's been banned from so many venues for inciting riots and for rampant antisemitism.'[47]

But Fadele's greatest contribution to the discourse around race and music came when he and Gavin Martin persuaded his *NME* colleagues to discard their myopia over Morrissey and present a clear-eyed view of the singer's right-wing flirtations. When Morrissey draped himself in a Union Jack and performed 'The National Front Disco' at a 1992 festival headlined by Madness – whose skinhead following had lingered – Fadele was in the audience. He persuaded the editorial team to abandon a planned Kylie Minogue cover and to run a shot of Morrissey clutching the British flag, splashed with the cover line: 'Flying the flag or flirting with disaster?'

'In agitated times,' wrote Fadele, 'when the twin spectres of fascism and ethnic cleansing are sweeping across Europe, and when there's been a return in England to the horrifying incidence of burning immigrants out of their homes, we must wonder why Morrissey has chosen this precise moment to fuel the fires of racism by parading onstage with a Union Jack and writing such ambiguous dodgy lyrics as "The National Front Disco" and "We'll Let You Know" on his recent album. Is he so starved of lyrical ideas that a touch of controversy is the best way to cover-up writer's block? Is he so completely fed up with the liberal consensus in the more compassionate side of the media that he's resorted to baiting the right-on crowd? Is there a sizeable degree of irony at work?'

The report earned Morrissey's bitter enmity: he refused to be interviewed by *NME* for twelve years. 'For what it's worth, I don't think Morrissey is a racist,' wrote Fadele in 1992. 'He just likes the trappings and the culture that surround the outsider element. He has some racist friends. And if he carries on this way, he'll have thousands more.'[48]

15
‘I should be doing that!’

Smash Hits Soars and *Boy’s Own* Gets on One, Matey

'A world free from all forms of cynical agenda, where wheezes were invented only for the sake of the wheeze, a world where U2 had finally "taken their place in the lineage of The Greats like the Thompson Twins".' So rhapsodized Sylvia Patterson about *Smash Hits*, which she joined in 1986 as its sales rose to the peak of one million per issue that it would hit within two years. Deputy editor Tom Hibbert continued to set the tone with his off-the-wall humour and loopy creations: the letters editor Black Type now had a supporting cast of fictional characters including Uncle Disgusting, Mr and Mrs Perkins and secretary Miss Pringle. These were embraced by the readers, who referenced them in letters and on the pen-pal page 'RSVP'.

'Hibbs was by some distance the most uniquely brilliant creative mind I had ever encountered,' Patterson wrote in her memoir *I'm Not With the Band*. 'A man about whom I knew nothing whatsoever, neither age nor background; though he did, I'd been told, test acid for a living in the seventies. Perhaps this had informed the sort of editorial sorcery he routinely conjured from the ether.'[1]

On the opposite side of Carnaby Street, *NME* hankered after the fun the magazine's staff were having. 'I used to stare out the window longing to be at *Smash Hits*,' David Quantick confessed. 'I'd be sat there typing, "The Blubbery Hellbellies have released a new single ..." thinking, "Why aren't I doing Spandau Ballet across the road? I should be doing that!"'[2]

But, as Patterson observed, *Smash Hits* journalists were no longer drafted in from the inkies but were 'indie kids, most in their early twenties, mostly Smiths apostles and John Peel devotees without a trace of indie snobbery, who also loved pop in all its forms'.[3]

These included Chris Heath. Nicknamed 'The Toff' because of his Oxbridge education, his thoughtful yet light-touch prose would eventually carry him to *Details*, *Rolling Stone* and *GQ*. Prior to that, he minted his insider reportage with the books *Literally* and *Pet Shop Boys versus Americ*a, in which he accompanied Neil Tennant and Chris Lowe on, respectively, their first world tour and live dates in the US.

On 'Ver Hits' – as the magazine called itself – he honed his approach with such pieces as a cover feature on a day in the promotional life of Norwegian heartthrobs A-ha: 'Six months ago this would probably have been *very* different: Mags, Morten and Pål would probably have smiled meekly every time they met all the important people – managing directors and so on – gathered around this table, but today quite the opposite is true. A-ha are the label's big new stars and so now everyone has to laugh at *their* jokes and congratulate *them* all the time. First the band are shown the sleeve and magazine ads for the new single (no-one mentions that it's far too late to make any changes even if the band hate them), then they're asked to choose a photo for a new picture disc. "You can use my head for the twelve-inch because it's so big," chortles Mags and everyone laughs. "It's a go-ahead guys! Let's do it!" he shouts sarcastically in a fake businessman's voice once they've chosen the photo, and everyone laughs again.'[4]

Despite such jollity, Mark Ellen decided to leave (he was replaced as editor by Steve Bush, who was Nick Logan's designer when *Smash Hits* was launched). Meanwhile, David Hepworth had overseen the launch of *Just Seventeen*, a preview of which – mixing pop features with affordable fashion and makeup tips – was given away with an issue of *Smash Hits*; it went on to be Britain's bestselling magazine for teenage girls. Now Ellen and Hepworth were given the go-ahead to trial a music monthly, kickstarted by the rapid takeup of CDs and the re-energizing of back catalogues by acts who appeared at Live Aid in 1985. 'The self-indulgent explanation was that we wanted a magazine we would like to write for and read,' said Hepworth. 'The proper publishing explanation was that there was an older demographic who were still interested in music but not going to read the inkies anymore.'

Discarding *Red*, *Music Review* and *Rock Review*, they settled on the more abstract *Q*, which could be explained as a reference to cueing up a CD or an abbreviation of an interviewer's question. The first issue – published in October 1986 to coincide with the busiest quarter for music sales – featured two giants. 'The music business had not yet succumbed to the worship of scale,' explained Hepworth, 'and therefore it was possible to get both Paul McCartney and Bob Dylan to give exclusive interviews for the first issue of a magazine which was only going to sell around 30,000 copies even if things went well. Then again, people weren't exactly queuing up to profile artists such as McCartney and Dylan at the time because *Q* had not yet invented rock nostalgia.'[5]

'*Q* was interesting because it was quite clear that there was a market for it,' said Chris Salewicz, who interviewed McCartney and wrote about former Clash members Mick Jones and Joe Strummer reuniting in the studio. 'I didn't see any contradiction in having [the Clash and McCartney] stories together. That wouldn't have been allowed at *NME*. And, because I'd published a positive book about him, McCartney gave an incredible interview.'

The former Beatle was afforded the courtesy of being sent dummy layouts. 'We basically said, "It's this kind of magazine," and he said, "Alright,"' recalled Hepworth, who felt Salewicz's piece gave McCartney an opportunity to dismantle his fluffy image. 'It was his chance to say, "I'm not just the bloke who wrote Yesterday; I'm a bit serious and, if anything, John was the one going home and in bed with his cocoa at half past nine." He really went off on one, with fantastically quotable stuff. We were very fortunate.'

Hepworth fared less well with Dylan: 'It was my worst nightmare; he wouldn't talk to me. And when Bob Dylan doesn't talk to you, ohhhhh ... it's something to tell the grandchildren. I sat in Bob's dressing room in Madison Square Garden while he played the guitar and studiously ignored me. And there was only him and me in the room. So we ran the story as, "Fuck! How rude is this?! Would you like to be here?" Mark's feeling was that you can always make a yarn out of anything.

'*Q* had a strong buzz right from the start. Every time we promoted it in the first few years, more people bought it and a high proportion of them stayed with it. We could get stars such as Elton John, Rod Stewart and Mick Jagger because they knew we would give them a fair crack of the whip, even though we reserved the right to raise a quizzical eyebrow at their lapses in self-awareness. The classic *Q* template was set by the interview with Elton John in issue three: "Stardom made a monster out of me; now I'm here to apologise and sell you my new album." It never failed.'[6]

Multiple images filled the cover: a break from the prevailing single portraits of acts. 'We wanted to give an idea of the range inside,' said Hepworth. 'We also didn't like the idea of just Bryan Ferry on the cover, because if you didn't like him you may not buy it. So we thought we'd do something that was a bit more like a contents page: someone zany over here, someone a bit wacky there. You could put over your attitude more.'

The first issue included a booklet listing the 100 best albums available on CD. 'Dire Straits certainly pushed it over the hill,' admitted Hepworth. 'I have to say the business case for *Q* was not as robust as it subsequently turned out to be. The feeling from the advertising department was, "You won't sell ads in a monthly," which proved to be completely wrong. Record companies loved it. The time seemed right. Live Aid had dragged rock from its catacombs and brought it blinking into the daylight of prime time [and] *NME* was passing through a phase when it seemed more determined than usual to alienate the casual reader.'[7]

Ellen and Hepworth insisted that publicists not sit in on interviews and that even powerful interviewees were never granted copy approval. This fed the notoriety of the feature for which *Q* is best remembered: Tom Hibbert's 'Who the hell does ... think he/she is?' – an often caustic and occasionally headline-making encounter with pop stars and celebrities from Margaret Thatcher to Jerry Lee Lewis, Ronnie Biggs to Ringo Starr. Positioned after the contents pages, it opened the magazine, said Hepworth, 'because the drumbeat was fame and what it does to people'.

'Who the hell ...?' was Ellen's idea. 'It was always going to be irreverent, but I don't think Mark knew how far it was going to go,' said Hibbert. 'He got really pissed off at me by the end because nobody would talk to him. I didn't get any trouble from record companies because I worked from home. Mark got it all. They'd ring up and complain about "this disgraceful article" and he'd have to deal with it.' Revered DJ John Peel, having hosted Hibbert at his Suffolk home, was among those who failed to see the funny side: '*Q* stitched me up with "Who the hell..?" They came down to talk to me and we were hospitable. I even asked them to wait until my kids came home from school so they could meet them. Then they wrote this piss-taking piece where they took the piss out of my dad, who's dead. I can't remember who wrote it, but he's a complete cunt. It's rather old-fashioned, but I thought it was a betrayal of our hospitality. We hadn't been nice to them in the hope they'd write a nice piece, but it was totally distorted and unfair.'

Bananarama also grumbled. 'They got really snotty,' Hibbert reported, 'and then tried to defend their position by saying I hadn't asked them enough horrible questions. David Crosby and Cliff Richard were brilliant, as was Johnny Rotten. We became friends after that. We used to live within two streets of each other so he used to come round and listen to old Neil Young records and drink beer.'

Hibbert was also let loose on the features section, for which he tracked down dented hero Roky Erickson, erstwhile leader of the 13th Floor Elevators, in Texas. 'Meeting him at his mother's house was really sad. I took him out for a meal, took him to a charity shop, but there was no communication. He'd point at a cuddly bear and ask, "What is that?" But I enjoy that weird situation more than a straightforward sit-down interview, because you can put more colour in when you write about it.'

Another sixties eccentric, Arthur Lee, prime mover of the great 1960s LA group Love, was distracted from Hibbert's interview by eccentric British racing commentator John McCririck on a hotel room TV. 'Arthur Lee was mad as a meat axe. He spent the whole interview asking, "What is this guy on?" I loved that.' And this was better than an interview with Roger McGuinn, 'who invented my life, basically, because I thought the Byrds were the best group ever, but when I met him he was a completely boring arsehole'.

Mat Snow was among those who jumped ship from the weeklies to *Q*: 'With *Smash Hits* and *The Face* before it, *Q* broke the stranglehold of the three-party music press. Obviously they were all staffed by refugees from *Sounds*, *Melody Maker* and *NME*. That the best writers from those papers joined showed how out of touch they were.

'Working there, I got to learn at the knee of Mark Ellen, who is interested in journalistic standards and saw no reason why we should be exempt from them because we wrote about rock music. He was interested in tone, balance and entertainment, not in first-person polemic, unlike *NME*. His vision for *Q* was very clear – he banned what he called "the perpendicular pronoun".'

Q also lured Lloyd Bradley, whose work had appeared in *Blues & Soul* and *NME*. A British Caribbean Londoner, Bradley – chef by day, sound system operator by night – became a journalist by sheer happenstance when he and fellow Funkadelic fan Chris Williams turned up outside the *Blues & Soul* offices in the hope of meeting their hero George Clinton, who was to review singles for the following week's issue. When they approached Clinton, he assumed they were journalists and invited them to join him. The magazine's staff, in turn, assumed they were part of the P-Funk legend's retinue, principally because they were Black. 'We spent the whole afternoon reviewing singles with George Clinton,' said Bradley. 'And when we said goodbye to him outside, he gave us tickets for his gig that night. Then the *Blues & Soul* guys said, "Aren't you going with him?" and we revealed we'd only just met him.' After the performance, Clinton invited Bradley and his friend to the Savoy hotel, where they chatted for three hours. 'George said he'd never met young Black British guys so didn't know what life was like for us, and asked loads of questions. I rang Bob [Kilbourn, *Blues & Soul* editor] and told him some of the things George had mentioned. He said, "You guys are pretty smart. Do you want some records to review?" When I reviewed four albums, I couldn't believe he didn't want them back!'

Interviewing the Godfather of Soul made for a sharp learning curve. 'I was crapping myself,' confessed Bradley, who found himself surrounded by veteran journalists. 'James Brown took no prisoners, so wasn't going to see that this kid was struggling. These older blokes were impressing him with how much they knew about his career, which he was soaking up. I think I asked him three questions and was desperately trying to write the answers down. It didn't occur to me to take a tape recorder.'[8]

Bradley survived to interview Teena Marie, War, Billy Preston and Syreeta before joining Neil Spencer's team at *NME*. There he faced an even greater challenge in the form of Peter Tosh: 'I was admitted to the hotel room to find the subject of my journey loudly, verging on violently, denouncing any suggested venue for a photo session. Nothing or nowhere, for a series of ludicrous reasons, was right. Finally, it is agreed that pictures are to be taken there, and optimistically I imagine that the camera lens will placate Tosh, and he will face the tape recorder with a happier disposition. Not so. After no more than half-a-dozen clicks, Tosh: "Why you take so much blood claat pictures?" Nick Knight: "Er ... it's my job." Tosh: "If you are a true professional then you should only need to take one picture and done!" Nick manages to finish the roll, packs up his gear and flees, presumably relieved to still be able to hold a camera, as Tosh is a very tall, powerful-looking man, and the look in his eye is a long way from the look of love.'[9]

Bradley also recognized Madonna's debt to Black music and her tough ambition. In the singer's first *NME* interview, centred on her debut single 'Everybody', he wrote: 'She's a disciple of the scratch'n'rap'n'break dance sessions held up and down the city, gathering with the faithful every Friday night at the Roxy as part of Afrika Bambaataa's much publicised Zulu Nation. However, more than being a mere camp follower, Madonna could be throwing this culture a much needed lifeline. Her current release, and forthcoming work, prove that since pestering the DJ at Danceteria to listen to her demo tape about a year ago, she has refined the rudiments of the style without ever losing sight of her mentors' visions. Teflon-coated electronic backing, strong on the repetitive computerised drum-beats, scratched and dubbed, yet through her impassioned vocals it becomes accessible to even the most mild-mannered disco fan.'[10]

While his White colleagues at *NME* geared up for the dreary 'hip-hop wars', Bradley got on with the job at hand, and championed new Black music as a presenter on pirate radio station Dread Broadcasting Corporation. And his addition to *Q*'s roster helped widen its rock-based scope, though he was equally comfortable interviewing Frankie Goes to Hollywood as he was analysing the impact of LL Cool J and Bobby Brown.

Q's sales rapidly rose north of 100,000 a month as readers gravitated to the punning wordplay seeded during the early years of *Smash Hits*. Ellen, art director Andy Cowles and the *Q* team produced a mickey-taking but affectionate take on their subjects; David Hepworth fondly recalls the caption 'The hoarse foreman of the apocalypse' on a photo of Robert Plant, while the pairing of King Crimson's Robert Fripp and post-punk singer Toyah Willcox was headlined 'Mr Chalk loves Mrs Cheese'.

Ellen and Hepworth imposed a strong line for photography after freelancer Steve Rapport returned from a session with a rock band. 'He had these moody, strangely lit pictures where you couldn't see what was going on, and told us that was the way in which they wanted to be seen,' said Hepworth. 'That's the way people were presenting themselves. *The Face* had invented this idea that photographs were there to project a mood. But we said to photographers, "We don't give a fuck about what they want to project. We want to see the story." So the classic *Q* photographic style was always the artist in context, like shooting the band from behind the amps so you can see the audience – the can of Coke next to the amp, the set list. And with informative captions. It was a documentary approach which became widely adopted.'

Another turning point was a review by *Smash Hits* graduate Dave Rimmer of an album by Japan singer David Sylvian. Ellen and Hepworth had instituted a star rating system, intended as an alternative to the often highly individual takes of the inkies. 'We'd told writers that this meant they had to stand aside from the music because the review was not purely their opinion,' said Hepworth. 'Dave's review came back with five stars and Mark and I said, "No. Sorry. David Sylvian does not rate five stars. He has not made a five-star album." It caused a bit of a to-do but I think we were right, because we put ourselves on the side of the readers rather than the writers. That's a big difference. If you're in the media, you work for the public. You're producing something they like and are excited about. So we docked a star. [The writers] got the hang of it.'

The relatively sober reviews section offered a contrast to the fireworks let off in features by the likes of Hibbert and Adrian Deevoy. 'The real reason readers bought *Q* was because it was a thrill-ride at the front and it had a good shopping guide at the back,' said Hepworth. 'That was the magazine's secret sauce. Nobody was trying to be hipper-than-thou or younger than they were, and nobody was trying to pretend they liked things that they didn't.'[11]

Eventually *Q*'s sales topped 200,000 a month, but not everyone was impressed by its matey approach. 'While it did its job very well, I found it rather smarmy,' said Barney Hoskyns. 'It took away the danger, glamour and mystery of music for me, because its tone was never to take anything seriously. *Q* was part of the Spinal Tapping of rock 'n' roll; all that "Sir Bonzo of DogBandshire". This came from the congruence of Mark Ellen's public school persona – as the deacon of rock 'n' roll, ha ha ha – and David Hepworth's rather pleased-with-himself grammar-school take.'

* * *

Q's domination of mainstream music publishing in the late 1980s, and the commensurate dwindling of the weeklies' influence, provided the space for specialist magazines, some selling no more than a few hundred copies an issue. These fused the energy of punk fanzines with professional visual presentation, as the desktop publishing revolution kicked in. *Bam Balam* publisher Brian Hogg was a driving force behind the information-packed *Strange Things Are Happening* – an offshoot of the Bam-Caruso reissue label that resurrected psychedelic obscurities. Hogg co-edited the glossy-covered magazine with the label's sleeve designer Phil Smee, who financed the publication. Contributors included musician and writer Richard Norris, who worked at the label and was later to score hits as half of electronic duo the Grid (the other being Dave Ball of Soft Cell).

'Initially we came up with the idea of Bam-Caruso Books,' said Hogg. 'We were writing and designing all this stuff, so thought it would be good to have a themed series: *British Folk Rock*, *The Blues Boom* ... There were six altogether, which we were going to produce at twelve-by-twelve inches, so you would put them on the shelf beside your albums.' But after a fruitless attempt to secure a publisher, Hogg and Smee channelled the material into a new magazine.

Alongside cult figures such as Nick Drake, *Strange Things* emphasized psychedelia, which meant it coincided with the advent of acid house and the interest of young rock groups like Primal Scream in the pharmaceutical sounds of the 13th Floor Elevators et al. For issue three, published in July 1988, Smee went gloriously overboard with chaotically colourized spreads that could be read only with the 3-D glasses stapled to one of the pages.

'We covered film and television, *The Man from U.N.CL.E.*, horror genre writers, a lot of stuff with music at the core,' recalled Hogg.

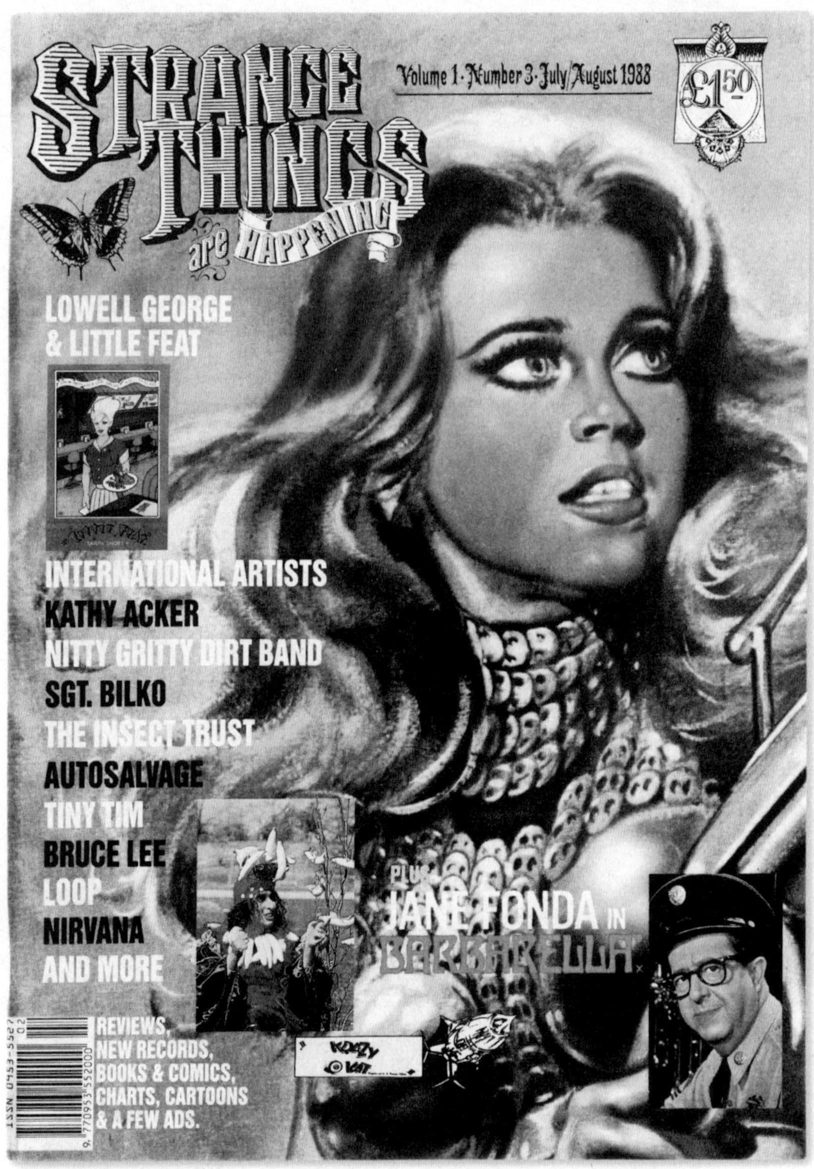

Strange Things Are Happening, vol. 1, no. 3, July/August 1988

'Through Richard [Norris], we had pieces on [experimental writer] Kathy Acker and early Creation records. He brought another perspective to the magazine. I'm very proud of what we did with *Strange Things*. For its time it was trailblazing.' However, cashflow problems restricted its run to six issues between 1988 and 1990. 'You only got paid by distributors after three issues,' explained Hogg. 'This put Phil in a financial bind and we had to stop doing it.' But he notes that those who took note of the magazine's breadth included David Hepworth and Mark Ellen when they came to launch *Mojo* a few years later.[12]

Six years before the arrival of *Strange Things*, the more serious and sometimes high-minded *The Wire* made its debut, concentrating on contemporary jazz and improvised music. 'Why this new magazine?' wrote Anthony Wood, who co-founded it with Chrissie Murray. 'Quite simply – as a country that has one of the largest jazz consumptions in Europe, it is poorly served by information, comment and opinion on the subject. The situation has become more pronounced by *Melody Maker*'s recent abandonment of jazz (sorry, Mike Oldfield, but a token eighth-of-a-page of news does not jazz coverage make). Meanwhile, the reverent gentlemen at *Jazz Journal* continue, at best, to admit only grudgingly that jazz has got beyond 1948; at worst, deny its current development. Add to this the recent rise in consciousness of jazz, especially among the under-twenty-fives, and the message is clear – a void has developed.'

The Wire took its name from a piece by British saxophonist Steve Lacy, 'to whose musical farsightedness the magazine is dedicated', Wood explained. 'Lacy – though standing at midpoint in jazz's evolution – has always looked back at the past and forward into the future when shaping his own music. This will broadly be the approach of *The Wire*.'[13]

The magazine shouldered *Melody Maker*'s original mantle: many of its readers were musicians, amateur and professional. Within a couple of years Murray and Wood received backing from maverick book publisher Naim Attalah, whose incorporation of the quarterly magazine into his Namara imprint enabled it to go monthly. This coincided with the promotion of Murray to editor, making her the world's first woman to hold that position at a jazz journal, some six decades after *Melody Maker* set the ball rolling. 'After years of neglect and decay,' declared Wood, 'jazz journalism and debate will be able to rise to the same heights which the music itself is currently experiencing in popularity. To the mass of new readers I will just say hang on tight because we're going to move fast ...'[14]

The Wire utilized some of the UK's most interesting journalists, including Brian Case, Max Jones, Eddie Prevost, Cynthia Rose, David Toop, Val Wilmer and David Widgery. And when Richard Cook became editor a couple of years later, he brought aboard Chris Bohn (who later succeeded Cook as editor), Paul Gilroy and Edwin Pouncey. As jazz writer John Fordham observed, Cook opened 'a specialized, sometimes uninviting publication to an audience drawn to classical, soul, reggae and pop as well as jazz'.[15]

Writer Mark Sinker said *The Wire* gave him 'the space and freedom to find my voice', although it 'paid the worst of all. Mostly I wrote about free improvised music and the more intransigent offshoots of post-punk'. Sinker recalled Cook's first editorial in 1985 as a call 'for a conversation able to handle everything from Oscar Peterson to Einstürzende Neubauten: to handle the collision of life-won high technique and smash-it-all iconoclasm'.[16]

By the early 1990s, the magazine was fulfilling that remit by covering hip-hop, modern classical, free improvisation and electronic music. 'I was responsible for commissioning all the record reviews, live reviews, book reviews,' said deputy editor Tony Herrington. 'There were basically two editorial staff: me and the editor and then a part-time designer. And that was it.' Herrington eventually became editor and publisher, and engineered a management buyout in 2000. 'Namara didn't really know much about *The Wire* so they were totally hands-off,' he recalled. 'We could pretty much do what we wanted, which is how I ended up being both publisher and editor, and of course I knew even less about what a publisher did than I knew about what an editor did.'[17] But with monthly sales of around 20,000, *The Wire* held its own as a bastion for serious analysis of music in the vanguard, and provided a model for others who wished to pursue an independent line.

Wire contributor Paul Bradshaw had written about reggae for Neil Spencer during his *NME* editorship. Spencer himself had spent

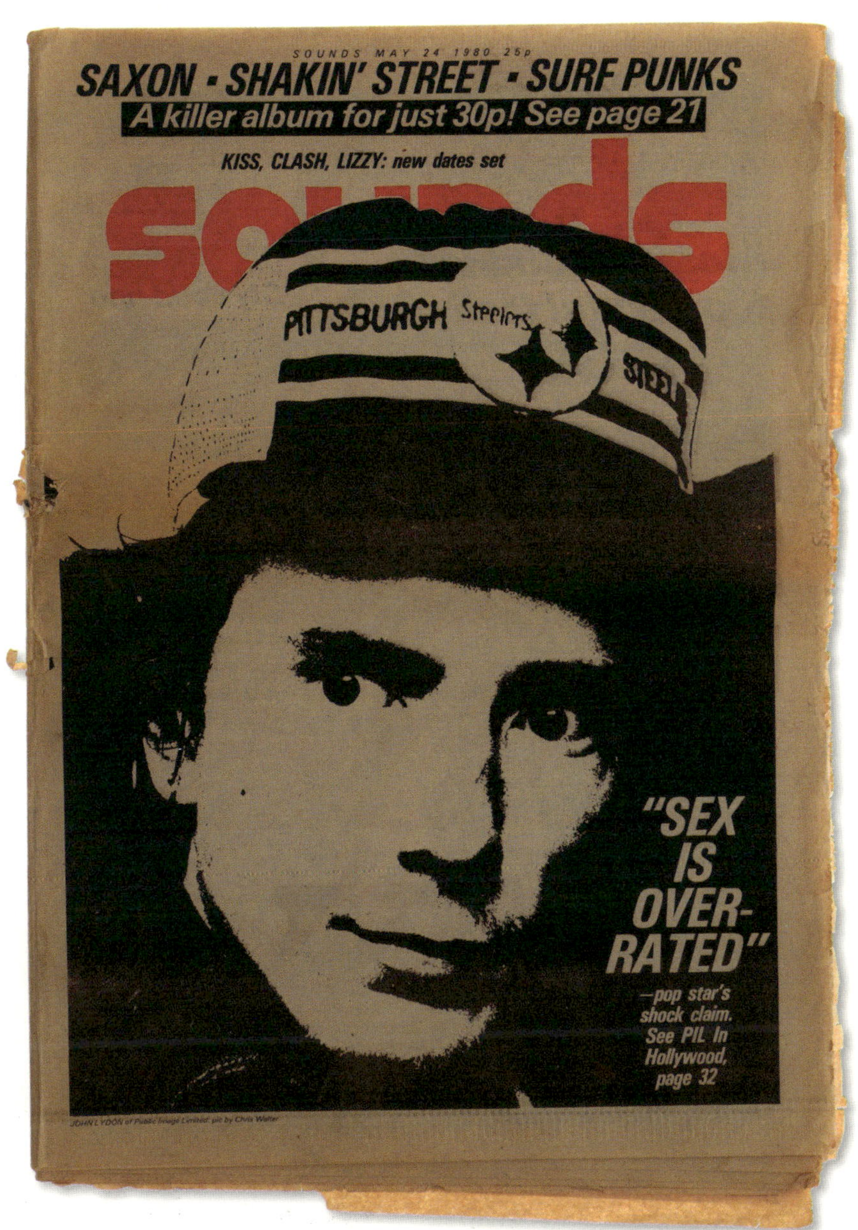

SOUNDS MAY 24 1980 25p

SAXON • SHAKIN' STREET • SURF PUNKS

A killer album for just 30p! See page 21

KISS, CLASH, LIZZY: new dates set

sounds

"SEX IS OVER-RATED"

—pop star's shock claim. See PIL In Hollywood, page 32

JOHN LYDON of Public Image Limited: pic by Chris Walter

12. *Sounds*, 24 May 1980

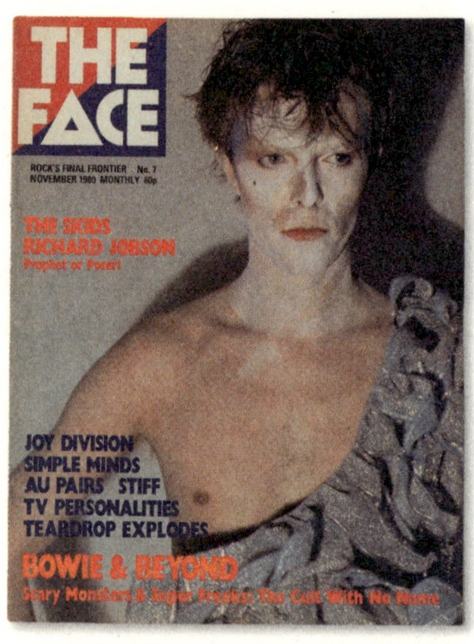

13. *The Face*, no. 7, November 1980

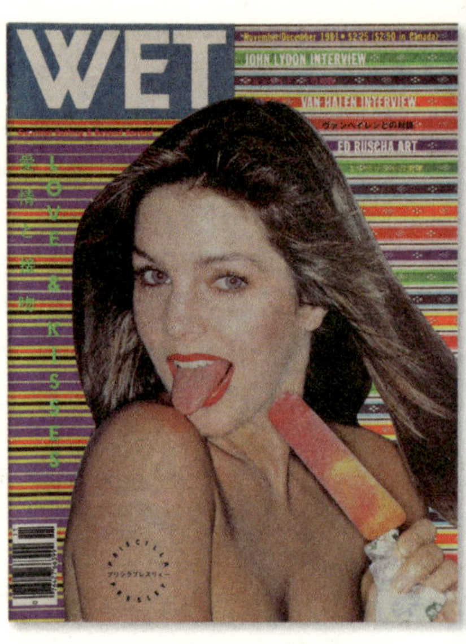

14. *WET*, November/December 1981

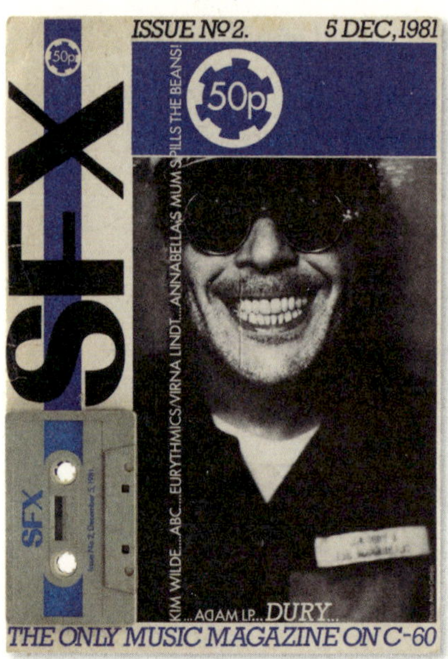

15. *SFX*, no. 2, 5 December 1981

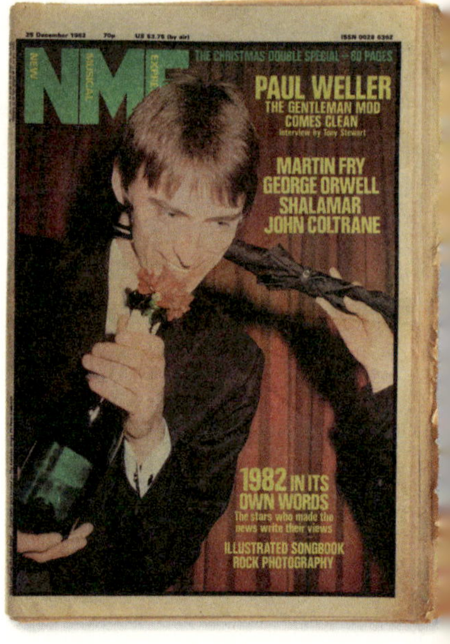

16. *NME*, 25 December 1982

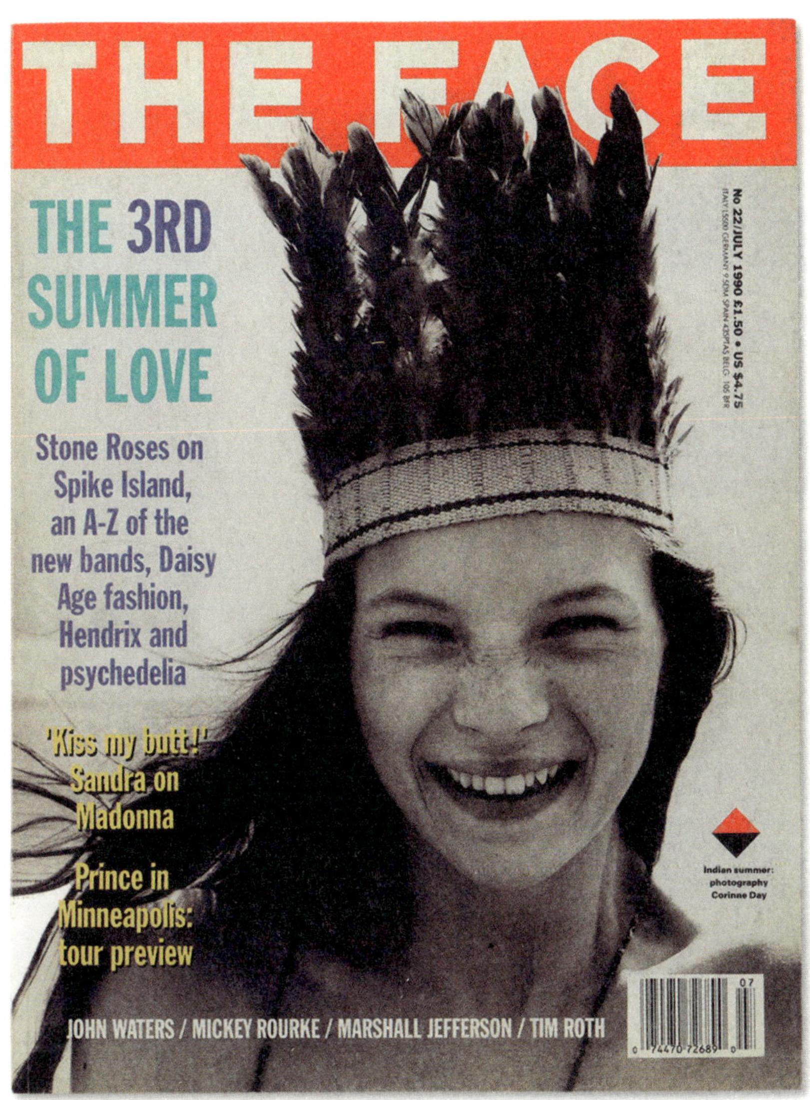

17. *The Face*, no. 22, July 1990

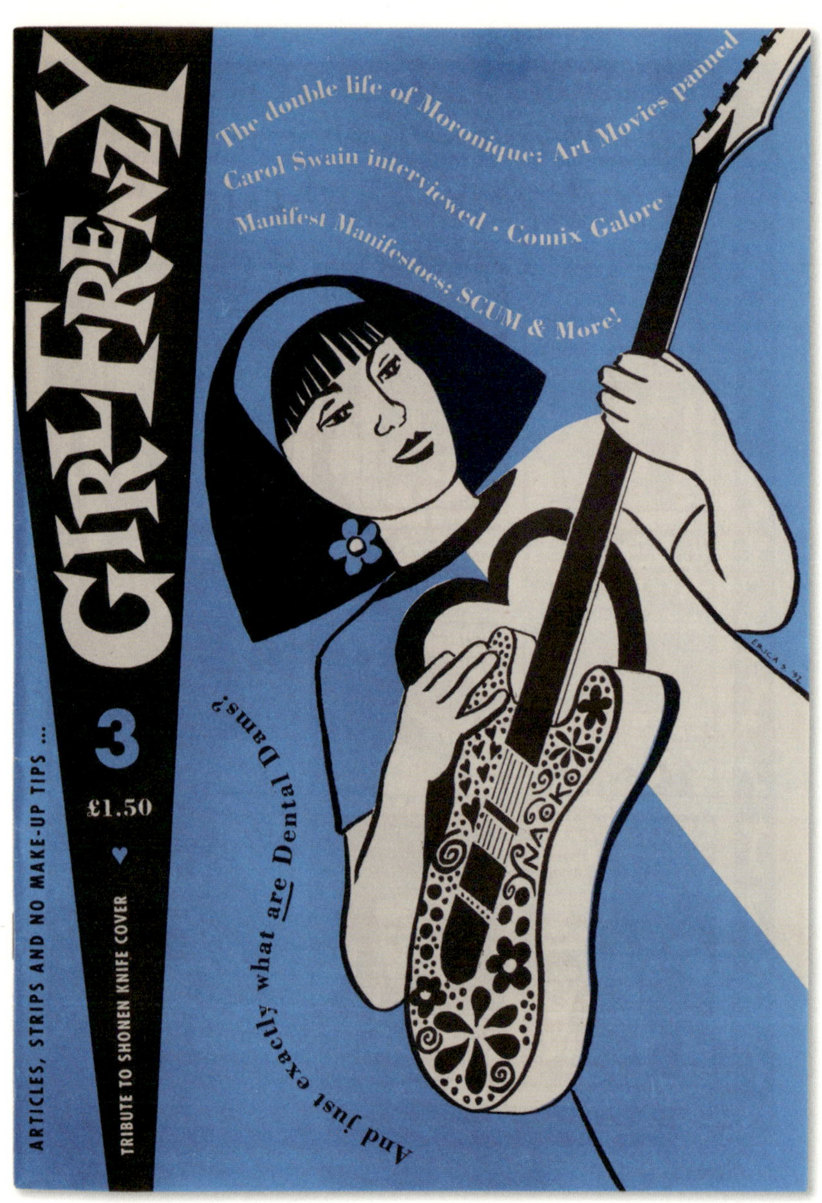

18. *Girlfrenzy*, no. 3, *c*. 1991/1992

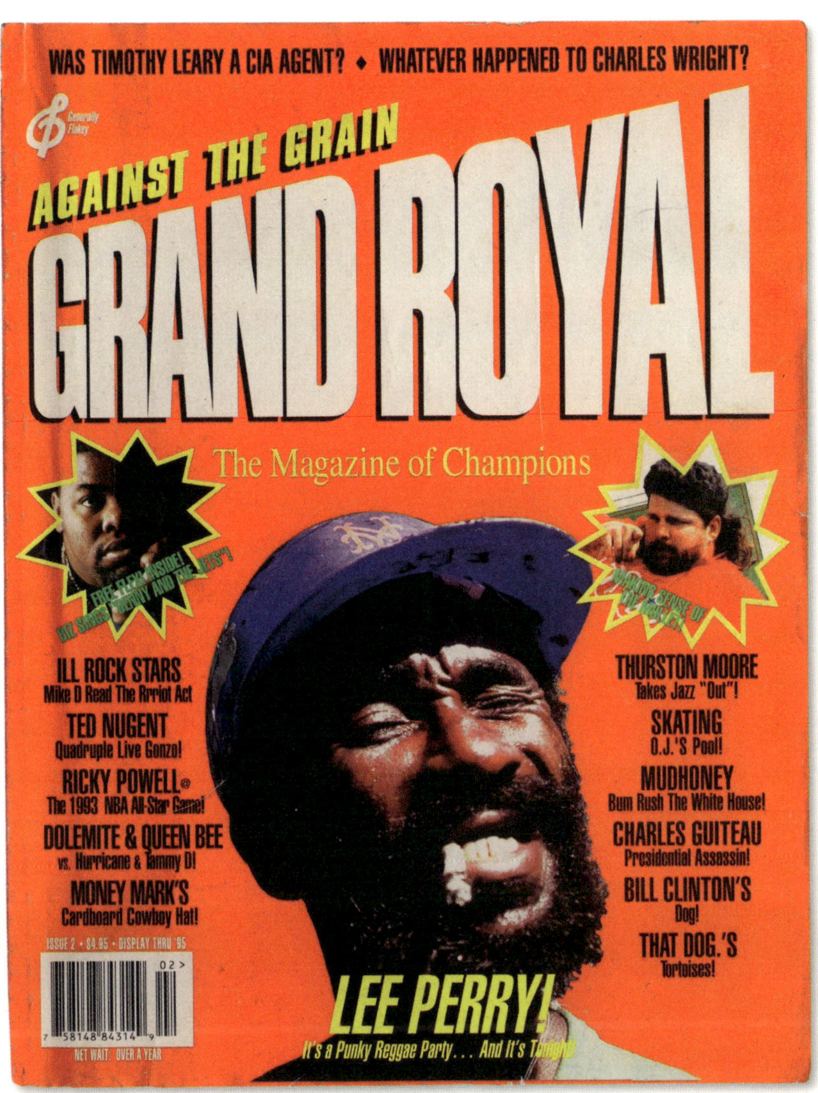

19. *Grand Royal*, no. 2, 1995

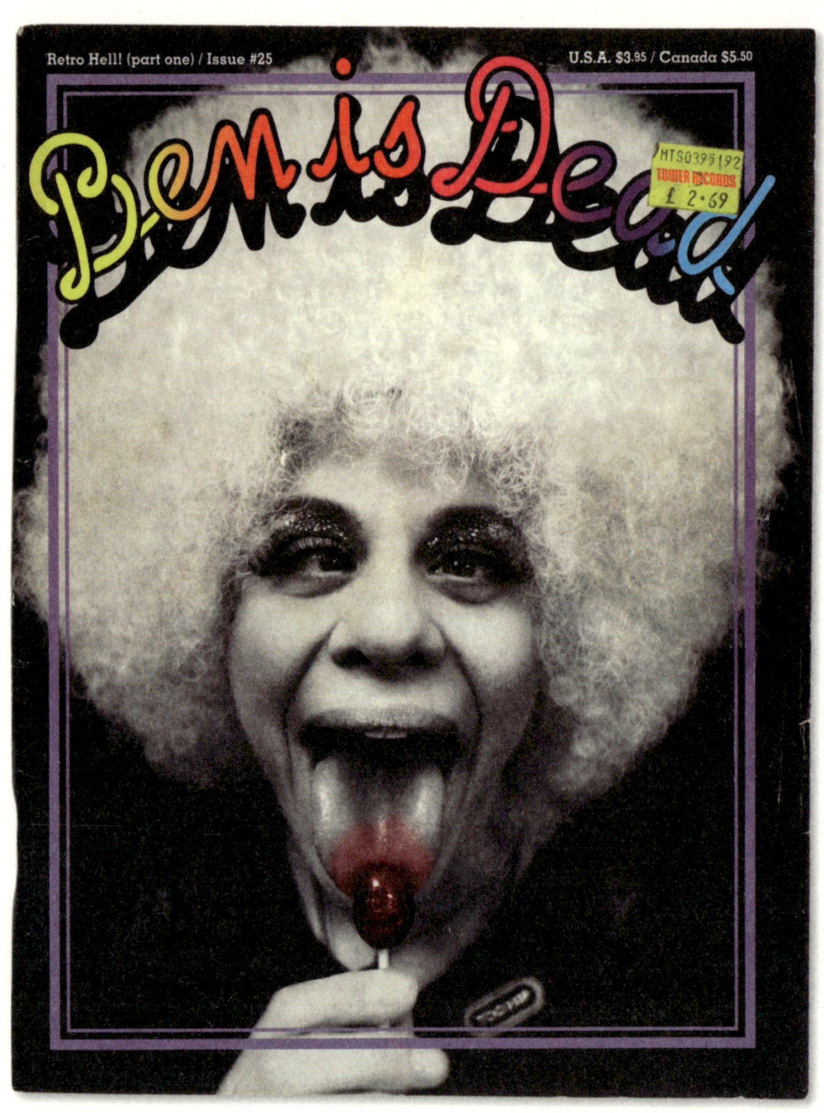

20. *Ben is Dead*, no. 25, 1995

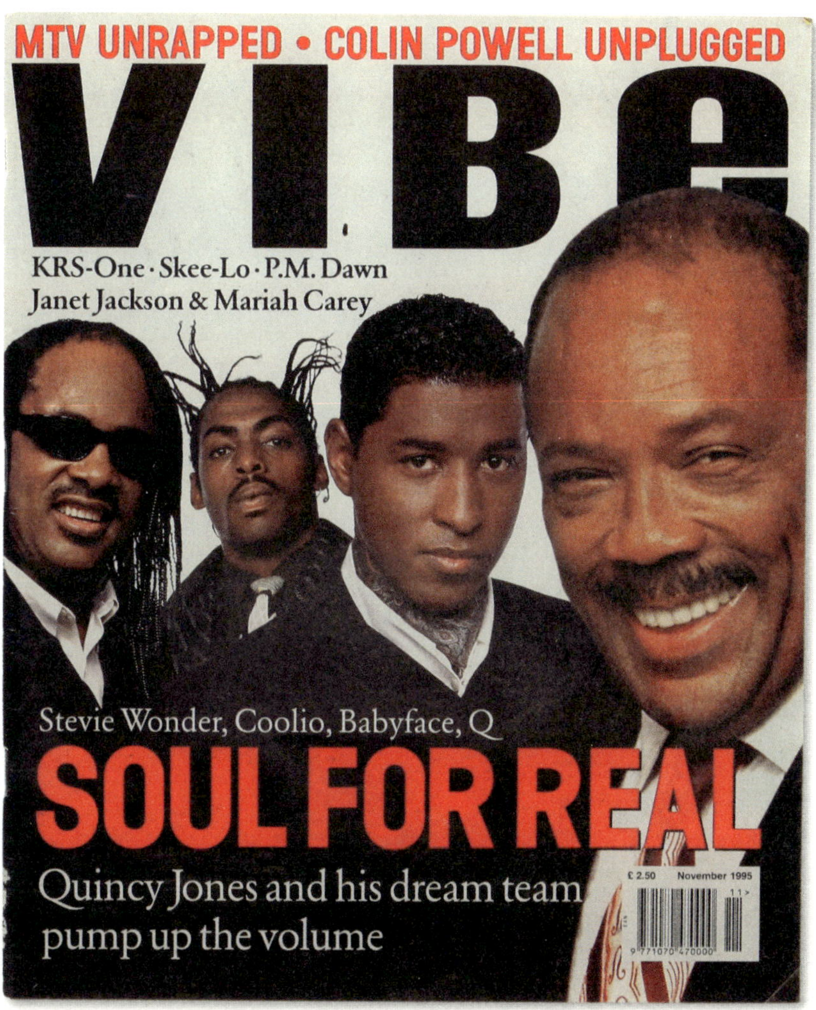

21. *Vibe*, November 1995

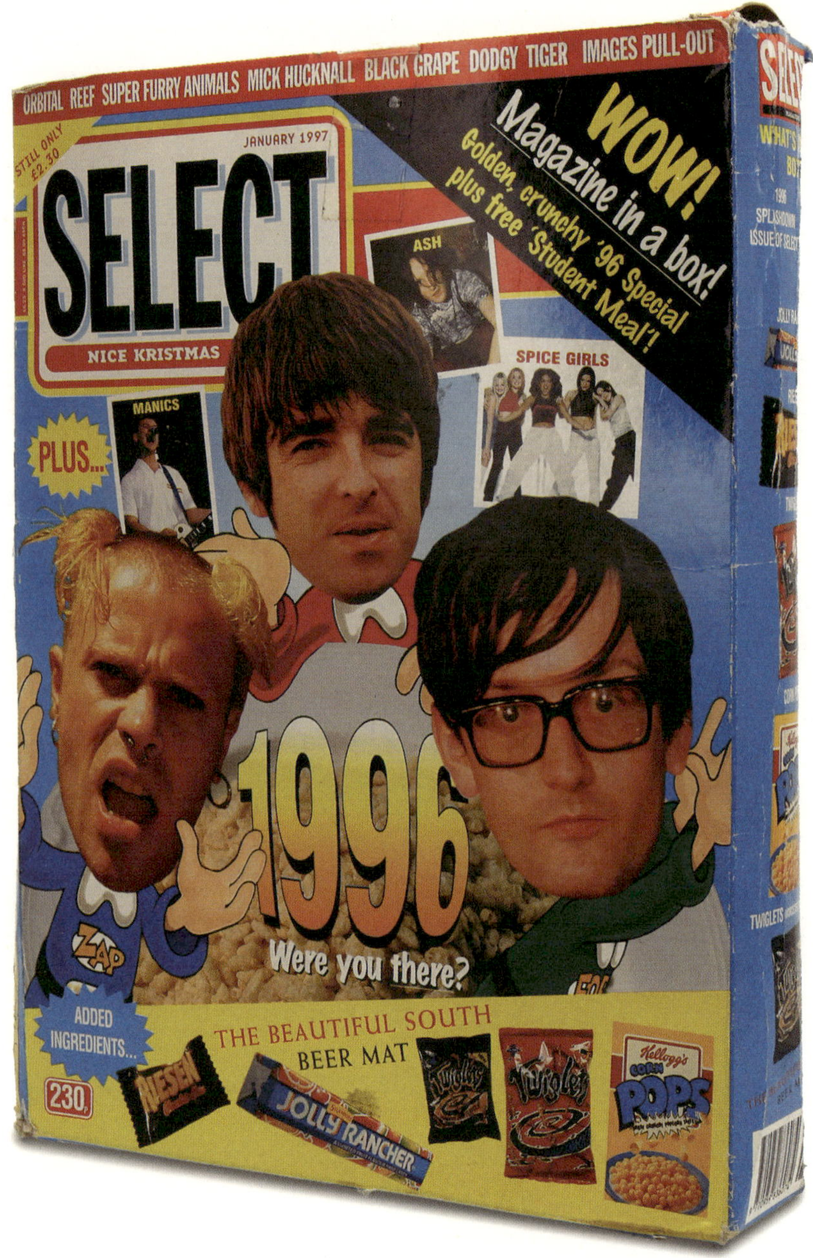

22. *Select*, January 1997

his post-*NME* years contributing to newspapers and helping Nick Logan launch his men's magazine *Arena*. 'My personal life improved and I started going out more because music was improving,' he enthused. 'I would go down the Wag [London club] to see Slim Gaillard. Jazz became hip. Soul became cred again. It was a much better time.' But Bradshaw was frustrated: 'No one was writing about what we were interested in: a connection between music of the African diaspora.'

So, in 1988, the pair united with fellow journalist Kath Willgress to found *Straight No Chaser*. Its turf, said Bradshaw, was 'anything from jazz to hip-hop to African music generally, Senegalese, Congolese, South African music, as well as Latin'.[18] The first issue's 1,000 copies were distributed via specialist shops and clubs during the acid-house-fuelled Second Summer of Love, whose multicultural nights included Soul II Soul at the Africa Centre. Meanwhile, Bradshaw's pirate radio confrere Gilles Peterson was making a name for himself as a DJ, playing the genres featured in *Straight No Chaser*. He duly launched the Talkin' Loud label, while Eddie Piller's Acid Jazz focused on funk and soul.

As well as Bradshaw, Willgress, Spencer and Peterson, contributors included James Lavelle, founder of the Mo'Wax label and dance collective UNKLE. The photography of Chris Clunn, Suki Dhanda, Liz Johnson Artur and Jonathan Oppong-Wiafe, and illustrations of Mitchy Bwoy and Ian Wright, were showcased in the magazine, which initially adopted a landscape format like the first issues of the trailblazing *i-D*.

The design was by Ian Swift, colleague of *The Face*'s art director Neville Brody. '[Neil] Spencer wanted Brody but, of course, got turned down,' recalled Swift. 'Brody was just too busy to take on a pro-bono. That's where I came in. It helped that I had my own Apple Macintosh.' The first issue – with 'The magazine of world jazz jive. The magazine tuned to the freedom principle' on the cover – emulated the designs of pioneers such as Reid Miles, who minted the look of jazz records in the 1950s for the Blue Note label. 'I thought, since hip-hop was sampling old music and turning it into something new, I'm going to do the same with the visuals,' said Swift. 'That was where it all started for me: the whole appropriation, visual remixing thing.'[19]

Straight No Chaser swerved the cerebral approach of *The Wire*, but was a self-consciously cool gathering of like-minded souls and experts. In stark contrast was *Boy's Own*, a soccer culture fanzine that osmosed into a piss-taking document of acid house and youth culture. Flagged as 'The only fanzine to get on one matey!', it began as a southern response to the Liverpudlian football 'zine *The End* (edited by Peter Hooton, later the leader of indie band the Farm). '*The End* colonised the borders between football, pop and fashion with incisive humour and subversive broadsides aimed at the London-centred homogeneity of eighties style culture,' wrote Matthew Collin in *Altered State*, his definitive book about the intertwining of ecstasy and clubbing. '*Boy's Own* followed Hooton's lead, but attacked from within. Its covers featured cheeky urchins with pit bull terriers and its prose was by turns hilarious (if you got the in-jokes) and vicious. *Boy's Own* fulfilled the role of agent provocateur, telling the scene in no uncertain terms exactly where it was going wrong.'[20]

The *Boy's Own* crew – Cymon Eckel, Terry Farley, Steven Hall, Steve Mayes and Andrew Weatherall – toiled by day in uninspiring jobs. Hall worked for British Airways, Farley was a gas-fitter and Weatherall a record shop assistant. Smart and funny, they and their friends were enraptured by soul and dance, football and style. 'While house music and ecstasy were the fuels powering the dance revolution, *Boy's Own* was the siren on top of the speeding vehicle, a loud satirical BLERRK screaming out at bystanders with little mercy for even its own scenesters,' wrote dance music historians Frank Broughton and Bill Brewster in their introduction to a bound volume of the magazine's twelve issues from 1986 to 1991. '*Boy's Own* represents a turning point in British youth culture. Acid house, with its origins in the casual world of beach-loving, E-smuggling hooligans, was when the suburbs stole the reins of popular culture from the middle-class art school grads who'd been hanging onto them since the late sixties.'[21]

Although it rarely sold more than 3,000 copies, *Boy's Own* cast an oversize shadow, propagated via club nights, parties, DJ sets, merchandising, record productions, remixes and eventually releases on their own label. But its openness to musical genres elevated it above club cliques. 'There's an attitude rather than a sound to the music,' explained Farley. 'It's all got a bit of spunk and a bit of life in it, whether it's Hank Williams or a rap record'[22] – hence a somewhat incongruous byline for Weatherall on an interview with folk-rock act Martin Stephenson and the Daintees in the first issue; a review of Primal Scream for *NME* under a pseudonym a couple of years later led to Weatherall producing the towering dance/rock amalgam *Screamadelica*. 'My and Steve Mayes's schooling was pretty non-existent,' Farley told dance music writer Stephen Titmus. 'We got Andrew in because he was a lot cleverer than us, could spell and knew proper grammar. Little did we know he was a lazy fucker and would always deliver his copy about five weeks late.'

Boy's Own's championing of the house music being nurtured in the gay clubs of Chicago and other US urban centres, Titmus pointed out, went against the grain of the London club scene dominated by the rare groove, funk and hip-hop of Gilles Peterson, Norman Jay and the Soul II Soul collective: 'Many viewed house negatively as simply another strain of gay disco ... Dancers wouldn't really know what to do with the boom-chick of house tracks, and the funky London strut that worked so well to rare groove just seemed out of synch with house's locked grooves.'[23]

But the importing of house by DJs Danny Rampling, Paul Oakenfold and Nicky Holloway, returning from Ibiza in the autumn of 1987, turned UK club culture on its head. And while *i-D* featured a smiley face – the symbol most associated with acid house – on its December 1987 cover, it was the *Boy's Own* issue published a couple of months later that solidified the first youth movement in a decade to cause a national media frenzy. The magazine's gossip column documented a 'poncho-wearing clubber outside Theatre of Madness club, central London, Monday night, 4.00 a.m.: "I don't mind telling you matey, I'm right on one and feel like I'm on holiday."'[24]

This preceded three pages headed 'Bermondsey goes Baleric' [*sic*], sparked by the rise of club nights Shoom and Future. A frontline report from Paul Oakenfold about his time in Ibiza was accompanied by a 'Get on one matey' chart that captured the scene's diversity, with the era-defining 'Acid Trax' by Phuture and 'Bango (to the Batmobile)' by the Todd Terry Project alongside Thrashing Doves' 'Jesus on the Payroll', U2's 'With or Without You', Cyndi Lauper's version of Marvin Gaye's 'What's Goin' On' and even John Lennon's 'Give Peace a Chance'. 'There is a real prejudice against this scene by the establishment of [London's] West End,' the feature concluded. 'Sure, fashion isn't important and maybe the dancers do look straight in style, but in attitude, no fucking way. Anyway if you ain't hip enough to enjoy the City of Angels on a Friday and then just to stick on your jeans and T-shirt the next night for a real rave, then bollocks, why are you reading *Boy's Own*?'[25]

References to the drug use that scandalized the tabloids were overt. '1987 was probably the best year to date for ecstasy,' wrote Oakenfold. 'It takes you up and gives you a feeling of freedom. You know what you're doing, you just feel more confident of love. People tend to take the drug and dance the night away.' To which somebody, presumably Farley, added: '(You hippie Oakenfold. Ed.)'.

As acid house took off, *Boy's Own* maintained its sardonic edge, tracking the 'mugs' and 'teds' it viewed as opportunists and bandwagon-followers, hence the slogan 'Better dead than Acid Ted'. Meanwhile Weatherall's salty editor's note – in the guise of 'The Outsider' – was a must-read. The seventh issue's was headlined, '*Boy's Own* – the fanzine that missed the boat' – a quote he attributed to rival publication *Soul Underground* ('Cheers chaps!').[26]

Soul Underground had been launched a year after *Boy's Own* by rare groove fans Darren Reynolds and David Lubich. Regulars at club nights and warehouse parties not covered by the mainstream press, they compiled the first issue on Reynolds's mother's kitchen table. All 850 copies were sold through specialist record shops.

'The first few editions seem a little crude now,' Lubich admitted, 'but, from the off, *Soul Underground* knew what it was about. We simply wanted to capture the essence of the music scene we loved, to treat it with some respect, and to write about it with passion and intelligence. And, more than anything, we wanted to be there first. That meant putting in the hours, building up a team of contacts. In those pre-internet days, social networking happened in the real world; our piece on the truly underground "Circle Line parties" came from a whisper overheard in a club queue. *Soul Underground* was also driven as much by the sources I rejected as those I sought out. This meant operating an effective bullshit detector, avoiding the hype merchants, PRs and sleazeballs who'd begun to smell money in this emergent scene – and who'd go on to dominate underground pop culture and more or less destroy it.'

By issue seven, the founders' relationship had fallen victim to the pressure of dealing with advertisers and labels tapping the market for the rap, electro, house, reggae and soul that had toppled rare groove. Reynolds exited and Lubich fell back on largely untested contributors. 'I went out to attract people with something to say,' he noted, 'even if they weren't too sure how to say it. *Soul Underground* would be the exact opposite of the cosy, smug, introverted and conservative magazines that nobody I knew read. While some of our contributors were experienced journalists, many had never seen their words in print before. What they had was passion, provocative opinions, incredible underground connections and record collections that put even my half-a-room of vinyl in the shade. A large chunk of my time was spent convincing DJs, musicians, scenesters and would-be journalists to have a go at writing – more or less the exact opposite of the normal editorial role of sending out rejection letters. A large part of the fun of running the magazine was seeing such a disparate group of people – soul boys, import junkies, rap obsessives, club promoters and borderline anarchists – come together.'[27]

Evolving from scrappy fanzine to stylish magazine, *Soul Underground* featured a regular cartoon strip satirizing youth culture by illustrator Bill Dew. Meanwhile, Lubich offered sober analyses of events such as the clampdown on pirate radio stations that were instrumental to dance music. In 1989, Home Secretary Douglas Hurd announced that, rather than providing FM licences to these operators, as had been previously indicated, new legislation would empower police activity. 'The pirates have been very naive,' Lubich wrote, 'as everyone knew that that the government wasn't going to hand out much in the way of FM contracts. The better stations have been forced to stay off the air with the promise of contracts that might never materialise. The DTI [Department of Trade & Industry] will be given more powers to do even more raids.'[28]

The magazine's international appeal was boosted by its New York editor, former *East Village Eye* publisher Leonard Abrams. 'He quickly built up a group of street-level writers and photographers and donated his feel for what was happening in music, his ear for high-quality gossip and a killer address book,' said Lubich. 'We even opened a New York office – in reality, a walk-in wardrobe in Leonard's Avenue A apartment. To this day, it amazes me to think that *Soul Underground* was being bought by Manhattan's DJs, musicians and music lovers.'[29]

Although the magazine also scored a first by covering the multicultural scene in Bristol that produced Massive Attack, it wasn't financially geared to survive the 1990 recession and consequent drop-off in advertising. After thirty-eight issues, Lubich pulled the plug early the following year.

16
‘We’ll take chances’

Spin Spins a New Line and *Grand Royal*, *Ray Gun* and *Ben Is Dead* Fly the Freak Flag

Chapter 16

Adult publishing scion Bob Guccione Jr was one of three music journalists attacked in Guns N' Roses' 'Get in the Ring'. Mick Wall of *Kerrang!* and Andy Secher of *Hit Parader* also fell foul of Axl Rose for unspecified offences. But Guccione was likely unruffled, having been raised in a family business built on *Penthouse*. His own stab at publishing immortality came in 1985, with *Spin*, 'an upbeat magazine without the politics and in love with rock 'n' roll and all its kindred spirits', he declared. 'We'll be open, unafraid, independent and unpretentious. We'll take chances and probably a few lumps. Most of all we'll be fun. A confession: *SPIN* is imperfect. It's rough-edged, restless, insatiably curious. A little aggressive, a little cocky. Youthfully uncompromising but maturely flexible. Romantic – definitely! Irreverent – sure. Unpredictable – yes. Very alive.'[1] These were big claims, but *Spin* almost immediately found its place as a street-level and more youthful *Rolling Stone*.

The first issue featured Madonna on the cover (four months before Guccione's father did the same with *Penthouse*, albeit with different pictures). But it also set out with an investigative edge: writer Ed Kiersh tracked down Ike Turner – erstwhile husband of Tina and a rock 'n' roll pioneer – who was then near-destitute and living on LA's margins. And while a roster that included British mainstays Chris Salewicz, Mick Farren, Jon Savage and Barney Hoskyns suggested the same old same old, an admirably diverse gallery of early cover stars included women (Tina Weymouth, Joan Jett, the Bangles), African Americans (Michael Jackson, Run-DMC) and acts with no US chart success whatsoever (Nick Cave). Screenwriter and author Jonathan Bernstein, who joined as a film critic, noted: 'The lack of cohesion in its cover choices – Nick Cave one month, Soul II Soul the next – and the fact that its stories dug a little deeper than just getting incapacitated with its subjects made it a more compelling read than the latest *NME*.'

'*Rolling Stone*'s midtown offices would've been an easy walk from my college campus at Fordham University in Lincoln Center, but I didn't think about applying there,' recalled broadcaster-to-be Lori Majewski, who joined as an intern in 1992. '*Spin*, whose offices at the time were located on 18th Street between Fifth and Sixth Avenues, was more downtown in every way. *Rolling Stone* felt very old-school – and, well, just old – whereas *Spin* was cool.

'Strong women emerged while I was working at the magazine: Kim Gordon, the Deal sisters of the Breeders, Tanya Donnelly and Belly, Juliana Hatfield, Liz Phair, Tori Amos, D'arcy from the Smashing Pumpkins. But the smartest of all may have been Courtney Love. Although she struck me as a coattail-rider of her rising rock star husband when I first spotted her on the front of post-feminist teen read *Sassy* in the summer of '92, by the time the Hole front woman scored her first solo *Spin* cover – the last issue of the magazine that I'd work on, it coincided with the release of 1994's *Live Through This* – she was very much deserving of her own spotlight.'[2]

While *Spin* kept it down 'n' dirty, *Details* evolved into a lifestyle glossy with some of the era's best American music writing. Just a few years before, attempts at Condé Nast to convert Annie Flanders's arty downtown newsprint bible into a mainstream title had been fraught, and coincided with the publishing house's major-domo Si Newhouse's interest in launching a US version of *The Face*.

When Newhouse first made his approach, Nick Logan insisted that his New York correspondent James Truman edit the magazine. 'Nick and I had a rather eccentric meeting with [Newhouse] at the Condé Nast offices and then over lunch at the Four Seasons restaurant,' said Truman. 'It was fairly obvious that the Condé Nast principals had little idea of why *The Face* was important, but to their credit they knew that it *was* important. So we discussed lots of arcane details – about frequency of publishing, demographic reach and even paper stock – without ever getting to what the magazine could be.'

In the event, Condé Nast decided not to proceed, but recruited Truman, first to work with Anna Wintour, then at *Details*. 'Newhouse told me that he'd lost faith in it as a viable proposition,' Truman recalled, 'and wanted me to take it over and turn it into the new [*Face*-style] magazine. I hated the idea and argued against it, since what I'd been working on was a completely different sensibility. Also, I liked *Details* and had friends there, and didn't want to be responsible for it being shut down.'

But Truman took over and, as he predicted, met resistance inside and out: 'Quite understandably, the readers of the old *Details* absolutely hated the new *Details*. The first six months of it were a disaster, since we quickly lost all the old readers and it was slow-going to build a new audience.' Truman felt the title was 'a liability, and not a good name for my magazine' but persevered, with editorial and commercial success. Infused with *The Face*'s core values – design-led accessibility and a finely honed approach to popular culture – *Details* provided strong coverage of the alternative music sector that crested with grunge.

David Bowie presided over September 1991's 'fall fashion special', featured rising stars of young American design. Meanwhile, Truman enlisted stars of the UK music press: Simon Reynolds hailed the emergence of techno, Len Brown wrote about Morrissey, Sean O'Hagan showcased U2, William Shaw encountered Depeche Mode, Ice Cube and Jesus Jones, and Tom Hibbert interviewed Tori Amos. 'I just feel the faeries in my stomach,' Amos told Hibbert. 'Are you certain this isn't simply indigestion?' he responded.

At the other end of the market were diverse fanzines and colourful monthlies, one of which, *Kicks*, gained cult status through its intense admiration for pre-Beatles American rock 'n' roll, rockabilly and early R&B, as conveyed in six heavyweight and humour-filled issues published between 1978 and the late 1980s. Its editors – Miriam Linna, who had been the drummer in the first line-up of the Cramps, and her partner, Billy Miller – took a sarky stance against the 'Limeys' who they believed had diluted the primal power of 1950s rock. They also used their Norton Records reissue label to celebrate the ramshackle delights of such outsider artists as the hillbilly rocker Hasil Adkins and the outrageously camp Little Richard precursor Esquerita.

The network of independent US titles also provided a bushwire for the scene that spawned Nirvana. Born from early 1980s hardcore, the magazines' snotty attitude and all-embracing love of the alternative meant their subject matter veered from William Burroughs spoken word tapes to Sun Ra bootlegs. The often functional layouts featured highly subjective interviews with never-heard-of mavericks, live reviews from a circuit untouched by *Rolling Stone*,

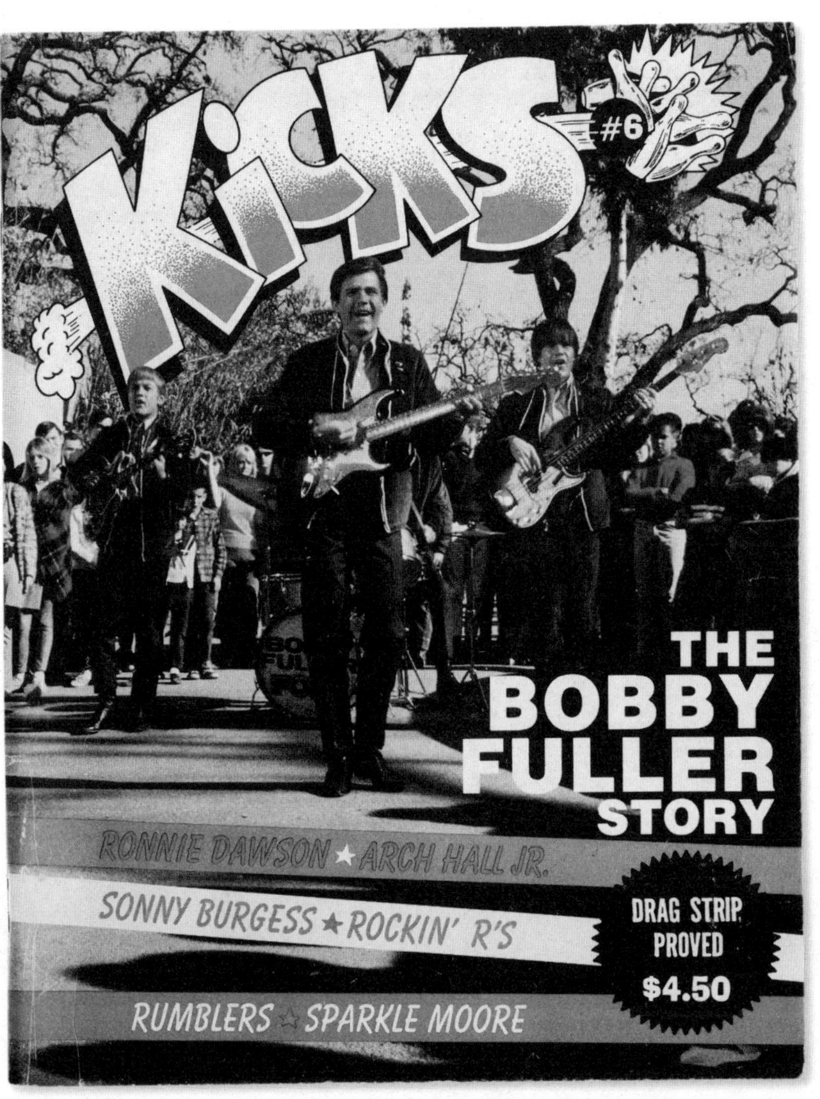

Kicks, no. 6, 1988

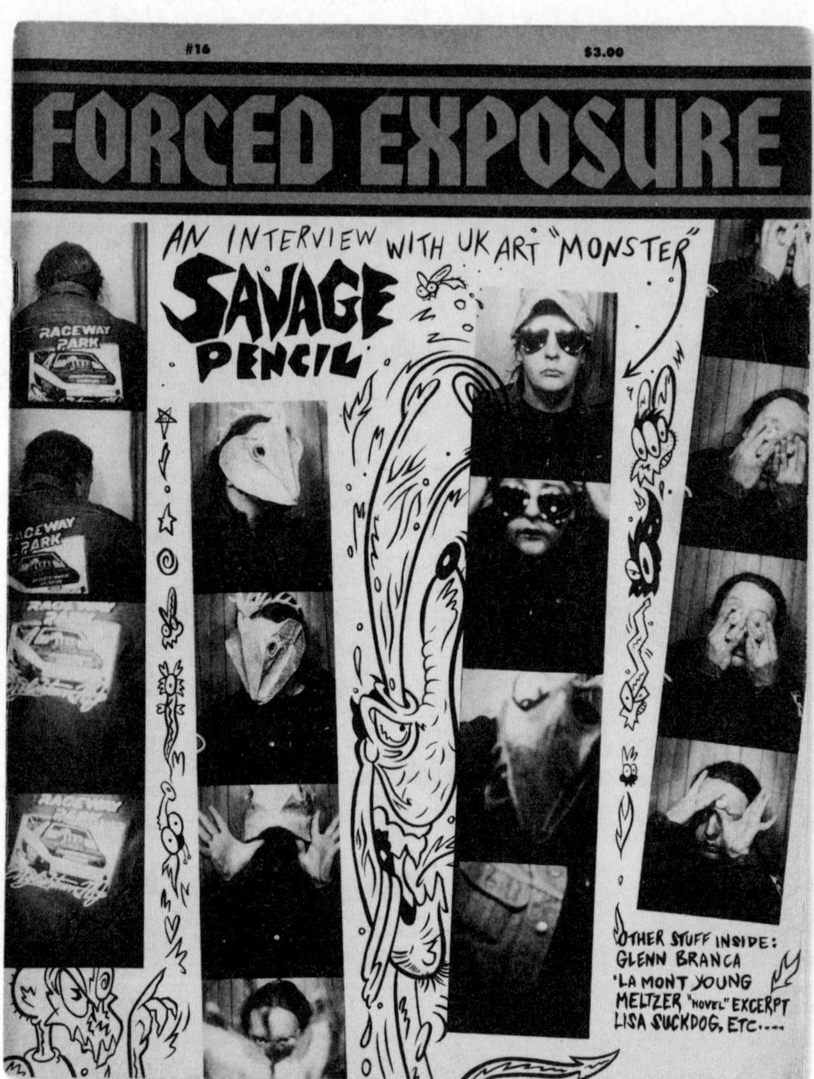

Forced Exposure, no. 16, 1990

and columns by the white-knuckle likes of producer and Big Black boss Steve Albini. Consequently, these titles became participants in, as well as documentarists of, the alternative scene.

Published in Massachusetts since the early 1980s, the sporadic *Forced Exposure* offered a memorable giveaway record: Sonic Youth's rock-crit hate song 'I Killed Christgau with My Big Fucking Dick'. 'I wasn't flattered to hear my name pronounced right,' responded Robert Christgau, who continued to give the band middling reviews until 1986's *Evol* ('The good parts are so good that for a while there I thought I was enjoying the bad parts'). Later, the West Coast-based *Flipside* operated its own label, releasing early tracks by Beck and other heroes of California's alternative scene.

Attracting national readership, *Maximum Rocknroll* kicked off in 1982 in San Francisco. By the 1990s, it was providing a tape of new tracks every week to public service broadcasters. Bravely, it refused to accept advertising from major record labels and independents that had distribution links to them. In 1993, 'coordinator' Tim Yohannan announced that the co-option of alternative music by major labels made the magazine even more determined to stay underground: 'Younger musicians are reacting to what's popular by getting back to a more grassroots punk attitude, and so are we.' And while the 'zine was printing 176 pages per fortnightly issue, he added, 'We've got ads backed up two, three months.'[3]

Cutting-edge sounds were a staple too for Minneapolis's *Your Flesh*. Founded in the early 1980s, by the next decade it had become glossier, catering for an arty crowd with leftfield poetry, prose and art alongside concert and record reviews. 'The reviews were just gorgeous, so beautifully written,' enthused British DJ John Peel. 'I liked the idea that they were expanding the language. I used to read the issues to my mother, who was a great appreciator of literature. Of course she had no idea what they were about, but she relished it. I'm not one of those people who wants the language to remain the same. The use of language in *Your Flesh* was just terrific.'

The magazine offered as much prominence to rap and hip-hop as it did to free jazz and experimental electronica, as evinced by an early 1990s review of Run-DMC and their protégés in New York: 'When Run-DMC finally appears at 3.00 a.m., born-again Christian

Jam Master Jay brings Onyx back out to reprise their antics with better sound and his blessing, and it takes almost fifteen more minutes to get them through one song. As it turns out, Onyx are one of Jay's developing commercial ventures, and if the lasers, posters, stickers and scooping onto the guest list of white writers who usually cover obscure rock bands all weren't enough to get the message across, Onyx are the official, endorsed, real East Coast hardcore shit of the summer.'[4]

The hardcore shit in magazine design on the opposite coast the following year was *Ray Gun*, created by a Santa Monica collective led by art director David Carson. His deliberately cluttered typography and abstract layouts earned Neville Brody's accolade, '*Ray Gun* is the end of print.' Often difficult to decipher – Carson set a boring interview with Bryan Ferry in the symbol font Zapf Dingbats – *Ray Gun* was headache-inducing, but its wilful attitude attracted such stars as Morrissey and Björk. 'They were the honey badger of music publishing,' wrote Liz Phair. '*Ray Gun* don't give a *fuck!*'

But even *Ray Gun*'s enviable production values were overshadowed by the Beastie Boys-backed *Grand Royal* (pl. 19), published in the first half of the 1990s and benefiting from budgets set by the hip-hop/rock stars. Each of the six issues is a perfect-bound, in-depth examination of the trio's eclectic and humour-filled interests; the aim, according to editor Bob Mack, was to 'take a retro stance sometimes, bringing to the fore our heroes from the past as well as from the present'.

Bruce Lee, Lee Perry and Fela Kuti retrospectives each ran to a dozen or more pages, while *Grand Royal* also applied its considerable chutzpah to a fashion spread based on the style of mulleted (and convicted) US tabloid staple Joey Buttafuoco and an encounter between rap magnate Russell Simmons and Jon Spencer Blues Explosion drummer Russell Simins, brought together simply because they had similar surnames. 'It's not a real magazine,' Bob Mack confessed. 'It's not on any production schedule. We don't have to bring it out monthly or whenever – just when we feel like it.'[5]

Equally idiosyncratic was *Ben Is Dead* (pl. 20), which began a run of thirty extraordinary issues in 1988. Edited and written by young women and contributors from marginalized communities,

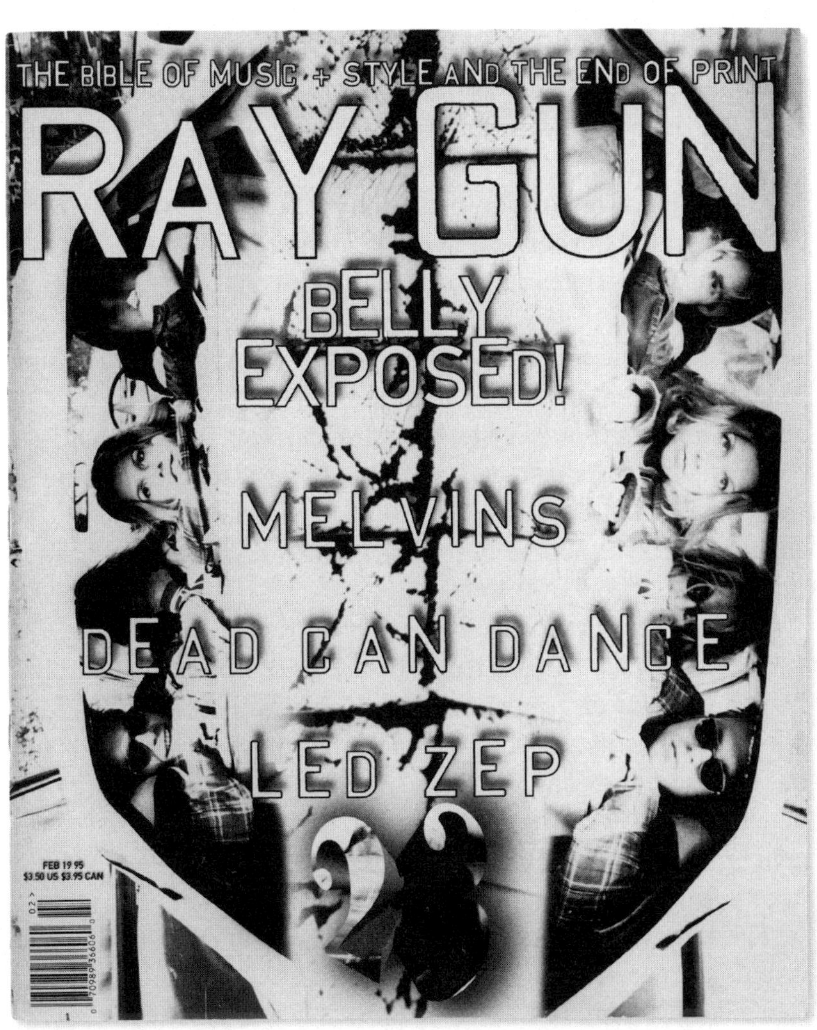

Ray Gun, February 1995

the LA-based magazine broke out from its beginnings as a punkish, free, black and white newsprint quarterly. 'Initially, music was the unifying theme,' explained Deborah 'Darby' Romeo, the graphics major who launched the magazine and named it in memory of her failed marriage to a French punk rocker whom she met while studying at the Sorbonne university in Paris.

Ten issues in, the summer 1990 *BID* dwelt on the theme 'Mother', inaugurating the magazine's most successful phase, in which Romeo dedicated successive editions to specific subjects. 'I loved punk, industrial, noise, the stuff coming from [Washington state indie label] Amphetamine Reptile, but wanted to look beyond that,' she said. 'Having a theme meant we could focus rather than being all over the place. There was also a slightly obsessive side to it; that thing of not being able to stop going off into different tangents and perspectives.'[6]

By the early 1990s, there were months between issues, the subjects of which ranged from 'Broke' and 'Obsessions and bad habits' to 'Modern transmissions and sensory overload' and the fake-news-predicting 'Disinformation'. They were packed with ads from underground labels and the faux-indies launched by the majors to cash in on the grunge boom. But *Ben Is Dead* viewed the genre uneasily, often mocking the corporate version of the messily organic grassroots movements they adored.

The magazine's political edge, wiseass humour and kaleidoscopic visuals garnered fans among their diverse interviewees, from Genesis P-Orridge to Simon Le Bon. 'We were lucky in that we found like-minded people with the same twisted sense of humour,' said co-editor Kerin Morataya, who joined a year or so after the magazine's launch. 'It kind of came together magically.'

Vanity Fair – snared by the *Ben Is Dead* spinoff *I Hate Brenda*, satirizing actress Shannen Doherty from *Beverly Hills, 90210* – appointed Romeo and Morataya as contributing editors. 'They took us to some fancy restaurant, nothing like we were used to, where the number of the booth where you sat indicated your social status,' said Morataya. When *Vanity Fair*'s all-powerful editor Tina Brown dropped by the table, Romeo sealed their reputation by addressing her as 'Tina Yothers' – star of the 1980s sitcom *Family Ties*.

Now deemed media professionals, Romeo and Moratay were disqualified when they entered a contest to edit an issue of the teen title *Sassy*. Undaunted, they assembled a *Sassy*-themed issue of *Ben Is Dead* and put President Clinton's fourteen-year-old daughter Chelsea on the cover. 'We thought Chelsea was gorgeous and deserved paying homage to,' said Romeo. 'People were so mean to her and that made me so incensed – she was just a kid. That's also the issue where we ran into Bob Dylan. We were interviewing some band in a recording studio and he walked past, so I encouraged my girl Friday, Jessy Jones, to ask him what *Sassy* meant to him. She barged into his studio uninvited and he pulled out an answer in one second: "Insolence"!'

The cornucopia of contributors included performance artist Vaginal Davis, a significant figure in LA's alternative society since the 1970s. 'She had so much influence on *Ben Is Dead* because of how huge she was in our world,' said Romeo. 'When we did a 'zine event in New York, we flew her in to host it and 1,000 people turned up. She was an amazing inspiration for all of us.' Inevitably, *Ben Is Dead*'s biggest seller was its 1992 'Sex' issue, which put local band Steakhouse on the cover and featured singer and writer Lydia Lunch, trans rockabilly artist Glen Meadmore, former Germs manager Nicole Panter, acid proselytizer Timothy Leary and radical writer Robert Anton Wilson.

'*Ben Is Dead* offered a sure and brilliant glimpse into the then-mystifying world of alternative culture,' said *LA Weekly*'s David Cotter. 'Each issue seemed more crassly erudite than the last ... [It] turned me on to artists and phenomena that were at once fascinating and terrifying.' In the wake of 1992's Los Angeles riots, Cotter noted, '*Ben Is Dead* published an issue that was stuffed to bursting with reportage that critiqued the media as much as the violence itself.' The cover featured graffiti on an LA sidewalk: 'BAD COP NO DONUT'.

Eventually, *BID* was threatened by the onset of the digital age. 'Everybody, including distributors, stopped paying their bills,' recalled Romeo, who lost $20,000 to just one company. 'The 'zines had no protection because we weren't part of conglomerates. Once the chips were down, it was easier to start stiffing us.' Last-minute support from *Larry Sanders Show* writer Paul Simms helped Romeo get to issue thirty, but *Ben Is Dead*'s time was up. Commercially savvy newcomers invaded its turf, including local rival *Boing Boing*, which offered a music-based mix and has continued into the digital age. Another survivor and evident descendant was *Vice*, formerly an unprepossessing giveaway published in Canada. 'We were much bigger than *Vice* back in the day,' notes Romeo. 'They were sending me their issues to get coverage and I was thinking, "What the heck is this shit – this fluffy, fashion, fake-punk thing?" But those guys were still ready to take it all on. I was over it.'[7]

* * *

'You launch something and the competition go, "It'll never work,"' noted David Hepworth. 'And then, when it works, they go, "Oh, we've got one of those." Which is how *Select* and *Vox* came into being.'

Spotlight's *Select* (pl. 22) was brainstormed over many months by *NME* and *Sounds* veteran Tony Stewart, who gathered a small team late in 1988. 'Tony phoned me to get in on "Project X" after he read a Van Morrison review of mine, which showed that maybe I had sufficient musical knowledge and the appropriate writing style,' said the *Sounds* writer David Cavanagh. 'He described the mag as mature and not at all emotional, without the dogmatic style you'd get with the weeklies. I said, "What, like *Q*?" and he said it was more like the kind of magazine you'd get with the *Sunday Telegraph*. "Q" was a verboten letter in the *Select* office.'

According to Cavanagh, who sadly died in 2018 at the age of fifty-four, the first dummy issue featured a cover story of David Byrne talking about his interest in Brazilian music. Cavanagh, who contributed a piece about John Lennon, thought it too sober and analytical. The publishers evidently took some convincing too: 'We didn't hear anything about Project X for a year, and suddenly it was on again. I was reviews editor and then deputy editor simply because there wasn't one.'[8]

Select launched in the summer of 1990, *The Face*'s so-called Third Summer of Love (pl. 17). Veterans Paolo Hewitt and Richard Cook were joined by younger writers such as Andrew Perry and Graham Linehan, the latter later the cowriter of TV comedy hits *Father Ted* and *The IT Crowd* and more recently a controversial online presence due to his views on trans issues. Once again, Lucy O'Brien was the female exception, having left *NME* way behind: 'As editor, Tony Stewart was as sweet as pie and no longer as daunting as when I first met him. I was film editor for a while. It was an interesting magazine because it was the first of the glossy monthlies to cover film and attempt to be more broadly based than *Q*.'

The market leader's existence was now acknowledged: 'The thing was to outdo them every month in the number and diversity of reviews,' said Cavanagh. 'Richard was good enough not to show up my deficiencies as a reviews editor and Paolo was really good – he wrote a fantastic cover story on Prince for the first issue.'

However, *Select* struggled to become a viable alternative to *Q*. 'The first issue sales were 100,000,' said Cavanagh. 'The next two did 50,000 and 30,000 respectively. Tony didn't tell me what was going on and I wasn't really there. I was always drunk and Tony was getting into champagne, so we were off our heads while we were running this extraordinarily unpopular magazine.'

Within months, sales capsized below 30,000: unsustainable for a magazine that was relatively expensive to produce. 'There was a laughter-in-the-dark atmosphere,' shuddered Cavanagh, 'because we were in the *Daily Express* building with *Sounds*, which was also seriously ailing at the time. Their main stories were about bootlegging or upcoming festivals, simply because they couldn't get a respectable artist to put on the cover. The record companies didn't want to know.'

While *Melody Maker*'s weekly sales hovered around 60,000, *Sounds*' sank beneath 40,000. Those of their stablemate *Record Mirror* fell off an even steeper cliff, as younger pop fans failed to show any interest in its glossy format featuring free, cover-mounted music. In April 1991 Spotlight elected to recast *Record Mirror* as a dance-music supplement within the pages of its weekly trade paper, *Music Week*, put *Sounds* out of its misery and sell *Select* and *Kerrang!* to Emap. 'Mike Sharman, the MD, announced that we should gather everything we needed because we were being bussed to Emap's headquarters,' recalled Cavanagh.

What was actually being sold was market share, Emap having already bought hard rock magazine *Raw* from an indie publisher.

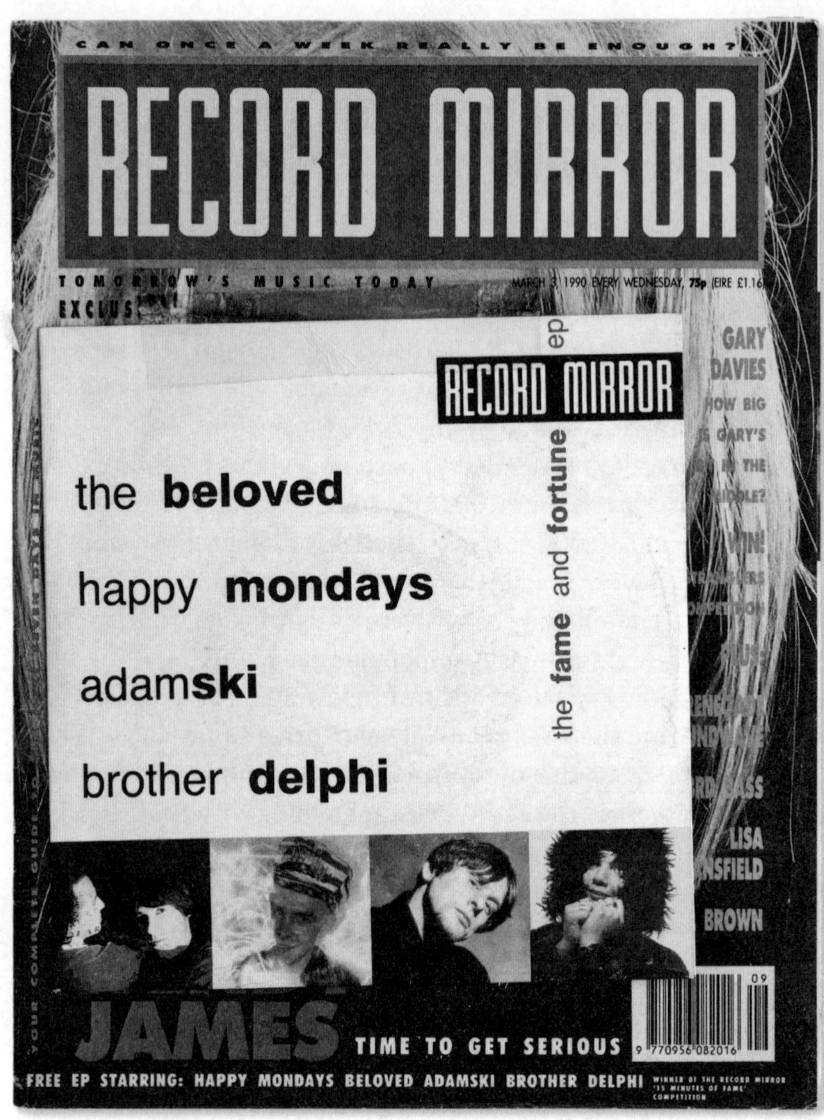

Record Mirror, 3 March 1990

'We wanted *Kerrang!*, after using *Raw* to get into the metal market,' explained David Hepworth. 'We had made it nearly impossible for Spotlight to publish *Kerrang!* profitably because we promoted *Raw* and they had to promote back, and that ate into their margins.'

Select could have become a casualty, but was remodelled into a less serious alternative to *Q*. 'There were tears and much gnashing of teeth at the start,' said Cavanagh, who informed a holidaying Tony Stewart of the takeover; Stewart subsequently edited the short-lived music magazine *Rage* for the soon-to-be-disgraced mogul Robert Maxwell. 'Then Mark Ellen stepped in as the man in charge. I got on well with him until he found out I liked to turn up at work pissed and leave early. There was more than one occasion when I turned up on acid. The behaviour was a little bizarre. I got bollocked a few times and it was politely suggested I might be more useful as chief feature writer.'

Ellen directed *Select* to focus on younger groups and genres, especially 'baggy', the catchall applied to the dance-injected rock of the Happy Mondays and Stone Roses. Helpfully, those bands were populated by colourful, quotable types such as Shaun Ryder and Ian Brown.

NME also leapt aboard the baggy bandwagon. Editor Alan Lewis appointed James Brown and encouraged him to bring in new writers and refocus on rock. 'To appropriate the words of Spinal Tap's Nigel Tufnell,' Brown observed, 'Alan Lewis is the man who turned music publishing up to eleven.' 'With Baggy, *NME* woke up again,' Quantick noted. 'I always used to say that *NME* did well when young white men with guitars are popular but they have no control over the world.'[9]

Quantick was by then writing humorous columns with former ranting poet Steven Wells. These attracted radio producer Armando Iannucci, who hired them to contribute to his BBC radio show *On the Hour*. There they worked with the cream of new British comedy, including Steve Coogan, Chris Morris, Stewart Lee and Richard Herring. Later, for the Edinburgh Festival, Quantick wrote a live show with Andrew Collins and Stuart Maconie called *Lloyd Cole Knew My Father*, based on their time at *NME*. 'We had an idea for a show about what it was *really* like,' said Quantick. 'Reviewing gigs that you had missed. Editing the letters page and making up letters, and the types of people who wrote in: the mysterious goth girl whose envelope, when tipped out, is full of tiny stars; the angry Morrissey hater. The history of all the people we'd met and the lies we'd told.'[10]

Quantick, Maconie and Collins were then recruited by Mark Ellen to *Select*. 'Mark had been paying close attention and Madchester [the baggy scene named after a Happy Mondays EP] had gone commercial by this time,' remembered David Cavanagh. 'I thought it childish but Mark said it was hilarious and we should use the glossiness and the colour of the magazine to our advantage. There were also bands like Ride, Lush, the Pixies and Primal Scream to do once every four or five months. [We waited] until the weeklies had made up their minds and then we came at them with a more considered viewpoint. It all made terrific sense.'

By the summer of 1991, with eye-catching cover stories such as a union of Primal Scream front man Bobby Gillespie with Kylie Minogue, the magazine hit its stride. Cavanagh dated the turning point to Ellen replacing a cover of Manchester supergroup Electronic, first with the Farm, then the Cure, one of alternative rock's biggest groups: 'I realised *Select* was going to survive that day. Mark's approach to press officers was, "This may be *Select* but I'm Mark Ellen." He'd come from *Q*, assimilated lots of knowledge of this music and was word-perfect on it. He transformed *Select* almost single-handedly. Within a year it was very healthy, with sales going from 28,000 to 80,000. It was the publication all the hip labels – the Creations and the Factorys – wanted to be in.'

Among the star writers was Miranda Sawyer, who had been part of *Smash Hits*' late eighties pomp, having been chosen by publisher Barry McIlhenny over another candidate, Jim Moir – who, considered 'too far out', instead pursued fame as comic Vic Reeves. A champion of pop, Sawyer added a new dimension to *Select*. 'As a general rule, men make better rock journalists, women better pop writers,' she observed. 'There's a fact-collecting aspect to the male psyche that is never happier than when listing the B-sides of the Byrds' five UK top forty hits, in chronological order ... I haven't got a clue about stuff like that. Who cares? But I can hear a hit at fifty paces, spot a pop star after one play of a tune.

'At *Smash Hits*, you took the music as read. What you were interested in was the stuff around it: the people who made it, where they lived, what they did, whether they had any interesting scars and whether they would put pineapples on their heads for the photoshoot. Sixty per cent nosiness, forty per cent cheekiness, plus jokes. Still a fantastic interviewing combination.

'Pop writing understands that pop is born within, and of, a living, breathing culture, and that this is what matters, rather than how the snare sound was achieved on track seven. It also allows that because of this, some performers are better discussed, rather than actively reviewed or interviewed. A great example of this is Kylie Minogue. Fantastic pop person – ace music, lovely outfits, slick entertainer, bottom as thing of beauty etc – but has she ever said anything of any interest whatsoever?'[11]

Select granted Sawyer a roving brief, from a very funny singles column to cover features. 'Shaun [Ryder] sits on the toilet with his pipe, smoking a rock of crack,' she reported of Happy Mondays' disastrous sessions for their album *Yes Please!* in Barbados. 'It's his tenth of the day. Each of the white, raisin-sized rocks contains about twenty-five grams of cocaine ... The Mondays chose Barbados – Shaun too – partly because they knew there was no heroin there. They'd thought there were no Class A drugs at all, just weed. Shaun has discovered otherwise. He hides in the toilet from the others, smokes crack, works on his lyrics.' Such pieces made Sawyer – then just twenty-six – the youngest winner of the Periodical Publishers' Association's Writer of the Year award.

This coincided with a breakthrough for *Select*. 'One magical day in the summer of 1993 the sales went over 100,000,' said Cavanagh, who acknowledged the role played by new editor Andrew Harrison. 'He is fantastically bright and, as he wrote in his application letter, he knew "when to buy a story and when to sell it".' Harrison recruited bright sparks he had known from university, including Clark Collis, Steve Hicks, Adam Higginbotham (later to edit *The Face*) and Andy Pemberton, who subsequently became *Q*'s editor. With Richard Lowe and William Shaw joining Sawyer among the *Smash Hits* alumni, *Select* acquired 'a slightly younger, Tom Hibbert sense of humour', said Cavanagh.

Less nimble was *Vox*, IPC's sister magazine to *NME*. It did however showcase Barbara Ellen, who had written for fanzines and *ZigZag* in the 1980s, and gravitated with ease to *NME*. There she proved more than a match for everyone from Madonna and Tori Amos to Guns N' Roses and the Stone Roses. 'When it was strong, the music press was engaged in cultural resistance, fighting off record companies' attempts to exploit it as an unofficial PR arm,' she reflected. 'The point was not blandly to regurgitate press releases; it was to listen, watch, assess, enthuse, refuse ... and sometimes childishly rip the piss just for the sheer hell of it. One big myth of music journalism was that writers secretly yearned to be in bands, when the vast majority couldn't care less. Whatever their brand of music journalism (and there were many churches, darling), these people considered themselves to be writers, part of the creative conversation in their own right. Which is why usually skint hacks felt justified in informing rich and famous rock stars that their latest album was a symphony of tripe; feeling, quite rightly, that this was all the "information" their readers required at that time. At the risk of sounding pretentious, isn't this cultural democracy in action, where wealth and commercial clout mean nothing and only quality counts?'[12]

Another *Vox* contributor, Lisa Verrico, proved equally adept interviewing Snoop Dogg, the Fall's Mark E. Smith and Jamiroquai's Jay Kay, and was among the first to spot the potential of Radiohead. 'We're always being asked to do [US radio] IDs,' Jonny Greenwood told her. 'Yesterday I got this fax saying, "Please record the following message: Hi, I'm Jonny from Radiohead. You're listening to those crazy heads on the radio and, hey, we're creeps."'[13]

But *Vox* rarely threatened either *Q*'s dominance or *Select*'s sizeable niche. David Hepworth initially viewed the monthly as a serious competitor but, he said, '*Vox* only prospered when *Q* was slightly off its game. When *Q* got back on its game, *Vox* went off it. They couldn't sustain it. Even when it was off the boil, *Q* always had the reviews section, which was valued by readers. You *had* to buy it. If you were interested in music and not buying *Q*, it was a bit of a contrary thing to do.'

* * *

Uninterested in the turf of the UK rock monthlies were a raft of female-led independent magazines. Documenting the early nineties Riot Grrrl movement, spearheaded by Huggy Bear and Bikini Kill, they included *Bust*, *Girlyhead* and *Girl's Life* in the US. In Britain, *Ablaze!* – founded in 1987 and based in the northern city Leeds – became an early champion of grunge before focusing on female bands and performers. That followed an epiphany for editor Karren Ablaze in the form of a 1992 show by Washington DC punk group Nation of Ulysses: 'They claimed not to be a band at all; they claimed to be a youth revolutionary group. Their ideology, their aesthetic, their insignia, their haircuts – all were inherently and explicitly political.' That night Ablaze wrote what she described as a 'girl power manifesto', part of which was reproduced in illustrator Erica Smith's fanzine *Girlfrenzy*. 'Shortly after that, Sally Margaret Joy wrote in *Melody Maker* the most inspiring piece I've ever read in a music paper, about Riot Grrrl in the States, and said it was happening here [in the UK] too. I made some phone calls – Riot Grrrl London had started! "Why don't you do something in Leeds?" they said to me. Shit – why not?'[14]

Ablaze made posters and circulated flyers, setting in motion a network of young female writers and musicians around the country. *Girlfrenzy* (pl. 18) was among the most accomplished of the publications, using illustrations to spread the message. One drawing showed a girl exposing her stomach with the message, 'Can you pinch an inch? Do you give a shit?' Meanwhile, a strip presented artist Kate Evans's memories of joining her mother and female friends at antinuclear protests in the 1980s.

An effective takedown of male rock hackery appeared in a strip entitled 'I married a music journalist', drawn by Erica Smith and based on the 'nasty experience' of a friend who had initially been impressed by the sex, drugs and rock 'n' roll lifestyle of her husband. His charms rapidly palled amid a barrage of boasts about encounters with the likes of Soundgarden and Lou Reed. In the strip, Catherine finally snaps when he mentions for the 666th time that he has interviewed Nick Cave: 'I went out, bought *NME* and *Melody Maker* and rolled them up. I went round and stuck one down his throat and the other up his arse.'[15]

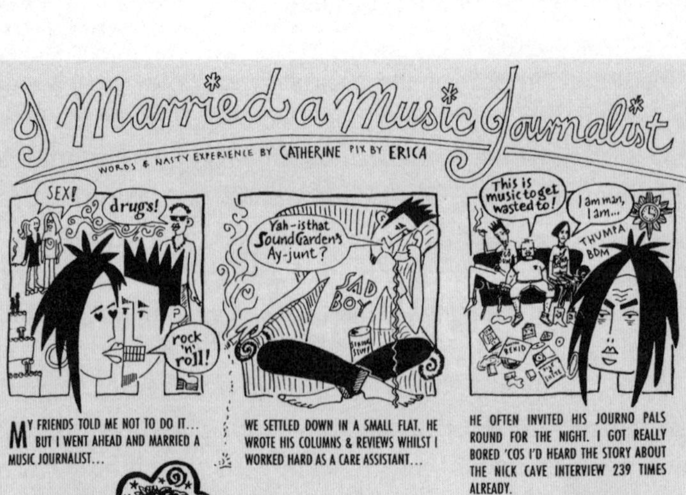

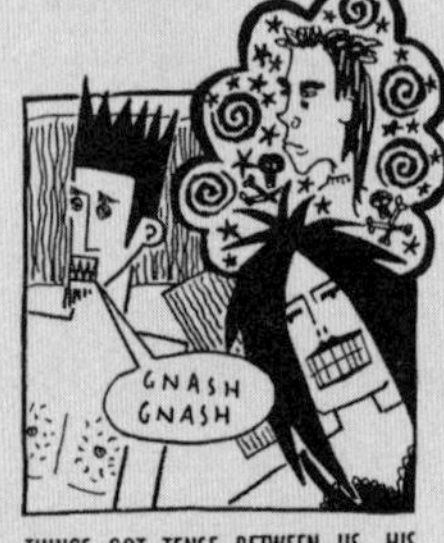

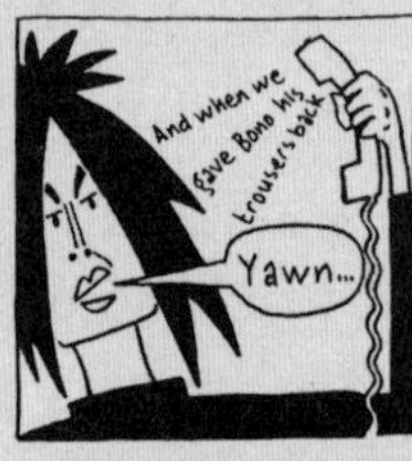

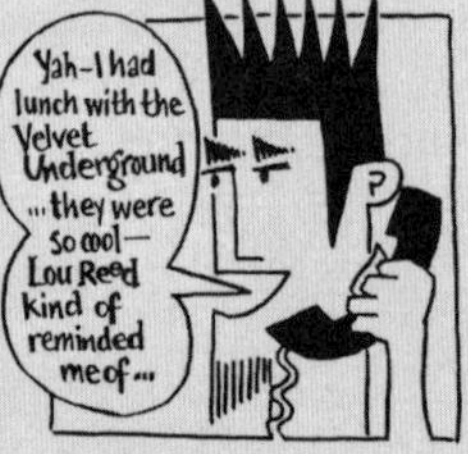

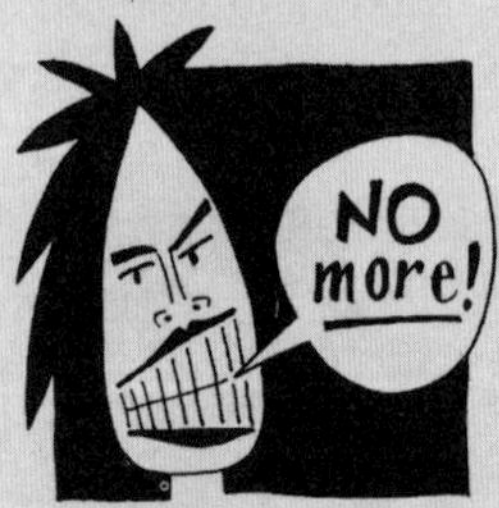

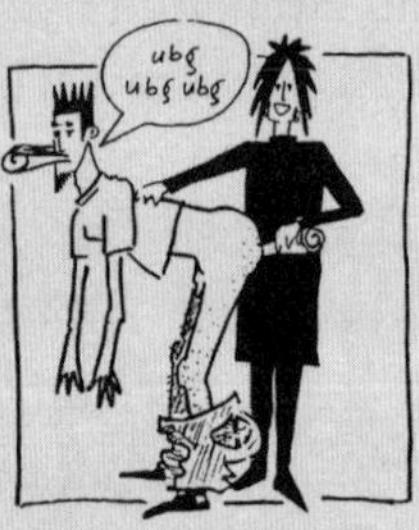

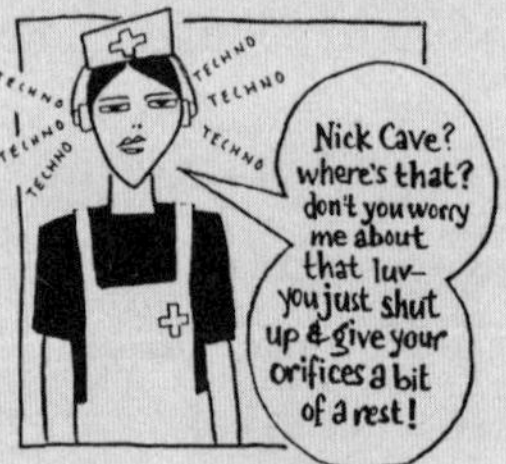

Girlfrenzy, no. 6, 1995, page 13

17
‘I remember thinking, “He doesn’t dance”’

Sheryl Garratt Steers *The Face*, Nelson George Does It First at *The Village Voice*, and *The Source* and *Vibe* Reshape Music Media

Always keen to flash their hip-hop credentials, the music monthlies were still overwhelmingly rock-oriented. In contrast, *The Face* continued to channel street-level developments into the mainstream, especially under new editor Sheryl Garratt. She had begun writing for Nick Logan's title in the mid-1980s, soon after the demise of the influential *Collusion* and the publication of her book with *Straight No Chaser*'s Sue Steward, *Signed, Sealed and Delivered: True Life Stories of Women in Pop*.

The exodus of longstanding contributors to Logan's men's magazine *Arena* in 1986 opened an opportunity for stand-out features by Garratt. These included a piece on the house music phenomenon, prompted by the release of a compilation by the DJ International label and a press trip to the tough Chicago neighbourhoods where the sound originated. 'Having flown a bunch of us out there, London Records took us to the DJ International office, which was full of white businessmen, and then set up interviews in some hotel with the people who appeared on the record,' Garratt recalled. 'I felt deeply unsatisfied; this was about music which came out of a club scene. Why were we in a hotel? I told Frankie [Knuckles, pioneering house DJ] that I wasn't getting the goods and he arranged to meet me at an address at midnight.'

Knuckles guided Garratt around the city's underground circuit, ending at the Muzic Box, where aficionados believe house music was created and where fellow pioneer Ron Hardy was manning the decks. 'As far as I know,' says Garratt, 'I was the only journalist who ever went there and saw him DJ. It was all-male and obviously I was the only white person there. It was an extraordinary place. I was so fired up when I wrote that piece.'

Though now distributed by Condé Nast and with a fresh look courtesy of the designers who succeeded Neville Brody, *The Face* was reliant on writers such as Garratt to keep it abreast of main competitor *i-D* and upstarts such as *Boy's Own*. 'I had known everyone who had done illegal warehouse parties,' she noted, 'and all of those who came in their wake through rare groove, the sound systems and acid house.'

But *The Face* – whose monthly sales had slid from the high nineties to 73,000 – was effectively now part of the media establishment, particularly since former staffers had become major names in the national papers: Tony Parsons at *The Sunday Times*, Julie Burchill at the *Mail on Sunday* and Jon Savage at *The Observer*. Realignment was required.

Nick Logan considered closing the magazine after the one hundredth issue in September 1988. Its job of capturing 1980s pop culture seemed complete, its circulation was unsteady and it took him away from his latest venture, *Arena*. The end of an era was expressed in the front cover description of *The Face* as 'the magazine of the decade', and the 200-page issue – with an innovative trifold cover – documenting the period 'from safe sex to acid house'.

Inside, heavy-hitters handled the era's sacred cows: Nick Kent took on Prince ('Let's not mince words. Without Prince, the 1980s would be even more unthinkably dead-arsed than they've already proven themselves to be') and Julie Burchill contributed a think-piece on Margaret Thatcher ('I don't believe in Thatcherism, but I do believe in Thatcher, given the options'). The latter aroused the ire of more than just readers: 'I stopped working for *The Face* after they printed that article saying how wonderful Mrs Thatcher was,' Jon Savage declared. 'I just resigned.' Elsewhere, the increasingly eccentric Michael Jackson was dissected by Sheryl Garratt and French contributor Phillip Manoevre, while a double-page spread mapped the chronology of London clubs from Billy's and Blitz to new nights such as Carwash, Enter the Dragon and Spectrum.

In the event, *The Face* stayed open, but the notion of calling time on its first eight years was driven home by the next issue. October 1988 was designated Volume 2, No. 1, with a cover photograph of DJ Tim Simenon from the sampledelic Bomb the Bass. Inside were features on Acid Jazz and Manchester's dance scene, while Garratt despatched writer Lindsay Baker and photographer Juergen Teller to New York to interview the Jungle Brothers, then advancing East Coast rap into new areas. 'Sheryl was very good at taking a suggestion,' said Baker, 'and working with you on refining it as an idea until it became a more wide-ranging piece.'[1]

Rave culture fell under Garratt's microscope in a brace of overviews at the turn of the 1990s. These explicitly refuted *The Face*'s original focus on urban elites, instead celebrating the rise of the regions amid the democratizing effects of dance culture. 'There was this feeling of being anti-wine bar, anti-cocktail bar,' said fashion writer Ashley Heath, 'in favour of sitting in cut-offs in a suburban pub garden listening to fantastic, uncool music.'[2]

'Sheryl had a clear idea of what she wanted to do,' said Richard Benson, who succeeded Garratt as editor in the mid-1990s. 'She felt things had become insular and played-out in terms of the eighties aesthetic, and had a vision of post-1988 youth culture that was more democratic. She knew that *The Face* shouldn't be about Soho anymore, but about the rest of the country.'[3]

In fact, the direction had come from Nick Logan, recalled Garratt: 'Nick had said to me, "You know these kids dancing around in fields? That's who we should be doing the magazine for now." I felt like he'd given me a mandate to push through everything I thought the magazine should be. When he'd talked about closing *The Face* on the hundredth issue, I understood that he was thinking about making a bold statement. But my point was, even then, "Something amazing is coming along and we ought to be around to address it." We also knew everything had to change. The circulation was going down and we needed to adjust to what was going on.'

'People were changing their attitude to the way they were dressing and socializing,' observed fashion photographer David Sims, 'and there were a lot of social structures which were eradicated for a short period of time. Rave culture made all that possible; we were just creating a visual to accompany that.'[4]

The first of Garratt's rave essays, written with Lindsay Baker, took readers on a nocturnal quest for a gathering entitled Biology: 'Promoters judge their success on the numbers they attract, not the names in the VIP room, and the clubbers come not to be seen but to hide in the crowd.'[5] In the second essay, Garratt explored attempts by local authorities and police to clamp down on gatherings of young people. Referencing the recent fall of the Berlin Wall, she wrote, 'When they begin to take holidays here over the next few years, Eastern European visitors may find some of Britain's restrictions on personal freedom strangely familiar.'[6]

A spellbinding portrait of sixteen-year-old Kate Moss, by photographer Corinne Day, introduced the July 1990 issue, which heralded 'the Third Summer of Love'. Inspired by the Happy Mondays, Stone Roses and Nirvana, Day – whose picture replaced a portrait of Sandra Bernhardt by Herb Ritts – was as interested in upturning hierarchies as Garratt: 'Fashion magazines had been selling sex and glamour for far too long. I wanted to instill some reality into a world of fantasy.'[7] Reality came crashing down when Garratt commissioned a report on a huge Stone Roses show at Spike Island in Cheshire, intended to prove their hastily acquired legendary status and encapsulate the spirit of the age. 'I thought we would find something in the crowd at Spike Island which would sum it all up,' she said, 'but the pictures weren't good enough. It may be seen as momentous now but Spike Island was a bit of a damp squib.'

Not long after the Third Summer of Love issue, Garratt recruited editorial assistant – and future features editor – Amy Raphael. 'I was quite taken aback at how tiny the staff was,' said Raphael, later an author whose subjects included Danny Boyle and Steve Coogan. 'I was also amazed that I could not only be around meetings where decisions were made about who was on the cover of the next issue, but could also contribute to them. Sheryl recognized the grafter in me. I wasn't in love with fashion or clubbing but I was completely obsessed with indie and rock music, living with a guy who was in a band, going to see bands every night and to Glastonbury every year. They used to laugh at me, because Glastonbury definitely wasn't cool then.'[8]

A decade after its launch, *The Face* was back in the game, although the next year was to prove challenging. Logan was diagnosed with cancer and spent months in recovery. Then a photo caption suggesting that Jason Donovan was gay led to a bitter legal battle that resulted in £200,000 in damages and legal costs being awarded to the Australian pop star. But the magazine's supporters – many high-profile figures – rallied round, offering financial support and public sympathy. Accepting Donovan's offer to waive fifty per cent of the damages, Logan, Garratt and their team remained on top of youth culture, with music at its heart, throughout the early 1990s.

* * *

'Nelson George did it first,' insists the website Afropunk. 'Whenever you think of all the fly shit a music writer has gone on to do in the wide world of media – magazines, book publishing, television, film, whatever – George is the first name that should come to mind. Indeed, if you are writing about contemporary music and culture today, you are walking a trail he's been blazing since the 1970s – especially if you're Black.'

Co-opted and exploited, music of Black origin – jazz, blues, swing, doo-wop, soul, funk, reggae, rap and hip-hop – formed the basis of most White rock and pop. Yet, throughout the decades, there were few opportunities for people of colour to write about music in the mainstream press. Only with the emergence of rap's powerful entrepreneurs in the 1980s and '90s were platforms created for reviewing and promoting their own music. Up until then, lifestyle titles such as *Jet*, *Ebony* and *Essence* had carried the weight, particularly in reporting the serial injustices of the civil rights era. But music was simply an element of their entertainment pages, not the focus.

Nelson George, however, became a driving force at the industry bible *Billboard* in the 1980s. He championed rap and hip-hop there and subsequently at *Village Voice*, becoming one of America's most influential journalists. And he traced his understanding of the struggle for recognition among Black artists to the 1978 Grammy awards, where titans such as Earth, Wind & Fire and Parliament-Funkadelic were overlooked while White British singer Leo Sayer's 'You Make Me Feel Like Dancing' won the best R&B song category (following a win by soft rocker Boz Scaggs the previous year). 'I was, like, so *this* is what it is,' he said.[9]

George started young: his book *The Nelson George Mixtape Vol 1* includes rejections from *Rolling Stone* and *Village Voice* to applications he sent while at college. 'I remember reading a *Rolling Stone* review of the Brothers Johnson album with their big hit "Stomp" on it,' he said. 'The guy kind of panned it and I remember thinking, "He doesn't dance." He was writing about it as if it was Bob Dylan, for the lyrical quality. That is not why anyone bought a Brothers Johnson record ... That was a big spur for me to go, "I can write about this music on a level where some of these people who are being paid to write about don't."'[10]

‘I remember thinking, “He doesn’t dance”’

His ambitions weren’t without precedent. Puerto Rican/Cuban Pablo Guzmán wrote for *Village Voice* and Black writer Vernon Gibbs covered Jimi Hendrix, Led Zeppelin, James Brown and Taj Mahal for *Crawdaddy*, *NME*, *Sounds*, *Black Music* and *Phonograph Record*.

Writing about music, George observed, ‘wasn’t a white-black divide. It was more a traditional-versus-innovation divide. Many of the people who were the institutions of the Black music business – who were deeply invested in R&B and funk – didn’t like, didn’t care, and didn’t think I should be covering hip-hop. Especially during the period all the way up until the late eighties. So a lot of the resistance was Black traditionalist, and that was also something that was in effect at places like *Amsterdam News* [one of America’s oldest Black newspapers, which gave George an early break]. If you tried to write for *Ebony* or *Essence*, it took a long time for them to believe it was valid.’[11]

Another role model was Vince Aletti, who covered disco for *Rolling Stone* and the trade magazine *Record World*, where George became Black music editor after interning at *Billboard*. While at college during that stint, George interviewed Chic, Van Halen, AC/DC, Ted Nugent and Foghat. When *Record World* closed, he returned to *Billboard* in 1982 and championed exciting new Black artists. ‘I pushed to update the title of the magazine’s soul chart,’ he recalled. ‘Prince wasn’t soul, nor was Kurtis Blow or Run-DMC. The direction of black music, one of the truest reflectors of our culture, had changed profoundly, as it always does.’[12]

He also published the prophetic book *The Death of Rhythm & Blues*, which viewed the African American music industry from a business perspective and set the careers of Chuck Berry, James Brown, Aretha Franklin and Michael Jackson in the context of the unstable world of Black-owned labels, broadcasters and retailers. His conclusions about the fragility of the culture within White American society were sobering, and he damned ‘Black America’s assimilationist obsession’ as ‘cultural suicide’.

An investor in his neighbour Spike Lee’s feature film debut *She’s Gotta Have It*, George also explored creative possibilities outside music writing. He began a regular column at *The Village Voice* in 1989 and, within a few years, was producing movies with Halle Berry and Chris Rock. Meanwhile, he compiled another book, *Buppies, B-Boys, Baps & Bohos*. 'It's clear to me,' he wrote, 'that four new African American character types have been crucial in shaping this country over the last twenty years ... There is the Buppie, ambitious and acquisitive, determined to savor the fruits of integration by any means necessary; the B-Boy, molded by hip-hop aesthetics and the tragedies of underclass life; the Black American Princess or Prince a/k/a/ Bap, who, whether by family heritage or personal will, enjoys an expectation of mainstream success and acceptance that borders on arrogance; and the Boho, a thoughtful, self-conscious figure like *A Different World*'s Cree Summer or Living Colour's Vernon Reid, whose range of interest and taste challenges both black and white stereotypes of African-American behaviour.'

The tensions arising from assimilation were detailed in *The Death of Rhythm & Blues*: 'Are Blacks selling out our culture to corporate America? Is our media elite using its new clout to promote the best aspects of the race or just pandering to Black folks' worst instincts? What do they owe their core audience? Aside from dollars, what is gained by reaching a white audience? Looking over the last twenty years, it's apparent that when confronted by crossover, assimilation and white standards of success, most African Americans have said, "Well, I guess they're all right by me." Even our most nationalist pop culturalists, people like Chuck D and Spike Lee, work within the established systems of capitalization and distribution. Both, for example, maintain total creative control over their work, but the only revenue stream that flows directly into their accounts is merchandising money.'[13]

George's erstwhile home, *The Village Voice*, provided a platform for another mould-breaking writer of colour. Native New Yorker Dr Carol Cooper started out writing for *SoHo Weekly News* and covered Joan Armatrading and Marvin Gaye for *Musician*. At the *Voice*, according to music editor Ann Powers, she 'deftly illuminated the R&B scene',[14] though a glance at Cooper's body of work shows that she has confidently handled music from Leadbelly to Coolio, via Green Day, Iggy Pop and Tori Amos.

'I cold-called or cold-pitched at any publication I liked; that's how I got my stories into print,' Cooper explained to rocksbackpages.com.

'Unlike a lot of other journalists who had a friend or a connection, which got them a foot in the door, 99.9 per cent of the time I did it myself because I was passionate, a really, really good researcher and knew what these publications didn't have or couldn't get in-house.' This persistence extended to *The Face*: she bought a cheap ticket to London and, armed with her clippings, tracked down Nick Logan and Paul Rambali. They awarded her a column, resulting in early and important pieces on Kid Creole and Prince.

'I had a point of view that they didn't have,' she said. 'There were artists, points of view and perspectives on life, culture and historical perspectives which I felt needed attention but weren't getting it. Being a college kid, I really wanted to address some of these things. I used to joke in the eighties that I was essentially rewriting the same piece over and over and over again. What I meant by that is that I had a point I wanted to make about history and – back in the time I couldn't say [this] out loud, but you can say now – white supremacy and what that was doing to culture. The only way I could do this was by covering that music and those scenes which made my point.' [15]

* * *

Public Enemy's 'Night of the Living Baseheads', the Ultramagnetic MCs' 'Watch Me Now' and Eric B & Rakim's 'Follow the Leader' were among the recommendations in a single-page newsletter promoting the college radio show Street Beat in 1988. Also in White Harvard students Dave Mays and Jon Shecter's *The Source* was a report from DJ battles at the New Music Seminar industry jamboree in New York.

Involved from the start was Raymond 'Benzino' Scott, a rapper friend of Mays from Boston's mixed neighbourhood Roxbury and a member of hip-hop group The Almighty RSO. When the students graduated, they moved to New York and transformed *The Source* into a full-colour affair. Billed as 'the magazine of hip-hop music, culture and politics', it documented stars from Snoop Dogg to Mike Tyson.

Shecter – now known as 'J. the Sultan' – assembled talented Black contributors including James Bernard, Robert Marriott, Ed

Young and Reggie Dennis. The latter had immersed himself in hip-hop and graffiti while growing up in Harlem, then devoured *The Village Voice*, *Spin* and the African American music and celebrity poster magazine *Word Up!* (the latter name-checked in the Notorious BIG's 'Juicy'). When he purchased issue three of *The Source*, he recalled, 'The course of my life was forever altered. This was the first time that a magazine ever spoke to me in a meaningful way. I had read a lot of good writing on hip-hop but *The Source* was the only place where the music and culture were being discussed in the proper context and with the proper enthusiasm. And it just got better.'[16] A 1989 issue celebrating a decade of rap, remembered Robbie Ettelson of hip-hop site uncut.com, 'had a massive impact on me in terms of both obsessing over obscure rap and reading about great records I'd never even heard of'.[17]

Dennis boarded *The Source* as an intern – 'I did the work no one else wanted to do. I shucked and jived and skinned and grinned' – and graduated to music editor when the magazine secured national distribution in 1991. Among his responsibilities was the 'Record Report' section, where new releases were awarded one to five microphones. These ratings were often hotly contested, and a four-and-a-half mics rating for Dr Dre's *The Chronic* – latterly acclaimed as a five-star classic – was perceived as a diss from the New York magazine to the West Coast rap community. The equally vital 'Unsigned Hype' section featured MCs who had yet to secure record deals, and included some of the first media mentions for the Notorious BIG, Canibus, Common, DMX, Eminem and Mobb Deep.

World-beating superstars and critically lauded albums made the early nineties pivotal for hip-hop, and *The Source* was the go-to choice for news-hungry fans. 'When Ice Cube left NWA, the first I'd heard of it was in his interview in *The Source*,' Dennis recalled. 'This was a pretty big news story but, since it wasn't a mainstream story, it wasn't really a story at all. But back then, it was felt that if *The Source* didn't cover certain things, then perhaps no one else would either. So that was the biggest influence the magazine had. We were in a position to sell water to people who were dying of thirst in the desert. The circulation was low in those days: maybe 40,000 copies printed. If you weren't at the record store when it arrived then maybe you didn't get a copy that month. There were riots in prisons all across the country because inmates were literally fighting over copies of the magazine. There were fistfights in record stores when cats simultaneously tried to grab the last copy on the rack.'

The Source's connection to its readers was strong. Dennis took a call from one who, traumatized by footage of the Rodney King beating, wanted to know how the magazine would cover the horrific episode and its ramifications for Black communities. 'During the first Gulf War I got a letter from a female soldier stationed in Saudi Arabia, requesting her subscription be forwarded to her wartime address,' he said. 'She wrote that, even though her unit was preparing to roll into Kuwait, they very much needed to know the latest hip-hop developments.' Dennis sent one hundred copies to be distributed around her base. A few weeks later he received a thank-you note and a container of Saudi Arabian sand.

'We were able to build up an enormous amount of goodwill, but for me it wasn't about celebrity access or perks,' he said. 'It was about being able to connect with people all over the country. It was like suddenly finding yourself surrounded by thousands of long-lost family members; folks who understood exactly where you were coming from – your tribe. We were simply the conduits for this energy.'

But factions swiftly developed at *The Source*. Dave Mays – who handled advertising and promotion – sided with Benzino and the rough-and-tumble RSO Almighty crowd. James Bernard and Reggie Dennis aligned with editorial head Jon Shecter. Tensions mounted when the magazine's awards ceremony was threatened with a boycott by rapper KRS-1, who questioned *The Source*'s credentials for judging hip-hop, and questions were asked about Mays's perceived conflict of interest in managing the Almighty RSO. Behind-the-scenes thuggery escalated when Dennis refused to include a review of an RSO EP. Then Mays – without informing the rest of the staff – inserted a three-page feature on the group in a 1994 issue as it was going to print. According to Dennis, in a thoroughgoing interview about the episode on the website HipHopDX, police were called after Shecter received threats and attempts at mediation descended into physical confrontation.

In the aftermath, Dennis, Shecter and six other staffers walked, leaving Mays and Benzino as the magazine's owners. The latter increasingly became its public face, particularly when he provoked bitter feuds with Dr Dre and his protégé Eminem; according to Benzino, Eminem represented the market manipulations of the racist music business's 'machine'.

Meanwhile, the bimonthly *Rap Pages* launched in 1992, editor Dane Webb intending to 'give *The Source* a run for its money'.[18] Declaring itself 'a magazine with an attitude', the first issue featured Ice Cube on the front: a sign of allegiance with the West Coast artists that some felt were not given their due by *The Source*. Webb was vocal about *Rap Pages*' mission to uplift the Black communities: in his first editorial, he urged, 'Spend less time drinkin' them damn 40s [forty-ounce bottles of malt liquor], spend less time on the corner and more time in them books.'[19]

The magazine went monthly in 1995 and was acquired by free speech champion and porn publisher Larry Flynt as part of his diversifying into titles covering photography, beauty, video games and – via *RIP* magazine – heavy metal. Under editor-in-chief Sheena Lester, *Rap Pages* showcased inventive layouts and striking front covers, including a portrait of the Notorious BIG in a crown – 'the King of New York' – just a few weeks before his 1997 murder. 'There was nary a cover concept, no matter how odd or unlikely, that *Rap Pages*' wildly imaginative edit squad couldn't somehow massage into viability, then, ultimately, reality,' said Lester, revealing that a shot of Goodie Mob emerging from a swamp was taken by sneaking onto government land. 'We talked Lauryn Hill into being slathered in sky-blue body paint from her ears to her ankles. We even persuaded a lovely young model named Shonda Santiago to let Ol' Dirty Bastard cup her bare breasts, to playfully kick *Rolling Stone*'s infamous 1994 Janet Jackson cover in its shins.'[20]

* * *

Keen to capitalize on the market opened up by *The Source* and *Rap Pages*, big players jumped on the bandwagon. Backed by the world-straddling Time Warner, veteran hit-maker Quincy Jones and his TV production partner David Salzman – whose joint successes included *The Fresh Prince of Bel-Air* – launched *Vibe* (pl. 21) in 1993. In featuring hip-hop, R&B, contemporary jazz and alternative rock, their aim, wrote academic Kembrew McLeod, was 'to create a crossover audience that would appear more friendly to advertisers and the financial backers'.[21]

An eleven-page plan for the magazine was drafted by Greg Sandow, music editor of *Entertainment Weekly*, who recalled being summoned to Time Warner's executive suite: 'This dapper guy in a suit and beautifully polished shoes says, "Does that mean we have to put black people on the cover?" It was a privately but not publicly stated policy at those magazines not to put black faces on the cover. Because, they said, covers with black faces didn't sell. I was speechless. The guy finally solved it himself. He says, "Wait a minute, we publish *Sports Illustrated*. We put Michael Jordan on the cover and people don't say, 'There's a black guy!'" Though maybe he needed a little more reassurance, because he turned to me and asked, "Is that how it is with rap guys?"'

While mooted names *Noise* and *Volume* were being rejected, *Vibe*'s heavyweight team was assembled by editor Jonathan Van Meter, a US *Vogue* graduate hailed by publishing executive Adam Moss as 'gay, white, but in his heart ... a fourteen-year-old black girl'.[22] Van Meter appointed senior editor Scott Poulson-Bryant, who had written a hip-hop column for *Spin*, and music editor Alan Light, who described *Vibe*'s raison d'etre as 'documenting the urban culture that had exploded during the previous decade'.[23] The contributors list was bolstered by Nelson George, Carol Cooper, Kevin Powell – another Rutgers alum, who had written for *Rolling Stone* and appeared on MTV's pioneering reality show *The Real World* – and Hilton Als, then a staff writer at *Village Voice* and subsequently *The New Yorker*'s theatre critic.

Positioned as '*Rolling Stone* for the nineties', *Vibe* benefited from Time Warner's deep pockets, with a $1 million test issue featuring Treach from Naughty By Nature on the cover. An enthusiastic reception laid the foundation for a $10 million rollout. Snoop Dogg appeared on the front of the first regular issue, but *Vibe* was too unfocused to establish an audience. Cover stars ranged from actors Wesley Snipes and Rosie Perez to George Clinton, En Vogue and Ice

Cube, with features sprawling from a celebration of the heady days of Paradise Garage to a report on transvestite thieves marauding around Florida. Generic White advertising – Sony MiniDisc, Calvin Klein jeans, Newport cigarettes – diluted the offer further.

There were also issues surrounding the colour of editor Jonathan Van Meter's skin, his sexuality and the fact that the magazine contained LGBTQ+-friendly material. 'The controversy in the field was, "Who is this white gay guy from *Vogue*?"' said Poulson-Bryant. 'I wasn't surprised a white guy was hired, and I felt he had some passion for the project.' But Van Meter's decision to replace an Eddie Murphy cover with one featuring Madonna and the sexuality-blurring basketball player Dennis Rodman brought things to a head. 'I called Madonna,' Quincy Jones recalled, 'and I said, "I'm telling you as a friend: it's not personal, but you cannot pander with an urban magazine this early." She said, "Quincy Jones, you and I can take over the world if we want to. See you around, pal." I haven't talked to her since then.'

Van Meter was incensed by the intervention and the lack of commercial thinking: 'Madonna was queen. You can't not put her on the cover. I couldn't conceive of killing the best cover story we had done so far. [Quincy and I] ended up having a fight on the phone, and I smashed my phone into a thousand pieces and cleared off the top of my desk onto the floor. I think I said, "I quit." I went home. And then the phone calls started. Everyone tried to get Quincy to change his mind. Even Madonna called me at home. She was really pissed.'[24]

The June/July 1994 *Vibe* featured Eddie Murphy on the cover and music editor Alan Light was elevated to the editor's post. In a turn of events that would have been familiar to *NME*'s Alan Smith and Nick Logan, Light was given three months to turn around the magazine's fortunes. Serendipitously, Prince agreed to his first interview in five years, giving Light breathing space to recruit Sheena Lester from *Rap Pages* to, she said, 'make his book more like our irreverent, edgy mix of hip-hop music and culture reporting, commentary and whatnot'.[25]

But Lester clashed with music editor Danyel Smith: 'The plan on [Smith's] watch was "to follow the pop charts". The words echoed in my ears like church bells. "Follow the pop charts?" I sure as hell didn't leave Los Angeles' loving embrace or haul my pregnant-with-twins behind from the big chair at *Rap Pages* to track pop audiences' fickle whims. The masses are asses, remember? Our chat made it clear the *Vibe* Danyel planned to create wasn't one I'd enjoy or thrive in. That was when I, as Large Professor so succinctly stated, started looking at the front door.'[26]

But appealing to the mainstream paid off when *Vibe*'s monthly sales topped 500,000. In an overview of Black music publishing, *The New Yorker*'s James Surowiecki observed: 'I find it hard to imagine that *Vibe* could have a bigger hip-hop fan editing its pages than Danyel Smith – who calls hip-hop "the most amazing thing that happened ever" – but it's certainly true that *Vibe*'s vibe is a long way from being hardcore.'

'We don't think of ourselves as a hip-hop or R&B magazine,' CEO Keith Clinkscales declared. '*Vibe* is a music magazine the way *Rolling Stone* is a music magazine. Our goal is to be as important as, if not more important than, *Rolling Stone*. What we want to emulate is not just their music coverage but also everything else they do.' By 'meandering happily' from superstars Mariah Carey and Will Smith to underground giant Silkk the Shocker, *Vibe* distinguished itself from *The Source* and other hip-hop titles. 'At a time when hip-hop and R&B are pretty much the whole story in pop music,' wrote a cultural commentator at the time, '*Vibe*'s range gives it, if not cultural authority, then at least a serious shot at becoming the definitive pop-music magazine.'[27]

Having split from *The Source*, Reggie Dennis and James Bernard launched the strictly hip-hop *XXL* in 1997. Intent on rivalling his alma mater, Dennis was also spurred by the business savvy spelled out on Jay-Z's 1996 debut album *Reasonable Doubt*: 'Had Jay-Z not been able to articulate the things he did, I certainly wouldn't have been inspired to go that extra mile and create the magazine that I did. It was hip-hop for grown ups: grown man stuff, responsibility, living with regrets and facing the consequences of your actions. It was about depth, subtlety and layers, and I knew that my next magazine would have to embody those qualities. But at the same time I wanted to put something out there that was bold, arrogant and would catch your eye. If a magazine is to live up to the name

XXL, then it has to be larger than life in every aspect, and Jay was well on his way to being that. He was the template. He opened the door that we pushed the magazine through.'[28] Jay was the cover star of the first issue and, having established a friendship with Dennis, returned the compliment: his 1997 track 'Imaginary Players' boasts, 'I got bail money/double X-L money'.

XXL flourished to rival *Vibe* and *The Source*, but Dennis and Bernard fell out with their publishers and exited. This opened a space for Sheena Lester after *Vibe*, and she set about creating a new visual identity for *XXL*, capped by a 1998 trifold cover headlined 'A great day in hip-hop'. This tribute to photographer Art Kane's 1958 *Esquire* image 'A great day in Harlem' replaced his jazz stars with a widescreen portrait of the 200 most important hip-hop artists and personalities, from Kool Herc, the Cold Crush Brothers, Grandmaster Caz and Grandmaster Flash and the Furious Five to A Tribe Called Quest, Busta Rhymes and Common – 'a moment of great cultural significance [and] a logistical nightmare-turned-miracle'.[29]

'*XXL* editorial meetings were, to me, always every week's highlight,' Lester explained. 'Interns' opinions were given equal weight as those of their titled supervisors. Spotting a skeptical lip curl or eyebrow raise from a junior staffer was always a treat for me at these sessions, as convener, since those telltale giveaways were surefire opportunities to coax out a contrary viewpoint that'd inform or deepen our discussions ... Once the subject of recreating the Art Kane photo interrupted the agenda, all else hit the back burner. But, surprisingly, this bright bunch needed to be convinced we could make it happen. [I was] genuinely taken aback at their reluctance. "It's not like Harlem is Mars; it's a couple miles up the street! Why can't we do it?"'[30]

Gordon Parks – who co-founded *Essence*, directed 1971's *Shaft* and chronicled the African American experience as *Life*'s only photojournalist of colour – was chosen to take the picture. But when *XXL*'s competitors got wind of the ambitious plan, Lester heard that her nemesis Danyel Smith had tried the 'chickenshit tactic' of informing managers and artists that they would be barred from *Vibe*'s pages if they attended. 'Everybody – *everybody* – recognized that Mr Parks's participation, his willingness to elevate this photo into his glorious portfolio, gave our shoot undeniable historic significance,' Lester observed. 'It transcended magazine rivalry.' She told *Vibe* CEO Keith Clinkscales: 'If she keeps trippin', we'll throw a goddamn press conference on the steps of *Vibe*'s building and call her raggedy ass out by name for being the sore fucking loser that she is!'[31] The shoot duly went ahead, sealing the credibility of hip-hop publishing that had bloomed over the past decade.

* * *

Across the country, *Urb* offered a laid-back Angeleno alternative to *XXL*, *The Source* and *Rap Pages*. Founded at the dawn of the 1990s by DJ and graffiti artist Raymond Roker, it covered rap, hip-hop, electronic music – especially releases from Europe – and streetwear. Writers included Hawaiian Chinese hip-hop expert Jeff Chang, who ran an independent label and worked with DJ Shadow and Blackalicious, and Joseph 'Jazzbo' Patel, later a film producer whose credits include the 2021 documentary hit *Summer of Soul*.

Jazzbo and DJ Shadow also contributed to *Urb*'s San Francisco counterpart *The Bomb Hip-Hop Magazine*, which DJ Dave Paul launched in 1991 to document the Bay Area's fertile underground. 'Before dating apps and search engines ruined San Francisco,' noted journalist Torii MacAdams, 'it was the most wonderfully weird city on earth: a hilly, wind-and-fog-chilled agglomeration of Summer of Love victims, Chinese immigrants, black radicals, gay bon vivants with wrists ranging from limp to heavily muscled, street gangs of every flavour, and *The Bomb*.' The latter, he wrote, '[was] probably the premier rap zine ... [its] Xeroxed style, smart-assed attitude, and limited-run flexidiscs closely mirroring the aesthetics of punk and hardcore 'zines'.[32]

Among *The Bomb*'s contributors were Cheo Hodari Coker, who later wrote the Notorious BIG biopic *Notorious*, and Dave Klein, who ran the Disney-owned Hollywood BASIC label and wrote the satirical column 'Gangsta Limpin'. Klein had also worked at Def Jam and Red Alert Productions and contributed to *The Source*. One Gangsta Limpin snipe – 'Fuck a TLC cover' – was taken to be a dig at *The Source* (that magazine having put the R&B trio on its front page) and led to an angry call from Jon Shecter, who derided *The*

Bomb as 'a stapled-together piece of shit'.[33] Cementing its strictly hip-hop stance, the magazine gave away flexidiscs featuring Dan the Automator and Peanut Butter Wolf, and masterminded the album *Bomb Hip-Hop Compilation* before folding in 1996.

As the *Bomb* ceased publication, the bimonthly hip-hop 'zine *Kronick* entered the field from the predominantly Black LA suburb West Adams, courtesy of young entrepreneur Meshack Blaq. '*The Source* and *Vibe* are good examples of hip-hop magazines well-staffed with black people, but the name at the top is white,' he told the *LA Times*. 'That means we're seeing the culture through white spectacles. That's where I come in. The respect I get from the artists. They give me more of themselves than they would a mainstream publication because they see me handling things from top to bottom.'[34]

Kronick pulled in advertising from Universal and Nike, while interviewees included Dr Dre, Kid Rock and Pharrell Williams. And Blaq claimed to be the last journalist to spend time with the Notorious BIG before the rapper was shot on leaving *Vibe*'s Soul Train Awards afterparty in 1997.

Short-lived but influential was *ego trip*, which ran for thirteen issues in the mid-1990s and traded in irreverent humour. Nas, Rakim and Method Man – the latter sporting fangs made from tinfoil – were among the cover stars of a magazine birthed as *Beat-Down Newspaper* by a group including Sacha Jenkins, who had run a graffiti 'zine and later became *Vibe*'s music editor. Fashion spreads mimicked grungy shoots appearing across the water in *The Face*, or were given a humorous spin: a street-style feature chronicling 'a day in the life of a wannabe playa' was headlined 'Ass-capades'. And such was *ego trip*'s impact that it inspired DJ Yoda and Dan Greenpeace to launch their own rap/skate/graffiti title, *Fat Lace*, which billed itself 'The magazine for ageing B-boys' and claimed to be the first to put Eminem on a front cover.

Less than a decade after *The Source* was launched as a one-sheet to promote a college radio show, Black American culture was reshaping the world's music media.

18
‘Club culture seemed more stylish’

From Superclubs and *Jockey Slut* to *Loaded* and the New Lad

Chapter 18

'The most important magazine in the world' was the verdict of Public Enemy's Chuck D on *Hip-Hop Connection* – the British title that, at its height, sold 60,000 copies a month. And readers returned the compliment by voting Public Enemy's *It Takes a Nation of Millions to Hold Us Back* the best album of all time. *Hip-Hop Connection*, launched in 1988, and the enduring *Blues & Soul*, which had long since absorbed *Black Music*, confirmed the appetite for specialist coverage of Black music – as did *Touch*, which featured a column by DJ and broadcaster Trevor Nelson.

Those titles, however, were outliers. The outward-looking nature of African American music media was rarely reflected in Britain's mainstream titles, which continued to focus on rock and zigzagged between hyping bands, coining absurd and short-lived subgenres such as 'the new wave of new wave' and picking over the bones of the 1960s and '70s.

Even *Smash Hits* was losing its lustre, with sales on a downward curve from a one-million high in 1989. 'We had an influx of new and very young readers last year,' explained publisher Rita Lewis in 1990. 'They were mad about Kylie Minogue, Jason Donovan and Bros, and ran around buying everything that had them in. When the crest of the wave is over, you lose readers.'[1]

But specialists such as *The Wire* and dance magazines reflected genuine advances, the latter devoting pages to a club network that threatened to outpace the tired concert circuit. 'I was lured away from guitars and gigs in sticky-floored student unions by the promise of a more sophisticated and exciting alternative,' said writer Alexis Petridis, features editor at the market-leading *Mixmag* and latterly music editor of *The Guardian*. 'Club culture seemed more stylish and fashion-conscious; its music more forward-thinking; its choice of intoxicants more thrilling than the obligatory pint of snakebite and black.'[2]

Mixmag started life in 1983 as a newsletter: American R&B trio Shalamar were on the cover of what was initially a mailout for DJs from the Disco Mix Club label. This produced megamixes and remixes of current hits, the meat and potatoes of DJs around the country, and so the first issue carried a cover-mounted megamix cassette.

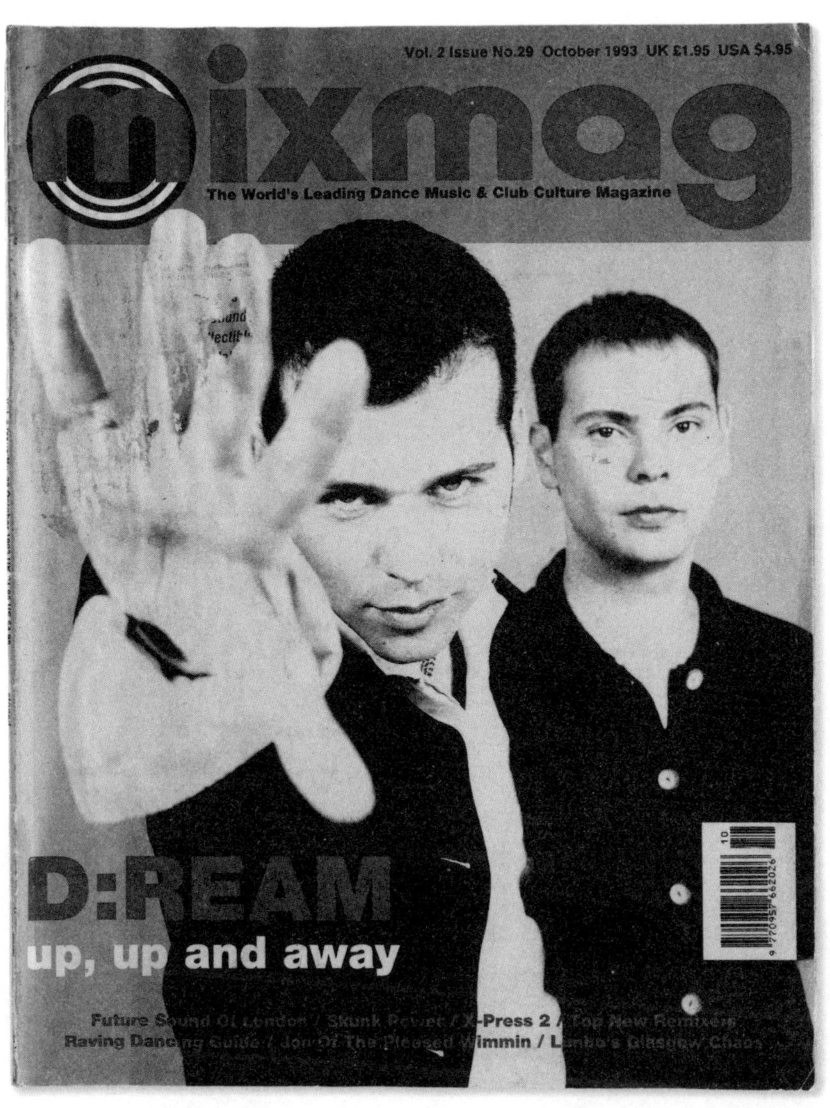

Mixmag, vol. 2, no. 29, October 1993

'I really wanted to write specifically about dance music, so I pestered *Mixmag* for work experience,' Petridis recalled. 'There were a lot of talented people there, but it was a relatively new music scene they were covering, with rules and standards very different from conventional rock music. So everyone was sort of busking it, making it up as they went along, which made it a very good environment to start your career in.'[3]

Exploding around the UK were 'superclubs': Ministry of Sound and Fabric in London, Gatecrasher in Sheffield, and Cream and Nation in Liverpool. Each drew thousands every weekend, then expanded to the Mediterranean holiday destinations of their clientele. This fresh lifestyle provided a readymade audience – and content – for new magazines. Meanwhile, boundaries were blurred by small but influential clubs like London's Heavenly Social and Metalheadz, the latter fronted by Goldie. The festival-style event Tribal Gathering in 1996 – which featured Carl Cox, the Chemical Brothers, Daft Punk, Goldie, Leftfield and Sasha – confirmed that dance music had crossed over and wielded as much power as rock.

With sales soaring above 80,000, *Mixmag* was swallowed by Emap in 1997 as the publisher again waged turf war with IPC. The latter's *Muzik* had launched two years earlier, with a £1.7 million marketing campaign, and covered garage, house, jungle, soul and techno with former *Melody Maker* man Chris 'Push' Dawes at the helm. The target audience, according to advertising journal *Campaign*, was 'eighteen to thirty-year-old men with disposable income who are obsessed with music and looking good'.[4]

Superclub Ministry of Sound crashed the sector with its monthly *Ministry* in 1998. Within a couple of years this was selling 90,000 per issue, not far behind *Mixmag*'s 106,000 and more than double *Muzik*'s total. But a battle for advertising took its toll. With owner James Palumbo diversifying into clothing, property and the Ministry of Sound record label, investment ran dry when revenues slumped at the turn of the century. The magazine closed just four years after its launch.

'Dance music in general is enduring a difficult time as ageing fans, who lived though the acid house era of the late eighties and the subsequent rise of superclubs such as the Ministry, fail to be replaced by a younger generation of clubbers,' reported *The Guardian*. Ministry creative director Mark Rodol added that the decision to close the magazine was not taken for financial reasons but because it had strayed too far from the image the company wanted to promote. He vowed that a new title would be 'about global youth culture as opposed to taking pills in a nightclub in the north of England'.[5]

But Ministry's next magazine, *Trash*, was pulled after a single issue. In contrast, *Jockey Slut* emerged in 1993 and survives today, publishing a bookazine dedicated to Andrew Weatherall on the DJ and producer's sudden death in 2020. This was apposite, since Weatherall's *Boy's Own* had been a major influence on *Jockey Slut* founders John Burgess and Paul Benney. 'When I left Manchester Poly with my 2:2 [degree],' said Benney, 'and *NME* said "no" to my job application, we decided to start our own magazine so that we could continue doing what we loved: going clubbing, meeting our favourite DJs and writing about them. The magazine grew over time, built a reputation for finding new music early and gave first covers to both the Chemical Brothers and Daft Punk. We also had a sense of humour – which was good, because running the mag nearly killed us.'

The magazine plugged into club culture via Burgess and Benney's weekly Bugged Out night in Manchester. As it grew into a major player, Bugged Out snared DJs from across the Atlantic, and – when it moved to Liverpool's Cream in the mid-1990s – attracted thousands of clubgoers. For the first issue of *Jockey Slut*, the duo persuaded Jon Savage to contribute a piece on experimental music, focusing on Britain's Aphex Twin and Norway's Biosphere. 'I got severely bored with being retro and started looking hard for a new kind of music that I knew would be out there,' Savage wrote, echoing his contribution to *Sounds*' New Musick issue twenty-five years previously. 'The Aphex Twin, Biosphere and others – Sandoz, Musicology, Cosmic Baby – are what I was looking for ... This music is part of a new way of looking at the world, a new language: minimal, cool, romantic, passionate.'[6]

As *Jockey Slut* progressed, Burgess observed, 'We only wrote about what we were passionate about. We left out who we didn't like. Being based in Manchester meant that PR people couldn't get to us. There was no, "Hey, let's go out for a glass of wine and then you'll write about my crap band!" Even at the end of it, we'd still refuse to give certain massive acts any oxygen if we didn't like them. Much to the annoyance of PR people.'[7]

* * *

Gay-friendly and evenly split between the sexes, readers of dance and clubbing magazines were young and diverse. And as expressions of sexuality relaxed after the oppressive Thatcher years, gay magazines that incorporated music flourished. Most appealing was *Boyz*, launched as a giveaway at the London Pride march in 1991 by the owners of the weekly *Pink Paper*. Aimed at young gay men, it was subsequently distributed nationally and – as editor Simon Gage admitted – mimicked *Smash Hits*, with vox pops about readers' sexual exploits and questions for celebrities such as 'What did you eat for breakfast?' The result shifted 25,000 copies a week.

The 1990s, suggested *Boyz* and *Pink Paper* photographer Mark C. O'Flaherty, were 'a golden age for the gay press. We did some really fun things'. Girl band Vanilla were covered in fake blood for a shoot in a seedy London hotel, while Republica singer Saffron appeared in clothes by cutting-edge designer Fabio Piras. 'We went to Bordeaux for a World AIDS Day shoot with Morcheeba, gave Siouxsie Sioux a makeover, fed Japanese crisps to [Texas front woman] Sharleen Spiteri and covered more of London Fashion Week than many "proper" magazines,' said O'Flaherty, who was also a contributor to *Melody Maker*. 'Under Simon Gage's editorship, we got to do whatever we wanted.'[8]

More weighty was *Attitude*, launched by publishing megacorp Northern & Shell in 1994. The first issue boasted a Boy George cover, a feature on performance artist Leigh Bowery, and twenty-four pages of fashion. In ensuing years, Madonna, Neil Tennant, Kylie Minogue, D:Ream, the Spice Girls, Gloria Estefan and Marc Almond were also cover stars. Such issues, said latterday publisher Darren Styles, 'read more like *Smash Hits*. It was quite pissy and passive-aggressive and, in terms of its view of authority, was up-and-at-'em, as would have been the political need then. We still had Section 28, which meant you couldn't speak about homosexuality in schools. Civil partnership, equal marriage – that was a distant dream at that point. So it *would* be antiestablishment and it *would* be angry, wouldn't it?'[9]

In the straight world, a less politicized generation of White males who had soaked up *NME*, *Melody Maker* and *Sounds* in their teens were now in their thirties. Above them were baby boomers, well into their middle years, who had come of age with rock of the 1960s. 'This is the first time there's been forty-something rock fans,' *Vox* editor Paul Colbert told *The Guardian*. 'There's a whole new audience.'[10] And fans young and old enjoyed the repackaged music that surfaced as record companies plundered their archives. 'The great thing about CDs – which nobody predicted – was that we got more music available than there had ever been before,' notes David Hepworth. 'Ancient Mississippi Fred McDowell records, German industrial techno, dance music, whatever. An incredible richness to be covered.' The likes of the cracked Syd Barrett and Skip Spence, the wild genius Lee Scratch Perry and the tragic Nick Drake and Tim Buckley were now ripe for reassessment.

'There was a tendency among eighteen-year-olds to develop a fascination for music made before they were born,' said Paul Du Noyer, editor of *Q* in the early 1990s. 'And at the same time [there was] a generation of middle-aged music fans who were not nostalgic and MOR in outlook but were curious about new music. I had this romantic notion of generation speaking unto generation.'

Q's sales now exceeded 170,000 a month; *Select* close to 100,000; *Vox* just over 80,000. All had embraced alternative acts such as Nirvana and the Cure, with token nods to dance music and clubbing. 'Being big and mainstream is nice,' Du Noyer observed, 'but it limits you to covering only mainstream music.' He was also keen to find a vehicle for journalists whose work he admired, and proposed *Mojo* – titled *Q Ultra* during development – to David Hepworth and Mark Ellen. 'There was a generation of writers who weren't being given the outlet they deserved,' he said. 'I thought of *Mojo* as a place I could bring in Jon Savage, who never had much of a place within the mainstream music press, as well as Charlie Murray and Nick Kent, and a newer breed as well.'

Paul McCartney, Bruce Springsteen and U2 had been crucial when *Q* launched in the mid-1980s but were now too old for that

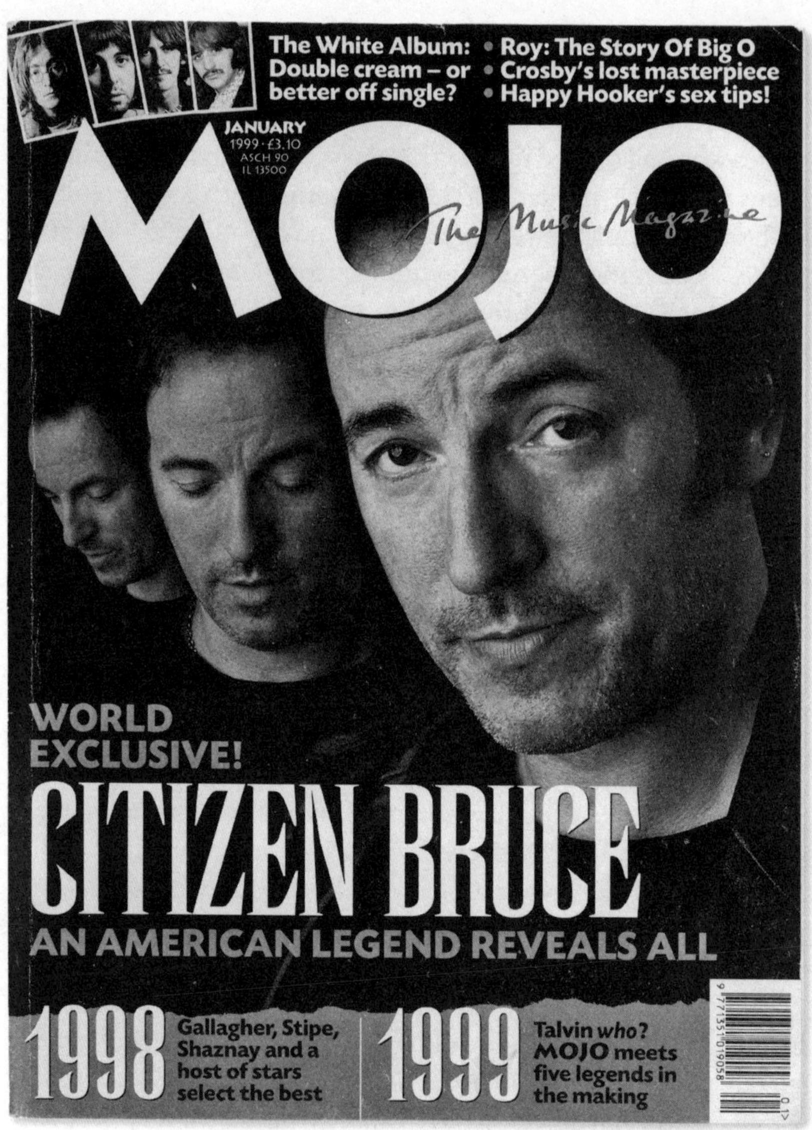

Mojo, January 1999

magazine's readers. 'Nonetheless,' Hepworth noted, 'there were still people interested in reading about them. That was the idea for *Mojo*: a magazine [where] you can write and read about classic rock acts in some depth.'

No fan of *Q*, Barney Hoskyns was on board from the first issue, published in 1993. Ellen's involvement, he suggested, was a 'subconscious atoning for what *Q* had done, which was [to] snuff out the real spirit of rock 'n' roll and package it as some chortlesome subject. I think *Mojo* represented a deep commitment to music and writing about it ... much more than cosy nostalgia. We decided we would allow writers to file impassioned and big pieces about obscure acts.'

Du Noyer and Ellen also recruited Jim Irvin, who had written for *Melody Maker* and sung with the 1980s band Furniture. For the design, Ellen requested 'something handcrafted and organic ... like the Band's second album'. Designer Andy Cowles duly 'bought lino and chisels and carved some graphics that looked like woodcuts'.[11]

A twenty-two-page story on a 1966 encounter between John Lennon and Bob Dylan was the centrepiece of *Mojo*'s first issue, and there were features on singer-songwriters Aimee Mann and Mary Chapin Carpenter. But the editorial lineup was determinedly male, although one *Sounds*/*Kerrang!* veteran was an exception. 'Paul was so open about what I could do,' said Sylvie Simmons, who would eventually develop *Mojo* features about Serge Gainsbourg into an incisive biography.

Initial expectations were for monthly sales of around 45,000, but *Mojo* earned higher numbers and international attention. 'The advertisers were attracted to it because the readership is of such high quality,' Du Noyer noted. '[The readers] are also very demanding and won't let you get away with anything sloppy, which is why writers are usually working at the top of their game at *Mojo*. I always fancied it as a global magazine. That's why I picked the name. It had a sense of the magic at the core of music and looked like a word French and Japanese people might get their tongues around.'

Richard Reigel compared *Mojo* to his alma mater *Creem*: 'I like the flashy, colourful format and the extensive coverage of artists, even when they're catering to my old-guyness by reliving the sixties on a monthly basis. *Mojo* has a good quotient of dry British humour too – so, while it's not quite *Creem*, it comes closer than any other current mag to that Boy Howdy ambience I miss so acutely.'[12]

Among the first contemporary cover stars were Oasis, who appeared a year into the magazine's run. Songwriter Noel Gallagher, Mark Ellen recognized, 'was *Mojo* all over. We'd just launched a magazine about songs, not albums; about the songwriters, not the band itself. It was searching for clues about how the great, deathless records were reconstructed, and I'd figured it was for people my age. Here was someone fourteen years younger who seemed to feel the same way.'[13]

That didn't stop *Mojo* becoming shorthand for a particularly male outlook, hence a woman's brush-off to her boyfriend in the British comedy *In the Loop*: 'And you can take your fucking back issues of *Mojo* with you!'[14] And, for some, the magazine represented what writer Ben Watson described as 'the conservatism of classicism'. In a book about Frank Zappa, he wrote: '*Mojo* magazine and classic rock in general is a celebration of music being nailed up in the lair of the accountant, only to be listened to through expensive systems, with all the fizzes and pops and memories of what its energy could actually mean digitally erased.'[15]

'We now have the *Mojo*-ification of music,' complained rocksbackpages.com editor Mark Pringle. 'Everything endlessly revisited and dug out; all kinds of mediocrities and obscurities from the sixties being treated as a Festival of Great Gods. This is antithetical to the spirit of the music they made, which was, to some extent about disposability. It was about, "Chuck out that forty-five [single], chuck out another" – and now suddenly we're in a sort of post-historical world where everything has to be endlessly revisited.'[16]

'*Mojo*-ification', to Liz Naylor, veteran of the 1970s fanzine scene and indie record labels, means 'people actually writing about music – which is a bit "juggling for radio", isn't it? To me, it's really boring ... At *Mojo* it's, "We're going to talk you through how the album was made." I guess if you're a musician, that's interesting, but it also sets up this thing where people who read it then aspire to be musicians. Which to me is a very pre-punk position of power – like, "Oh, if only I could be Rick Wakeman. But I can't."'[17]

Mojo's blessing and curse was its mainly male readership, but Sylvie Simmons noted that younger journalists who rose through the ranks later in the 1990s actively strove to diversify, by driving coverage away from staples such as the Beatles and Led Zeppelin. 'There are a lot more females working there now,' she said. However, she pointed, too, to a survey conducted during Mat Snow's mid-1990s editorship that confirmed ninety per cent of the audience were male. 'They are very wary,' she noted, 'of scaring off their core readership.'

* * *

Sexism, sport, drug-taking, boozing, non-PC humour and general adolescent misbehaviour were the hallmarks of New Lads: the mid-1990s males who evidently felt threatened by social and cultural progress over the preceding decade. And the magazine that wrapped its arms around the phenomenon and stoked its fires was *Loaded*, IPC's lifestyle monthly that covered music, comedy, clubbing and travel but was dominated by 'babes', booze and soccer. This cocktail proved intoxicating for young British men whose less charming characteristics were legitimized by mediagenic editor James Brown, a former editor of *NME* with a feel for pop culture and an irreverent sense of humour.

Loaded was the latest in the series of innovations introduced by IPC's Alan Lewis over three decades. And Brown insists the publisher deserves the kudos for having added to the mix the element for which *Loaded* became noted: 'Lewis came up to me three days before launch and said, "James, you have everything young men like: music, football, clubs, humour. But you haven't got women." Then he promptly ripped out a page about Rod Stewart and stuck in a picture of Liz Hurley in La Perla underwear.' The picture caused a stir in the national papers, earning *Loaded* hundreds of column inches of free promotion.

'What fresh lunacy is this?' Brown mused in his inaugural address. '*Loaded* is a new magazine dedicated to life, liberty and the pursuit of sex, drink, football and less serious matters ... *Loaded* is for the man who believes he can do anything, if only he wasn't hungover.'[18] The first issue, in May 1994, sold 59,400 copies. Eight months later sales exceeded 100,000.

The pain was keenly felt at Wagadon, publishers of *The Face* and *Arena*, where John Stoddart's photograph of Hurley had been rejected. *Loaded*, said Richard Benson, soon to be editor of *The Face*, 'made us look old-fashioned and up ourselves in terms of cultural positioning. It felt like the zeitgeist was moving on.'

However, for the time being, *The Face* maintained its place on the frontline. 'There was definitely a conscious anti-eighties spirit,' said Benson. 'I remember, in a meeting, us all criticising a cheesy Southern Comfort ad for having an eighties aesthetic of success as opposed to nineties reality; actual life as it was lived in Britain. One of the overlays was the strongly felt sense that there was too much interest in American popular culture.' And the magazine benefited from Amy Raphael's appreciation for grunge. '*The Face*, like all youth culture magazines, had a bigger opportunity to flourish when something exciting [was] happening locally,' said deputy editor Charles Gant. 'It was slightly challenging when the thing that was happening had inconveniently come from Seattle. I think we did a very good job of dealing with that because Amy established a personal connection with those artists.'[19]

Raphael's enthusiasm led to Courtney Love appearing on *The Face*'s cover in February 1993, despite her band Hole having spent just a single week in the UK charts. Seven months later came photographer David Sims's striking cover shot of a kohl-eyed Kurt Cobain in a floral print dress (for images inside, he donned a Tigger suit). Exhausted by the pressures of fame and quizzed about his heroin usage, Cobain told Raphael: 'I'm not addicted any more. But I'll always be a junkie.' She later revealed that they also talked about Cobain's belief that happiness could be achieved only in death.

Meanwhile, Richard Benson identified Suede as the British group with which *The Face* could align: 'They had that Bowie, London thing down, so expressed a Britishness. The Happy Mondays and the Stone Roses had been very much about being "northern". Not that there's anything wrong with that – I'm from up north – but it was time for something more all-embracing.'

Kurt Cobain's April 1994 suicide signalled the end of the need to focus on America. Writer Gavin Hills even submitted a piece that described Nirvana as overrated, Cobain as a cop-out and grunge as worthless music peddled by US entertainment giants. Editor Sheryl Garratt declined to publish that (it turned up instead in the slacker title *The Idler*), but the issue of *The Face* that came out immediately after Cobain's death expressed a new British bullishness, with Blur's Damon Albarn and a Union Jack on the cover and the headline 'Brit up your ears'. Inside was a guide to the provocateurs who would constitute the Young British Artists movement with which Britpop was twinned, including Damien Hirst, Gary Hume, Sam Taylor-Wood and Gavin Turk.

'If a rock band was going to feature in *The Face*, they had to do something different,' Garratt explained. 'They weren't just going to be lined up for five minutes against a wall for the photograph, but [would] have to commit to a day in the studio, sometimes doing uncomfortable things. Like when Blur sat astride a roll of carpet, which appeared as a rocket in the magazine.'

Britpop was the phenomenon that outgrew the music press. 'We suffered quite badly,' said *Melody Maker* stalwart Allan Jones. 'You may think the music weeklies thrived during that period, but *MM* certainly didn't. We started to lose readers even though we were right in the thick of it, famously doing the first Suede cover before their first single came out. The problem was that the coverage was ubiquitous. The Gallagher brothers were all over the [*Daily*] *Mirror* and you couldn't pick up a magazine of any kind – from *Angler's Weekly* to *Motorbike Rider* – without seeing coverage of Blur, Oasis or Pulp.'

The October 1995 release of Oasis's album *(What's the Story) Morning Glory?*, said David Cavanagh, 'changed the music press in this country forever'. *Q* had thrown its weight behind Blur rather than Oasis in the media-constructed battle between south and north, art school against working-class estate, experimental sounds and Kinksian lyricism versus Beatles-based rock 'n' roll. 'The readers loved Blur and they had commercial appeal,' explained Cavanagh. 'Their albums had depth and lots of sixties references. Oasis were regarded as a band for the lads down the corridor at *Select*.' *Q* had given Oasis's debut *Definitely Maybe* a 140-word review with no photograph in 1994, and followed it with a two-page report that interviewed no group members. For Blur's 1995 album *The Great Escape*, *Q* likened lyricist Damon Albarn to Orwell and Dickens, but Cavanagh granted *Morning Glory* just three stars, describing the lyrics as meaningless: 'They scan; they fill a hole; end of story. They say nothing much about anything.'[20] 'I'd heard about [the album] from John Harris, who joined *Select* from *NME*, and he'd slated it, saying it was hilarious, that it was shit and they'd get sued for every song,' said Cavanagh. 'I heard it, liked about half of it and wrote what has gone down in history as a slag-off.'

Inconveniently, the Oasis album went to number one and stayed in the top five for thirty-five weeks, utterly eclipsing Blur. This meant that Noel and Liam Gallagher's presence was required at the Q Awards, to receive the gong for the year's best album. 'At that point,' Cavanagh recalled, '*Q* got the response, "Oh, okay, we see: you want Liam and Noel to come and pick up an award for an album which you said was no good." They were told, "Ah! One of our freelancers said it was no good. *We* love it!" Then you had all these people, who'd slagged it off for three months, saying it was great. I didn't get any work for three months. A lot of people saw the bus leaving and wanted to get on it. I preferred walking.'

The titles that liked to think they defined musical tastes were

forced to bow to market forces. 'Oasis and a lot of other bands became *Q* property,' said Cavanagh. 'Pulp and the kings of Britpop – Supergrass, Black Grape – were on the *Q* covers, which left *Select* with slim pickings: the Foo Fighters and [Stone Roses spin-off] the Seahorses. They were in the same position as *Melody Maker* in regard to *NME*: angling for the same groups but not getting them because their sales didn't justify it. *Select* was fucked and they weren't alone – it hit *Vox* and *Melody Maker*. Here was a band [and] a genre which appealed to all the readers of all the magazines, from *Smash Hits* to *Mojo*, and those with the biggest circulations won out.'

'Britpop never did us any favours,' agreed Allan Jones of *Melody Maker*. 'We probably lost some of our heartland readers who were used to more considered writing. Britpop was brash, so the coverage assumed this rather shrill quality.' *Melody Maker* also suffered from the exit of Simon Reynolds, Chris Roberts and, most significantly, Caitlin Moran. Ultimately the best-known writer to emerge from Britain's music press in the 1990s, Moran had cut a swathe through the boysy domination of the *Maker*'s pages. 'Not as good-looking as supposed rivals Take That, not as dance-driven

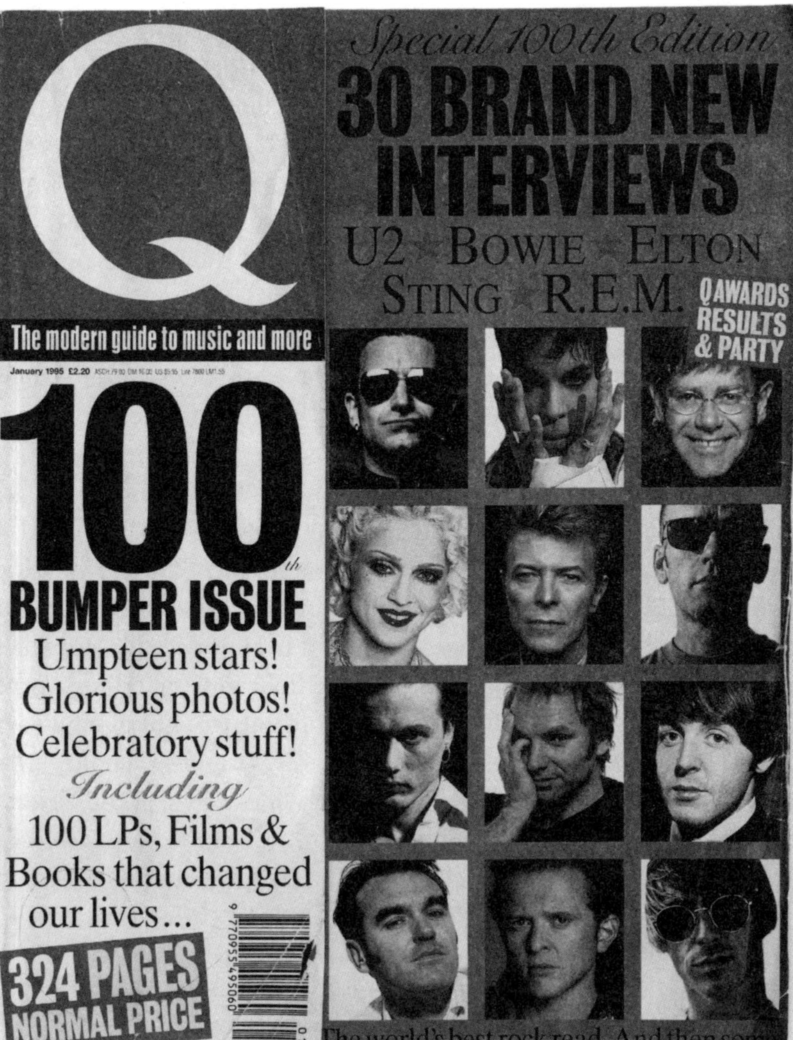

Q, January 1995

as U-U-U-Utah Saints, and absolutely *shite* at writing lyrics,' she wrote of London bad boys East 17. 'What the fuck's *"I wanna do it 'til my belly rumbles"* supposed to make a lass think? I know the way to a man's heart is through his stomach, but that's *ridiculous.* But hell, look at the sales. It's enough to make Bob Mould weep. Yup, East 17, princelings of sampladelic pop-rap and the EMF it's probably still not okay to like, have captured the beered-up-lads-'aving-a-night-out *and* the lasses-cruising-for-a-shagging markets impeccably ... *The Maker*'s here because the East End Shagging Machines have released a cover of the Pet Shop Boys' ennui-laden "West End Girls", and we love the Pet Shop Boys. The occasional lyrical idiosyncrasy notwithstanding, we're also quite partial to East 17 themselves. Plus, we're rather curious as to what real *Smash Hits*-style, moist-knicker-inducing Pop Stars are like.'[21]

Moran graduated to TV presenting and earned a patronizing profile by Beatles biographer Hunter Davies: 'She's not very tidy. Just look at the state of her basement flat in Hampstead. More like a squat. She herself is squatting, on the floor in front of her Apple Mac laptop, price £4,000. There is no furniture, not even a sofa or chair. The floor is totally covered – dirty clothes, books, CDs, records, mugs, dishes, half-empty bottles, messages, notes, tickets, photos and dead ashtrays, full to the brim. Somewhere, amid all this debris, are three large cheques. She remembers them coming, she remembers opening the envelopes, but now she can't find them. Her boyfriend, Taylor [Parkes, fellow *Melody Maker* writer], is searching for them. They have run out of cash, even though these days Caitlin is earning around £50,000 a year.'[22]

Moran's novel *How to Build a Girl* is rooted in her music press past. 'I was that pioneer girl, a fat, teenaged journalist in London, and so is [the book's heroine] Johanna,' she told Goodreads. 'A lot of mistakes that she makes are things I stole from other people's lives. There's a really famous journalist [called] Julie Burchill, who started working for *NME* when she was sixteen. She was a hot working-class girl from Bristol with a flash of lipstick and dark hair, who wrote these really rebarbative pieces and became more famous than most of the bands that she interviewed, and was the centre of this gang. When I was writing about Johanna, I thought it'd be far more fun to make her like Julie Burchill than me. Because when I was a teenage music journalist, I'd just stand in the corner of the magazine, really shy, going, "I really like Crowded House. Would anyone like to be my friend?"'[23]

Moran later married *Melody Maker* contemporary Peter Paphides, who similarly tracked the twists and turns of pop in the early to mid-1990s and became *The Times*'s rock critic. He also turned to book writing, translating his experiences as the child of immigrants in Birmingham in the 1970s into the award-winning memoir *Broken Greek*. But the qualities these writers brought to the world's oldest music paper had all but disappeared by the end of the decade. 'Something was missing, and our readers spotted it before some of us,' said Allan Jones. 'They had been buying us for our eulogies on Mark Eitzel and American Music Club, but now we were saying, "Menswe@r – what a super group." If I had to put Menswe@r on the cover one more time I would have shot myself or somebody was going to suffer.'

In 1996 Jones interviewed the alt-country group Lambchop. 'It occurred to me as I was writing it up that the readers *Melody Maker* was supposed to be reaching wouldn't get it,' he lamented, 'so I gave up.' The only sections of the paper to which he contributed enthusiastically were its film and book reviews: 'We were getting access to people we'd never have expected. We covered [novelist] Don DeLillo the first time he came to the UK, mainly because none of the broadsheets had heard of him. I did Elmore Leonard, John Carpenter, a whole bunch of people.'

Interest from readers encouraged Jones and editorial director Alan Lewis to pull the material out of *Melody Maker* and expand on it for a new monthly, *Uncut*. Debuting in 1997, it represented IPC's response to the success of *Mojo* and Jones's allergic reaction to Britpop. The cover stars were often the same as those of its Emap rival – Dylan, Springsteen, Pink Floyd – but *Uncut* developed a USP by dedicating huge space to its subjects. Meanwhile, Jones's back-page memories of encounters with the good, the bad and the ugly in *Melody Maker*'s heyday provided an opportunity for scores to be entertainingly settled.

19
Sex and Hollywood Spell Danger

FHM Roars while *The Face* Crashes, *Select* Spirals and Time is Called on *Melody Maker*

Sex and Hollywood Spell Danger

Sex and Hollywood spelled danger for the once dominant monthlies. *Uncut* juggled movie and music coverage, while *Q* ceded its film content to a sister title, *Empire*. Meanwhile, *For Him Magazine*, which had limped along since the mid-1980s, was reinvigorated as the sex-oriented *FHM*, which swiftly became more than a match for *Loaded*. Inevitably, Felix Dennis crashed the party with *Maxim*, intended as a 'less puerile Loaded' that was 'more edgy than the advertiser-friendly *FHM*'.[1] The strategy paid off: international versions survived well into the 21st century. Where board approval at Emap and IPC could stymie the lightning reflexes required to stay one step ahead, Dennis noted, 'The joy of an independent company is its ability to turn on a sixpence.'[2]

Such manoeuvring also impacted *The Face*. By the spring of 1996, Nick Logan's magazine's circulation was sliding from an all-time high of 128,000, new titles denting its ability to charge premium advertising rates. Newsagent racks were jammed with youth culture magazines such as *Blow*, *Code*, *Herb Garden*, *The Idler*, *Straight No Chaser*, *Touch*, *Sleazenation* and direct competitor *Dazed & Confused*. '*Dazed* came at *The Face*,' says the latter's editor Richard Benson. 'They aggressively marketed themselves, which is something Nick had never done ... *Dazed* very astutely worked the newness factor. With *Loaded*, we could position ourselves as the more intelligent option to advertisers. *Dazed* were more difficult to pin down. I felt they were inflicting damage to our reputation.'

More than thirty years into his career, Logan's judgment faltered. He turned down an approach from Canadian journalist Tyler Brûlé to back his magazine *Wallpaper*, which cast a sophisticated eye over architecture, design, interiors and travel. Then, in 1997, as Britpop peaked with *Vanity Fair*'s 'London swings again' issue (featuring, on the cover, Oasis's Liam Gallagher and actress Patsy Kensit on a bed of Union Jack sheets), guitar-playing Tony Blair became prime minister of the first Labour Party government since 1979 – the year Logan began mapping out *The Face*. 'There's something about New Labour coming in which gives me the creeps when I look back,' said Richard Benson. 'Our sales started to collapse, yet there was the pressure of finding content because the issues were getting bigger and bigger. We felt we had to maintain the editorial ratio, so there'd be ten, eleven features in each issue. I cringe when I look back at things like Gorky's Zygotic Mynci, a terrible indie band who helped fill a gap.'

Logan launched the women's magazine *Frank*, aimed at 'upmarket, urban women who are stylish and unconventional'. The first issue sold a promising 120,000, largely thanks to enduring interest in the man who had overseen *NME*'s 1970s reinvention and conceived *Smash Hits*, *The Face* and *Arena*. But Logan underestimated the ferocity of his rivals; it was reportedly suggested to fashion photographers that their work would be unwelcome at *Vogue* if they shot for *Frank*. Sales faltered while editorial discontent grew.

Meanwhile, relations frayed at *The Face*. The focus on *Frank*, and the importing of well-paid staff from high-end titles such as *Vogue*, rubbed existing employees up the wrong way, and the accidental drowning of contributor Gavin Hills at the age of thirty-one darkened the mood further. In the second half of 1997, sales toppled dramatically. 'Pop-culturally, the planets weren't as aligned as they had been,' said deputy editor Charles Gant. 'There didn't seem to

be something strong coming along to replace Britpop.' This malaise was reflected in run-of-the-mill cover choices, driven by PR rather than an instinct for the new and fresh. Such was the competition from *Loaded*, *FHM* and *Q* that *The Face* could no longer afford to go out on a limb and miss the big names that drove newsstand sales.

With *Frank* foundering (it closed in 1999) and *The Face* and *Arena* embattled, Logan risked the house in 1998 on a new men's title, *Deluxe*, edited by Andrew Harrison, fresh from editing *Select*. '*Deluxe* is here because a group of people got tired of being told that the same clapped-out subjects were the be-all and end-all of men's interests,' Harrison declared when the magazine launched with Jarvis Cocker on the cover. 'They got bored of pro-celebrity shark-fishing and Z-list actresses in their knickers. The world is more interesting and more complicated than all that.'[3] But when *Deluxe* fell far short of a 150,000 circulation target – itself a third of what *Loaded* sold every month – in came more photographs of women. While neither Z-list nor in their knickers, they were presented as 'babes'. Within months, the magazine was put out of its misery.

Sex and Hollywood Spell Danger

A poisoned chalice awaited *Select* graduate Adam Higginbotham when he was appointed editor of *The Face* in 1998. Amid the circulation's downward spiral, and with a mutinous editorial team, he was charged with introducing a more populist approach. But he faced tough competition in a crowded market and a lull in youth culture.

Unsupported by staff and management, Higginbotham tried to innovate, creating a text-only cover for an issue about drugs. But neither this nor more predictable cover stars Blur, Kate Moss, Robbie Williams and the Manic Street Preachers could prevent him lasting just ten months in the post.

Adding insult to injury, in 1999 *Loaded* was declared 'the publishing phenomenon of the decade', with sales peaking at around 450,000. Meanwhile, the market leader *FHM* – edited by Nick Logan's brother-in-law Mike Soutar, who had worked at *Smash Hits* in the early days – was shifting a staggering 775,000. *The Face* limped along with 50,000 and was sold by Logan to Emap in 1998 before folding in 2004, having never regained its position as a must-read. Seven years later, Logan still bore the bruises. 'Whatever you do, don't go into publishing,' he told the young editors of the literary compendium *Bad Idea*. 'That is my ultimate advice. It is not what you think it is.'[4]

* * *

'There are more hip-hop magazines than ever before, they're more popular than ever before, and they're bristling with more ads than ever before, indicating a belief on the part of mainstream advertisers that hip-hop can no longer be seen as a niche market,' declared *New York* magazine in 1999. The previous year, 80 million hip-hop albums had been sold, Lauryn Hill had been nominated for ten Grammy awards (of which she won five) and *XXL* had been launched – as had *Blaze*, which *Vibe*'s parent company established to take on *The Source*. *Vibe* itself sold around 650,000 copies a month, making it the music press's second biggest seller after *Rolling Stone* (1.2 million).

When *Vibe* editor Alan Light was switched to *Spin* (then pulling in 500,000 readers and generating $20 million a year in turnover), his successors were Danyel Smith, then Emil Wilbekin, who was at the helm when *Vibe* won a National Magazine Award for excellence. 'We beat out *The New Yorker*, *Wired*, *Jane* and *Gourmet*,' he told *Billboard*. 'It was a coup and a tipping point for *Vibe*, hip-hop and black media. In my acceptance speech, I talked about giving voice to the voiceless.'[5]

The stakes had become high. *Blaze* editor Jesse Washington claimed that Wyclef Jean of the Fugees pulled a gun on him after a bad review ('I carry a guitar, not a gun,' Jean responded. 'I attack with my pen, not a pistol. I'm all about making music. The editor of *Blaze* is all about selling magazines.') Washington also said that he was attacked by producer Deric "D-Dot" Angelettie when *Blaze* exposed Angelettie as the true identity of the Bad Boy label's comic foil the Madd Rapper. 'Writers and editors say other rappers have lashed out because they didn't make the cover of publications, didn't like what was printed about them or didn't like the photos that appeared in magazines,' reported the *New York Times*. 'Some journalists say they are careful not to be acerbic – or to do anything that would set off an artist – when they profile rappers or critique new CDs. Some journalists, speaking on the condition of anonymity, say rappers are sometimes allowed to see stories and layouts before they go to press.'

Black journalists were particularly at risk. '[The artists] don't respond to us the same way they do to mainstream media,' noted *XXL* editor Sheena Lester, who said she had been threatened by Tupac Shakur over an editorial in her previous magazine *Rap Pages*. 'They would never do what they did to Jesse [Washington] to Joe Levy, the music editor at *Rolling Stone*. What happened with Jesse was so horrifying, I couldn't sleep. I mean, beat up in his office!'

But such incidents were not restricted to the Black community. Around this time, Marilyn Manson and his bodyguards were charged with an assault on *Spin*'s executive editor Craig Marks (the shock rocker having objected to being replaced on *Spin*'s cover by another Manson, Garbage singer Shirley). And Selwyn Hinds noted that *The Source* suffered no such violence during his tenure in the late 1990s: 'I've dealt with situations that were very tense. But in our case, diplomacy, conversation and mediation have always prevailed.'[6]

* * *

Sonic the Hedgehog drove another nail into the coffin of the British music press. Where once young fans counted the days until the new *Smash Hits*, now they sat with fingers glued to computer consoles. This made them ideal consumers of both the online platforms and nascent social media gobbling advertising revenue and – waiting in the wings – the MP3s and file-sharing services that would put an end to the commercial value of music itself.

'Music lost its place in the imagination of youth, at least in Britain,' observed Paul Du Noyer. 'It became one more competing leisure pursuit for all but a few die-hards and was no longer the be-all and end-all of what it was to be young here.'

Globe-straddling pop in the shape of the Spice Girls and Britney Spears, and an obsession with celebrity in titles such as *Heat*, left the music press with a dwindling constituency. 'When the Spice Girls were really happening, they'd be on the cover of every magazine in a way that Boyzone and Travis would never be,' noted David Hepworth, one of *Heat*'s masterminds.

IPC launched nme.com in 1996, but free access irked former contributors such as Mat Snow, who saw it as an example of the company's 'bad stewardship of the whole music market. The website is its principal problem since it gives you for free something which the paper should be selling: an updated gig guide and news pages'.

The publisher also shuttered *Vox* in 1998 after eight years of vying against the dominant *Q*. A year later, Emap closed *Select*. 'No matter how many features we did on Destiny's Child, people still thought we were a magazine about Oasis,' said Alexis Petridis, who had joined *Select* as editor from stablemate *Mixmag*. 'We were forever associated with a music in decline.' One of the factors was the anodyne copy that resulted from the vice-like grip publicists now exerted over their clientele. 'You don't get to go round the band's house, shoot up heroin with them and throw up on their doorstep, as Nick Kent did with Keith Richards,' noted Petridis. 'You could never get away with stuff like Lester Bangs's infamous interviews with Lou Reed, where the journalist tells him he's useless and they basically scream at each other for two hours. You'd just be ushered out of the room by the press officer.'[7]

Two months after *Select*'s closure, IPC bowed to the inevitable and shut down the seventy-four-year-old *Melody Maker*. The publication that at its height had sold 300,000 a week could, at the death, muster only 20,000. The axe was wielded by Alan Lewis, after a period of chaos that included the decision to shift *Melody Maker's* editor Steve Sutherland to pole position at *NME* – an appointment that sparked a staff walk-out and a wave of resignations. Among those who exited was the talented Mary Anne Hobbs, setting herself on a path to broadcasting prominence, most recently as a music and cultural presenter on BBC 6 Music.

Lewis had tried to differentiate *Melody Maker* by introducing glossy colour covers with pop-culture subjects including Gillian Anderson of *The X-Files* and various Spice Girls and All Saints. 'They changed the format and inherently changed the direction,' observed Allan Jones from his perch as editor of *Uncut*. 'When it relaunched in 1999, the editor Mark Sutherland (no relation) made no bones about chasing the *Smash Hits* market. Of course the readers started drifting away again, much as I'd lost readers earlier when we had to cover Britpop.'

Charles Shaar Murray believed *Melody Maker* fell victim to pop music's loss of potency: 'The best band name of the last fifteen years was Pop Will Eat Itself. Now pop is no longer eating itself; it's excreting itself. While there is still good music being made, I can't see pop ever mattering again the way it did then. Pop is now another part of the entertainment industry. Maybe it always was, but there was a time when it seemed to mean much more, and that was a time when I was fortunate to be part of the circus.'

'I was expecting it four or five years ago,' said Caroline Coon of the closure. 'The music papers weren't at the vanguard of culture; they were sexist, homophobic and they didn't like dance culture. They weren't relevant.' And so *Melody Maker*'s existence, threaded over nearly three-quarters of a century, came to a close. And with it so did the story of the sector that defined the 20th century's music press.

Epilogue

The first years of the 21st century following the demise of *Melody Maker*, *Select* and others were not kind to print publications in general and the music press in particular. Hip-hop, however, retained its grip on commercial sales in the last hurrah before the widespread adoption of free downloads tanked advertising rates and readership circulations.

The magazines that championed and benefited from the genre – principally *Vibe* and *The Source* – completed their progression into all-encompassing lifestyle titles, with websites enhancing the print offer. By 2003 *Vibe* was widely understood as 'more than just a music magazine'; the following year it even branched into the women's market with the quarterly beauty, entertainment and dating-fixated *Vibe Vixen*. 'By keeping its remit broad, *Vibe* has capitalised on the expansive swathe hip-hop culture has cut into mainstream sensibilities,' wrote Angus Batey in *The Times*.[1]

The Source also sold well, its popularity bolstered by the penchant for controversies. At the heart of these was the divisive figure of Raymond 'Benzino' Scott, who was eventually ousted with founder Dave Mays in 2006 by private equity investor Black Enterprise/Greenwich Street. More litigation against the pair was directed by former editor-in-chief Kim Osoro; she won a harassment claim and returned to the position in 2012. Though Osoro left after a year, the owner North Star Group ploughed on and, as of 2021, *The Source* was published as a biannual or annual publication with a circulation estimated at 175,000.

Rolling Stone maintained its dominance as the paper of pop culture record bolstered by Wenner Media's controlling stake; it also owned staples *US Weekly* and *Men's Journal*. But it no longer made the news for its music content, let alone celebrity reporting;

the biggest *Rolling Stone* stories to break through concerned investigations into the factors behind the global financial crash of the late 2000s and alarming revelations about the US military's role in Afghanistan.

By 2014 the publication was exposed to the depredations being experienced across the sector when the loss of a defamation case over a retracted story about a gang rape at the University of Virginia seriously winged its credibility. Three years later Jann Wenner sold forty-nine per cent of his company's share in *Rolling Stone* to Singapore music platform Bandlab Technologies for $40m ahead of the magazine's 50th anniversary. Soon the remaining fifty-one per cent was gobbled up for a reported $50m by the car manufacturing heir Jay Penske, who had previously acquired entertainment industry bible *Variety* and fashion's *WWD*. In 2019, Penske Media took full control by buying out Bandlab.

In the teeth of the Covid-19 pandemic Penske announced launches of Chinese and UK editions to add to the dozen versions already in existence around the world. The first British issue, with

three different covers featuring British band Bastille, UK singer Sam Fender and *No Time to Die* star Lashana Lynch, was published in September 2021 via a deal with Stream Publishing, owner of LGBTQ+ title *Attitude*.

Much earlier, a challenge to *Vibe*, *The Source* and *Rolling Stone* came from *Blender*, the sardonic monthly which had been launched in 1999 by Felix Dennis to capitalize on the popularity of *Maxim*. Such a bold move into what was seen as a moribund sector prompted the *New York Times* to run the headline, 'Is Felix Dennis mad?'.

American journalist Nina Munk's prediction that, 'just as *Maxim* made the older men's magazines look and feel stodgy and snooty, *Blender* promises to be younger and more inclusive than its competitors'[2] was borne out by healthy sales responding to sparky copy produced by the team under British editor-in-chief Andy Pemberton.

American advertising writer Simon Dumenico recognized that '*Blender*, like *Maxim*, is not a serious magazine, and has no intentions of becoming one. It is simply yet another Dennis-produced form of Short Attention Span Theatre, and it succeeds quite nicely at that.'[3] But when physical sales of music started to fall rapidly midway through the decade, the jig was up for *Blender*, which, like so many other titles, became a casualty of the financial crash.

'Amid the carnage, magazine advertising revenues plummeted,' recalled US journalist Aaron Gilbreath in a 2018 piece headed 'Where have all the music magazines gone?' for the website longreads.com. 'Total ad pages dropped from 255,667 in 2007 to 172,240 by 2010. Magazine newsstand sales had been declining before the recession, but magazines' advertising revenues precipitously fell from $13.9 billion in 2008 to $10 billion in 2009. To streamline operations, magazines restructured sales departments and reduced print schedules and staff.'[4]

The oldest surviving music paper, which had looked to be on shaky ground for years, survived into the second decade of the 21st century. Initially, *NME* succeeded by riding the return to fashionability of rock a few years earlier with the emergence of a new wave of New York-based post-punk-influenced groups led by the Strokes and Yeah Yeah Yeahs. Their early exploits were chronicled by such new journalists as Lizzy Goodman, who posted about their gigs online before switching to *Rolling Stone* and *NME* and later writing the definitive account of these groups in her 2017 oral history *Meet Me in the Bathroom*.

Yet the life-span of the most prominent group was relatively short, as US journalist Andy Greenwald pointed out to Goodman: 'The Strokes weren't really that big. Everyone needed them to be that big and desperately wanted them to be that big, but they kind of weren't.'[5] Nevertheless, the group lit a fire fanned by the North American pugnacity that greeted the tragedy surrounding the 9/11 terrorist attacks and coincided with groups ranging from such fellow travellers as the White Stripes and the Vines to Southern boogie merchants Kings of Leon and Vegas God-squadders (and the ultimate victors in gaining stadium rock superstardom) the Killers.

It was the music of these and other similar acts that enabled *NME* to regain lost ground after editor Ben Knowles, who was in the job for about a year, was replaced by the ambitious Conor McNicholas in 2002. Taking his cue from such front-of-house predecessors as James Brown, McNicholas astutely tied the paper's flag to the new indie mast, manifested in such exciting fresh bands as the messy and drug-addled Libertines, Scotland's sharp Franz Ferdinand, the West Country's prog-prone Muse and the angular sounds and clever wordplay of Sheffield's Arctic Monkeys.

As these crossed over, so the publication once again lost its cachet and a poorly received redesign in 2008 heralded McNicholas's exit. His successor was Krissi Murison, the first female editor in the paper's six-decade existence; but glossy full-colour front pages and a fuller embrace of celebrity, entertainment and film failed to paper over the cracks and Murison was out by 2012. Three years later, the person who took her job, Mike Williams, oversaw first the abandonment of a cover price – free copies flagging up such pop stars as Rihanna soon littered the streets and platforms of transport links – and then, in 2018, the decision by owner Time Inc. to halt publication altogether. The following year, Time sold the paper along with *Uncut* to Bandlab, which was divesting itself of the *Rolling Stone* stake at the time.

Against these financial transactions, a symptom of a music criticism malaise was the tendency among writers, and US journalists in particular, to tie themselves in ideological knots, not least about the value of the world-beating pop stars who were created by the super-connected online environment: since Avril Lavigne, say, did not conform to the pieties that insisted on authenticity, was she worthy of attention?

This in turn led to the trend for what became known in music journalism as 'poptimism', which, according to *The Guardian*'s Ian Gormely, came of age in 2014, 'led by the unlikely figure of Taylor Swift. Making the transition out of Nashville, Swift's latest album, *1989*, is a poptimistic curve ball that ignores the dance-urban trend and replaces it with something more ambitious.'[6]

But poptimism couldn't help save swathes of music papers. *Spin* relinquished its print model in 2012, while, in British terms, the launch that hammered home the redundancy of the music press had appeared a decade or so previously. *Heat* positioned celebrity as the central focus and was the brainchild of Mark Ellen and David Hepworth, the pair who had done so much to activate the sector. It echoed the decision by Nick Logan to accentuate lifestyle over music with *The Face* decades earlier.

Ellen and Hepworth subsequently left Emap to found monthly *The Word* (later *Word*), which favoured text over imagery and ran for more than a hundred issues, receiving plaudits from media watchers but suffering from the particular pressures of independent publishing. It was shuttered in 2012, though continues as a podcast and regular live events under the umbrella banner of Word In Your Ear (altered to the digital Word In Your Attic during the coronavirus pandemic).

The onset of the pandemic in spring 2020 was cited as one of the factors in the decision to close *Q*, the self-titled 'world's greatest music magazine', which Ellen and Hepworth had set up thirty-four years before. According to Ellen Pierson-Hagger in Britain's *New Statesman*, this didn't mean that the music press was dead. Rather, she found that publishing in the sector had once again become a niche activity, citing such UK magazines as *Gold Flake Paint*, *DIY*, *Crack*, which published German and Dutch editions, and the free *Loud & Quiet* and *In Stereo*. 'Fewer permanent, full-time writing jobs means that music journalism is an ever-more exclusive industry, with many freelance writers relying on other work to flesh out their income,' wrote Pierson-Hagger.

Gold Flake Paint's editor Tom Johnson told her: 'The disposable weekly/monthly music press of days gone by was very news-led and almost tabloid-y. There was a very irreverent style of writing, quite cocky. I see us much more as a platform for sharing stories than the objective pulling apart of music. We only want to exist to push the things that we think are worth people investing their time in.'[7]

Despite the substantial odds stacked against them over the course of the 2000s and 2010s, music magazines continued to emerge, albeit on a micro level. In the UK, the fertile grime and dubstep scene was reflected in a rash of titles, including the excellent small-format *Woofah*. Meanwhile, the enduring *Electronic Sound* began as an iPad-only magazine in 2013 before switching to print in 2016. As editor Mark Roland told retailer and website magculture.com, interest in print publications was analogous to the uptake in vinyl records. 'The response to our first print version has been overwhelming,' said Roland.[8]

Even as I was finalizing this book, word came of yet another prominent music launch, a new title from the founders of *Jockey*

Slut: according to its publisher, *Disco Pogo* is 'a beautifully designed and printed, twice-yearly heavyweight print magazine, featuring the best music writers covering the best new electronic music, whilst also looking back on key moments and artists from the last 50 years. It will include beautifully written longform articles, original photography from the scene's best photographers and some archive content from the original *Jockey Slut*. It will also have a sense of humour.'

According to such exponents as Lizzy Goodman, 'the role of the critic is very different now. There used to be profile writers and critics. That has changed. Music journalism isn't really journalism about music anymore, it's culture journalism.'[9] Add to this the inbuilt obsolescence of the publishing process. 'Magazines rise and fall,' said Aaron Gilbreath. 'They lose relevance, their founders move on, or get revamped or shut down by new owners. The internet has shaped how current generations speak about music.'[10] This has been led by such outlets as the Quietus and Pitchfork, which have built on the earlier work of such sites as salon.com to provide informed and intelligent music criticism.

However attractively written and perceptive their copy, this cannot replicate the impact of the music press at its height, according to Simon Reynolds. 'The music papers I grew up on offered a concentrated, all-enveloping experience,' wrote Reynolds in 2014, ironically for Pitchfork's quarterly print spin-off. 'Few online magazines have been able to create this effect of enclosure and focus. On the internet, newspapers and magazines are permeable and the reader's attention is too often fatally distracted by the adjacencies of any given webpage to everything else in the online universe. Hyperlinks, those editorially self-inflicted wounds, encourage interruptions to the reading process, diversions that may never return to the main road.'[11]

On *Q*'s closure in 2020, founder David Hepworth sent a message to the music business. 'You're going to miss the music press,' he wrote. 'Why? Because it did one thing you failed to value. Through its lens it made your acts seem exciting and larger than life, even when they weren't.'[12]

Notes

Chapter 1

1 Godbolt, Jim, *A History Of British Jazz, 1919–50* (Quartet Books, 1984)
2 Fordham, John, Dancing on the edge: what was life really like for black jazz bands in 1930s Britain? (*The Guardian*, 4 February 2013)
3 Hylton, Jack, The prophets of doom (*The Melody Maker*, Vol. 1 No. 1, January 1926)
4 Grimshaw, Emile, The banjo and tenor-banjo in modern dance orchestras (*The Melody Maker*, Vol. 1 No. 1, January 1926)
5 Moore, Hilary, *Inside British Jazz: Crossing Borders of Race, Nation and Class* (Routledge, 2007)
6 'White' is capitalized in this book in accordance with anti-colonial academic Musab Younis's conclusion that the use of the capital 'draws attention to the fact that what we are describing is a social position'. Younis has cited philosopher Kwame Anthony Appiah's view that 'the point of the capital letter isn't to elevate. It is to situate.' See Younis, Musab, To Own Whiteness (*London Review of Books*, 10 February 2022).
7 McKay, George, Jazz, Race and JB Souter's The Breakdown (georgemckay.org, 26 January 2018)
8 Jackson, Edgar, Editorial (*The Melody Maker*, January 1927)
9 Anonymous, Where the fair sex fails (*The Melody Maker*, May 1928)
10 Johnstone, Nick, *Melody Maker: History of 20th Century Popular Music* (Bloomsbury, 1999)
11 Two big bands wiped out by the Nazis (*The Melody Maker*, 27 May 1933)
12 'Mike', 'Mike' sees signs of a white revival (*The Melody Maker*, 23 September 1933)
13 As cited in Frith, Simon, Playing with real feeling: making sense of jazz in Britain (*New Formations*, Spring 1988)
14 Mathison Brooks, Percy, Record circles (*The Melody Maker*, 29 July 1933)
15 Davies, Lawrence, *British Encounters with Blues and Jazz in Transatlantic Circulation c.1929–1960* (thesis submitted for degree of Doctor of Philosophy in Musicology, King's College London, 2 January 2018)
16 Dope cigarette peddling among British musicians (*Melody Maker*, 22 February 1936)
17 Johnstone, 1999
18 Melody Maker buys Rhythm (*Melody Maker*, 9 November 1935)
19 Nelson, Stanley, *All About Jazz* (Heath, Cranton, 1934)
20 Mathison Brooks, Percy, Our job now! (*Melody Maker*, 9 September 1939)
21 Rubinstein, William D., Jolles, Michael and Rubinstein, Hilary L., *The Palgrave Dictionary of Anglo-Jewish History* (Palgrave MacMillan, 2011)
22 As cited in Johnstone, 1999
23 As cited in Baade, 2011
24 *Musical Express*, 6 January 1950
25 Long, Pat, *The History of the NME: High times and low lives at the world's most famous music magazine* (Portico, 2012)
26 Wilmer, Val, *Mama Said There'd Be Days Like This: My Life in the Jazz World* (The Women's Press, 1989)
27 Voce, Steve, Obituary: Max Jones (*The Independent*, 4 August 1993)
28 All quotes by Chris Welch are from a 2001 interview with the author unless otherwise indicated
29 Voce, 1993
30 All quotes by Maurice Kinn are from interviews with the author 1998–99 unless otherwise indicated

Chapter 2

1 hwww.broadcasting-history.ca/personalities/sonin-ray
2 East, Ken, A personal history of the British record industry 23 – Percy Dickins (vinylmemories.wordpress.com, 28 January 2016)
3 Long, 2012
4 Announcing ... The New Musical Express out on March 7! (*Musical Express*, 22 February 1952)
5 East, 2016
6 East, 2016
7 Announcing the first record hit

parade (*New Musical Express*, 14 November 1952)

8 Long, 2012

9 Williams, 2002

10 Hepple, Peter, Simon Blumenfeld – Columnist, author, playwright, theatre critic, editor and former light entertainment editor of *The Stage* (*UK Press Gazette*, 5 May 2005)

11 Mills, Peter, *Media and Popular Music* (Edinburgh University, 2012)

12 *Reports of Patent, Design, Trade Mark and Other Cases, Vol. 73* (Patent Office, 1956)

13 As cited in Johnstone, 1999

14 As cited in Long, 2012

15 Ibid

16 Ibid

17 All quotes by Mick Farren are from a 2001 interview with the author unless otherwise indicated

18 Gorman, Paul, *In Their Own Write: Adventures in the Music Press* (Sanctuary Publishing, 2002)

19 *The Sound of the City* was published by Sphere Books in 1971. All quotes by Gillett are from 1999 and 2000 interviews with the author unless otherwise indicated

20 John, Elton with Petridis, Alexis, *Me* (Macmillan, 2019)

21 Johnstone, 1999

22 Ibid

23 A history as rich as jazz itself (About *DownBeat*, downbeat.com)

24 All quotes by Harvey Kubernik are from a 2001 interview with the author unless otherwise indicated

25 Savage, Jon, The Columbus Day riot: Frank Sinatra is pop's first star (*The Guardian*, 11 June 2011)

26 Harrison, Martin, editor/designer, *Elvis Presley 1956: Photographs by Marvin Israel* (Harry N. Abrams Inc. Publishers, 1998)

27 England Jr, Ralph W., A theory of middle class juvenile delinquency, *The Journal of Criminal Law, Criminology and Police Science*, 1960

28 Betrock, Alan, *Hitsville: The 100 Greatest Rock 'n' Roll Magazines 1954–68* (Shake Books, 1991)

29 Ibid

30 Weisberg, Jessica, Mavis Gallant's double-dealing literary agent (*The New Yorker*, 11 July 2012)

31 Moser, Margaret, Dreamsville: Gloria Stavers, 16 Magazine and the roots of rock journalism (*The Austin Chronicle*, 30 November 2007)

32 Unless otherwise indicated, all quotes from Randi Reisfeld and Danny Fields are from their book *16 Magazine: Who's Your Fave Rave?* (Boulevard Books, 1997)

33 Ibid

34 Marsh, Dave, preface, *16 Magazine: Who's Your Fave Rave?* (Boulevard Books, 1997)

Chapter 3

1 Marsh, 1997

2 Ibid

3 As cited in Reisfeld and Fields, 1997

4 Gorman, 2001

5 Moser, 1999

6 Steele, Karen, About Gloria (gloriastavers.typepad.com/blog/Gloria-stavers.html)

7 Ibid

8 Long, 2012

9 Abrams is credited with identifying the new demographic in his study *The Teenage Consumer: Middle Class and Working Class Boys and Girls* (LPE, 1961)

10 Savage, Jon, The magazine explosion (*The Observer*, 6 September 2009)

11 Sinatra, Frank, Jazz has no colour bar! (*Melody Maker*, 19 October 1958)

12 This is what they did to Miles Davis (*Melody Maker*, 12 September 1959)

13 All quotes by Keith Altham are from a 2000 interview with the author unless otherwise indicated

14 All quotes by John Broven are from a 2001 interview with the author unless otherwise indicated

15 Gorman, Paul, Blues explosion (*Mojo*, October 2002)

16 Gorman, 2002

17 Welch, Chris, Obituary: Ray Coleman (*The Independent*, 13 September 1996)

18 Michael Watts on Melody Maker + Swamp Dogg + Cramps (rockbackpages.com podcast episode 65, 2019)

19 bjorner.com/bob.htm

20 Williams, Richard, Obituary: Penny Valentine (*The Guardian*, 13 January 2003)
21 Wilmer, 1989
22 Williams, 2003
23 Laing, Dave, Obituary: Bob Houston (*The Guardian*, 14 October 2005)
24 Houston, Bob, Bob Dawbarn: jazz trombonist and music journalist who was the original raver (*The Guardian*, 26 October 2000)
25 All quotes by Berenice Kinn are from a 1999 interview with the author unless otherwise indicated
26 Sutherland, Steve, The gig that time forgot (*The Independent*, 6 January 2006)
27 Savage, 2009
28 All quotes by Tony Tyler are from a 2001 interview with the author unless otherwise indicated

Chapter 4

1 Avery, Kevin, *Everything Is an Afterthought: The Life & Writings of Paul Nelson* (Fantagraphics Books, 2011)
2 Christgau, 2011
3 Gorman, 2001
4 Moser, 1999
5 Jim Delehant biography, rocksbackpages.com
6 Betrock, 1991
7 Reidy, Darren, Sex, drugs & rock criticism: Richard Goldstein on the sixties (*Rolling Stone*, 29 May 2015)
8 McDonnell, Evelyn, Live through this: a pioneering rock critic looks back with love and sorrow on the 1960s (*Los Angeles Review of Books*, 25 June 2015)
9 Reidy, 2015
10 All quotes by Lisa Robinson are from a 2001 interview with the author unless otherwise indicated
11 Gorman, 2001
12 All quotes by Greg Shaw are from a 2001 interview with the author unless otherwise indicated.
13 DeRogatis, Jim, *Let It Blurt: The Life & Times of Lester Bangs, America's Greatest Rock Critic* (Bantam Doubleday, 2000)
14 Ibid
15 All quotes by Lenny Kaye are from a 2001 interview with the author unless otherwise indicated
16 McDonnell, 2015
17 Gorman, 2001
18 Draper, Robert, *The Rolling Stone Story: The Magazine That Moved a Generation* (Mainstream, 1990)
19 Hagan, Joe, *Sticky Fingers: The Life & Times of Jann Wenner and Rolling Stone Magazine* (Penguin Random House, 2017)
20 Ibid
21 Weir, David, Wenner's world (salon.com, 20 April 1999)
22 Hagan, 2017
23 Draper, 1990
24 Weir, 1999
25 Drury, Colin, Jann Wenner: That's me in the picture (*The Guardian*, 27 October 2017)
26 Nick Kent on *NME* (rocksbackpages.com podcast episode 93, February 2021)
27 Hagan, 2017
28 Gorman, 2001
29 Ibid
30 DeRogatis, 2000
31 Ibid
32 Gorman, 2001
33 Hagan, 2017

Chapter 5

1 Loyd Grossman, rock critic + Brian May audio + (Dixie) Chicks (rocksbackpages.com podcast episode 79, summer 2020)
2 Frere-Jones, Sasha, *Out of the Vinyl Deeps: Ellen Willis on rock music* (University of Minnesota Press, 2011)
3 Tucker, Ken, From the Vinyl Deeps, Ellen Willis wrote about rock (NPR, 1 June 2011)
4 Frere-Jones, 2011
5 Ibid
6 Gorman, 2001
7 Christgau, Robert, Pioneer days (Dean of American Rock Critics, 21 November 2011)
8 Ibid

9 McDonnell, Evelyn, Out of the Vinyl Deeps – Ellen Willis on rock music (*New York Times*, 10 June 2011)
10 McDonnell, Evelyn, The feminine critique: the secret history of women and rock journalism (in *Rock She Wrote: Women Write About Rock, Pop and Rap*, Plexus, 1995; an earlier version appeared in *The Village Voice* Rock & Roll Quarterly, autumn 1992)

Chapter 6

1 All quotes by Ian MacDonald are from a 2000 interview with the author unless otherwise indicated
2 Williams, Richard, John and Yoko's Wedding Album issued (*Melody Maker*, 15 September 1969)
3 As cited in The Wedding Album (jpgr.co.uk/sapcor11.html)
4 As cited in Johnstone, 1999
5 Walsh, Alan, UFOs are landing in my garden (*Melody Maker*, 15 June 1968)
6 As related to Mark Ellen and David Hepworth (Word In Your Attic podcast, 29 December 2020)
7 All quotes by Allan Jones are from a 2001 interview with the author unless otherwise indicated
8 All quotes by Jerry Gilbert are from a 2000 interview with the author unless otherwise indicated
9 All quotes by Nick Logan are from a 2012 interview with the author unless otherwise indicated
10 Long, 2012
11 Gorman, 2001
12 Punessen, Ines, Women Writing Rights: The discrimination of female journalists (Women Writing Rights: The discrimination of female journalists. index.html, 2013)
13 Farren, Mick, *Give the Anarchist a Cigarette* (Jonathan Cape, 2001)
14 Fountain, Nigel, *Underground: The London Alternative Press 1966–74* (Comedia, 1988)
15 Gorman, 2001
16 Green, Jonathon, *All Dressed Up: The Sixties and the Counterculture* (Jonathan Cape, 1998)
17 Fountain, 1988
18 Ibid
19 All quotes by Tony Elliott are from a 2018 interview with the author unless otherwise indicated
20 Fountain, 1988
21 All quotes by Jonathon Green are from a 2001 interview with the author unless otherwise indicated
22 As cited in Hewison, 1986
23 Neville, Richard, *Hippie Hippie Shake: The dreams, the trips, the trials, the love-ins, the screw-ups ... the Sixties* (Bloomsbury, 1995)
24 Ibid
25 Green, Jonathon, *Days in the Life: Voices from the English Underground 1961–71* (Pimlico, 1988)
26 Fountain, 1988
27 Ibid

Chapter 7

1 DeRogatis, Jim, *Let It Blurt: The Life and Times of Lester Bangs* (Bloomsbury, 2000)
2 *Creem*, January 1970
3 All quotes by Danny Sugerman are from a 2001 interview with the author unless otherwise indicated
4 All quotes by Jaan Uhelski are from a 2001 interview with the author unless otherwise indicated
5 DeRogatis, 2000
6 Gillett, Charlie, So you wanna be A rock 'n' roll writer (Keep a Carbon!) (*Rock File* 1, 1972, from http://www.rocksbackpages.com/Library/Article/so-you-wanna-be-a-rocknroll-writer-keep-a-carbon)
7 Everyone's a critic: the lost Lester Bangs interview (rockcritics.com, 23 March 2013)
8 Tosches, Nick, from a reading at A Tribute To Lester Bangs, The Poetry Project, Church of St Mark's in-the-Bowery, 15 May 1992
9 Tosches, Nick, Spirit in flesh: God-crazed hippies reap boffo BO (*Creem*, November 1971)
10 Woods, Scott, Metal Guru: Inside Mike Saunders' brain (rockcritics.com, July 2001)

11 *IT* No. 91, 5–19 November 1970 (As cited in *Strange Days*)
12 Charlesworth, Chris, My first day at *Melody Maker*, 4 May 1970 (justbackdated.blogspot.com, 4 May 2020)
13 Sinker, Mark, editor, *A Hidden Landscape Once a Week: the unruly curiosity of the UK music press 1960s-80s in the words of those who were there* (Strange Attractor Press, 2018)
14 Michael Watts on *Melody Maker* + Swamp Dogg + Cramps (rockbackpages.com podcast episode 65, 2019)
15 Watts, Michael, Flashback: 22 January 1972 (*The Guardian*, 22 January 2006)
16 Hollingworth, Roy, David Bowie: Cha ... Cha ... Changes – a journey with Aladdin (*Melody Maker*, 12 May 1973)
17 Charlesworth, Chris, My second day at *Melody Maker*, 5 May 1970 (justbackdated.blogspot.com, 5 May 2020)
18 Williams, Richard, Colourful critic who embarked on a mission to become a rock star (*The Guardian*, 22 March 2002)
19 As cited in Welch, Chris, Roy Hollingworth (*The Independent*, 22 March 2002)
20 Charlesworth, Chris, My third day at *Melody Maker*, 6 May 1970 (justbackdated.blogspot.com, 6 May 2020)
21 Williams, Richard, Roxy in the rock stakes (*Melody Maker*, 7 August 1971)
22 Williams, Richard, Roxy Music (*Melody Maker*, 12 February 1972)
23 As cited in Williams, Richard, Dave Godin (*The Guardian*, 20 October 2004)
24 Savage, Jon, Dave Godin interview #1 (jonsavage.com/compilations, 11 February 1995)
25 Williams, 2004
26 Gene Clark + Mick Hucknall + Mick Brown on Spector & Soul (rocksbackpages.com podcast episode 65, 8 November 2019)
27 Colli, Beppi, An interview with Pete Frame, 1999 (*Clouds & Clocks*, 12 August 2003)
28 All quotes by Pete Frame are from a 2001 interview with the author unless otherwise indicated
29 Colli, 1999
30 All quotes by Barney Hoskyns are from a 2000 interview with the author unless otherwise indicated
31 Gillett, *Rock File* 1, 1972
32 Colli, 1999
33 Gillett, *Rock File* 1, 1972
34 Russell, Tony, Dave Laing obituary (*The Guardian*, 24 January 2019)
35 Gillett, *Rock File* 1, 1972
36 Laing, Dave, Bob Houston (*The Guardian*, 14 October 2005)
37 Laing, Dave, Words (*Let It Rock*, October 1972)
38 Russell, 2019
39 All quotes by John Peel are from a 2000 interview with the author unless otherwise indicated
40 Long, 2011

Chapter 8

1 Long, 2012
2 Smith, Alan, Message from NME editor Alan Smith (*New Musical Express*, 5 February 1972)
3 Sinker, 2018
4 York, Peter, The post-punk mortem (*Harper's & Queen*, July 1977; reprinted in *Style Wars*, Sidgwick & Jackson, 1980)
5 Kent, Nick, *Apathy for the Devil* (Faber & Faber, 2011)
6 Ibid
7 Ware, Gareth, Nick Logan: 'A new crisis never seemed far away' (*DIY Magazine*, 23 February 2013)
8 Ward, Steven, El David: Saint Dalton shoots his mouth off (rockcritics.com, May 2001)
9 McCoy, Dave, Portrait of the director as a young critic (*Guardian Unlimited*, November 2000)
10 Hoskyns, Barney, The great lig in the sky: the legendary rock writers convention of 1973 (Rock's Backpages, June 2006)
11 *Columbia Journalism Review*, February 1974
12 Ward, Stephen, From jester to Lester (rockcritics.com, March 2001)
13 All quotes by Lisa Robinson are from a 2000 interview with the author unless otherwise indicated

14 Robinson, Lisa, *There Goes Gravity: A Life in Rock & Roll* (Riverhead, 2014)
15 Know your rock writer: Nick Kent (*Rock Scene*, May 1975)
16 Dear Wayne (*Rock Scene*, October 1974)

Chapter 9

1 Hynde, Chrissie, *Reckless: My Life as a Pretender* (Ebury, 2015).
2 Hynde, Chrissie, Everything you'd rather not know about Eno (*New Musical Express*, 2 February 1974)
3 Hynde, Chrissie, David Cassidy: terminal fandom (*New Musical Express*, 8 June 1974)
4 Sinker, 2018
5 Hynde, 2015
6 Webb, Julie, Queen (*New Musical Express*, 16 March 1974).
7 Webb, Julie, T. Rex (*New Musical Express*, 26 January 1974)
8 Farren, Mick and Rowley, Chris, Inflation, gloom, depression, dread (*New Musical Express*, 14 September 1974)
9 Tyler, Andrew, Our man in lost wages (*New Musical Express*, 17 August 1974)
10 Mock advert (*New Musical Express*, 10 August 1974)
11 Jones, Dylan, editor, *Meaty Beaty Big & Bouncy: Classic Rock Writing from Elvis to Oasis* (Sceptre, 1997)
12 DeRogatis, 2000
13 Nick Kent on *NME* (rocksbackpages.com podcast episode 93, February 2021)
14 Kent, Nick, The mighty Pop vs the hand of blight (*New Musical Express*, 3 May 1975)
15 Burchill, Julie, *I Knew I Was Right* (William Heinemann, 1998)
16 Who's Ruskin??? (*New Musical Express*, 30 November 1974)
17 rocksbackpages.com podcast episode 93, February 2021
18 Michael Watts on *Melody Maker* + Swamp Dogg + Cramps audio (rockbackpages.com podcast episode 65, 2019)
19 Sinker, 2018
20 Gayle, Carl, The real music – the rebel music (*Let It Rock*, July 1973)
21 Sinker, 2018
22 Sigerson, Davitt, Tom Moulton, father of the disco mix (*Black Music*, January 1976)
23 Sinker, 2018
24 Gayle, Carl, The Upsetter part 2 (*Black Music*, February 1975)
25 Gayle, Carl, Oh, what a rat race ... (*Black Music*, May 1976)
26 Sinker, 2018
27 Jones, Allan, If you ask me (*UK Press Gazette*, 29 July 2007)
28 Watts, Michael, Caroline Coon: the underground angel of mercy ... (*Melody Maker*, 30 January 1971)
29 All quotes by Caroline Coon are from a 2001 interview with the author unless otherwise indicated
30 Steward, Sue and Garratt, Sheryl, *Signed Sealed Delivered: True Life Stories of Women in Pop* (Pluto Press, 1984)
31 Coon, Caroline, Inside the Bay City Rollers camp (*Melody Maker*, 13 September 1975)
32 Suzi Quatro & Olivia Newton-John: dolly mixture (*Melody Maker*, 20 July 1974)
33 Punessen, 2013
34 Ibid

Chapter 10

1 Steward & Garratt, 1984
2 Valentine, Penny, Godzilla and I (*Street Life*, 21 February 1976)
3 Sinker, 2018
4 Walters, Idris, Dub: reggae's cutting edge (*Street Life*, 1 November 1975)
5 Valentine, Penny, Imagine a life full of heroes & villains & fools (*Street Life*, 1 November 1975)
6 Valentine, Penny, Godzilla and I (*Street Life*, 21 February 1976)
7 Valentine, Penny, A question of survival: rock 'n' roll women (*Street Life*, 6 March 1976)
8 Sinker, 2018
9 Szymanksi, Rick, Would you buy a rubber T-shirt from this man? (*Street Life*, 1–14 May 1976)
10 Sinker, Mark, Ites Reel (www.patreon.com/posts/ites-reel-being-21446722, 16 September 2018)

Notes

11 Taylor, Angus, Interview: Chris Lane, reggae writer (United Reggae, 13 March 2013)
12 Gilroy, Paul in Sinker, 2018
13 Reel, Penny, From the dread depths of despair (*New Musical Express*, 7 February 1976)
14 Phillips, Kate, Queen Elizabeth College All Night Christmas Ball (*New Musical Express*, 27 December 1975)
15 Spencer, Neil, Don't look over your shoulder but the Sex Pistols are coming (*New Musical Express*, 21 February 1976)
16 McCain, Gillian and McNeil, Legs, *Please Kill Me* (Abacus, 1997)
17 All quotes by Mary Harron are from a 2001 interview with the author unless otherwise indicated
18 Harron, Mary, The Ramones – rock & roll – the real thing (*Punk*, January 1976)
19 Editorial (*Punk*, January 1976)
20 McCain and McNeil, 1997
21 cited in Harron, Mary, Punk is just another word for nothin' left to lose (*The Village Voice*, 28 March 1977)
22 Jackson, Connor, Forty years later Punk magazine rises from the dead (*The Village Voice*, 29 January 2016)
23 Is your fave rave rock star old enough to be your father? (*New Musical Express*, 24 January 1976)
24 Farren, Mick, The kids are not necessarily alright (*New Musical Express*, 1 March 1975)
25 Farren, Mick, The titanic sails at dawn (*New Musical Express*, 19 June 1976)
26 Farren, Mick, *Give the Anarchist a Cigarette* (Jonathan Cape, 2001)
27 Jones, Allan, Sex Pistols (*Melody Maker*, 10 April 1976)
28 Singleton, Phil, Jonh Ingham: Exclusive interview for God Save The Sex Pistols (sex-pistols.net, February 2012)
29 MacDonald, Michael Patrick, Vivien Goldman (*Bomb*, 17 June 2016)
30 Gilroy, 2018
31 All quotes by Vivien Goldman are from a 2001 interview with the author unless otherwise indicated
32 Barbara Charone on the Who + Keef Richards + Chelsea FC (rocksbackpages podcast episode 54, 2020)
33 Ingham, Jonh, The Sex Pistols are four months old ... (*Sounds*, 24 April 1976)
34 Tennant, Neil, Terrorise your audience the Pistols way (*New Musical Express*, 8 May 1976)
35 Coon, Caroline, Punk rock: rebels against the system (*Melody Maker*, 7 August 1976)
36 Murray, Charles Shaar, Sex Pistols, Clash, Buzzcocks: Screen on the Green, London (*New Musical Express*, 11 September 1976)
37 Joyce, Cynthia, Litchat with Nick Hornby (salon.com, 14 October 1996)
38 All quotes by Paul Du Noyer are from a 2001 interview with the author unless otherwise indicated
39 Burchill, Julie, *I Knew I Was Right* (William Heinemann, 1998)
40 All quotes by Tony Parsons are from a 2001 interview with the author unless otherwise indicated
41 York, 1977
42 Burchill, 1998
43 Ibid
44 Morrissey, Steven, Aero-vision (*Melody Maker*, 6 September 1975)
45 Morrissey, Steven, Gasbag (*New Musical Express*, 18 June 1976)
46 Bruno, Peter, Follett, Angela, Saunders, Red, Huddle, Roger and others, Gasbag (*New Musical Express*, 11 September 1976)
47 Rachel, Daniel, *Walls Come Tumbling Down: The Music and Politics of Rock Against Racism, 2 Tone and Red Wedge* (Picador, 2016)
48 Clapton, Eric, Dear Everybody (Letters, *Sounds*, 11 September 1976)
49 Huddle, Roger, Anti-fascism: that was then, this is now (*Socialist Review*, June 2004)
50 Daniel, 2016
51 Ibid
52 Williams, Eliza, Rock Against Racism movement celebrated at Impressions Gallery in Bradford (*Creative Review*, June 2016)
53 Front page (*Temporary Hoarding 1*, spring 1977)
54 Daniel, 2016
55 Whitman, Lucy, Rock Against Racism (lucywhitman.com/rock-against-racism)

56 Sharon, Never mind the people here's the bollocks (*Temporary Hoarding 4*, winter 1977)
57 Daniel, 2016
58 Gregory, Ruth, in Sinker, 2018
59 Sinker, 2018
60 Gilroy, Paul, in Shelton, Syd, *Rock Against Racism* (Autograph ABP, 2015)

Chapter 11

1 Kent, Nick, Ramones (*New Musical Express*, 15 May 1976)
2 Brian Hogg: Bam Balam, Strange Things Are Happening (Rock Writ podcast, 21 March 2021)
3 Perry, Mark, editor, *Sniffin' Glue: The Essential Punk Accessory* (Sanctuary, 2000)
4 Ibid
5 All quotes by Lindsay Hutton are from a 2001 interview with the author unless otherwise indicated
6 Savage, Jon, Sex Pistols: Screen on the Green, London (*Sounds*, 9 April 1977)
7 Salewicz, Chris, Poly Styrene obituary (*The Independent*, 23 October 2011)
8 Suck, Jane, Dropped intuh the fun house: impressions of the Roxy (*Sounds*, 12 February 1977)
9 Suck, Jane, True Life Romance presents ... The day a young gurl's dream came true (*Sounds*, 29 October 1977)
10 Suck, Jane, Roxy Music's Greatest Hits (*Sounds*, 5 November 1977)
11 Gorman, 2001
12 Burchill, 1998
13 Savage, Jon, Fanzines: pure pop art for now people (*Sounds*, 14 January 1978)
14 Savage, Jon, Stranglers, No More Heroes (*Sounds*, 24 September 1977)
15 All quotes by Chas de Whalley are from a 2001 interview with the author unless otherwise indicated
16 Savage, Jon, New musick (*Sounds*, 26 November 1977)
17 Needs, Kris, *Needs Must* (Virgin Books, 1999)
18 Ward, Steven, Caught with his trousers down: the Ira Robbins interview (rockcritics.com, May 2001)
19 Schwartz, Andy, Remembering Alan Betrock (*The Village Voice*, 7 April 2001)
20 Ejercito, Karlynne, V. Vale (*Bomb*, 27 July 2015, bombmagazine.org/articles/v-vale/)
21 Meltzer, Richard, Cocktails with Claude (*LA Weekly*, 12 December 1979)
22 Mullen, Brendan, Obituary: Claude Bessy 1947–2001 (*LA Weekly*, 2 October 2001)
23 Young, Charles M., Rock is sick and living in London (*Rolling Stone*, 29 October 1977)
24 Punessen, 2013
25 Logan, 2013
26 Logan, 2016
27 All quotes by Paul Rambali are from a 2016 interview with the author unless otherwise indicated
28 Neil Tennant's *Smash Hits* Christmas (BBC Radio 4, 24 December 2012)
29 Hill, Stephen, in Forster, Laurie and Harper, Sue, editors, *British Culture & Society in the 1970s: The Lost Decade* (Cambridge Scholars Publishing, 2010)

Chapter 12

1 Reel, Penny, A dread's tale (*New Musical Express*, 14 October 1978)
2 York, Peter, Little magazines: the big story (*Harper's & Queen*, August 1977)
3 Long, 2012
4 Darling, Andy, Danny Baker interview (*FHM*, May 1994)
5 Baker, Danny, *Going to Sea in a Sieve: The Autobiography* (Weidenfeld & Nicolson, 2012)
6 York, Peter, *Style Wars* (Sidgwick & Jackson, 1980)
7 Frere-Jones, Sasha, New as foam, old as rock: the music criticism of Ian Penman (*Bookforum*, December/January 2020)
8 Reynolds, Simon, *Rip It Up and Start Again: Post Punk 1978–84* (Faber & Faber, 2005)
9 Morley, Paul, In the terminal zone (*New Musical Express*, 14 July 1979)
10 Morley, Paul, What a long predictable trip it's become (*New Musical Express*, 20 March 1981)
11 Frere-Jones, December/January 2020

Notes

12 Penman, Ian, ABC: A-Z Club, Bayswater, London (*New Musical Express*, 24 October 1981)
13 Ian Penman on Prince + Charlie Parker + ZZ Top (rocksbackpages.com podcast episode 40, 2019)
14 Long, 2012
15 Fox, Killian, NME: 60 years of rock history ... and four front covers that define their eras (*The Guardian*, 26 February 2012)
16 Baker, Danny, *Going Off Alarming: The Autobiography Vol. 2* (Weidenfeld & Nicolson, 2014)
17 Rose, Cynthia, Brian Eno: into the spirit world (*New Musical Express*, 20 July 1980)
18 All quotes by Garry Bushell are from a 2001 interview with the author unless otherwise indicated
19 All quotes by Paolo Hewitt are from a 2000 interview with the author unless otherwise indicated
20 Sinker, 2018
21 All quotes by Tom Hibbert are from a 2000 interview with the author unless otherwise indicated
22 Ellen, Mark, Tom Hibbert obituary (*The Guardian*, 2 September 2011)
23 Ellen, Mark, *Rock Stars Stole My Life: A Big Bad Love Affair with Music* (Coronet, 2014)
24 Rose, Cynthia, No news meant New Music News ... for a while (*New Musical Express*, 20 December 1980)

Chapter 13

1 Logan, Nick, *The Face*'s Greatest Hits in pictures (*The Guardian*, 4 December 2011)
2 Ibid
3 All quotes by Sheryl Garratt are from a 2015 interview with the author unless otherwise indicated
4 All quotes by James Truman are from a 2016 interview with the author unless otherwise indicated
5 Katz, Robin, Maverick or madman? (*Evening Standard*, 1 May 1980)
6 All quotes by Steve Taylor are from a 2016 interview with the author unless otherwise indicated
7 Punessen, 2013
8 www.rocksbackpages.com/Library/Writer/deanne-pearson
9 All quotes by Robert Elms are from a 2016 interview with the author unless otherwise indicated
10 Glick, Beverley, How I played my part in inventing the New Romantics (beverleyglick.com, 26 September 2013)
11 Page, Betty, The New Romantics – a manifesto for the eighties (*Sounds*, 13 September 1980)
12 York, Peter and Jennings, Charles, *Peter York's Eighties* (BBC Books, 1995)
13 Ibid
14 Hill, 2010
15 Simpson, Dave, How we made *Smash Hits* magazine (*The Guardian*, 6 August 2018)
16 Sinker, 2018
17 Simpson, 2018
18 Mark Ellen (*Mouth*, 20 March 2015; themouthmagazine.com/2015/03/20/mark-ellen)
19 Ellen, 2014
20 Rimmer, Dave, *Like Punk Never Happened: Culture Club and the New Pop* (Faber & Faber, 1985)
21 Ellen, 2014
22 Neil Tennant's *Smash Hits* Christmas (BBC Radio 4, 24 December 2012)
23 Neil Tennant on Smash Hits + Pet Shop Boys + Andy Weatherall (rocksbackpagespodcast.com podcast episode 63, February 2020)
24 Neil Tennant's *Smash Hits* Christmas, 2012
25 Tennant, Neil, The new adventures of Malcolm McLaren (*Smash Hits*, 6 January 1983)
26 Daly, Steven, Pet Shop Boys' Neil Tennant (1996), Rock's Backpages Audio (retrieved 12 May 2021 from rocksbackpages.com/Library/Article/pet-shop-boys-neil-tennant-1996)
27 Tennant, Neil, in Frith, Mark, editor, *The Best of Smash Hits* (Sphere, 2006)
28 Neil Tennant's *Smash Hits* Christmas, 2012
29 rocksbackpagespodcast.com podcast episode 63
30 Simpson, 2018

Notes

Chapter 14

1 From an interview with the author, 2012
2 All quotes by Steve Taylor are from a 2016 interview with the author unless otherwise indicated
3 Jobey, Liz, There's a new kid on the block to take on Time Out (*The Observer*, 27 September 1981)
4 Lott, Tim, Flexipop!'s shameless pop legacy (*The Guardian*, 4 February 2010)
5 Star Hits staffers Q&A Part 2 (mulletsihaveloved.wordpress.com, 8 July 2014)
6 *Star Hits* editors David Keeps and Suzan Colón answer your questions! (mulletsihaveloved.wordpress.com, 4 June 2014)
7 Fricke, David, Editorial (*Star Hits* Vol. 1 No. 4, May 1984)
8 mulletsihaveloved.wordpress.com, 2014
9 Keating, Matt, My mentor: Phil Alexander (*The Guardian*, 27 May 2006)
10 All quotes by Sylvie Simmons are from a 2016 interview with the author unless otherwise indicated
11 Cook, Richard, Everywhere man (*New Musical Express*, 25 September 1982)
12 Hudson, Mark, A tribute to Evening Standard critic and pioneer spirit Sue Steward (*Evening Standard*, 31 August 2017)
13 Sinker, 2018
14 Ibid
15 Kirk, Chris, What a difference a gay makes (*Collusion* No. 4, February–April 1983)
16 Harvey, Steven, Behind the groove: New York City's disco underground (*Collusion* No. 5, September 1983)
17 Klemesrud, Judy, Ann Flanders: new fashion voice (*New York Times*, 10 February 1985)
18 Koren, Leonard, *Making WET: The Magazine of Gourmet Bathing* (Imperfect Publishing, 2012)
19 Heller, Steven, *WET*: Of course there was a 'gourmet bathing' magazine in the 70s (*The Atlantic*, 12 July 2012)
20 All quotes by Glenn O'Brien are from a 2001 interview with the author unless otherwise indicated
21 McCoy, 2000
22 Ward, Steven, The Rev. Charles M. Young calms down, grows up, and sings the joys of middle age (rockcritics.com, February 2001)
23 Ward, Steven, Whatever happened to rock critic Paul Nelson (rockcritics.com, March 2000)
24 Draper, 1990
25 All quotes by Anthony DeCurtis are from a 2001 interview with the author unless otherwise indicated
26 Cohen, Rich, The rise & fall of *Rolling Stone* (*The Atlantic*, December 2017)
27 Davies, Jim, 200 issues of The Face (*Campaign*, 7 February 1997)
28 All quotes by Lesley White are from a 2016 interview with the author unless otherwise indicated
29 White, Lesley, Dexys Midnight Runners: fact and fiction (*The Face*, September 1982)
30 Rimmer, 1984
31 Long, 2012
32 Hanna, Lynn, Fashion passion! The year that style revolted (*New Musical Express*, 19 December 1981)
33 All quotes by Mat Snow are from a 2001 interview with the author unless otherwise indicated
34 Richard Cook 1957–2007 (rocksbackpages.com, 27 August 2007).
35 War on pop (*New Musical Express*, 8 September 1984)
36 Quantick, David, That Emmy Award winners party in full (Word In Your Ear, 5 July 2021)
37 Rai, Amrik, The Smiths (*New Musical Express*, 17 October 1983)
38 All quotes by Lucy O'Brien are from a 2001 interview with the author unless otherwise indicated
39 Beaumont-Thomas, Ben and Snapes, Laura, 'Pete Doherty tried to get out of the car at 80mph': the stories behind NME's greatest covers (*The Guardian*, 9 March 2018)
40 Brown, Len, *Meetings with Morrissey* (Omnibus, 2009)
41 Ibid
42 Quantick, 2021
43 Ibid
44 Gambotto-Burke, Antonella, Interview with Morrissey (*Sounds*, 20 April 1985)
45 Mercer, Mick, The Lost ZigZag (www.mickmercer.com/pdfs/the_mick_56.pdf)

46 Jonze, Tim, 'He was a groundbreaker and visonary': music writer Dele Fadele remembered (*The Guardian*, 14 September 2020)
47 Fadele, Dele, The enemy without (*New Musical Express*, 16 May 1987)
48 Fadele, Dele, Caucasian rut (*New Musical Express*, 2 August 1992)

Chapter 15

1 Patterson, Sylvia, *I'm Not With the Band: A Writer's Life Lost in Music* (Sphere, 2017)
2 Quantick, 2021
3 Patterson, 2017
4 Heath, Chris, A day in the life of A-ha (*Smash Hits*, 1 January 1986)
5 Hepworth, David, Why we should mourn the loss of Q magazine (*New Statesman*, 22 July 2020)
6 Ibid
7 Ibid
8 Lloyd Bradley plus etched solid-brass Michael Jackson party invite (Word In Your Attic, 8 April 2021)
9 Bradley, Lloyd, A tiff with Tosh (*New Musical Express*, 21 May 1981)
10 Bradley, Lloyd, In time with the perfect beat (*New Musical Express*, 26 March 1983)
11 Ibid
12 Rock Writ, 2021
13 Wood, Anthony, A message on The Wire (*The Wire*, Summer 1982)
14 Wood, Anthony, A giant step (*The Wire*, Summer 1984)
15 Fordham, John, Richard Cook (*The Guardian*, 25 September 2007)
16 Sinker, 2017
17 Watson, Steve, A very odd, slightly strange, idiosyncratic mutant (*Stack*, October 2019)
18 Wang, Grace, Ancient to future: interplanetary sounds in Straight No Chaser (*Stack*, August 2018)
19 Tan, Ken, On following your instincts (creativeindependent.com, 25 September 2019)
20 Collin, Matthew and Godfrey, John, *Altered State: The Story of Ecstasy Culture and Acid House* (Serpent's Tail, 1997)
21 Broughton, Frank, and Brewster, Bill, *Boy's Own: the complete fanzines 1986–92* (boysownproductions.com, 2018)
22 Farley, Terry, Boy's Own (*Snub TV*, BBC2, 1990)
23 Titmuss, Stephen, Boy's Own: A History (*Resident Advisor*, 12 January 2010)
24 Give us a line (*Boy's Own* No. 5, Spring 1988)
25 Oakenfold, Paul and others, Bermondsey goes Baleric (*Boy's Own* No. 5, Spring 1988)
26 Weatherall, Andrew, The outsider (*Boy's Own* No. 7, Spring 1989)
27 Lubich, David, Soul Underground: the story (davidlubich.net, 6 May 2018)
28 Goddard, Grant, *KISS FM – From Radical Radio to Big Business: The Inside Story of a London Pirate Radio Station's Path to Success* (Radio Books, 2011)
29 Lubich, 2018

Chapter 16

1 Guccione Jr, Bob, Editorial (*Spin*, March 1985)
2 Majewski, Lori and Bernstein, Jonathan, Spin 30: Kurt, Courtney & cassettes: we worked at *Spin* in the early '90s (spin.com, 27 April 2015)
3 All quotes by Tim Yohannon are from a 1993 interview with the author unless otherwise indicated
4 Christe, Ian, Run DMC/Onyx/Boss, Palladium, NYC (*Your Flesh*, Summer 1993)
5 All quotes by Bob Mack are from a 1993 interview with the author unless otherwise indicated
6 All quotes by Darby Romeo are from 2020 interviews with the author unless otherwise indicated
7 Gorman, Paul, We were a collection of people in a good way (WePresent, May 2020)
8 All quotes by David Cavanagh are from a 2000 interview with the author unless otherwise indicated
9 Word In Your Ear, 2021
10 Quantick, 2021
11 Sawyer, Miranda, My life as a pop chick (*The Observer*, 21 September 2003)

12 Ellen, Barbara, Farewell *NME* – irreverent, acerbic, essential. At least when I was there! (*The Observer*, 11 March 2018)
13 Verrico, Liza, Citizen Insane (*Vox*, November 1993)
14 Ablaze, Karren, Girl love & girl action (*Girlfrenzy*, 1995)
15 Smith, Erica and Catherine, I married a music journalist (*Girlfrenzy*, 1995)

Chapter 17

1 All quotes by Lyndsey Baker are from a 2016 interview with the author unless otherwise indicated
2 All quotes by Ashley Heath are from a 2013 interview with the author unless otherwise indicated
3 All quotes by Richard Benson are from a 2014 interview with the author unless otherwise indicated
4 Cotton, Charlotte, editor, *Imperfect Beauty: The Making of Contemporary Fashion Photographs* (V&A Publishing, 2000)
5 Garratt, Sheryl and Baker, Lyndsey, The We generation (*The Face*, December 1989)
6 Garratt, Sheryl and Taggart, Chris, HM Government vs Acid House (*The Face*, February 1990)
7 Cotton, Charlotte, 2000
8 All quotes by Amy Raphael are from a 2016 interview with the author unless otherwise indicated
9 Aku, Timmtohep, Nelson George: The Afropunk interview (Afropunk, 14 February 2020)
10 Nelson George on the death of R&B + Jimmy Jam and Terry Lewis (rocksbackpages.com podcast episode 105, June 2021)
11 Aku, 2020
12 George, Nelson, *Buppies, B-Boys, Baps & Bohos: Notes on Post-Soul Black Culture*, HarperPerennial, 1992)
13 George, Nelson, Buppies, B-Boys, Baps & Bohos (*The Village Voice*, 17 March 1992)
14 Flanagan, Andrew, Former *Village Voice* editors and writers remember its outsized impact on music (*The Record*, 25 August 2017)
15 Carol Cooper on New York Sounds (rocksbackpages.com podcast episode 102, 2020)
16 J-23, *The Source* magazine (early 90s): the greatest story never told (hiphopdx.com, 18 April 2005)
17 Ettelson, Robbie, Looking back at the first 100 issues of *The Source* (unkut.com, 31 January 2021)
18 Lester, Sheena, Editorial (*Rap Pages*, February 1996)
19 Webb, Dane, Black is back, and we're all in (*Rap Pages*, February 1992)
20 Lester, Sheena, The game changer: the greatest day in Harlem 20th anniversary tribute (*Respect*, September 2018)
21 McLeod, Kembrew, in Jones, Steve and Baker, Susan S., *Pop Music and the Press* (Temple University Press, 2002)
22 Charnas, Dan, 'We changed culture': an oral history of *Vibe* magazine (*Billboard*, 27 September 2018)
23 Light, Alan, editor, *The Vibe History of Hip-Hop* (Plexus, 1999)
24 Charnas, 2018
25 Lester, 2018
26 Ibid
27 Surowiecki, James, Hip-hopped up (*New York*, 5 April 1999)
28 J-23, *The Source* magazine (early 90s): Mays Benzino and a gun (hiphopdx.com, 18 April 2005)
29 McLeod, 2002
30 Lester, 2018
31 Ibid
32 MacAdams, Torii, A history of hip-hop zines (daily.redbullmusicacademy.com, 2 June 2015)
33 Dave 'Funken' Klein – Gangsta Limpin forever! (bomphiphop.com/limpin.htm)
34 Wollock, David, Bringing the newz to the hip-hop confederacy (*LA Times*, 25 August 2002)

Chapter 18

1 Smash Hits ABCs (*Marketing Week*, 23 February 1990)
2 Petridis, Alexis, The road to Wigan Pier (*The Guardian*, 3 October 2003)

3 Petridis, Alexis, I used to dream about owning every record in the world (*The Guardian*, 2 June 2018)
4 IPC reveals plans for dance-music launch (*Campaign*, 10 March 1995)
5 Gibson, Owen, Ministry of Sound: the UK's largest independent record label (*The Guardian*, 25 October 2002)
6 Savage, Jon, Aphex Twin: Selected ambient works 1985–92; Biosphere: Microgravity (*Jockey Slut*, January 1993)
7 Baines, Josh, The story of Jockey Slut: the greatest magazine you've probably never read (vice.com, 4 November 2015)
8 O'Flaherty, Mark C., Instagram post (8 August 2021)
9 Clarke, Cameron, Never-say-die Attitude: a boundary-pushing magazine 300 issues on (thedrum.com, 21 August 2018)
10 Sullivan, Caroline, Rock of ages (*The Guardian*, 29 October 1993)
11 Ellen, 2014
12 Ward, 2001
13 Ellen, 2014
14 Emma Messinger to Ollie Reeder (*In the Loop*, dir. Armando Iannucci, 2009)
15 Watson, Ben and Leslie, Esther, editors, *Academy Zappa: Proceedings of the First International Conference of Esemplastic Zappology* (SAF Publishing, 2001)
16 Sinker, 2018
17 Ibid
18 Brown, James, Editor's note (*Loaded*, May 1994)
19 All quotes by Charles Gant are from a 2013 interview with the author unless otherwise indicated
20 Cavanagh, David, Blatant (*Q*, November 1995)
21 Moran, Caitlin, East 17: sex induction hour (*Melody Maker*, 19 June 1993)
22 Davies, Hunter, Meet Caitlin Moran, newspaper columnist, television presenter, novelist, scriptwriter, pop music pundit ... and typical teenage slob (*The Independent*, 23 October 1994)
23 Gross, Jessica, Caitlin Moran on the working class, masturbation and writing a novel (Longreads, 25 September 2014)

Chapter 19

1 Dennis, Felix, The wayward child who conquered the world (*Maxim*, 18 April 2009)
2 Ibid
3 Griffiths, Anna, Wagadon's *Deluxe* Set For Men's Mid-Market (*Campaign*, 20 March, 1998).
4 Roberts, Jack and Stacey, Daniel, *Bad Idea: The Anthology* (Portico Books, 2008)
5 Charnas, 2018
6 Williams, Monte, Irate rappers give journalists a combat beat (*New York Times*, 22 December 1998)
7 Mulholland, Gary, Quick – smash up a hotel room (*The Guardian*, 20 February 2001)

Epilogue

1 Batey, Angus, The Hip-Hop Years (*The Times*, 23 October 2003)
2 Smith, Russ and Strausbaugh, John, Q&A with *Blender* editors (salon.com, 1999)
3 Dumenico, Simon, Felix Dennis Takes on Redbook (salon.com, May 2001)
4 Gilbreath, Aaron, Where Have All The Music Magazines Gone? (Longreads, December 2018)
5 Goodman, Lizzy, The Last Moment of the Last Great Rock Band, *Vulture* (May 2015)
6 Gormely, Ian, Taylor Swift Leads Poptimism's Rebirth (*The Guardian*, 3 December 2014)
7 Pierson-Hagger, Ellen, The music press isn't dead (*New Statesman*, 27 July 2020)
8 Morley, Madeleine, Electronic Sound #2 (magculture.com, 26 May 2016)
9 Rooney, Connor, Meet Me In The Bathroom: An interview with Lizzy Goodman, http://sbpress.com/2018/05/meet-me-in-the-bathroom-an-interview-with-lizzy-goodman/
10 Gilbreath, Aaron, Where Have All The Music Magazines Gone? (Longreads, December 2018)
11 Reynolds, Simon, Worth Their Wait (*Pitchfork Quarterly*, 2 September 2014).
12 Hepworth, David, Why we should mourn the loss of *Q* magazine (*New Statesman*, 22 July 2020)

Acknowledgments

In the making of this book I am grateful to Sophy Thompson, Ben Hayes and the team at Thames & Hudson, and to my agent, Maggie Hanbury.

I am especially thankful to Barney Hoskyns and Mark Pringle at rocksbackpages.com. I am also grateful to all of those who have made a difference in the long story of the music press, including but not limited to the following interviewees and contributors:

Keith Altham, Lindsay Baker, Richard Benson, Julie Burchill, Garry Bushell, Roy Carr, David Cavanagh, Robert Christgau, Richard Cook, Caroline Coon, Carol Cooper, Ian Cranna, Cameron Crowe, David Dalton, Anthony DeCurtis, Fred Dellar, Paul Du Noyer, Chuck Eddy, Ben Edmonds, Mark Ellen, Robert Elms, Mick Farren, High Fielder, Danny Fields, Ben Fong-Torres, Pete Frame, Simon Frith, Charles Gant, Sheryl Garratt, Jerry Gilbert, Charlie Gillett, Vivien Goldman, Jonathon Green, John Harris, Mary Harron, Ashley Heath, David Hepworth, Paolo Hewitt, Tom Hibbert, Bill Holdship, Lindsay Hutton, Allan Jones, Lenny Kaye, Maurice Kinn, Harvey Kubernik, Nick Logan, Pat Long, Ian MacDonald, Bob Mack, Dave Marsh, John May, Richard Meltzer, Barry Miles, Charles Shaar Murray, Glenn O'Brien, Lucy O'Brien, Mark C. O'Flaherty, Tony Parsons, John Peel, Paul Rambali, Amy Raphael, Richard Reigel, Simon Reynolds, Ira Robbins, Lisa Robinson, Darby Romeo, Chris Salewicz, Jon Savage, Greg Shaw, Pete Silverton, Sylvie Simmons, Pennie Smith, Mat Snow, Neil Spencer, Danny Sugerman, Phil Sutcliffe, Steve Taylor, Jerry Thackray, David Toop, James Truman, Steve Turner, Tony Tyler, Jaan Uhelszki, Andrew Weatherall, Marc Weingarten, Chris Welch, Chas de Whalley, Lesley White, Mark Williams, Paul S. Williams, Richard Williams, Scott Woods, Tim Yohannon and Peter York.

This book is dedicated to Caz Facey for her affection, love, patience and unqualified support.

Picture Credits

All publications illustrated in this book are taken from the Paul Gorman Archive. They have been reproduced in their actual condition to emphasize the fact that they are historical objects.

Page 88 Time Out London. Photo Ray Stevenson; **119** © 2022 NME Networks; **139** © 2022 NME Networks. Photo © Pennie Smith; **149** © 2022 NME Networks. Photo © Joe Stevens; **237** H Bauer Publishing; **303** Courtesy David Carson; **314** Catherine Lupton. Illustration Erica Smith; **340** H Bauer Publishing.

Plate 3 © Estate of Richard Neville; **8** Rolling Stone, © 1973 and Trademark ® Rolling Stone LLC. All rights reserved. Used by permission. Photo Henry Diltz; **11** H Bauer Publishing; **13** Photo Edward Bell; **16** © 2022 NME Networks. Photo © Peter Anderson; **17** Corinne Day/Trunk Archive; **18** Illustration Erica Smith; **21** Vibe Media Publishing LLC. © 1995, All rights reserved. Used by permission.

Author photo Toby Amies

Every effort has been made to identify copyright holders and obtain their permission for the use of copyright material. Any errors or omissions that are drawn to the publisher's attention will be corrected in future editions of the book.

Index

Page numbers in *italic* refer to the illustrations in the text.

Index

Index

Index

Index

Index

Index

First published in the United Kingdom in 2022 by Thames & Hudson Ltd,
181A High Holborn, London WC1V 7QX

First published in the United States of America in 2022 by Thames & Hudson Inc.,
500 Fifth Avenue, New York, New York 10110

Designed by Daniel Streat, Visual Fields

British Library Cataloguing-in-Publication Data
A catalogue record for this book is available from the British Library

Library of Congress Control Number 2022931903

ISBN 978-0-500-02263-4

Printed and bound in China by RR Donnelley